Applying Ibn Khaldūn

The writings of Ibn Khaldūn, particularly the *Muqaddimah (Prolegomenon)*, have rightly been regarded as being sociological in nature. For this reason, Ibn Khaldūn has been widely regarded as the founder of sociology, or at least a precursor of modern sociology. While he was given this recognition, however, few works went beyond proclaiming him as a founder or precursor to the systematic application of his theoretical perspective to specific historical and contemporary aspects of Muslim societies in North Africa and the Middle East. The continuing presence of Eurocentrism in the social sciences has not helped in this regard: it often stands in the way of the consideration of non-Western sources of theories and concepts.

This book provides an overview of Ibn Khaldūn and his sociology, discusses reasons for his marginality, and suggests ways to bring Ibn Khaldūn into the mainstream through the systematic application of his theory. It moves beyond works that simply state that Ibn Khaldūn was a founder of sociology or provide descriptive accounts of his works. Instead it systematically applies Ibn Khaldūn's theoretical perspective to specific historical aspects of Muslim societies in North Africa and the Middle East, successfully integrating concepts and frameworks from Khaldūnian sociology into modern social science theories. *Applying Ibn Khaldūn* will be of interest to students and scholars of sociology and social theory.

Syed Farid Alatas is Head of the Department of Malay Studies and Associate Professor of Sociology at the National University of Singapore. His books include *Democracy and Authoritarianism: The Rise of the Post-Colonial State in Indonesia and Malaysia* (Macmillan, 1997), *Alternative Discourse in Asian Social Science: Responses to Eurocentrism* (Sage, 2006) and *Ibn Khaldūn* (Oxford University Press, 2012).

Routledge advances in sociology

1. **Virtual Globalization**
   Virtual spaces/tourist spaces
   Edited by David Holmes

2. **The Criminal Spectre in Law, Literature and Aesthetics**
   Peter Hutchings

3. **Immigrants and National Identity in Europe**
   Anna Triandafyllidou

4. **Constructing Risk and Safety in Technological Practice**
   Edited by Jane Summerton and Boel Berner

5. **Europeanisation, National Identities and Migration**
   Changes in boundary constructions between Western and Eastern Europe
   Willfried Spohn and Anna Triandafyllidou

6. **Language, Identity and Conflict**
   A comparative study of language in ethnic conflict in Europe and Eurasia
   Diarmait Mac Giolla Chríost

7. **Immigrant Life in the U.S.**
   Multi-disciplinary perspectives
   Edited by Donna R. Gabaccia and Colin Wayne Leach

8. **Rave Culture and Religion**
   Edited by Graham St. John

9. **Creation and Returns of Social Capital**
   A new research program
   Edited by Henk Flap and Beate Völker

10. **Self-Care**
    Embodiment, personal autonomy and the shaping of health consciousness
    Christopher Ziguras

11. **Mechanisms of Cooperation**
    Werner Raub and Jeroen Weesie

12. **After the Bell**
    Educational success, public policy and family background
    Edited by Dalton Conley and Karen Albright

13. **Youth Crime and Youth Culture in the Inner City**
    Bill Sanders

14. **Emotions and Social Movements**
Edited by Helena Flam and Debra King

15. **Globalization, Uncertainty and Youth in Society**
Edited by Hans-Peter Blossfeld, Erik Klijzing, Melinda Mills and Karin Kurz

16. **Love, Heterosexuality and Society**
Paul Johnson

17. **Agricultural Governance**
Globalization and the new politics of regulation
Edited by Vaughan Higgins and Geoffrey Lawrence

18. **Challenging Hegemonic Masculinity**
Richard Howson

19. **Social Isolation in Modern Society**
Roelof Hortulanus, Anja Machielse and Ludwien Meeuwesen

20. **Weber and the Persistence of Religion**
Social theory, capitalism and the sublime
Joseph W. H. Lough

21. **Globalization, Uncertainty and Late Careers in Society**
Edited by Hans-Peter Blossfeld, Sandra Buchholz and Dirk Hofäcker

22. **Bourdieu's Politics**
Problems and possibilities
Jeremy F. Lane

23. **Media Bias in Reporting Social Research?**
The case of reviewing ethnic inequalities in education
Martyn Hammersley

24. **A General Theory of Emotions and Social Life**
Warren D. TenHouten

25. **Sociology, Religion and Grace**
Arpad Szakolczai

26. **Youth Cultures**
Scenes, subcultures and tribes
Edited by Paul Hodkinson and Wolfgang Deicke

27. **The Obituary as Collective Memory**
Bridget Fowler

28. **Tocqueville's Virus**
Utopia and dystopia in western social and political thought
Mark Featherstone

29. **Jewish Eating and Identity Through the Ages**
David Kraemer

30. **The Institutionalization of Social Welfare**
A study of medicalizing management
Mikael Holmqvist

31. **The Role of Religion in Modern Societies**
Edited by Detlef Pollack and Daniel V. A. Olson

32. **Sex Research and Sex Therapy**
A sociological analysis of Masters and Johnson
Ross Morrow

33. **A Crisis of Waste?**
Understanding the rubbish society
Martin O'Brien

34. **Globalization and Transformations of Local Socioeconomic Practices**
Edited by Ulrike Schuerkens

35. **The Culture of Welfare Markets**
The international recasting of pension and care systems
Ingo Bode

36. **Cohabitation, Family and Society**
Tiziana Nazio

37. **Latin America and Contemporary Modernity**
A sociological interpretation
José Maurízio Domingues

38. **Exploring the Networked Worlds of Popular Music**
Milieu cultures
Peter Webb

39. **The Cultural Significance of the Child Star**
Jane O'Connor

40. **European Integration as an Elite Process: The Failure of a Dream?**
Max Haller

41. **Queer Political Performance and Protest**
Benjamin Shepard

42. **Cosmopolitan Spaces**
Europe, globalization, theory
Chris Rumford

43. **Contexts of Social Capital**
Social networks in communities, markets and organizations
Edited by Ray-May Hsung, Nan Lin, and Ronald Breiger

44. **Feminism, Domesticity and Popular Culture**
Edited by Stacy Gillis and Joanne Hollows

45. **Changing Relationships**
Edited by Malcolm Brynin and John Ermisch

46. **Formal and Informal Work**
The hidden work regime in Europe
Edited by Birgit Pfau-Effinger, Lluis Flaquer, & Per H. Jensen

47. **Interpreting Human Rights**
Social science perspectives
Edited by Rhiannon Morgan and Bryan S. Turner

48. **Club Cultures**
Boundaries, identities and otherness
Silvia Rief

49. **Eastern European Immigrant Families**
Mihaela Robila

50. **People and Societies**
Rom Harré and designing the social sciences
Luk van Langenhove

51. **Legislating Creativity**
The intersections of art and politics
Dustin Kidd

52. **Youth in Contemporary Europe**
Edited by Jeremy Leaman and Martha Wörsching

53. **Globalization and Transformations of Social Inequality**
Edited by Ulrike Schuerkens

54. **Twentieth Century Music and the Question of Modernity**
Eduardo De La Fuente

55. **The American Surfer**
Radical culture and capitalism
Kristin Lawler

56. **Religion and Social Problems**
Edited by Titus Hjelm

57. **Play, Creativity, and Social Movements**
If I can't Dance, It's not my Revolution
Benjamin Shepard

58. **Undocumented Workers' Transitions**
Legal status, migration, and work in Europe
Sonia McKay, Eugenia Markova and Anna Paraskevopoulou

59. **The Marketing of War in the Age of Neo-Militarism**
Edited by Kostas Gouliamos and Christos Kassimeris

60. **Neoliberalism and the Global Restructuring of Knowledge and Education**
Steven C. Ward

61. **Social Theory in Contemporary Asia**
Ann Brooks

62. **Foundations of Critical Media and Information Studies**
Christian Fuchs

63. **A Companion to Life Course Studies**
The social and historical context of the British birth cohort studies
Michael Wadsworth and John Bynner

64. **Understanding Russianness**
Risto Alapuro, Arto Mustajoki and Pekka Pesonen

65. **Understanding Religious Ritual**
Theoretical approaches and innovations
John Hoffmann

66. **Online Gaming in Context**
The social and cultural significance of online games
Garry Crawford, Victoria K. Gosling and Ben Light

67. **Contested Citizenship in East Asia**
Developmental politics, national unity, and globalization
Kyung-Sup Chang and Bryan S. Turner

68. **Agency without Actors?**
New Approaches to collective action
Edited by Jan-Hendrik Passoth, Birgit Peuker and Michael Schillmeier

69. **The Neighborhood in the Internet**
Design research projects in community informatics
John M. Carroll

70. **Managing Overflow in Affluent Societies**
Edited by Barbara Czarniawska and Orvar Löfgren

71. **Refugee Women**
Beyond Gender versus Culture
Leah Bassel

72. **Socioeconomic Outcomes of the Global Financial Crisis**
Theoretical discussion and empirical case studies
Edited by Ulrike Schuerkens

73. **Migration in the 21st Century**
Political economy and ethnography
Edited by Pauline Gardiner Barber and Winnie Lem

74. **Ulrich Beck**
An introduction to the theory of second modernity and the risk society
Mads P. Sørensen and Allan Christiansen

75. **The International Recording Industries**
Edited by Lee Marshall

76. **Ethnographic Research in the Construction Industry**
Edited by Sarah Pink, Dylan Tutt and Andrew Dainty

77. **Routledge Companion to Contemporary Japanese Social Theory**
From individualization to globalization in Japan today
Edited by Anthony Elliott, Masataka Katagiri and Atsushi Sawai

78. **Immigrant Adaptation in Multi-Ethnic Societies**
Canada, Taiwan, and the United States
Edited by Eric Fong, Lan-Hung Nora Chiang and Nancy Denton

79. **Cultural Capital, Identity, and Social Mobility**
The life course of working-class university graduates
Mick Matthys

80. **Speaking for Animals**
Animal autobiographical writing
Edited by Margo DeMello

81. **Healthy Aging in Sociocultural Context**
Edited by Andrew E. Scharlach and Kazumi Hoshino

82. **Touring Poverty**
Bianca Freire-Medeiros

83. **Life Course Perspectives on Military Service**
Edited by Janet M. Wilmoth and Andrew S. London

84. **Innovation in Socio-Cultural Context**
Edited by Frane Adam and Hans Westlund

85. Youth, Arts and Education
Reassembling subjectivity through affect
Anna Hickey-Moody

86. The Capitalist Personality
Face-to-face sociality and economic change in the post-communist world
Christopher S. Swader

87. The Culture of Enterprise in Neoliberalism
Specters of entrepreneurship
Tomas Marttila

88. Islamophobia in the West
Measuring and explaining individual attitudes
Marc Helbling

89. The Challenges of Being a Rural Gay Man
Coping with stigma
Deborah Bray Preston and Anthony R. D'Augelli

90. Global Justice Activism and Policy Reform in Europe
Understanding when change happens
Edited by Peter Utting, Mario Pianta and Anne Ellersiek

91. Sociology of the Visual Sphere
Edited by Regev Nathansohn and Dennis Zuev

92. Solidarity in Individualized Societies
Recognition, justice and good judgement
Søren Juul

93. Heritage in the Digital Era
Cinematic tourism and the activist cause
Rodanthi Tzanelli

94. Generation, Discourse, and Social Change
Karen R. Foster

95. Sustainable Practices
Social theory and climate change
Elizabeth Shove and Nicola Spurling

96. The Transformative Capacity of New Technologies
A theory of sociotechnical change
Ulrich Dolata

97. Consuming Families
Buying, making, producing family life in the 21st century
Jo Lindsay and JaneMaree Maher

98. Migrant Marginality
A transnational perspective
Edited by Philip Kretsedemas, Glenn Jacobs and Jorge Capetillo-Ponce

99. Changing Gay Male Identities
Andrew Cooper

100. Perspectives on Genetic Discrimination
Thomas Lemke

101. Social Sustainability
A multilevel approach to social inclusion
Edited by Veronica Dujon, Jesse Dillard, and Eileen M. Brennan

102. Capitalism
A companion to Marx's economy critique
Johan Fornäs

103. Understanding European Movements
New social movements, global justice struggles, anti-austerity protest
Edited by Cristina Flesher Fominaya and Laurence Cox

104. Applying Ibn Khaldūn
The recovery of a lost tradition in sociology
Syed Farid Alatas

Applying Ibn Khaldūn

The recovery of a lost tradition in sociology

Syed Farid Alatas

Routledge
Taylor & Francis Group
LONDON AND NEW YORK

First published 2014
by Routledge
2 Park Square, Milton Park, Abingdon, Oxon OX14 4RN

and by Routledge
711 Third Avenue, New York, NY 10017

Routledge is an imprint of the Taylor & Francis Group, an informa business

British Library Cataloguing in Publication Data
A catalogue record for this book is available from the British Library.

Library of Congress Cataloging in Publication Data
Alatas, Farid, Syed.
Applying Ibn Khaldun : the recovery of a lost tradition in sociology / Syed Farid Alatas.
pages cm. – (Routledge advances in sociology; 104)
Includes bibliographical references and index.
1. Ibn Khaldun, 1332-1406. 2. Sociology–Arab countries–History.
3. Islamic sociology–History. 4. Social sciences–Philosophy–History.
5. Sociology. I. Title.
HM477.A68A43 2013
297.2'7–dc23 2012047974

ISBN: 978-0-415-67878-0 (hbk)
ISBN: 978-0-203-09359-7 (ebk)

Typeset in Times New Roman
by Deer Park Productions

Printed and Bound in the United States of America by
Edwards Brothers Malloy

To my late father,
Syed Hussein bin Ali bin Abdullah bin Muhsin Alatas
(1928–2007)

Contents

Preface

Ibn Khaldūn is a scholar about whom so much has been written but whose perspective has also been greatly neglected. This book is a contribution to the application of Khaldūnian theory to specific historical cases. It is in the area of application that Ibn Khaldūn has remained, for the most part, marginal.

My interest in Ibn Khaldūn started during my late teens as a result of listening to my father, the late Professor Syed Hussein Alatas, speak about this North African scholar as an original thinker and founder of what in the modern period came to be known as sociology. My father also made frequent references to Ibn Khaldūn in his various writings and the name was etched in my mind as a result. When I was studying at university I developed a greater interest in Ibn Khaldūn. This resulted in several term papers as well as a few journal article publications towards the end of my graduate career. By that time, I had already realized that while there were many publications, symposia and discussions on Ibn Khaldūn, research in one particular area was lacking. There was no school of Khaldūnian sociology or social science to speak of. While it would be possible to refer to countless numbers of social scientists who have adopted the theoretical perspectives of Marx, Weber or Durkheim and developed schools of thought and traditions after these founding fathers, the same cannot be said in reference to Ibn Khaldūn. I finally came to the conclusion that it was necessary to go beyond claiming that Ibn Khaldūn was a precursor of the modern social sciences, a founder of sociology, or an Orientalist tool used to justify colonialism. There were sufficient empirical materials from West Asian and North African history that could be used to test Ibn Khaldūn's theory of the rise and decline of states. This book, then, is an attempt to systematically apply Ibn Khaldūn's theory to specific historical and contemporary empirical cases.

I have used some material from previously published papers on Ibn Khaldūn, although most of this book consists of new material. The following papers have been used as sources in this book: "The Historical Sociology of Muslim Societies: Khaldūnian Application", *International Sociology*, 22, May 2007; "Ibn Khaldūn and the Ottoman Modes of Production", *Arab Historical Review for Ottoman Studies*, 1(2), 1990; "A Khaldūnian Perspective on the Dynamics of Asiatic Societies", *Comparative Civilizations Review*, 29, 1993; and "Ibn Khaldūn and Contemporary Sociology", *International Sociology*, 21, November 2006.

Various individuals and institutions were extremely helpful to me during various stages of my research and writing on Ibn Khaldūn. I would like to thank the Volkswagen Foundation for a grant that allowed me to travel to Egypt and Tunisia between 1996 and 1999 to meet scholars and use the libraries there. In connection with this, I must express my gratitude to the late Professor Joachim Matthes, who introduced me to the Volkswagen Foundation and was extremely supportive of my application for a grant from them. I would also like to thank Professor Mahmoud Dhaouadi, who was a gracious host to me when I was in Tunis and with whom I had many discussions about the sociology of Ibn Khaldūn. I would also like to thank Professor Mohamed Talbi for having kindly met me and given me advice regarding my research. I must also thank the White Fathers, or Pères Blancs, of Tunis, who gave me access to their specialist library from where I obtained many useful papers about Ibn Khaldūn, many of which are cited in this book. In Egypt it was Professor Mona Abaza of the Amercian University in Cairo who gave me a place to stay while I was making use of the library of the AUC and meeting some scholars based in Cairo. I also wish to thank Professor Saad Eddin Ibrāhīm, former president of the Ibn Khaldūn Center for Development Studies, with which I was affiliated while doing fieldwork in Cairo.

Another country to which I travelled frequently and obtained much material on Ibn Khaldūn is Turkey. Professor Recep Şentürk of the Center for Islamic Studies (ISAM), Istanbul, was very kind to host me on several occasions. Recep had also organized symposia on Ibn Khaldūn in Istanbul. The first took place in 2006, where I suggested that an organization devoted to promoting studies on Ibn Khaldūn be established. This was followed up by Professor Şentürk, who established the International Ibn Khaldūn Society with a view to convening a meeting on Ibn Khaldūn every three years in Istanbul. Another Turk who was very helpful was Professor Ş. Tufan Buzpınar, who was kind and patient enough to translate passages on Ibn Khaldūn from his own Turkish language publications. I should also express heartfelt gratitude to Professor Mehmet İpşirli of Fatih University, Istanbul, for having introduced me to the research files of the *İslâm Ansiklopedisi* (*Encyclopaedia of Islam*) project of ISAM. Finally, I must thank staff at the library of the Institute of Political and International Studies (IPIS), Tehran, who provided me with a number of Persian sources concerning Ibn Khaldūn.

In Singapore, the library staff at the Central Library of the National University of Singapore were, as always, extremely kind, helpful and efficient when it came to obtaining materials via inter-library loan or document delivery. Thanks must also go to two of my research assistants from the Department of Malay Studies at NUS, that is, Ms Sharifah Husainah and Ms Nurul Fadiah Bte Johari, who helped me with some library work. Thanks are also due to Mr Syafiq Borhannuddin from the Centre for Advanced Studies on Islam, Science and Civilization (CASIS) at the Universiti Teknologi Malaysia, who assisted me in obtaining some works on Ibn Khaldūn from Malaysian libraries.

No amount of words is sufficient when it comes to thanking my family members for the love and warmth that they provide. My mother, S. Zaharah Alatas and Babsy at our home in Kuala Lumpur continue to give me much support in my intellectual and other pursuits. My wife Mojgan Shavarebi, and children Syed Imad Alatas, Sharifah Afra Alatas and Syed Ubaydillah Alatas always provide the peace and tranquillity needed to concentrate. My father, the late Syed Hussein Alatas, was the reason that I took Ibn Khaldūn seriously and it is to him that this book is dedicated.

Introduction

Ibn Khaldūn as a sociologist

The basic argument of this book is that there is a modern sociology to be reconstructed from the writings of 'Abd al-Raḥmān ibn Khaldūn that would have much relevance to the study of history and contemporary society, but that this reconstruction and application has generally not taken place because of the relative neglect of Ibn Khaldūn as a theorist.

One of the most conspicuous features of Orientalism, a persistent feature that has survived for centuries, is the neglect of the theoretical authority of so-called Oriental thinkers. Although the critique of Orientalism and related problems such as Eurocentrism in the social sciences and humanities has been around since at least the latter part of the nineteenth century,[1] the serious consideration of the thought of seminal non-Western thinkers as sources of theories and concepts that are applicable to historical and empirical data is largely absent. The task of studying alternatives to Orientalist constructions is the logical result of the critique of Orientalism but has, with a few exceptions, not been undertaken. This is particularly true of the fields of Islamic, Middle Eastern and North African studies. The present study focuses on the historical sociology of a thinker whose theoretical authority over his subject matter and potential relevance to times and places beyond his own have been largely neglected.

Why should a social thinker like Ibn Khaldūn be excluded from the serious study of the history of sociology, sociological theory or historical sociology? A quick review of contemporary histories of social thought and social theory will reveal that very little attention is given to non-Western precursors of sociology or non-Western social thinkers who were contemporaneous with the European founders of the discipline. Nineteenth- and early-twentieth-century Western sociologists, on the other hand, were more aware of the role of non-Western thought in the development of Western sociology as a discipline. This interest will be found to have waned in most of the twentieth century up till today.

The nineteenth century European founders of sociology such as Marx, Weber and Durkheim had such an impact on the development of sociology and the other social sciences that many theories and models derived from their works were applied to areas outside of Europe: that is, to the non-Western world. The same attitude was not applied to non-Western social thinkers. Without suggesting that

European or Western ideas have no relevance to non-European realities, this chapter suggests that multicultural sources of sociological thought and theory should be considered.

The study of the rise and decline of states, of dynastic succession and the role of religion in the Muslim East and West (*al-mashriq* and *al-maghrib*), have yet to benefit from a systematic application of the theory of Ibn Khaldūn. The chief reason for this is that Ibn Khaldūn has always been at the margins of the modern social sciences and, at most, regarded as a precursor of modern sociology, but not a sociologist in his own right. Consequently, his work on history and his elaboration of the science of society (*'ilm al-'umrān*), deemed by him as a prerequisite for the study of history, has rarely been seriously considered as a basis for a modern Khaldūnian sociology.

Ibn Khaldūn died 600 years ago, but his ideas have endured. Nevertheless, there is a way in which he has been appropriated, resulting in his somewhat marginal status in contemporary sociology.

What is being said here with regard to the state of Ibn Khaldūn studies in the West holds equally true for the Arab and Muslim worlds. Since the education systems in the Muslim world are mirror images of those in the West, it follows that the problems of Eurocentrism are defining features of the social sciences there as well, with the added dimension that in the Muslim world Eurocentrism implies alienation from the Muslim tradition of scholarship. An examination of sociological theory syllabi in many Muslim countries illustrates just this point. I have seen course outlines for introductory and advanced courses on classical social thought and social theory in universities in Egypt, Jordan, Yemen, Bangladesh, Indonesia and Malaysia and have found this alienation to be a persistent theme.[2] There is a remarkable lack of diversity across these countries as far as the teaching of sociological theory is concerned. There is an overwhelming emphasis, often exclusive attention, to nineteenth- and early-twentieth-century European and North American male theorists such as Marx, Weber and Durkheim. This is as if to say that there was an absence of European and American women, or Asian, African and Latin American men and women, who theorized about the state of society during the same period.

The bulk of research and writing on Ibn Khaldūn consists of (1) biographical details of his life; (2) descriptive restatements of his general theory of state formation or discussions on specific concepts contained in his work; (3) comparisons between his theory and that of the founders of modern Western social science; (4) references to his historical narrative of North Africa (*al-maghrib*) as a source of historical data and information on the region; and (5) analyses of the methodological foundations of his writings. There has been very little by way of theoretical applications of Ibn Khaldūn's theory of state formation to empirical historical situations. This is partly due to the continuing presence of Eurocentrism in the social sciences that stands in the way of the consideration of non-European (for European read also American) sources of theories and concepts. This is, in fact, the manner in which Ibn Khaldūn's thought is marginal to the modern social science. While he is well known and often referred in those areas of study to which he is relevant, there is a profound indifference or neglect of the theoretical applicability of his ideas.

This book provides an overview of Ibn Khaldūn and his sociology, discusses reasons for his marginality, and suggests ways to bring Ibn Khaldūn into the mainstream through the systematic application of his theory. The point is to move beyond works that simply state that Ibn Khaldūn was a founder of sociology or provide descriptive accounts of his works. By Khaldūnian sociology I am referring to theoretical applications that include the integration of concepts and frameworks from Khaldūnian into modern social science theories.

The life of Ibn Khaldūn

'Abd al-Raḥmān bin Muḥammad bin Muḥammad bin al-Ḥassan bin Muḥammad bin Jābir bin Muḥammad ibn Ibrāhīm bin 'Abd al-Raḥmān bin Khaldūn (732–808 AH/1332–1406 AD) is probably the most well known among Muslim scholars both in the Muslim world and the West as far as the social sciences are concerned. Much is known about Ibn Khaldūn's life because of his autobiography, which accounts for his life up to the year 1405, about a year before he died. Born in Tunis into the house of Khaldūn (Banū Khaldūn), he traces his descent to an Arab tribe from the South Arabian region of the Ḥaḍramawt. His ancestors had settled in Seville, Andalusia, in the early period of the Arab conquest of the Iberian Peninsula. They left Andalusia for the Maghrib (North Africa) after the Reconquista, settling in Tunis in the seventh/thirteenth century.[3] One of the more prominent of Ibn Khaldūn's ancestors was one Kurayb who is said to have revolted against the Umayyads towards the end of the ninth century and established a quasi-independent state in Seville.[4] It is known that the Banū Khaldūn played an important role in the political leadership of Seville.

Khaldūn bin 'Uthmān established himself in Carmona, Andalusia with a small group of Ḥaḍramīs where the family was founded. Two sons of Khaldūn, Kurayb and Khālid, were active participants in successful revolts against the Umayyad rulers in Seville towards the end of the third/ninth–tenth century.[5] By this time, the house of Khaldūn had established itself as an eminent family of politicians and men of knowledge. Kurayb was eventually killed but the Khaldūns remained in Seville during the entire Umayyad period, gaining prominence once again after the conquest of Seville by Ka'b ibn 'Abbād, when they were given ministerial and other high posts in the latter half of the fifth/eleventh century. During this period, Ibn 'Abbād entered into an alliance with the Almoravid (1053–1147) ruler of North Africa, Yūsuf ibn Tāshfīn, and together they defeated Alfonso VI, king of Castille (479 AH/1086 AD).[6]

Almoravid rule over Andalusia gave way to that of the Almohads (1147–1275), where the Banū Khaldūn continued to enjoy authority under the rule of Abū Hafs, chief of the Hintāta tribe, who became the ruler of Seville and western Andalusia.[7] As Almohad power began to decline and its territories fell gradually into the hands of the king of Castille, Abū Zakariyyā, the grandson of Abū Ḥafṣ, emigrated to Tunis (Ifrīqiyā) in 620 AH/1202 AD, of which he declared himself an independent ruler. During the same time Banū Khaldūn left Seville, fearing Christian encroachment on the city, and settled in Ceuta, off the North African coast, which was under Ḥafṣid rule.[8] Then, the fourth grandfather of Ibn Khaldūn, al-Ḥasan bin Muḥammad, joined Abū Zakariyyā' in Bona (in present-day Algeria), enjoying his protection and patronage. Abū Zakariyyā' died in Bona in 647 AH/1247 AD and was succeeded by his son al-Mustanṣir Muḥammad, who was in turn succeeded by his son, Yaḥyā in 675 AH/1277 AD. The throne was eventually seized by the brother of Al-Mustanṣir, Abū Isḥāq, who appointed Abū Bakr Muḥammad, Ibn Khaldūn's great-grandfather, Director of Finances (*'amal al-ashghāl*). Later on, Sultan Abū Isḥāq named Muḥammad, the historian's grandfather, Chamberlain to the Crown Prince, Abū Fāris.[9]

At this time, the authority of the Ḥafṣids began to weaken and a pretender to the throne, Ibn abī 'Imārah, seized power, murdered Abū Bakr ibn Khaldūn and confiscated his wealth. Ibn Khaldūn's grandfather, Muḥammad, remained at the Ḥafṣid court until Tunis was taken by Abū Yaḥyā ibn al-Liḥyānī, during which time Muḥammad was appointed chamberlain for a while. He died in 737 AH/1337 AD.[10] This Khaldūnian predilection for office continued in the family after they had left Anadalusia for North Africa. They settled in Tunis, where Ibn Khaldūn was born.

Ibn Khaldūn's life is usually divided by historians into three periods. The first, of 20 years, was that of his childhood, youth and education. Ibn Khaldūn then spent the following 23 years continuing his studies and working for various rulers. He spent the third period of 31 years as a scholar, teacher and magistrate.[11]

Born in the month of Ramaḍān in the year 732 AH/1332 AD, Ibn Khaldūn studied the various Islamic sciences such as Qur'anic recitation and its styles, Qur'anic orthography, Malikite jurisprudence, the hadith or traditions of the Prophet, and poetry. He studied under several well-known scholars and also received the *ijāzah* or permission to transmit teachings in language and law from Shams al-Dīn abū 'Abdallāh Muḥammad bin Jābir bin Sulṭān al-Qaysī al-Wādīyāshī, the greatest hadith authority of Tunis.[12] The Marinids' hold over Tunis under Abū al-Ḥasan and his son, Abū 'Inān, was precarious and intermittent and ended a decade later when the Ḥafṣids regained power. While this would have seemed to be a period of political instability, Ibn Khaldūn gained in terms of his education because of the availability of great scholars who accompanied Abū al-Ḥasan to Tunis as part of his retinue. During the second period of his life, Ibn Khaldūn was involved in a great deal of political adventure and intrigue.

During the reign of the Ḥafṣids, Ibn Khaldūn was appointed to the post of Master of the Signature (*Ṣāhib al-'Alāmah*) by the powerful chamberlain, Abū Muḥammad ibn Tāfrāgīn. Ibn Khaldūn was not happy in this position as he missed his intellectual pursuits under the various masters that he had studied with previously, many of whom had left Tunis or died during the Great Plague in 748 AH/1348 AD, which took Ibn Khaldūn's parents as well.[13]

Ibn Khaldūn had to wait for an opportune moment to abscond from the despot Ibn Tāfrāgīn. This moment came in 753 AH/1352 AD. The ruler of Constantine, Abū Zayd, grandson of Sultan Abū Yaḥyā, amassed his troops and marched on Tunis. He was met by Ibn Tāfrāgīn and his forces, accompanied by the young and newly appointed Master of the Signature. Ibn Khaldūn managed to steal away from the Tunisian camp and slowly travelled to the west, seeking refuge and help along the way. In Tlemcen he met up with Sultan Abū ʻInān, who warmly welcomed him and in Batha' was given a reception such as he had never seen by the Chamberlain Ibn abī ʻAmr, whom he then accompanied to Bougie to witness and participate in the conquest of that city. Ibn Khaldūn stayed in Bougie until the end of 754 AH/1353 AD.[14]

Upon his return to Fez, Sultan Abū ʻInān began to assemble men of learning, during which time, Ibn Khaldūn says, his name was mentioned in the course of the selection of scholars for participation in discussions and consultation. He was eventually appointed to the scientific council of the sultan in 755 AH/1354 AD.[15] This gave Ibn Khaldūn the opportunity to meet with scholars from the Maghrib and Andalusia who visited the court of Fez, many of whom are listed by Ibn Khaldūn and include various well-known personalities. There was the master Muḥammad bin al-Ṣaffār, originally from Marrakesh and the foremost authority of his time on the Qur'an. There was also the grand cadi (*qāḍī*) of Fez, Muḥummad al-Maqqarī from Tlemcen, and the scholar of the intellectual and rational sciences, Muḥammad bin Aḥmad al-Sharīf al-Ḥasanī, also known as al-ʻAlawī.[16]

Whenever a situation was unfavourable to him, Ibn Khaldūn would try to leave. For example, he wished to leave Fez and return to Tunis. The ruler of Fez was reluctant to let him go for fear that he may collude with his enemy, the ruler of Tlemcen. Ibn Khaldūn was eventually allowed to leave on condition that he did not go to Tlemcen. He chose to go to Andalusia where he entered into the service of the ruler of Granada, Sultan Muḥammad. There Ibn Khaldūn met with the famous vizier and renowned writer and poet, Ibn al-Khaṭīb.[17]

When Ibn Khaldūn fell out of favour with Sultan Muḥammad, he moved to Bougie in North Africa in the middle of 766 AH/1365 AD, where he was appointed Chamberlain (*wilāyat al-ḥijābah*). His duty was to manage the affairs of the state and the relations between the sultan and his subjects.[18] Ibn Khaldūn reports that he was extremely well received with much pomp and ceremony. He was met by a procession and the inhabitants of Bougie rushed to touch his robe and kiss his hands. He found it to be a memorable day indeed. Ibn Khaldūn says that he deployed all his effort at managing the affairs of the ruler. In addition to his duties as Chamberlain, he was also put in charge of the Friday sermon at the mosque of the citadel.[19]

As happened before, after a while things did not proceed smoothly. Antagonism developed between Muḥammad and his cousin, Sultan Abū al-ʻAbbās, the ruler of Constantine. The sultan had set his sights on the conquest of Bougie, which he marched on in 767 AH/1366 AD and defeated and killed Muḥammad. Some of the inhabitants of the city asked Ibn Khaldūn to take power and proclaim one of the sons of Muḥammad as ruler. He refused and instead handed over Bougie to Abū al-ʻAbbās, who continued to have Ibn Khaldūn serve in his former position.[20]

Such was the life of Ibn Khaldūn until he finally decided to withdraw to a life of scholarship. This took place in the isolated fort, the Qalʻat Ibn Salāmah in Algeria. It is here that the third period of Ibn Khaldūn's life begins. Ibn Khaldūn held posts in many of the courts of the Maghrib and Andalusia. Ibn Khaldūn lived during the period of the political fragmentation and cultural decline of the Arab Muslim world. The picture of chaos and disintegration that Ibn Khaldūn grew up with must have influenced the development of his thought. The uncertainties of politics and the lure of scholarship, as well as a number of unsuccessful stints in office, finally led to his withdrawing into seclusion to write his introduction to the study of history. The previous period of politics and intrigues had given way to reflection on the meaning and pattern of history. The result of four years of isolation was the *Muqaddimah* or *Prolegomenon* to his larger work on the history of the Arabs and Berbers. This was completed in 1378 and introduces what he believed to be a new science that resembles what is now called sociology. He says, "I completed its introduction following that unusual method (*al-naḥw al-gharīb*) I was guided to by that retreat."[21]

Ibn Khaldūn began to be celebrated as the author of the *Muqaddimah*. One of Ibn Khaldūn's biographers, Maḥāsin ibn Taghribirdī, tells us that Ibn Khaldūn lectured at the Grand Mosque of al-Azhar.[22] Another biographer, al-Sakhāwī, relates that the people of Cairo received him with honour and spent much time with him.[23] He lectured on the hidith and jurisprudence and also on topics that the *Muqaddimah* was concerned with. This was related, among others, by the historian Taqī al-Dīn al-Maqrīzī who had attended Ibn Khaldūn's lectures when he was a young man[24] and was possibly his follower as well.[25]

Ibn Khaldūn was in Egypt during Timur's invasion of Syria. He became a reluctant member of an Egyptian expedition that aimed to repel the Tartar's forces. When the fighting between the two sides resulted in a stalemate, Ibn Khaldūn decided to attempt to seek a way out by meeting Timur. Ibn Khaldūn's audience with Timur consisted of a long conversation between the two. Timur was reportedly curious about the history of North Africa.[26] According to Fischel, an account of the meeting between Timur and Ibn Khaldūn by the biographer of Timur, Aḥmad ibn Muḥammad ibn 'Arabshāh, suggests that it was unlikely that Timur had heard of Ibn Khaldūn. Timur knew about Ibn Khaldūn only when he appeared before him. Timur had apparently remarked to the other Egyptians present, "This man [Ibn Khaldūn] is not from your country", something Timur gathered from Ibn Khaldūn's dress.[27] Despite having just become acquainted with Ibn Khaldūn's work, Timur was evidently impressed enough by the latter's knowledge to ask him to compose a work on North African history for him.[28] Talbi speculates on an interesting idea that Ibn Khaldūn may have considered Timur as "'the man of the century' who possessed enough *'aṣabīyyah* to unite the Muslim world and change the direction of history".[29]

It is possible that Ibn Khaldūn questioned the terms of the surrender of Damascus with Timur. It was not very long after the meeting that Damascus surrendered.[30] Enan, however, reports that the historian al-Maqrīzī gives a different account of these events. According to him, it was the judge Taqī al-Dīn ibn Mufliḥ al-Ḥanbalī who negotiated with Timur over the surrender of Damascus. According to this account it was Ibn Mufliḥ who convinced the chiefs to capitulate and it was he who obtained the guarantee of safety. But Timur broke his word and arrested

Ibn Mufliḥ and set Damascus on fire.[31] Enan says that this was confirmed by Ibn Iyās, who said that Ibn Mufliḥ was chosen as the negotiator because he spoke the Turkic dialect of Timur.[32] Enan does state, however, that there is no reason to doubt Ibn Khaldūn's version of events, which is not inconsistent with the possibility that Ibn Mufliḥ also took part in negotiations with Timur.[33] Ibn Khaldūn referred to Timur, in his conversations with him, as the sultan of the world and that the world had not seen a comparable ruler since Adam.[34] Talbi suggests that Ibn Khaldūn considered that Timur was the ruler whose *'aṣabīyyah* (group feeling) was sufficiently great to reunite the Muslim world.[35]

Ibn Khaldūn spent his last days in Cairo, where he was appointed to the post of Malikite judge for a total of six times. He was reappointed to the post of judge in the latter part of 803 AH. He died on the 26th of Ramaḍān 808 AH/16 March 1406 AD, just a few weeks after his sixth and final appointment.

The works of Ibn Khaldūn

Ibn Khaldūn's greatest work, and the one that is relevant to the modern discipline of sociology, the *Muqaddimah*, forms a part of his monumental study, the *Kitāb al-'Ibar Dīwān al-Mubtadā' wa-l-Khabar fī Ayyām al-'Arab wa-l-'Ajam wa-l-Barbar* (*Book of Examples and the Collection of Origins of the History of the Arabs and Berbers*), an empirical work on the history of the Arabs and Berbers in several volumes. The *Muqaddimah* or *Prolegomenon* was written as the introduction to the *Kitāb al-'Ibar*. Ibn Khaldūn understood the *Muqaddimah* to be the explanation of the underlying causes and inner meaning of that history, while the *Kitāb al-'Ibar* was the descriptive part of his history. It is the study of the underlying causes and inner meaning of history that Ibn Khaldūn referred to as both *'ilm al-'umrān al-basharī* (the science of human social organization) or *'ilm al-ijtimā' al-insānī* (the science of human society). The structure of the *Kitāb al-'Ibar* is as follows.

- A short Introduction (*muqaddimah*). This is not the *Prolegomenon*, which had also come to be referred to by the title *Muqaddimah*. The Introduction discusses the excellence of historiography as well as the various errors to which historians are prone.
- Book One (*Kitāb al-Awwal*), dealing with society and its characteristics, covers topics such as authority, government, modes of making a living, and the crafts and sciences.
- Book Two (*Kitāb al-Thānī*) covers the history of Arab as well as non-Arab dynasties such as the Persians, Syrians, Copts, Israelites, Nabataeans, Greeks, Byzantines and Turks.
- Book Three (*Kitāb al-Thālith*) deals with the history of the Berbers of North Africa, focusing on royal authority and dynastic succession.
- What came to be known as the *Muqaddimah* or *Prolegomenon* is the entirety of Book One consisting of six chapters (*faṣl*).
- Ibn Khaldūn's autobiography, *Al-Ta'rīf bi-Ibn Khaldūn Mu'allif Hādha al-Kitāb, wa Riḥlatuhu Gharban wa-Sharqan* (*Information on Ibn Khaldūn,*

Author of this Work, and His Travels East and West), which appears separately in published versions, was originally attached to the end of the *Kitāb al-'Ibar*.[36]

The present study

Apart from biographies, many works that present overviews of the thought of Ibn Khaldūn do so in the context of bestowing a precursor status to Ibn Khaldūn. At least two generations of sociologists in the Arab and Muslim world wrote on Ibn Khaldūn as a precursor of modern sociology. 'Abd al-'Azīz 'Izzat wrote a thesis in 1932 entitled *Ibn Khaldun et sa science sociale* under the direction of Fauconnier and René Maunier in France,[37] and another work comparing Ibn Khaldūn and Emile Durkheim.[38] 'Ali 'Abd al-Wāḥid Wāfī, also of that generation, did a comparative study of Ibn Khaldūn and Auguste Comte and wrote a well-known piece on Ibn Khaldūn as the founder of sociology.[39] Syed Hussein Alatas from Malaysia also referred to Ibn Khaldūn as having established the principles of modern sociology.[40] In fact, for some, to write on Ibn Khaldūn became something of an inaugural act for entry into the profession of sociology, as noted by Roussillon and Abaza.[41] It is interesting to note that the famed Egyptian novelist and social thinker Taha Hussein, who himself wrote a doctoral dissertation on Ibn Khaldūn, regarded the claim that Ibn Khaldūn was a sociologist as an exaggeration.[42]

There are a few historical exceptions to what has been said above. These can be divided into at least three genres. The first regards Ibn Khaldūn's *Muqaddimah* as an originally conceived philosophy of history.[43] The second seeks to extract what we may call a neo-Khaldūnian sociology, as it were, from Ibn Khaldūn's works.[44] The third is critical of approaches that seek to view Ibn Khaldūn's work anachronistically through modern lenses and attribute to him a modern sociological imagination.[45] Nevertheless, there are no long-standing debates surrounding each of these positions. As a result, theoretical interest in Ibn Khaldūn has not been able to sustain itself to any appreciable degree. In place of a more sophisticated theoretical assessment of Ibn Khaldūn's writings are simplified caricatures of his work. For example, Lacoste suggests that most authors who studied the *Muqaddimah* reduce Ibn Khaldūn's thought to a psychologistic cyclical theory of state formation founded on the simplistic distinction between nomadic and sedentary society.[46]

This book addresses itself to the second genre: that is, the specification of a general Khaldūnian historical sociology. While it is not within the scope of this book to elaborate a general Khaldūnian sociology, the aim is to provide examples of systematic applications of Ibn Khaldūn's theory of state formation to specific historical and empirical cases, most of which lie outside of his own time and geographical focus. These applications can be seen as a prerequisite for the development of a general Khaldūnian sociological theory, the relevance of which can be extended to regions and contexts outside of those that concerned Ibn Khaldūn directly. The reconstruction of Ibn Khaldūn's theory itself is deemed necessary as existing discussions on his thought, though extensive, varied and valuable, tend to treat his theoretical and empirical work separately. They elaborate on his theory by drawing upon his *Muqaddimah* or discuss or refer to his historical data presented in the *Kitāb al-'Ibar*. Furthermore, such works tend to be innocent of political economy, failing to relate the dynamics of state formation in Ibn Khaldūn's theory to questions of class and the ownership and control of the means of production. The aim in the present study is to raise certain problems in the study of state formation in parts of the Muslim world and elsewhere as distinctly Khaldūnian problems that can be approached by applying a framework that integrates Ibn Khaldūn's theory of state formation with modern concepts in sociology. I propose to do this by selecting a number of historical cases of state formation. There have been many historical and sociological studies of state formation in the Middle East, North Africa, Central Asia, the Indian sub-continent and China, areas where a Khaldūnian model has potential applicability and may provide the empirical ground on which to develop a general Khaldūnian sociology.

The meta-theoretical context of this study has to do with the state of the social sciences in the South. While the theoretical critiques of the social sciences such as the theories of Orientalism, Eurocentrism, intellectual imperialism and academic dependency are well known, the logical consequences of these critiques, such as the prescriptions for autonomous social sciences or alternative discourses, are not widely understood in mainstream academic circles and are rarely put into practice even in the South. This study offers Ibn Khaldūn as an exemplar for a sociology of and for the South by way of an application of his ideas to concrete historical cases.

This study revolves around the *Muqaddimah*, Ibn Khaldūn's prologue to his empirical history, the *Kitāb al-'Ibar Dīwān al-Mubtadā' wa-l-Khabar fī Ayyām al-'Arab wa-l-'Ajam wa-l-Barbar* (*Book of Examples and the Collection of Origins of the History of the Arabs and Berbers*). This book goes beyond merely proclaiming that Ibn Khaldūn was the founder or precursor of sociology. The writings of Ibn Khaldūn, particularly the *Muqaddimah*, have rightly been regarded as being sociological in nature. For this reason, Ibn Khaldūn has been widely regarded as the founder of sociology, or at least, a precursor of modern sociology. While he was correctly given this recognition, however, few works went beyond proclaiming him as a founder or precursor to the systematic application of his theoretical perspective to specific historical and empirical aspects of Muslim societies in North Africa and the Middle East. This is partly due to the continuing presence of Eurocentrism in the social sciences, which stands in the way of the consideration of non-Western sources of theories and concepts. This book corrects this imbalance by systematically applying Ibn Khaldūn theoretical perspective to specific historical and contemporary aspects of Muslim societies in North Africa and the Middle East. As such, it is a contribution to the multicultural origins of the discipline of sociology.

Ibn Khaldūn has always been noted as a founder of sociology and other social sciences, but this was more the case in the nineteenth and early twentieth centuries. Today, there is much less appeal to heritage both in the Arab-Muslim world and in the West. As noted above, even when there was a historical interest in Ibn Khaldūn, it was not for his work as a source of theoretical sociology that had potential to be brought into the discipline of modern sociology. Where Ibn Khaldūn is taken up more seriously in Islamic, Middle Eastern or North African studies or where he is referred to by scholars in non-Eurocentric contexts, theoretical and methodological work on Ibn Khaldūn is rarely attempted. It is almost exclusively social thought originating from Western Europe and North America that continues to be the focus of teachers and students of sociology and the history of social thought and theory.

The organization of the book is as follows. Chapter 1 introduces Ibn Khaldūn's discourse on the errors of historians up to his time. It is his keen observations of the faults of historians that led him to consider the need for a new science that may avoid the pitfalls of the existing historiography. Chapter 2 introduces the *Muqaddimah* by way of discussing its structure and aims, and provides a cursory sketch of his theory of society and his basic epistemological position. It provides a theoretical overview of Ibn Khaldūn's framework for the study of state formation, with reference to both the theory as well as his methodology. Chapter 3 discusses the reception of Ibn Khaldūn among modern sociologists in the nineteenth and twentieth centuries, particularly during the formative period of the discipline of sociology. This chapter also provides an account of the marginal status of Ibn Khaldūn, situating him between the polar opposites of Eurocentrism and Islamization of knowledge project. I suggest here that a Khaldūnian tradition was in the making but failed to develop through to today. This failure can be attributed to the problem of Eurocentrism in the social sciences as well as to a nativistic orientation to be found among some social science communities in the Muslim world. The rest of the book is concerned with elaborating the form that a Khaldūnian sociology might take. The chapters that follow outline the new science as Ibn Khaldūn conceived it and discuss applications of the Khaldūnian framework to empirical cases from various historical periods and geographical regions.

Chapters 4 to 8 provide examples of how Ibn Khaldūn's theory of state formation may be applied to different historical and contemporary situations. Chapter 4 looks at pre-modern applications of Ibn Khaldūn, drawing on examples from his followers in the Arab East and West as well as the Ottoman Empire where they asked Khaldūnian questions about their own history. Chapter 5 discusses Ibn Khaldūn's theory of state formation as a theory of Muslim reform and provides a critique of this theory, suggesting that it is psychologistic. Here, I turn to the application of Ibn Khaldūn to the study of Muslim reform and suggest that Ibn Khaldūn's theory of state formation is indeed a theory of Muslim reform, a reading conveyed by the Khaldūnian term *taghyīr al-munkar*. This raises the idea of the possibilities for a Khaldūnian sociology of Muslim reform. Chapters 6 and 7 attempt to correct the imbalance identified in Chapter 5 by integrating a mode of production framework into Ibn Khaldūn's theory of state formation, using the examples of the Ottoman and Safavid political economy. Chapter 8 brings the discussion to the modern period and discusses several ways in which Ibn Khaldūn's theory of state formation has been applied to understand the rise and demise of modern states. Chapter 9 makes some general remarks on the development of

Khaldūnian sociology and the importance of the role of teaching, research and other academic activities in promoting the ideas of a nearly forgotten sociological theorist. It concludes with some comments on the issue of Ibn Khaldūn and the future of autonomous sociology.

There is a need to go beyond claiming that Ibn Khaldūn is a precursor of the modern social sciences or seeing him as a tool for the justification of colonial rule among Orientalists. There are clearly areas for the further development of sociology that seriously take the ideas of Ibn Khaldūn into account. This book is about the possibilities of developing Khaldūnian sociology, a sociology that can be applied to historical and contemporary empirical cases.

1 The errors of history and the new science

Introduction to the *Muqaddimah*

The problematization of history as the basis for sociology

The basis of Ibn Khaldūn's new science of society was his critique of the state of historiography among the historians of the Arab East and West up to his time. His critical mind can be gauged from comments that he made in his autobiography regarding his own family tree, the accuracy of which he doubted. The autobiography begins with an observation of an error in the record of his family's genealogy. Assuming that it were true that the first Khaldūn migrated to Andalusia during the time of the Arab conquest, there would be some 20 generations between him and his ancestor. However, according to the family tree there were ten generations that separated them. Ibn Khaldūn figured that ten generations would not have covered the span of 700 years that separated him from the first Khaldūn, if it was considered that three generations appeared per century. He reckoned that it was more likely that 20 generations separated him from the first Khaldūn, if there were three generations per century.[1] The failure to apply such logic to the reports of history was among the more serious errors committed by historians that Ibn Khaldūn cited. The *Muqaddimah*, completed in 1378, was written to create a theoretical framework that would allow for a reconstruction of history that avoided the errors common to the historiography of his time. Furthermore, the *Muqaddimah* serves as an introduction to his larger empirical work on the history of the Arabs and Berbers, the *Kitāb al-'Ibar*. In the foreword he gives us the rationale for this work. He notes that history is something that both the learned and ignorant are able to understand. The all-important distinction between the surface (*ẓāhir*) aspect of history as distinguished from its inner meaning (*bāṭin*) is made.

> For on the surface history is no more than information about political events, dynasties, and occurrences of the remote past, elegantly presented and spiced with proverbs. It serves to entertain large, crowded gatherings and brings to us an understanding of human affairs. (It shows) how changing conditions affected (human affairs), how certain dynasties came to occupy an ever wider space in the world, and how they settled the earth until they heard the call and their time was up.

> The inner meaning of history, on the other hand, involves speculation and an attempt to get at the truth, subtle explanation of the causes and origins of existing things, and deep knowledge of the how and why of events.[2]

The *Kitāb al-'Ibar* in Ibn Khaldūn's terms, therefore, covers the surface phenomenon of history in that it details the history of the Arab and Berber dynasties of the Arab East (the Mashriq) and Arab West (the Maghrib). The inner meaning of history, on the other hand, is dealt with in the *Muqaddimah*, the *Prolegomenon* and the first book of Ibn Khaldūn's voluminous *Kitāb al-'Ibar*.

While there were outstanding historians among the Muslims of the past, later historians introduced untruths and even gossip which were passed on to succeeding generations of historians. The false and the nonsensical in history were not rejected, as historians tended not to look into the causes and origins of events and conditions. The problem here for Ibn Khaldūn was the lack of a critical perspective. This absence allowed for errors and weak assumptions to predominate in historical information. For Ibn Khaldūn, the discipline of history had come to be dominated by unqualified and unoriginal historians who failed to distinguish the surface phenomena of history from its inner meanings.

> Blind trust in tradition is an inherited trait in human beings. Occupation with the (scholarly) disciplines on the part of those who have no right is widespread. But the pasture of stupidity is unwholesome for mankind. No one can stand up against the authority of truth, and the evil of falsehood is to be fought with enlightening speculation. The reporter merely dictates and passes on (the material). It takes critical insight to sort out the hidden truth; it takes knowledge to lay truth bare and polish it so that critical insight may be applied to it.
>
> Many systematic historical works have been composed, and the history of nations and dynasties in the world has been compiled and written down. But there are very few (historians) who have become so well known as to be recognized as authorities, and who have replaced the products of their predecessors by their own works.[3]

The tradition-bound historians copied the work of earlier historians without paying due attention to the origins of phenomena and changes in conditions over time. Their main objective was to preserve historical information as they received it, without seeking explanations of causes and origins, and make judgements as to the truth of falsehood of reports.

> They do not turn to the beginning of the dynasty. Nor do they tell why it unfurled its banner and was able to give prominence to its emblem, or what caused it to come to a stop when it had reached its term. The student, thus, has still to search for the beginnings of conditions and for (the principles of) organization of (the various dynasties). He must (himself) investigate why the various dynasties brought pressures to bear upon each other and why they succeeded each other. He must search for a convincing explanation of the

elements that made for mutual separation or contact among the dynasties. All this will be dealt with in the Introduction to this work.[4]

Having made some preliminary remarks on the study of history in the foreword, Ibn Khaldūn proceeds to make further elaborations on the errors to which historians are prone to making in the short introduction to the *Kitāb al-'Ibar*. The discipline of history requires not only a sound command of numerous sources but also a good speculative mind. Historical information cannot be trusted in its plain transmitted form. A lack of knowledge of customs, the fundamentals of politics, and the nature of human social organization, coupled with the failure to apply the comparative method, results in the commission of errors in the reporting of events.[5] Ibn Khaldūn provides many illustrations of these errors.

For example, he notes that the renowned historian al-Mas'ūdī, and many others, reported that Moses' army of Israelites consisted of more than 600,000 arms-bearing men in battle. Al-Mas'ūdī failed to consider if it were indeed possible for an army of that size to do battle. Such a large army in battle would extend much beyond the field of vision. Ibn Khaldūn notes that this was the case with battle formations during his time and that this fact was sufficient to testify to the situation of the past. Furthermore, Ibn Khaldūn notes that the fact that the Persians had far greater territory under their rule can also be used as a gauge of the size of Moses' army. If the Persians commanded greater territory it stands to reason that their army was larger than that of the Israelites. We would be more confident in accepting this argument when it is known that the Persians under Nebuchadnezzar defeated the Israelites. Nebuchadnezzar was only a governor in the Persian realm. The total number of Persian troops amounted to about 200,000 men. Even if Nebuchadnezzar had commanded all of these 200,000 men, it is unlikely that he went into battle against 600,000 Israelites. Ibn Khaldūn also suggests that it was unlikely that the Israelites could have amounted to so many men, as it was improbable that the descendants of one man, Israel, could have attained such a great number within just four generations.[6]

Another example of erroneous statements by historians is from the history of the kings of Yemen and the Arabian Peninsula, the Tubba's. They are said to have conducted raids of Ifrīqiyā and the Berbers of North Africa. One of the Tubba' kings, Afrīqus bin Qays bin Ṣayfī, was said to have massacred the Berbers. It was further claimed that it was Afrīqus who gave the name "Berber" to them. Upon hearing what was to him an unintelligible language, he asked what that "*barbarah*" was. It was also claimed in many accounts that Afrīqus left some Ḥimyar tribes in the Maghrib which intermarried with the indigenous population and gave rise to the Ṣinhājah and Kutāmah tribes. It thus became widely believed that these two tribes were descendants of the Ḥimyar. It was also said of the Tubba's that their last ruler, As'ad abū Karib, and his sons raided, routed and slaughtered the Byzantines, Persians and Chinese.

Ibn Khaldūn says that these claims about the Tubba' are baseless. In fact, their realm was restricted to the Arabian Peninsula. As they were surrounded by the ocean on three sides, the only access they had to the Maghrib was via the Suez.

It was unlikely that the army of the Tubba's could have travelled to the Mediterranean unless he controlled the region between the Red Sea and the Mediterranean. This is because of the needs of food, fodder and shelter. Ibn Khaldūn notes that there are no reports of wars between the Tubba's and those who controlled the region, such as Amalekites, Canaanites, Copts and Israelites. There were also no reports that the Tubba's ever took control or possession of the land of territory of the Persians and Byzantines.[7]

Yet another example cited by Ibn Khaldūn is the historians' denial of the 'Alid origins of the Shi'i 'Ubaydī (Fātimid) caliphs of Qayrawan and Cairo. These historians questioned the authenticity of the 'Ubaydī descent from Imām Ismā'īl bin Ja'far al-Ṣādiq. The facts are as follows. Abū 'Abdallāh al-Muḥtasib, a religious leader among the Kutāmah Berbers, was well known as a supporter of the 'Alids. He pushed for the Kutāmah to recognize the 'Alids 'Ubaydallāh al-Mahdī and his son, Abū al-Qāsim. Fearing repercussions from those unhappy with their popularity, the two fled to Egypt and then to the Maghrib. Eventually, however, the Shi'i victory over the Aghlabids in Qayrawan and their influence throughout Ifrīqiyā and the Maghrib, Yemen, Egypt, Syria and the Hijaz meant that the 'Ubaydī dynasty reached a level comparable to that of the Abbasids. The 'Ubaydī dynasty lasted for 270 years. During this period their partisans and supporters continued to believe firmly in their descent from Ismā'īl bin Ja'far al-Ṣādiq. Even after the passing of the dynasty, people considered that the descendants of the 'Ubaydīs had legitimate claims to the caliphate. Ibn Khaldūn says that the degree of devotion to the 'Ubaydīs over a period of more than 270 years could not be explained had there been any doubts among the followers regarding their 'Alid origins. Ibn Khaldūn expresses amazement that the renowned theologian Abū Bakr al-Bāqillānī supported the denial of the 'Alid origins of the 'Ubaydīs. Ibn Khaldūn held that al-Bāqillānī's position was irrational. If his view regarding their 'Alid origins was due to his consideration of the 'Ubaydīs as heretical Shi'ah, his denial of their origins does not change the objectionable nature of their beliefs.[8]

It was the supporters of the Abbasids who propagated the denial of the 'Alid origins of the 'Ubaydīs in their effort to ingratiate themselves with their ('Ubaydī) enemies, the Abbasid caliphs. This denial also aided the Abbasids in their efforts to contain the Kutāmah Berbers, the supporters of the 'Ubaydīs, who had wrested Syria, Egypt and the Hijaz from the Abbasids. Eventually, the judges of Baghdad drafted an official statement denying the 'Alid ancestry of the 'Ubaydīs. Ibn Khaldūn reports that many prominent men and religious scholars witnessed the document. Their testimonies were based on what people in Baghdad, pro-Abbasid partisans, generally believed regarding the genealogy of the 'Ubaydīs. This was simply reported by the historians without considering its truth value.[9]

Ibn Khaldūn's purpose in carrying out lengthy discussions of the errors of historians is to point out the prerequisites for writing history which accords with the truth. At the outset of Book One of the *Kitāb al-'Ibar* – the *Muqaddimah* – the various errors of historians as charged by Ibn Khaldūn are enumerated.

Seven reasons are given as to why untruth afflicts information reported by historians.

The first is partiality or partisanship for opinions, sects or schools. A non-objective scholar will not devote to the information collected its due share of critique and reconstruction. The second reason is the reliance on transmitters. In the Islamic tradition, there is a discipline concerned with personality criticism (*al-jarḥ wa-l-ta'dīl*) which assesses the probity, accuracy, thoroughness and reliability of transmitters of the prophetic traditions.[10] Ibn Khaldūn's point here has to do with the over-reliance on transmitters to the point of failing to assess the possibility of an event or plausibility of an argument.

A third reason is scholars being unaware of the purpose of an event. Ibn Khaldūn claims that many transmitters seem to be ignorant of the significance of the real meaning of their observations or the reported facts. The transmitted information is assumed to have a significance that is wrongly attributed to it, resulting in falsehood. An example of this is the danger of projecting the present on to the past.

A historian who has studied the facts of the past may remain unaware of the changes in conditions that warrant an interpretation different from what he had in mind. His being unaware of these changes results in his applying his knowledge of the present conditions to the historical information of the past, thereby constructing an erroneous account. An example cited by Ibn Khaldūn is the position of judges in the past and during his own time. Certain erroneous conclusions were often drawn by those who read about the role of judges in society. They assumed that the office of the judge was the same in earlier times as it was during theirs. In the past, as for example during the period of the Umayyad dynasty in Spain, the office of the judge was no mere administrative rank. The position of judge was given to those who shared in the *'aṣabiyyah* or group feeling of the dynasty. Judges accompanied the army during its campaigns and were entrusted with vital affairs of state beyond the scope of judges in later times. The situation changed after the Arab dynasty in Spain weakened and its group feeling and the mutual cooperation that accompanied it eroded. At that point the office of the judge was more of an administrative rank and was far less important than it used to be. Being ignorant of changing conditions over time may lead some to imagine that the position of judges in the past was as insignificant as they were later.[11]

A fourth reason that makes untruths unavoidable in historical information is the presence of erroneous assumptions as to the truth of a report. This is a result of the reliance on transmitters. Many examples of fictitious accounts accepted as truths and transmitted by historians were furnished by Ibn Khaldūn, some of which were discussed above.

Fifth, there is the problem of the ignorance of how conditions correspond with reality. The transmitter reports on conditions without being aware of whether or not the various aspects attached to those conditions belong to its essence or are artificial distortions of normal phenomena. The sixth reason is the desire to praise those in positions of authority and high rank. In this case, information may not be truthful as the objectives are not to report the truth but to ingratiate those who report to people of standing and power.[12]

The seventh and most important reason for the prevalence of untruths in historical reports is ignorance of the nature of the conditions of human society. Every phenomenon has a nature peculiar to it, and is distinguished by its essences (*dhāt*) as well as the accidental conditions (*a'rāḍ*) that are attached to it. The student of history must know the nature of conditions and events in order to know what is possible and what is impossible. This will in turn help her to separate the truthful from the spurious or false.[13] Without this ability, there will be the tendency to accept absurd information. Ibn Khaldūn gives many examples of these absurdities.

There was the story, transmitted by al-Mas'ūdī, of Alexander and the sea monsters who allegedly obstructed and prevented him from building Alexandria. Alexander dived into the bottom of the sea in a glass box, drew pictures of the monsters he saw, built metal effigies of these monsters and placed them in the area of construction. The monsters, upon seeing the effigies, fled, thereby permitting Alexander to complete the building of Alexandria. The fact that it would be impossible for a person to spend a long time under water in a box due to the depletion of oxygen supply was not considered by the transmitter.[14] Another absurd story is that transmitted by al-Bakrī about the "Gate City". According to the account, the city had such a large area that it took more than 30 days to go around it and had 10,000 gates. Ibn Khaldūn considers this to be an untruth. Having 10,000 gates would not enable the city to provide security and protection to its citizens. It is unlikely that anyone would have built such a city with so many points of access.[15]

Only knowledge of the nature of society allows for a critical approach in research. This approach is superior to those that rely upon the personality criticism of transmitters. Ibn Khaldūn does not suggest that personality criticism should be dispensed with altogether but that it is to be resorted to only if it has been established whether or not the fact or event reported is itself possible. The absurdity of a report or an illogical interpretation may be sufficient grounds to cast doubt on the reliability of the information. In order to establish the truth and soundness of reports of events and facts, it is necessary to assess the conformity or lack of conformity of that which is reported with the general conditions of a given society. It becomes necessary, therefore, to investigate if it is possible that the reported event or fact could have taken place. Such investigation has priority over personality criticism. Here Ibn Khaldūn makes a distinction between "what is" and "what ought to be". The "correct notion about something that ought to be can be derived only from (personality criticism), while the correct notion about something that was (*al-akhbār 'an al-wāq'āt*) can be derived from (personality criticism) and external (evidence) by (checking) the conformity (of the historical report with general conditions)".[16]

If it is accepted that right from wrong in historical information can be established on the grounds of the inherent possibility or absurdity of an event or fact, it follows that the basic rule would be to study human society (*al-ijtimā' al-basharī*), for it is such study that will enable us to assess if reported facts were possible or not. The study of society should distinguish between those aspects that form the essence (*dhāt*) of society, those that are its accidents (*a'rāḍ*), and those that cannot be attached to it: that is, those properties that are never part of what makes a society. We would then have a method that would allow us to distinguish truth from falsehoods and absurdities in historical information by the application of logical demonstration. The study of society would provide us with a yardstick with which we may measure claims to truth in the works of historians.[17] What Ibn Khaldūn proposed is actually a radically different way of writing history. He was suggesting what was then a new field, one that he deemed a necessary requirement for the study of history.

> Therefore, today, the scholar in this field needs to know the principles of politics, the (true) nature of existent things, and the differences among nations, places, and periods with regard to ways of life, character qualities, customs, sects, schools, and everything else. He further needs a comprehensive knowledge of present conditions in all these respects. He must compare similarities or differences between the present and the past (or distantly located) conditions. He must know the causes of the similarities in certain cases and of the differences in others. He must be aware of the differing origins and beginnings of (different) dynasties and religious groups, as well as of the reasons and incentives that brought them into being and the circumstances and history of the persons who supported them. His goal must be to have complete knowledge of the reasons for every happening, and to be acquainted with the origin of every event. Then, he must check transmitted information with the basic principles he knows. If it fulfills their requirements, it is sound. Otherwise, the historian must consider it as spurious and dispense with it. It was for this reason alone that historiography was highly considered by the ancients, so much so that al-Ẓabarī, al-Bukhārī, and, before them, Ibn Isḥāq and other Muslim religious scholars, chose to occupy themselves with it. Most scholars, however, forgot this, the (real) secret of historiography, with the result that it became a stupid occupation. Ordinary people as well as (scholars) who had no firm foundation of knowledge, considered it a simple matter to study and know history, to delve into it and sponge on it. Strays got into the flock, bits of shell were mixed with the nut, truth was adulterated with lies.[18]

Having thoroughly read the works of the past historians, Ibn Khaldūn says with his characteristic humour:

> When I had read the works of others and probed into the recesses of yesterday and today, I shook myself out of that drowsy complacency and sleepiness. Although not much of a writer, I exhibited my own literary ability as well as I could, and, thus, composed a book on history. In (this book) I lifted the veil from conditions as they arise in the various generations. I arranged it in an orderly way in chapters dealing with historical facts and reflections. In it I showed how and why dynasties and civilization originate. I based the work on the history of the two races that constitute the population of the Maghrib at this time and people its various regions and cities, and on that of their

> ruling houses, both long- and short-lived, including the rulers and allies they had in the past. These two races are the Arabs and the Berbers.[19]

What prompted Ibn Khaldūn to write the *Kitāb al-'Ibar*, apart from the intellectual reasons discussed thus far? An additional note appended to the end of the Introduction gives us an idea of Ibn Khaldūn's state of mind when he was writing the *Muqaddimah*. He refers to history as discussions of events that are specific to a particular age or people and cover the general conditions of regions, places and nations. Such was the case with the work of al-Mas'ūdī, who wrote on geography and the sects and customs of the Arab and non-Arab peoples. His work became a standard reference for later historians. Al-Mas'ūdī was followed by al-Bakrī, who wrote principally on routes and provinces. Al-Bakrī did not write about other matters, as not much had changed since the time of al-Mas'ūdī. Ibn Khaldūn notes, however, that by his time the situation, particularly in the Maghrib, had changed dramatically. An influx of Arabs physically and economically displaced the original Berber population, a process that began in the fifth (eleventh) century. Then a devastating plague in the eighth (fourteenth) century affected the Arab East and West, bringing much destruction to whole populations. Cities were in ruins, and dynasties were weakened. To Ibn Khaldūn it seemed as if "the voice of existence in the world had called out for oblivion and restriction, and the world had responded to its call".[20] This general change of conditions required a fresh approach to the study of history. It was necessary to do what al-Mas'ūdī did for his time: that is, to record the condition of the world as it is now, taking into account the changes in peoples, customs, beliefs and regions.[21] We may look at this as a modest restatement of Ibn Khaldūn's objectives, for what he does is more than merely record the changes that society underwent.

The science of human society

Ibn Khaldūn wrote the *Muqaddimah* in order to clarify the proper method for the study of history: that is, the method that would enable the scholar to ascertain true events from false narratives and to assess the probability and possibility of the events of history.[22] It is this method and subject matter that he refers to as the science of human social organization (*'ilm al-'umrān al-basharī*) or the science of human society (*'ilm al-ijtimā 'al-insānī*). Ibn Khaldūn considered existing historical works to be fraught with errors and unfounded assumptions, as we saw above. In order to know if what was reported to have happened in history really did happen, it is insufficient to depend solely on the reliability of transmitters, the nature of the sources and other such technical criteria. Rather it is also necessary to know something about the nature of society. This requires going beyond the outer forms (*ẓāhir*) of facts and reports to the inner meaning (*bāṭin*) of history, that is, the explanation of cause and effect.[23]

The *Muqaddimah* is dedicated to delineating the errors of historians and, more importantly, presenting the proper theory and method for the study of history. Therefore, underlying whatever substantive concerns Ibn Khaldūn had with history was his interest in elaborating a new science of society.

This new science was necessitated by Ibn Khaldūn's discovery of problems surrounding the nature of historical studies up to his time. An understanding of the relationships between the state and society, group feeling or solidarity, and the question of the development of society require an understanding of the nature of society which Ibn Khaldūn approached by way of the study of the constituent elements of society, such as economic life and urban institutions, the organizing ability of the state, and solidarity or group feeling (*'aṣabiyyah*), the primary factor affecting societal change.[24] The above can be said to be the elements of Ibn Khaldūn's general sociology, applicable to all types of societies, nomadic or sedentary, feudal or prebendal, Muslim or non-Muslim.

The *Muqaddimah* was conceived by Ibn Khaldūn to be an integral part of the larger *Kitāb al-'Ibar*, which comprises three books. The *Muqaddimah* is the first book of the *Kitāb al-'Ibar* and deals with the merit of the new science of human society and its methods. The *Muqaddimah* was written to fulfil the need for better and sounder historical theories and methods that provided a means of separating truth from fiction. Ibn Khaldūn's substantive concern was with the history and dynasties of the Arabs, Israelites, Persians, Greeks, Byzantines, Turks and Berbers.[25] These are dealt with in Books Two and Three. Dealing with such substantive history, however, was dependent on, as El-Azmeh put it, a master science,[26] or what Ibn Khaldūn called the science of human society. Mere reliance on the reporting of facts by transmitters, however reliable they may be, was insufficient as a method. The effort to establish what was probable and possible among the events of history required an independent science that "has its own peculiar object – that is, human social organization and society".[27]

Ibn Khaldūn conceived of his new science of human society as consisting of a number of sub-areas, as follows: (1) society (*'umrān*) in general and its divisions; (2) bedouin society (*al-'umrān al-badawī*), tribal societies (*qabā'il*), and primitive peoples (*al-waḥshiyyah*); (3) the state (*al-dawlah*), royal (*mulk*) and caliphate *(khilāfah)* authority; (4) sedentary society (*al-'umrān al-ḥaḍarī*), cities; and (5) the crafts, ways of making a living, occupations. These areas can be seen to cover what in modern terms would encompass human or social ecology, rural sociology, political sociology, urban sociology, and the sociology of work.[28]

It was this effort – that is, to distinguish between the more popular narrative history on the one hand and history as a science that investigates the origins and development of society on the other – that resulted in his discovery of the science of human society, or what we may call sociology. Ibn Khaldūn saw his new science as a "vessel for philosophy, a receptacle for historical knowledge", as it dealt with the origins and causes of historical phenomena.[29]

Ibn Khaldūn was very conscious of the uniqueness of his science of human society, noting that it did not belong to existing disciplines such as rhetoric or politics, although it shared some similarities with them.[30] He saw his work as constituting a unique contribution informed by a familiar if hidden wisdom.[31] He notes:

> Such is the purpose of this first book of our work. (The subject) is in a way an independent science. (This science) has its own peculiar object – that is, human civilization and social organization. It also has its own peculiar problems,

> that is, explaining the conditions that attach themselves to the essence of civilization, one after the other. Thus, the situation is the same with this science as it is with any other science, whether it be a conventional or an intellectual one.
>
> It should be known that the discussion of this topic is something new, extraordinary, and highly useful. Penetrating research has shown the way to it.[32]

The new science: a theory of state formation

The substantive interest of Ibn Khaldūn, in both the *Muqaddimah* and the *Kitāb al-'Ibar*, lies in the explanation of the formation and decline of Maghribian and Arab states. He was more confident and thorough in his work on North Africa, as he had direct access to primary materials on the Maghrib, unlike the second-hand information he had on the Arab East.[33]

Ibn Khaldūn approached his study of the rise and fall of the various North African states by focusing on the essential differences in social organization between pastoral nomadic and sedentary societies in terms of their social organization. Central to understanding these differences is the concept of *'aṣabiyyah*, often translated as group feeling, solidarity or social cohesion. Ibn Khaldūn's thesis was that groups with strong *'aṣabiyyah* could establish political rule over those with weak *'aṣabiyyah*.[34]

He saw nomadic civilization as naturally evolving towards sedentary civilization not in the sense that the one gives way to the other but rather in the sense that the organization of sedentary life, with its cities' relatively luxurious lifestyle and high culture, is the goal of bedouin life. In other words, human societies tend to change from being pastoral nomadic to sedentary. This change involved the fundamental role of *'aṣabiyyah* or group feeling. Only a society with a strong *'aṣabiyyah* could establish domination over one with a weak *'aṣabiyyah*. In this context, *'aṣabiyyah* refers to the feeling of solidarity among the members of a group that is derived from the knowledge that they share a common descent. As we shall see, however, descent is not the only consideration. Because of superior *'aṣabiyyah* among the bedouin, they could defeat sedentary people in urban areas and establish their own dynasties. Having done so, they became set in the urban ways of life and experienced great diminution in their *'aṣabiyyah*. With this went their military strength and their ability to rule. This left them vulnerable to attack by fresh supplies of pre-urban bedouins with stronger social cohesion, due to their *'aṣabiyyah* being intact. The group with the stronger *'aṣabiyyah* replaces the weaker settled group. But the relationship is not one of the domination of the settled areas or the cities by the tribes. Rather it is a relationship of dominance in the other direction, of which there are two important aspects. First, the nature of the existence of the tribesmen makes them dependent on the cities for the basic necessities of life. Second, the tribes are dependent on a religious leader or saint (*walī*) who interprets religion for them. The propaganda of religion is such that the call to fulfil the commands of God results in the tribesmen adopting praiseworthy qualities and to desire to fight for a cause as defined by religion. Under the religious leader, they become united as a social organization and develop a following and, eventually, royal authority.

The social cohesion expressed by the concept of *'aṣabiyyah* is only partly derived from agnatic ties in tribal social organizations. While all tribal groups have stronger or weaker *'aṣabiyyah* based on kinship, religion can also bring about such social cohesion, as was the case with the Arabs who needed Islam in order to subordinate themselves and unite as a social organization. But beyond this social psychological aspect of *'aṣabiyyah*, there are its material manifestations.

Another fundamental concept in Ibn Khaldūn's work is that of *mulk* (royal authority). Royal authority is not the same as leadership. Leaders may be obeyed in leadership, but the leader is generally unable to force people to accept his rulings. It is only with royal authority that the ruler has the ability to force others to accept his rulings, for royal authority refers to superiority and the power to rule by force.

Because of *'aṣabiyyah*, a tribal chieftain will be obeyed by his followers, a precondition for achieving royal authority. But it is not merely the psychological feeling of cohesion that achieves this. *'Aṣabiyyah* refers to the authority that is wielded by the chieftain that derives, in addition, from his material standing as a result of profits from trade and appropriation from plunder and pillage. For Ibn Khaldūn, then, *'aṣabiyyah* referred to (1) kinship ties; (2) a socially cohesive religion such as Islam that provided a shared idiom legitimizing the chieftain's aspirations for *mulk*; and (3) the strength of the chieftain through trade, booty, pillage and conquest.

Once a tribe founds a dynasty and its members assume the various positions of the ruling class, the conditions for the decline in *'aṣabiyyah* are established. There are at least two general ways in which this takes place. One is where the second generation of tribesmen who founded the dynasty experience a change from the desert ethic to an outlook fostered by the sedentary lifestyle, from a state of scarcity to luxury, and from a state in which everybody shared and benefited from whatever successes the community had to one in which one man, the ruler, claims all the glory for himself. Thus, the strength of the group feeling is eroded to a great extent. By the third generation, *'aṣabiyyah* disappears completely.

It is not only the relatively luxurious life of sedentary society that causes an erosion in *'aṣabiyyah* but also when the ruler, in gaining near absolute control over his people, arrogates to himself all royal authority. He excludes his people and prevents them from having a share in the royal authority. In other words, when a tribal group establishes a dynasty and its authority becomes legitimate the ruler can dispense with *'aṣabiyyah*. The ascendant ruler then rules with the help not of his own people but rather that of other tribal groups who have become his clients. The ruler attempts to exclude the supporting tribe from power. The ability of a tribal chieftain to maintain *'aṣabiyyah* under these circumstances is diminished.

When we speak of diminishing *'aṣabiyyah*, then, we refer to the circumstances under which a chieftain is no longer able to command tribal support (1) by appealing to kinship and/or other ties, (2) due to the corrosion in social cohesion that results either from luxurious urban life or from attempts by the ruler to dispense with *'aṣabiyyah*. As *'aṣabiyyah* decreases, the power of the ruling dynasty erodes until it is finally conquered by another tribal group with superior *'aṣabiyyah*. And so the cycle repeats itself. As noted by El-Azmeh, *'aṣabiyyah* is "that which makes a group a power group".[35] Because of superior *'aṣabiyyah* among the bedouin, they could defeat sedentary people in urban areas and establish their own dynasties. The final manifestation of *'aṣabiyyah* was the dynasty or *al-dawlah*.[36] Having achieved this, the bedouin became set in the urban ways of life and experienced great diminution in their *'aṣabiyyah*. With this went their military strength and their vulnerability to attack and conquest by tribal groups from the outside. The cycle of rise and decline was estimated by Ibn Khaldūn to take approximately four generations.

The bulk of the *Muqaddimah* is devoted to elaborating a theory of state formation and decline. This is presented in the course of three major sections (*faṣl*): that is, Sections Two to Four. Section Two deals with the nature of nomadic society, the superiority of tribal social solidarity (*'aṣabiyyah*) or group feeling, the role of kinship and blood ties in group feeling, and the natural inclination of nomadic society to attaining royal authority (*mulk*) and establishing a dynasty. Section Three focuses on the development and decay of royal authority, the role of religion in this, the various groups and forces that figure in dynastic decline, and the mode of origin and disintegration of dynasties. Section Four highlights a number of aspects of the nature of sedentary civilization.

In Chapter 2 I provide an elaborate account of Ibn Khaldūn's theory of state formation.

2 Ibn Khaldūn's theory of state formation

There are three components of Ibn Khaldūn's sociology of human society. These are (1) the premises or *muqaddimāt* of the science of human society; (2) the theory of the rise and decline of states; and (3) the method employed in the critique of historiography as well as the elaboration of the theory of rise and decline. In what follows, I shall be making some reference to Ibn Khaldūn's premises of his new science and the methods he used. However, the greater focus will be on his theory of the rise and decline of states, as it is this that is most relevant to our effort to apply his perspectives to the specific historical and empirical cases.

The *muqaddimāt* of the science of human society

The *Muqaddimah* (*Prolegomenon*) is informed by certain basic assumptions (*muqaddimāt*, sing. *muqaddimah*) that function as premises of Ibn Khaldūn's entire work on history. The premises are assertions whose demonstration does not fall within the scope of the new science.[1] Six *muqaddimāt* are listed but the two that are the most relevant to Ibn Khaldūn's study of society are as follows. First, human society is necessary.[2] Humans have a need to live together for the sake of companionship and for the satisfaction of basic needs. This also results from their natural disposition towards cooperation.[3] Second, humans are influenced physically, psychologically and socially by the physical environment.[4] Given that human beings are influenced by their physical environment and that their ability to think results in the development of the sciences and crafts and the various modes of making a living, differences in the physical environment would result in different modes of making a living. These are found in the two major types of society that Ibn Khaldūn deals with: pastoral nomadic or bedouin society (*al-'umrān al-badawī*) and sedentary society (*al-'umrān al ḥaḍarī*). Ibn Khaldūn's theory of the rise and decline of states revolves around the relationship between the two types of social organization (*'umrān*) and the various modes of making a living that they represent.

The nature of dynasties in turn was examined by Ibn Khaldūn in terms of the types of authority wielded by states, that is, kingship (*mulk*) and caliphate (*khilāfah*) authority. The single most important concept for understanding the nomadic-sedentary dialectic and the impact of this on state formation is that of *'aṣabiyyah*, a type of social cohesion or group feeling. Ibn Khaldūn's theory of the rise and decline of states is a theory of weak and strong *'aṣabiyyah*. Nomadic groups with strong *'aṣabiyyah* had the prerequisites to establish states because they could dominate over groups with weak *'aṣabiyyah*. Nevertheless, the establishment of state and dynasty by a particular tribal group and its subsequent settlement and sedentarization in villages and cities results in the erosion of its *'aṣabiyyah*, thereby leaving the group susceptible to attack and defeat by a new influx of pre-sedentary tribes.

The methods of the new science

We have seen in Chapter 1 that Ibn Khaldūn viewed the traditional method of assessing historical accounts for their accuracy as problematic because of what he would have regarded as an obsession with the reliability of sources and the characters of the transmitters of information. Ibn Khaldūn thought it necessary to focus on the inherent possibility or absurdity of reported events and conditions which in turn required knowledge of the nature of human society. The truth and reliability of reported facts and events can be logically demonstrated from what is known about the nature of society. It is therefore the method of demonstration (*burhān*) that occupies the most important place in Ibn Khaldūn's theory of society. It is also here that we can place him squarely within the classical Islamic tradition, which considered the method of demonstration to be the most reliable in terms of yielding certain knowledge.

Ibn Khaldūn did not introduce a new method in his scholarship. He was heir to the philosophers of Islam who studied and improved upon the Greek methods of argumentation. However, his application of the method of the philosophers to historical phenomena was new. As Hodgson put it, Ibn Khaldūn's science was meant to be "a self-consistent body of demonstrable generalizations about historical change, generalizations which would in turn be based on premises taken from the demonstrated results of 'higher', i.e., more abstract, sciences – in this case chiefly biology, psychology, and geography".[5] These premises were the six *muqaddimāt* mentioned above: that is, assertions whose demonstration does not fall within the scope of the new science.

The term "method", according to Mahdi,[6] refers to what Ibn Khaldūn and others in the classical Islamic tradition understood as *manṭiq*: that is, the rules that enable one to distinguish right from wrong. The ability to make this distinction rests on the skills with which definitions (*ḥudūd*) that provide the essence (*māhiyāt*) of things are arrived at and arguments that lead to judgement or apperception (*taṣdīqāt*) are made.[7] Animals and humans alike perceive the *sensibilia* by the five senses (*al-ḥawās al-khamsa*). Where humans differ from animals is in their ability to abstract universals (*kulliyāt*) from the *sensibilia*. Knowledge is either conception (*taṣawwur*) – that is, the perception of the essence of things – or it is apperception (*taṣdīq*). Conception does not involve the exercising of judgement. Apperception, on the other hand, does involve judgement or assent in order to establish the correspondence between the concept and the object to which the concept refers. The goal of apperception is knowledge of the realities of things (*ḥaqā'iq al-ashyā'*).[8] Knowledge as conception (*taṣawwur*), or the perception of the essence of things, refers to the knowledge of universals, of which there are five. These are: genus (*jins*), difference (*faṣl*), species (*nū'*), property (*khāṣah*), and general accident (*'arḍ al-'ām*).[9] Ibn Khaldūn says:

> Every event (or phenomenon), whether (it comes into being in connection with some) essence or (as the result of an) action, must inevitably possess a nature peculiar to its essence as well as to the accidental conditions that may attach themselves to it. If the student knows the nature of events and the circumstances and requirements in the world of existence, it will help him to distinguish truth from untruth in investigating the historical information critically. This is more effective in critical investigation than any other aspect that may be brought up in connection with it.[10]

According to the philosophical tradition that Ibn Khaldūn belonged to, knowledge comes from knowing the essence (*dhāt*) as well as accidents (*a'rāḍ*) of phenomena. To know something is to be able to distinguish between the essence of a phenomenon and its accidental properties. Essences of things are spoken of in terms of genus, species and difference. When this rule is applied to history, it requires the historian to distinguish between what is essential and natural from what is accidental to events and conditions.

The process of abstraction proceeds until the highest universal is reached. For example, the perception of humans results in the abstraction of the species (*nū'*) to which humans belong. At another level, the comparison between human beings and animals is made resulting in the abstraction of the genus (*jins*) to which both humans and animals belong. The comparisons proceed in this way until the highest genus is reached: that is, substance (*jawhar*). After this point, no further abstractions can be made.

This process of abstraction may take place in the right or wrong way. For this reason, the field of logic was developed in order that the methods of logic could be understood and presented in a systematic manner to aid the process of analogical reasoning (*qiyās*). The Muslims followed Aristotle in recognizing five kinds of analogical reasoning.[11]

1. Demonstration (*burhān*), which refers to the kind of analogical reasoning, the syllogism, that produces certain knowledge, and the conditions that must be satisfied for yielding certain knowledge.
2. Dialectics (*jadal*) or disputation, which refers to analogical reasoning that aims to silence an opponent. It does not yield certain knowledge as its premises are not certain ones. Dialectics may include deductive, inductive or other forms of arguments.
3. Rhetoric (*khiṭābah*), which refers to reasoning and the use of forms of speech that are directed to influencing people. It is directed towards influence or persuasion rather than instruction.

4. Poetics (*shi'ir*), which is reasoning that teaches the invention and use of parable (*tamthīl*) and similes (*tasbīh*) with the aim of stirring the imagination, inspiring and encouraging people.
5. Sophistry (*safsaṭah*), which is a form of reasoning that teaches the opposite of truth and aims to confuse and deceive an opponent. It is, of course, a method to be avoided.

Ibn Khaldūn belonged to a tradition that regarded demonstrative methods as the best way to ascertain the truth. The arguments in demonstration proceed from premises that are certain and they produce certain knowledge. This was the method Ibn Khaldūn employed in the *Muqaddimah*.

Demonstration was not the only method employed by Ibn Khaldūn. His critique of historical writing of scholars that preceded him was not premised on true, self-evident and primary statements. Rather, his critique employed the dialectical method. Ibn Khaldūn used this method to expose the weaknesses of historical writing. The aim in employing this method was not to formulate true, self-evident and primary premises. Dialectical arguments are often founded on weak premises or opinions that may be true or false. The purpose of the dialectical argument is to refute or accept the opinions. The argument attempts to do so by revealing the absurdity of opposing opinions. In other words, a dialectical argument is purely logical in that it does not necessarily proceed from true premises.

Ibn Khaldūn was critical of the tendency among some scholars, such as Fakhr al-Dīn ibn al-Khaṭīb and Afḍal al-Dīn al-Khūnajī, to reduce logic to a discipline in its own right, rather than regard it as an instrument for the other sciences. For Ibn Khaldūn's own work, methods of demonstration and dialectics were tools that he employed for the critique of the existing historical scholarship up to his time and the development of his new science of human society.

It is also important to point out that while Ibn Khaldūn's methods were not new, his approach was novel to the extent that it was materialist in orientation. He placed a great deal of emphasis on the role of material factors in accounting for the differences between nomadic and sedentary societies. Ibn Khaldūn was very much aware that he had developed a new science and a novel approach to the study of history:

> It should be known that the discussion of this topic is something new, extraordinary and highly useful. Penetrating research has shown the way to it. It does not belong to rhetoric, one of the logical disciplines (represented in Aristotle's *Organon*), the subject of which is convincing words by means of which the mass is inclined to accept a particular opinion or not to accept it. It is also not politics, because politics is concerned with the administration of home or city in accordance with ethical and philosophical requirements, for the purpose of directing the mass toward a behavior that will result in the preservation and permanence of the (human) species.
>
> The subject here is different from that of these two disciplines which, however, are often similar to it. In a way, it is an entirely original science. In fact, I have not come across a discussion along these lines by anyone.[12]

But, it should be stressed that Ibn Khaldūn's originality is in fact not to be found at the epistemological level. Ibn Khaldūn merely applied methods of argumentation already known and well developed among Muslim philosophers, theologians and scholars of jurisprudence. Ibn Khaldūn's originality lies in the application of these methods to the critique of the science of history of his time and the generation of a new science that was to be applied to the study of history.

Theory of state formation

These are the chief features of Ibn Khaldūn's historical sociology of the state, which attempts to explain the rise and decline of dynasties in terms of the interaction and cyclical conflict between two types of society or social organization: pastoral nomadic and sedentary society. The very conditions that make for sedentary society and the possibility for rule and the development of kingship also give rise to factors that eventually result in the undermining of *'aṣabiyyah*, the erosion of kingship and finally the decline of the state.

For Ibn Khaldūn, it is the mode of making a living (*al-ma'āsh*) that explains the differential organization of social life. For those for whom agriculture or animal husbandry is their principal mode of making a living, they live in desert areas and do not lead much more than a subsistence-level lifestyle. An increase in wealth means that nomadic peoples may live above subsistence levels, settle in towns and cities, and partake of the culture of sedentary people, including good cuisine, the fine arts, elaborate architecture and an overall higher level of comfort and luxury. The mode of making a living corresponds to level of wealth.[13] Pastoral nomads are further differentiated into those who make their living from raising sheep and cattle and those who are dependent on camels. The former are shepherds (*shāwiyyah*), who only venture far into the desert if good pastures are available and include the Turks and Turkomans. Nomads who are dependent on camels have to go deeper into the desert where camels can find sustenance. Among the camel nomads are the Kurds, Turkomans and Turks in the East and the Arabs, Berbers and Zanātah in the West. The Arabs, however, venture further into the desert than the other groups, as their dependence on camels is far greater and they rely less on sheep and cattle like the Kurds, Turkomans, Turks and Berbers.[14]

According to Ibn Khaldūn, nomadic and sedentary societies do not merely happen to be two types of society that coexist and interact with each other. The fact that most of the inhabitants of cities originate from the bedouin suggests that nomadic society is the precursor to sedentary society:

> It has thus become clear that the existence of Bedouins is prior to, and the basis of, the existence of towns and cities. Likewise, the existence of towns and cities results from luxury customs pertaining to luxury and ease, which are posterior to the customs that go with the bare necessities of life.[15]

Following from this observation are some interesting points about the difference between nomadic and sedentary societies that are vital for the development of Ibn

Khaldūn's theory of state formation. He suggests that nomadic people are morally better (*khayr*) than sedentary people. His argument seems to be one about materialism. The soul is born in a natural state but acquires good or evil through socialization. Ibn Khaldūn reasons that nomads are closer to being in a natural state than sedentary people, as they restrict themselves to the bare necessities of life. The nomadic soul is first affected by good and finds it difficult to acquire evil. The sedentary soul, on the other hand, is introduced to evil much earlier because it is born into a context of luxury and worldly success.[16] Another important difference between these two types of societies is that nomadic people are braver than sedentary people. The relatively more luxurious lifestyle of sedentary people affords them a life of ease. They do not carry weapons for protection and do not hunt for their sustenance. A feature of the sedentary lifestyle is that there are relevant authorities that provide protection. Furthermore, the division of labour is such that sustenance is provided for in sedentary life. Bedouin society, on the other hand, lacks the facilities available to their sedentary counterparts. They must necessarily hunt and carry weapons for their protection:

> They watch carefully all sides of the road. They take hurried naps only when they are together in company or when they are in the saddle. They pay attention to every faint barking and noise. They go alone into the desert, guided by their fortitude, putting their trust in themselves. Fortitude has become a character quality of theirs, and courage their nature. They use it whenever they are called upon or an alarm stirs them. When sedentary people mix with them in the desert or associate with them on a journey, they depend on them. They cannot do anything for themselves without them. This is an observed fact. (Their dependence extends) even to knowledge of the country, the (right) directions, watering places, and crossroads.[17]

We have already noted Ibn Khaldūn's views on the superiority of nomadic over sedentary groups in terms of morality and courage. He further notes that nomadic people also have the edge over sedentary people in terms of group feeling. Group feeling facilitates mutual defence and social activities. At the same time, every social group requires a power to exercise restraint over it. The superior ruler is the one with the stronger group feeling such that he can exert authority and command the obedience of the others in the group. This superiority is kingship (*mulk*). If a particular tribe has several houses and, therefore, many group feelings, it is the superior or stronger group feeling that rules.[18]

Sedentary people are further disadvantaged because of their over-reliance on law. The nature of sedentary life is such that the majority of people are dominated by a minority. When this domination is accompanied by intimidation and injustice, it destroys the fortitude and power of resistance of the people. Punishment as a means of enforcing laws diminishes the fortitude of a people because of the humiliation that it brings about. For example, laws that are implemented with the objective to educate and instruct may unintentionally result in the lowering of fortitude because people come to rely more on rules and regulations rather than on their own abilities. In general, therefore, there is a higher degree of fortitude among the bedouin in comparison with sedentary societies. Ibn Khaldūn notes exceptions such as the men around the Prophet Muḥammad. They were known to be observant of the laws but had also great fortitude. This was because the restraining influence came from within, as a function of their faith and belief, rather than being imposed upon them from without.[19]

Unlike sedentary people, the bedouin are constituted by strong, tightly knit communities. Although the restraining influence among the bedouin tribes is derived from their leaders, their shaykhs, this is a function of the high degree of respect and veneration they generally enjoy among the tribesmen. The dwelling areas of the bedouins are defended against outside aggression by militia composed of the youths of the tribe who are well known for their courage. Their ability to defend and protect the bedouin depends very much on the degree to which they are a close group of common descent. This not only gives them greater courage, it causes them to be feared by their enemies since it is known that affection for the kin group is far more important than anything else. As Ibn Khaldūn notes, "compassion and affection for one's blood relations and relatives exist in human nature as something God put into the hearts of men. It makes for mutual support and aid, and increases the fear felt by the enemy".[20]

'Aṣabiyyah has been the subject of much discussion and translated as a variety of terms, such as solidarity, group feeling, *esprit de corps*, group loyalty and blood binding.[21] Perhaps which term we use is less important than understanding the meaning attached to the term. By *'aṣabiyyah* Ibn Khaldūn meant a sense of common cause and destiny, and the binding ties of loyalty that are founded to a great extent but not exclusively on blood ties. The solidarity derived from *'aṣabiyyah* gave internal cohesion to a group of leaders who were usually genealogically related and who strove together to found a dynasty.[22] Ibn Khaldūn observed that there are three types of relationships that make up *'aṣabiyyah*. These are blood ties (*ṣilat al-raḥim*), clientship (*walā'*), and alliance (*ḥilf*).[23] The type of *'aṣabiyyah* that is found in any given society is determined by the preponderance of each element. The most powerful type of *'aṣabiyyah* is the one that is founded on close blood ties. Such *'aṣabiyyah* creates the strongest feelings of solidarity and is the most powerful and reliable. This type of *'aṣabiyyah* lasts only as long as the kinship factor in social ties remains important. As kinship declines, however, affiliation and clientship may take over as the more dominant factors in group relations, resulting in weaker forms of *'aṣabiyyah*.

'Aṣabiyyah as a function of kinship ties is the most potent type. Social groups with stronger kinship ties have stronger *'aṣabiyyah* and are superior to the extent that their levels of mutual aid and affection are greater. Kinship ties yield *'aṣabiyyah* only if the idea of common descent is clear and unambiguous and manifests itself in the form of mutual aid and affection.[24] The leadership of a people is vested in those who are from the same descent group. In addition, the leader has the superior group feeling, which each individual in the group is ready to follow and obey.[25] This is because the leader has a house (*al-bayt*) and the

attribute of nobility (*al-sharaf*). The house and nobility are prerequisites of group feeling and effective leadership.

> This is because nobility and prestige are the result of (personal) qualities. A "house" means that a man counts noble and famous men among his forebears. The fact that he is their progeny and descendant gives him great standing among his fellows, for his fellows respect the great standing and nobility that his ancestors acquired through their (personal) qualities.[26]

This in turn facilitates mutual aid and affection. The knowledge of having noble ancestors and the prestige that such knowledge brings to members of the group serve to strengthen the group.

The nature of sedentary life, on the other hand, is such that it causes an erosion of *'aṣabiyyah* to the extent that it results in the weakening of tribal affiliations. Nobility disappears and this goes along with the dissipation of group feeling.[27] When the group feeling and nobility of the ruling house diminish, their clients, followers and slaves who had attached themselves to that house may assume the house and nobility of their masters. In other words, it is a derived house and nobility, and not house and nobility that proceeds from their own kinship or blood ties.[28] Ibn Khaldūn gives the example of the Barmecides, who belonged to a Persian house but later became clients of the Abbasids. The factor that decided their nobility and rise to power was not their descent but their position as followers of the Abbasids.[29]

The prestige (*al-ḥasb*), and along with that, the ability of a house to rule, generally lasts for no longer than four generations in one lineage.

> It reaches its end in a single family within four successive generations. This is as follows: The builder of the glory (of the family) knows what it cost him to do the work, and he keeps the qualities that created his glory and made it last. The son who comes after him had personal contact with his father and thus learned those things from him. However, he is inferior in this respect to (his father), in as much as a person who learns things through study is inferior to a person who knows them from practical application. The third generation must be content with imitation and, in particular, with reliance upon tradition. This member is inferior to him of the second generation, in as much as a person who relies (blindly) upon tradition is inferior to a person who exercises independent judgement.
>
> The fourth generation, then, is inferior to the preceding ones in every respect. This member has lost the qualities that preserved the edifice of their glory. He (actually) despises (those qualities). He imagines that the edifice was not built through application and effort. He thinks that it was something due his people from the very beginning by virtue of the mere fact of their (noble) descent, and not something that resulted from group (effort) and (individual) qualities. For he sees the great respect in which he is held by the people, but he does not know how that respect originated and what the reason for it was.

> He imagines that it is due to his descent and nothing else. He keeps away from those in whose group feeling he shares, thinking that he is better than they. He trusts that (they will obey him because) he was brought up to take their obedience for granted, and he does not know the qualities that made obedience necessary. Such qualities are humility (in dealing) with (such men) and respect for their feelings. Therefore, he considers them despicable, and they, in turn, revolt against him and despise him. They transfer (political) leadership from him and his direct lineage to some other related branch (of his tribe), in obedience to their group feeling, as we have stated. (They do so) after they have convinced themselves that the qualities of the (new leader) are satisfactory to them. His family then grows, whereas the family of the original (leader) decays and the edifice of his "house" collapses.[30]

The four generations can be described as the builder, the one who has personal contact with the builder, the one who relies on tradition, and the destroyer. Ibn Khaldūn believed that the rule of four generations generally held true, although it did happen that a house collapsed in fewer than four generations or managed to last for five or six generations in a state of decline and decay.[31]

Once a house declines, another from among the same descent may arise to take its place. The ultimate end of group feeling is the attainment of rule via kingship. The tribe that represents the group with the superior group feeling may attain kingship either by acquiring actual and direct control of the state or providing assistance to the ruling dynasty. For a people whose group feeling remains resilient, kingship may be transferred from one branch of the people to another. Kingship "continues in a particular nation until the force of the group feeling of (that nation) is broken and gone, or until all its groups have ceased to exist".[32] Therefore, kingship in a particular nation (*ummah*) remains within that nation until the group feeling of the entire nation diminishes:

> This can be illustrated by what happened among the nations. When the royal authority of 'Ād was wiped out, their brethren, the Thamūd, took over. They were succeeded, in turn, by their brethren, the Amalekites. The Amalekites were succeeded by their brethren, the Ḥimyar. The Ḥimyar were succeeded by their brethren, the Tubba's, who belonged to the Ḥimyar. They, likewise, were succeeded, by the Adhwā'. Then, the Muḍar came to power.
>
> The same was the case with the Persians. When the Kayyanid rule was wiped out, the Sassanians ruled after them. Eventually, God permitted them all to be destroyed by the Muslims.
>
> The same was also the case with the Greeks. Their rule was wiped out and transferred to their brethren, the Rūm (Romans).
>
> The same was the case with the Berbers in the Maghrib. When the rule of their first rulers, the Maghrāwah and the Kutāmah, was wiped out, it went to the Ṣinhājah. Then it went to the Veiled (Ṣinhājah), then to the Maṣmūdah, and then to the (still) remaining Zanātah groups.

> This is how God proceeds with His servants and creatures.
>
> All this has its origin in group feeling, which differs in the different groups. Luxury wears out the royal authority and overthrows it, as we shall mention later on. When a dynasty is wiped out, the power is taken (away) from (the members of that dynasty) by those people whose group feeling has a share in the (established) group feeling, since it is recognized that submission and subservience (by others) belong to (the established group feeling) and since people are used to the fact that (the established group feeling) has superiority over all other group feelings. (The same group feeling,) now, exists only in those people who are closely related (to the outgoing dynasty), because group feeling is proportionate to the degree of relationship. (It goes on that way until,) eventually, a great change takes place in the world, such as the transformation of a religion, or the disappearance of a civilization, or something else willed by the power of God. Then, royal authority is transferred from one group to another – to the one that God permits to effect that change. This happened to the Muḍar. They gained superiority over nations and dynasties, and took power away from all the people of the world, after having themselves been kept out of power for ages.[33]

Once a particular group establishes its superiority over other groups of the same people who share in that group feeling, it then is able to establish its superiority over other group feelings. If it succeeds in overpowering another people, the two group feelings come into close contact with each other, with the defeated group feeling providing additional strength to the victorious group feeling. As the ruling dynasty grows senile and declines, and if there is no one from among those who share in its group feeling to defend it, the new group feeling assumes rule and attains kingship.[34]

Once a dynasty is in power, it dispenses with and marginalizes the very group feeling that facilitated its rise to power and establishment. In a state in which kingship has been exercised over several generations and through different dynasties, the leaders are followed for their own personal attributes rather than for reasons to do with group feeling. In dispensing with group feeling, the rulers then resort to rule with the aid of clients who belong to groups that have different lineages. For example, the Abbasids under al-Mu'tasim and his son al-Wāthiq ruled with the help of the Persians, Turks, Daylams, Seljuks and others as their clients. As was typical of such arrangements, in time the clients gradually gained control of provincial areas until the caliphs retained control of only Baghdad before the dynasty finally disintegrated.[35] In other words, the ruler eventually turns against his own people. Once the dynasty is established, the people of his own group feeling are brought into the administrative services of the state. They, however, pose a danger to him as they are potential usurpers. He therefore feels the need to be independent of the people of his group feeling. These positions are substituted by clients and followers who are brought into the inner circle and given important positions in the administrative services of the state.[36]

Ibn Khaldūn discusses two ways in which *'aṣabiyyah* is eroded. One is where the second generation of the ruling tribe that founded the dynasty becomes assimilated into sedentary culture and urban living, which involves a life of relative luxury and the development of a kind of sedentary indolence. As the ruling tribe settles to a life of sedentary existence, a hierarchy also develops among them, with some having political office or land and others having lesser positions, authority and property. In sum, the ruling tribe experiences a change "from the desert attitude to sedentary culture, from privation to luxury, from a state in which everybody shared in the glory to one in which one man claims all the glory for himself while the others are too lazy to strive for (glory), and from proud superiority to humble subservience. Thus, the vigour of group feeling is broken to some extent", and is dissipated by the third generation.[37] Ibn Khaldūn sees luxury as a crucial factor impeding the ability to rule:

> The reason for this is that, when a tribe has achieved a certain measure of superiority with the help of its group feeling, it gains control over a corresponding amount of wealth and comes to share prosperity and abundance with those who have been in possession of these things (for a long time). It shares in them to the degree of its power and usefulness to the ruling dynasty. If the ruling dynasty is so strong that no one would think of depriving it of its power or sharing (its power) with it, the tribe in question submits to its rule and is satisfied with whatever share in the dynasty's wealth and tax revenue it is permitted to enjoy. Hopes would not go so high as to (think of) the royal prerogatives or ways to obtain the (royal authority. Members of the tribe) are merely concerned with prosperity, gain, and a life of abundance. (They are satisfied) to lead an easy, restful life in the shadow of the ruling dynasty, and to adopt royal habits in building and dress, a matter they stress and in which they take more and more pride, the more luxuries and plenty they obtain, as well as all the other things that go with luxury and plenty.[38]

The result is the loss of the toughness of desert life and the weakening of *'aṣabiyyah*, fortitude and courage.

The second way in which *'aṣabiyyah* declines is when the tribal chieftain, now a ruler of a new dynasty, attempts to dispense with *'aṣabiyyah*. He takes measures to alienate his tribesmen by excluding them from important offices and positions. This comes from the realization that members of the ruling tribe are potential usurpers of power. Thus, the "ruler gains complete control over his people, claims royal authority all for himself, excluding them; and prevents them from trying to have a share in it".[39] The ruler instead rules with the help of other tribal groups and develops a patron–client relationship with them.

In Ibn Khaldūn's theory, religion has the function of supplementing the power and authority that a dynasty obtains from *'aṣabiyyah*. Religion does this by creating a zealousness that enables the people who share in a group feeling to transcend jealousies and inspire them to fight for common goals. The lethal combination of *'aṣabiyyah* and religion enables the group to fight against and even defeat armies many times their size.[40] Ibn Khaldūn is careful to point out that as potent a force as religion is, it still requires the support of group feeling if it is to play a role in state formation. He quotes the hadith of the Prophet, "God sent no prophet who did not enjoy the protection of his people", to support this idea.[41]

Ibn Khaldūn further observes that for the Arabs, religion seemed to be a necessary condition for them to obtain kingship and establish a dynasty.

> The reason for this is that because of their savagery, the Arabs are the least willing of nations to subordinate themselves to each other, as they are rude, proud, ambitious, and eager to be the leader. Their individual aspirations rarely coincide. But when there is religion (among them) through prophecy or sainthood, then they have some restraining influence in themselves. The qualities of haughtiness and jealousy leave them. It is, then, easy for them to subordinate themselves and to unite (as a social organization). This is achieved by the common religion they now have. It causes rudeness and pride to disappear and exercises a restraining influence on their mutual envy and jealousy. When there is a prophet or saint among them, who calls upon them to fulfill the commands of God and rids them of blameworthy qualities and causes them to adopt praiseworthy ones, and who has them concentrate all their strength in order to make the truth prevail, they become fully united (as a social organization) and obtain superiority and royal authority. Besides, no people are as quick (as the Arabs) to accept (religious) truth and right guidance, because their natures have been preserved free from distorted habits and uncontaminated by base character qualities.[42]

Because of the nature of sedentary society, the characteristics of nomadic life that facilitated the establishment and consolidation of the dynasty, that is, an austere lifestyle, morality, courage and fortitude, diminish. Sedentary life is the last stage of society, during which time it begins to decay.[43] Once decay sets in, it cannot be reversed.[44] Although kingship is very much a product of group feeling, the role of economic factors is given a great deal of attention by Ibn Khaldūn. In fact, the decline of a dynasty is an outcome of the erosion of group feeling as it interacts with economic factors. During the early years of a dynasty, the ruling class develops a taste for luxury. The envy of the ruler towards his family and relatives who share in his group feeling leads to their being alienated. As they are seen by him to be potential usurpers of power, they are marginalized and even eliminated. The ruler elevates in their place an inner circle of clients and followers among whom a new group feeling develops. This new group feeling, however, lacks the force of the older one as it is not founded on kinship ties.[45] Ibn Khaldūn continues:

> The ruler thus isolates himself from his family and helpers, those who have natural affection (for him). This (in turn) is sensed by the people of other groups. Very naturally, they become audacious vis-à-vis the ruler and his inner circle. Therefore, the ruler destroys them and persecutes and kills them, one after the other. The later people of the dynasty follow the tradition of the former in that respect. In addition, they are exposed to the detrimental effect of luxury that we have mentioned before. Thus, destruction comes upon them

> through luxury and through being killed. Eventually, they no longer have the coloring of (their) group feeling. They forget the affection and strength that (used to) go with it. They become hirelings for the military protection (of the dynasty). They thus become few in number. As a consequence, the militia settled in the remote and frontier regions becomes numerically weak. This, then, emboldens the subjects in the remote regions to abandon the cause (of the dynasty) there. Rebels who are members of the ruling family and other (types of rebels) go out to these remote regions. They hope that under these circumstances, they will be able to reach their goal by obtaining a following among the inhabitants of the remote regions of the realm. (They hope that) they will be secure from capture by the (government) militia. This (process) keeps on and the authority of the ruling dynasty continues gradually to shrink until the rebels reach places extremely close to the center of the dynasty. The dynasty then often splits into two or three dynasties, depending on its original strength, as we have stated. People who do not share in the group feeling of (the dynasty) take charge of its affairs, though they obey the people who do share in the group feeling of (the dynasty) and accept their acknowledged superiority.[46]

An example is the Umayyads. At one time the rule of the Umayyads extended to Andalusia, India and China. As their group feeling eroded, they were replaced by the Abbasids who marginalized and eliminated the descendants of Abū Ṭālib, the 'Alids, thereby destroying the previous group feeling. The Abbasid dynasty itself split into a number of dynasties as the Aghlabids in Ifrīqiyā and the Andalusians developed their own followings in these areas.[47]

When a ruling dynasty is at an advanced stage of disintegration, the rise of a new dynasty may take place in one of two ways. One is when provincial governors of the disintegrating dynasty gain control of the outlying areas, founding new dynasties there. For example, in Andalusia, the Umayyad dynasty disintegrated into several principalities or *ṭawa'if*, ruled by former Umayyad provincial governors. When the Abbasids were at an advanced stage of decay, the Samanids took control of the outer regions such as Transoxiana, the Hamdanids of Mosul and Syria, and the Tulunids of Egypt. The second way that a new dynasty emerges is when rebels from a neighbouring nation and tribe, riding on the prestige of their own group feelings, conquer a decaying state.[48]

Authority and the economy

The distinction that Ibn Khaldūn makes between caliphate authority (*khilāfah*) and kingship is an important sociological contribution. The exercise of caliphate authority meant that the ruler was able:

> to cause the masses to act as required by religious insight into their interests into the other world as well as in this world. (The worldly interests) have bearing upon (the interests in the other world), since according to the Lawgiver (Muḥammad), all worldly conditions are to be considered in their

> relation to their value for the other world. Thus, (the caliphate) in reality substitutes for the Lawgiver (Muḥammad), in as much as it serves, like him, to protect the religion and to exercise (political) leadership of the world.[49]

Kingship, on the other hand, refers to the ability to rule by force:

> We have also mentioned before that according to their nature, human beings need someone to act as a restraining influence and mediator in every social organization, in order to keep the members from (fighting) with each other. That person must, by necessity, have superiority over the others in the matter of group feeling. If not, his power to (exercise a restraining influence) could not materialize.[50]

Kingship for Ibn Khaldūn is something natural and inevitable. Once the stage of social organization has been reached, there is the need for a restraining influence to be exercised over humans owing to their being naturally aggressive and unjust.

> The weapons made for the defense of human beings against the aggressiveness of dumb animals do not suffice against the aggressiveness of man to man, because all of them possess those weapons. Thus, something else is needed for defense against the aggressiveness of human beings toward each other. It could not come from outside, because all the other animals fall short of human perceptions and inspiration. The person who exercises a restraining influence, therefore, must be one of themselves.[51]

Kingship refers to the ability to dominate over humans and to have power and authority over them, in order to restrain one against the other. Kingship is a natural quality of humans and absolutely necessary to their survival.

Ibn Khaldūn makes a distinction between two types of kingship: *mulk siyāsī* (royal authority) and *mulk ṭabī'ī* (unbridled kingship).[52] Royal authority is kingship that "causes the masses to act as required by intellectual (rational) insight into the means of furthering their worldly interests and avoiding anything that is harmful (in that respect)".[53] In royal authority, life is not regulated according to the "*bon plaisir*" of the ruler.[54] When authority is combined with a strong and intact *'aṣabiyyah* – that is, when power wielded by the ruler is founded not on unbridled kingship but on the acceptance of his legitimacy – it is royal authority. As *'aṣabiyyah* disintegrates and the element of kinship is replaced by alliance and clientship, another kind of authority is established, that is, natural or unbridled kingship. Unbridled kingship "causes the masses to act as required by purpose and desire (of the rulers)".[55] It is a type of authority that is wielded by force in which the private interests of the ruler are prioritized and the well-being of the public is of secondary importance.[56]

In Ibn Khaldūn's theory of the rise and decline of states, there is a close relationship between politics and economy. The decline of a dynasty is not only a social-psychological phenomenon involving the dissipation of group feeling.

Wealth interacts with the functions of the state in ways that are peculiar to the declining phase of the dynasty. Kingship calls for a luxurious lifestyle that requires ever-increasing expenditure on salaries and allowances. As the expectations of the military elite continue to grow, the ruler is under pressure to increase taxes and duties and may even resort to the confiscation of property.

Ibn Khaldūn's account of the interplay between economy and polity, as noted by Ernest Gellner, reminds one of a Keynesian-type notion of the multiplier.[57] Ibn Khaldūn, however, does not blame the middle class for inadequate aggregate demand, but rather the governmental propensity to save at a time of weak private investment:

> Now, if the ruler holds on to property and revenue, or they are lost or not properly used by him, then the property in the possession of the ruler's entourage will be small. The gifts which they, in their turn, had used to give to their entourage and people, stop, and all their expenditures are cut down. They constitute the greatest number of people (who make expenditures), and their expenditures provide more of the substance of trade than (the expenditures of) any other (group of people). Thus (when they stop spending), business slumps and commercial profits decline because of the shortage of capital. Revenues from the land tax decrease, because the land tax and taxation (in general) depend on cultural activity, commercial transactions, business prosperity, and the people's demand for gain and profit. It is the dynasty that suffers from the situation and that has a deficit, because under these circumstances the property of the ruler decreases in consequence of the decrease in revenues from the land tax. As we have stated, the dynasty is the greatest market, the mother and base of all trade. (It is the market that provides) the substance of income and expenditures (for trade). If government business slumps and the volume of trade is small, the dependent markets will naturally show the same symptoms, and to a greater degree. Furthermore, money circulates between subjects and ruler, moving back and forth. Now, if the ruler keeps it to himself, it is lost to the subjects.[58]

There is a strong correlation between the political down-cycle of a dynasty and the economic down-cycle. In the early stages of the dynasty, taxation produces larger revenues from relatively smaller assessments. Towards the end of a dynasty the reverse holds true. During the early years of a dynasty, taxes are limited to those required by religious law. In its later stages, the rulers emulate the sedentary lifestyle of their predecessors and increase taxes and duties in order to obtain higher tax revenue.[59] There comes a point where the assessments increase beyond what is equitable, resulting in a halt to economically productive activities. Tax revenues in turn decrease and individual imposts are increased to make up the difference, further exacerbating the downturn in production.[60] In periods of kingship of the unbridled type, people are in constant danger of having forced labour, duties not required by Islamic law, imposed upon them, and their property confiscated.

The interplay between the economy and politics is described by Ibn Khaldūn:

> The ruler, then, must impose duties on articles sold in the markets, in order to improve his revenues. (He does so,) because he sees the luxury of the urban population testifying to their prosperity, and because he needs the money for the expenditures of his government and the salaries of his soldiers. Habits of luxury, then, further increase. The customs duties no longer pay for them. The dynasty, by this time, is flourishing in its power and its forceful hold over the subjects under its control. Its hand reaches out to seize some of the property of the subjects, either through customs duties, or through commercial transactions, or, in some cases, merely by hostile acts directed against (property holdings), on some pretext or even with none.
>
> At this stage, the soldiers have already grown bold against the dynasty, because it has become weak and senile, as far as its group feeling is concerned. (The dynasty) expects that from them, and attempts to remedy and smooth over the situation through generous allowances and much spending for (the soldiers). It cannot get around that.
>
> At this stage, the tax collectors in the dynasty have acquired much wealth, because vast revenues are in their hands and their position has widened in importance for this reason. Suspicions of having appropriated tax money, therefore, attach to them. It becomes common for one tax collector to denounce another, because of their mutual jealousy and envy. One after another is deprived of his money by confiscation and torture. Eventually, their wealth is gone, and they are ruined. The dynasty loses the pomp and magnificence it had possessed through them.
>
> After their prosperity is destroyed, the dynasty goes farther afield and approaches its other wealthy subjects. At this stage, feebleness has already afflicted its (former) might. (The dynasty) has become too weak to retain its power and forceful hold. The policy of the ruler, at this time, is to handle matters diplomatically by spending money. He considers this more advantageous than the sword, which is of little use. His need for money grows beyond what is needed for expenditures and soldiers' salaries. He never gets enough. Senility affects the dynasty more and more. The people of (other) regions grow bold against it.
>
> At each of these stages, the strength of the dynasty crumbles. Eventually, it reaches complete ruin. It is open to domination by (any) aggressor. Anyone who wants to attack it can take it away from those who support it. If this does not occur, it will continue to dwindle and finally disappear – like the wick of a lamp when the oil is exhausted, and it goes out.[61]

Towards applying Ibn Khaldūn

Ibn Khaldūn worked out an elaborate theoretical scheme that he abstracted from the facts of the history of North Africa and the East. His objective was to understand the dynamics of the rise and decline of states. The main features of his theory can be summarized as follows.

Strong *'aṣabiyyah* or group feeling is a prerequisite for a group to found a house with the attribute of nobility (*sharaf*). Only such houses are able to found a dynasty. Various dominant group feelings may compete until one emerges victorious. The superiority of a group feeling is materially expressed in terms of kingship. The idea of group feeling or social cohesion conveyed by the term *'aṣabiyyah* is partly derived from agnatic ties in tribal social organizations. All tribal groups have stronger or weaker *'aṣabiyyah* based on kinship. But pastoral nomadic tribes have the edge in terms of the strength of their *'aṣabiyyah*. Living in the desert bestows upon the bedouin positive qualities such as courage and fortitude. These qualities are enhanced by the high degree of *'aṣabiyyah* that the nomads have. What makes *'aṣabiyyah* so potent as a social and political force is that it is a form of solidarity or social cohesion that is founded on the knowledge of its members that they share a common descent. Ibn Khaldūn believed that the form of solidarity based on *'aṣabiyyah* was far more powerful and effective than other forms of solidarity. The stronger the *'aṣabiyyah*, the more closely knit the group and the greater the degree of mutual support and aid. The *'aṣabiyyah* of the bedouin was more intact than that of sedentary people, giving them a higher degree of fortitude and mutual support. However, the *'aṣabiyyah* of the new dynasty and its social network of family members and tribes tends to dissipate once the people become sedentarized for various reasons that have to do with the nature of sedentary life.

The interaction between religion and *'aṣabiyyah* was noted by Ibn Khaldūn. Religion had been instrumental in creating a kind of trans-tribal *'aṣabiyyah*. This was true of the Arab tribes of the Arabian peninsula during the time of the Prophet Muḥammad, who subordinated their individual group feelings to religion and united on a trans-tribal basis. Contributing to the social psychological dimension of *'aṣabiyyah* is the authority enjoyed by the chieftain as a result of his control over resources derived from profits from trade and appropriation from raiding activities. For Ibn Khaldūn, then, *'aṣabiyyah* (1) referred to kinship ties; (2) was buttressed by a socially cohesive religion such as Islam, which provided a shared orientation and legitimized the leader's aspirations for power and authority; and (3) was characterized by the strength of the leader being derived from trade, booty, pillage and conquest.

Ibn Khaldūn was, of course, referring to tribal groups for which *'aṣabiyyah* had a specific meaning: that is, the feeling of solidarity or cohesion among the members of a group that is derived from the knowledge that they share a common descent. The *'aṣabiyyah* of the bedouin was held to be stronger and this enabled them to militarily and morally defeat sedentary people, those settled in and around urban areas, and establish their own dynasties. After a new dynasty was established, however, the ruling tribesmen gradually became absorbed into a sedentary lifestyle and experienced an erosion of their *'aṣabiyyah*. In other words, sedentary life was antithetical to a strong *'aṣabiyyah* and had the effect of reducing the strength of group feeling. With the reduction in group feeling went the military strength of the tribesmen and the dynasty they supported. Their ability to rule was compromised.

The cycle is completed when the dynasty is conquered by a group of pre-sedentary tribes with their *'aṣabiyyah* intact, who replace the weaker, sedentarized ones.

A dynasty generally lasts for four generations. Power may transfer within a nation to another group that shares in the same group feeling, or kingship may be passed on to an entirely new people. The ruling tribes and elites are replaced on a cyclical basis but the system remains stable. This is the nature of the Khaldūnian cycle.

The objective of this book is to apply Khaldūnian theory to cases other than those dealt with by Ibn Khaldūn in the *Muqaddimah* and the rest of the *Kitāb al-'Ibar*. Ibn Khaldūn bequeathed to us a model that may serve as a reference point for the study of society, possibly an alternative to European and American theoretical models.[62] This requires our having a certain attitude towards Ibn Khaldūn's work, an attitude according to which we may "lift Ibn Khaldūn from his time",[63] and consider merging his ideas and concepts with those of the modern social sciences. Doing this also requires that we distinguish the general categories developed by Ibn Khaldūn from those that he applied to the specific case of the history of the Maghrib.[64]

The application of the theory requires a detailed account of it, such as the one presented above, as well as attention to ideas and concepts not addressed by Ibn Khaldūn but which are deemed necessary to the application. For example, Ibn Khaldūn does not conceptualize the economic systems of the dynasties or regions he deals with. A definition of the economic systems of the states to which we are applying Ibn Khaldūn's theory may allow us to better explain the rise and decline of dynasties within the Khaldūnian framework. It would help to provide the relevant economic context of the function of *'aṣabiyyah* and kingship, and the wielding of royal authority. This can be achieved by, for example, introducing the concept of mode of production into the application of the Khaldūnian framework to Ottoman and Safavid history to provide the economic base in which *'aṣabiyyah* and authority operate. These will be presented and elaborated in Chapters 6 and 7. In the next chapter, however, I turn to a discussion on why a systematic Khaldūnian sociology did not develop in the modern period.

3 Ibn Khaldūn and modern sociology

An aborted tradition

Ibn Khaldūn has not been taken seriously enough by the various disciplines in the social sciences, particularly sociology, of which, it is often claimed, he is the founder. This is true both of the West and the Muslim world. While it is not true that there were no followers of Ibn Khaldūn in the Muslim world and in pre-modern times, a Khaldūnian tradition in the science of human society, as Ibn Khaldūn called it, or the modern social sciences, never developed. In the modern period, when there was more interest in Ibn Khaldūn, his works were generally not seen as sources of theories and concepts to be applied to the study of historical and contemporary empirical realities. Although Ibn Khaldūn has been hailed in many quarters as a precursor and founder of sociology, a Khaldūnian sociology has yet to develop.

I suggest that a serious obstacle to the development of a Khaldūnian sociology is the Eurocentric nature of social science education in most of the world. Eurocentrism defines the content of education in such a way that the origins of the social sciences and the question of alternative points of view are not thematized. It is this lack of thematization that makes it highly unlikely that the works of non-European thinkers such as Ibn Khaldūn would be given the same attention as European and American social theorists such as Marx, Weber, Durkheim and others. Eurocentrism is a thought-style that is not restricted to Europeans. The social sciences are taught in the Third World in a Eurocentric manner. In the Muslim world, this has contributed to the alienation of social scientists from their scholarly tradition. Courses in sociology and the other social sciences generally do not attempt to correct the Eurocentric bias by introducing non-Western thinkers such as Ibn Khaldūn. In this chapter I show how Eurocentrism and the resulting marginalization of non-Western ideas in the history and teaching of sociology obstruct the emergence of a Khaldūnian social theory and suggest what conditions must be fulfilled in order that Khaldūnian sociology may develop.

After an account of the Western discovery of Ibn Khaldūn, I will explain how the prevalence of Eurocentrism in the social sciences functions to obstruct the development of a Khaldūnian perspective in mainstream sociology. I then turn to a discussion of one reaction to Eurocentrism in the Muslim world: that is, the Islamization of knowledge project. This project had generally failed to consider and systematically develop Ibn Khaldūn as an exemplar for an alternative sociology founded on the Islamic tradition. As a result, a Khaldūnian sociology remains virtually undeveloped in both mainstream social science and what is referred to as Islamic sociology.

The western discovery of Ibn Khaldūn

Ibn Khaldūn's first appearance in Europe can be traced to 1636, to a Latin translation of Ibn 'Arabshāh's *Fī Akhbār Taymūr 'Ajā'ib al-Maqdūr* (*Viate et rerum gestarum Timuri, qui vulgo Tamerlanes dicitur, Historia*). In this work 'Arabshāh mentions the historic meeting between Ibn Khaldūn and Tamerlane, the Mongol warrior and conqueror.[1] In the latter part of the seventeenth century a biography of Ibn Khaldūn appeared in d'Herbelot's *Bibliotheque Orientale*.[2] However, it was then more than 100 years before translations of Ibn Khaldūn appeared. A French translation of extracts of Ibn Khaldūn's works, undertaken by Silvestre de Sacy, appeared in 1810.[3] Joseph von Hammer-Purgstall published extracts of the *Muqaddimah* in German (1818, 1822).[4] William MacGuckin de Slane's French translation of the *Muqaddimah* appeared between 1862 and 1868.[5] The incorporation of Ibn Khaldūn into modern social science is incomplete. There was more serious attention to Ibn Khaldūn in mainstream sociology in the nineteenth century than there is today. Several Western scholars in the nineteenth century recognized Ibn Khaldūn as a founder of sociology.[6]

In conflict theorists such as Ludwig Gumplowicz (1838–1909) and Franz Oppenheimer (1864–1943), we find more serious students of Ibn Khaldūn. In his *Sociological Essays*, Gumplowicz devoted an entire chapter to Ibn Khaldūn, referring to him as an Arab sociologist of the fourteenth century. Oppenheimer was referred to by Becker and Barnes as the "reviver of Ibn Khaldūn".[7] Becker and Barnes themselves, in their chapter titled "Struggle over 'The Struggle for Existence'", recognized him as an early conflict theorist and one "who emphasized causal principles in history at a time when 'providential' viewpoints everywhere held sway".[8] They had also referred to Ibn Khaldūn as the first writer, after Polybius, to apply the equivalent of modern ideas in historical sociology.[9]

An interesting example of the European revival of Ibn Khaldūn that has implications for the attempt to incorporate Ibn Khaldūn's ideas into the modern social sciences is an article by the Spanish philosopher José Ortega y Gasset, appearing in 1934: "Ibn Khaldūn reveals the secret to us: thoughts on North Africa". Ortega reflects on Melilla, a city in North Africa, conquered by the Spaniards at the end of the fifteenth century. For Ortega, what presented itself as an intellectual problem was the fact that Melilla was for centuries, up to his own time, enclosed within its own walls, having no relations or only hostile relations with the countryside.[10] Ortega says that Europeans had to ask a native of Africa for the solution to the problem. The answer could not come from Europeans, who operated according to a different conception of history from that required for understanding Africa. But despite their having studied and written historical books, native Africans were generally not thinkers.[11] Ibn Khaldūn is then named by Ortega as an eminent exception, who has a clear and insightful mind in the way of the Greeks.

Ibn Khaldūn reveals to us that the apparent chaos of events in North Africa can be understood in terms of the coexistence of two ways of life: the nomadic and sedentary.[12] Ortega notes that for Ibn Khaldūn state and society in North Africa are radically separated. Herein lies the secret of historical change. Two completely different human types create each social group. Government is created by nomadic groups while society is the creation of sedentary peoples. The nomads, with a higher level of moral discipline and greater courage, are able to get the better of sedentary people and take control of cities. They create states. But the states they found are transitory because the nomads in the cities become infected by the "virus of softness".[13] The weakened, sedentarized nomads are now at the mercy of fresh supplies of nomadic invaders. The process is repeated every three generations or about 120 years.[14] This is the basis of Ibn Khaldūn's philosophy of history which Ortega regarded at the same time as the first sociology.[15]

The secrets revealed to us by Ibn Khaldūn are useful not only for the understanding of Melilla and its relationship with the countryside; they can also tell us something about life in Spain itself. For example, Castile has elements of Berber culture. The house of the Castilian peasant is similar to the *kabylia* house and the form of dress bears resemblance to the *djelaba*.[16] Ortega also suggests that Ibn Khaldūn's theory can be applied to the rise of the Wahhabi movement in the Arabian peninsula. Ortega was wrong in attributing the extremist orientation of the Wahhabi movement to Islam itself. He says:

> The Muhammadan faith is instrinsically polemic, warring. First of all, they believe that others have no right to believe what they believe not. Rather than monotheism the psychologically exact name of this religion should be "non-polytheism". Within Muhammadanism there are periodically new forms of archi-puritanism. One of them is Wahhabism …[17]

Clearly, Ortega here betrays an Orientalist understanding of Islam. Nevertheless, he was correct about the utility of Ibn Khaldūn's theory for our understanding the rise of the Saudi Wahhabi state and the role of Wahhabi orientations in that.[18]

Although we may speak of the beginnings of a modern Khaldūnian sociological tradition if we refer to the works of scholars such as Oppenheimer and Ortega, or those who came after them such as Lacoste and Gellner,[19] this tradition has yet to develop, whether in the Muslim world or in the West.

As the modern social sciences spread across the Arab world from the nineteenth century onwards, there were a handful of Muslim and Western scholars who began to use Khaldūnian categories to study the historical and contemporary realities of their societies. Among the Muslims influenced by Ibn Khaldūn were the reformers Jamāl al-Dīn al-Afghānī, Muḥammad 'Abduh and Rashīd Riḍā.[20] In our times, scholars such as Muḥammad 'Ābid al-Jābirī and Ali Oumlil have attempted to understand Ibn Khaldūn's thought in a non-Eurocentric manner.[21] While these studies are not applications of Ibn Khaldūn to historical or empirical contexts, they are nevertheless important theoretical appraisals of his work that seek to understand Ibn Khaldūn in terms of the categories and concepts of his own time, a prerequisite for any serious attempt to develop such Khaldūnian applications. Western scholars who have attempted applications of Khaldūnian theory to Muslim history and society include Ernest Gellner and Yves Lacoste.

Becker and Barnes, in their *Social Thought from Lore to Science*, first published in 1938, devote many pages to a discussion of the ideas of Ibn Khaldūn, recognizing that he was the first to apply modern-like ideas in historical sociology.[22] Perhaps the most important contribution of Ibn Khaldūn was summed up by Barnes as follows:

> But the most important of the innovations of this interesting writer was his grasp of the unity and continuity of the historical process. In sharp contrast to the static conceptions of the prevailing Christian historiography, he grasped the fundamental conception that the stages of civilization are always in a constant process of change, like the life of the individual. He pointed out clearly the co-operation of psychic and environmental factors in this process of historical development. All in all, Khaldun, rather than Vico, has the best claim to the honor of having founded the philosophy of history, and his view of the factors involved in the historical process was sounder and more modern than that of the Italian of three centuries later.[23]

Baali cites Sorokin, Gumplowicz, Barnes and Becker as being among those who recognize the Arabic contribution to the field of sociology.[24]

Ibn Khaldūn has been compared with many Western scholars who lived after him but who were said to have originated similar ideas. Let us consider the parallels between Ibn Khaldūn and Auguste Comte (1798–1857), the founding father of sociology, as discussed by Baali.[25]

1. Each believed that they had created something new. Ibn Khaldūn called his new science *'ilm al-'umrān al-basharī* (the science of civilization) or *'ilm al-ijtimā' al-insānī* (the science of human society), whereas Comte called it sociology.
2. Comte wanted to emancipate society from theological and metaphysical conceptions. Similarly, Ibn Khaldūn aimed to purge the study of society of metaphysical explanations and emphasized objective and reliable information.
3. Both attempted to discover laws of social life. Therefore, they understood their respective disciplines as being predictive.
4. They both believed that it was necessary to have knowledge of the past in order to understand the present: that is, the historical method.
5. Both emphasized a historical method and did not propose statistical methods.
6. Both distinguished their sciences from what preceded them.
7. Both believed that human nature is the same everywhere.
8. Both recognized the importance of social change.

The obvious question that arises, which was raised by Baali, is: was Comte familiar with the writings of Ibn Khaldūn?

Theories as to how Comte may have come to know of the works of Ibn Khaldūn include: that Comte would have come across the French translations noted above; that he would have heard of Ibn Khaldūn through his Egyptian students; that he had read Montesquieu, who had read Ibn Khaldūn in the original Arabic. But it is only speculation that Comte was indirectly influenced by Ibn Khaldūn.

The possibility of the influence of Ibn Khaldūn on Marx and Engels has been discussed elsewhere.[26] Some assumptions can be made as to how Engels may have come to know of the works of Ibn Khaldūn: he, like Comte, may have come across the French translations; he may have heard of Ibn Khaldūn through Marx, as Marx cited de Slane's translation in some reading notes he made on Algeria in the early 1880s;[27] and Engels describes cyclical change in his reading of European history prior to the medieval period, quite similar to that of Ibn Khaldūn.

In a footnote from 1894–95, Engels makes a classic Orientalist statement in his contrast between Christianity and Islam:

> Islam is a religion adapted to Orientals, especially Arabs, i.e., on one hand to townsmen engaged in trade and industry, on the other to nomadic bedouins. Therein lies, however, the embryo of a periodically recurring collision. The townspeople grow rich, luxurious and lax in the observation of the "law". The bedouins, poor and hence of strict morals, contemplate with envy and covetousness these riches and pleasures. Then they unite under a prophet, a Mahdi, to chastise the apostates and restore the observation of the ritual and the true faith and to appropriate in recompense the treasures of the renegades. In a hundred years they are naturally in the same position as the renegades were: a new purge of the faith is required, a new Mahdi arises and the game starts again from the beginning. That is what happened from the conquest campaigns of the African Almoravids and the Almohads in Spain to the last Mahdi of Khartoum who so successfully thwarted the English. It happened in the same way or similarly with the risings in Persia and other Mohammedan countries. All these movements are clothed in religion but they have their source in economic causes; and yet, even when they are victorious, they allow the old economic conditions to persist untouched. So the old situation remains unchanged and the collision recurs periodically.[28]

In both Europe and the Muslim world, religion was held to be merely a disguise for movements that had economic causes. But in the case of the Christian West the movements attacked an antiquated economic order, contributed to its overthrow and took Europe to a higher stage of development; whereas in the Muslim world the economic order remained untouched. What is of more relevance to us here, however, is the Khaldūnian nature of Engels' statement. While Engels makes no reference to Ibn Khaldūn it is quite likely that both he and Marx were aware of Ibn Khaldūn's works. As Hopkins notes, Engels may have been attracted to Ibn Khaldūn because of what Engels might have seen as a materialistic approach in the *Muqaddimah*.[29] For example, Ibn Khaldūn states that differences among groups are due to the different modes of making a living.[30]

Bousquet suggests that Engels had read de Slane's translation of the *Muqaddimah*, but turned Ibn Khaldūn on his head when he asserted the primacy of economic life rather than the Khaldūnian political cycle of prosperity-decadence.[31] While Engels probably borrowed from Ibn Khaldūn, neither he nor Marx had thought about how to incorporate the Khaldūnian framework into their own conceptual scheme. The task of the elaboration of a Khaldūnian sociology requires thinking along these lines. However, Marx and Engels failed to relate this to one of their own concepts, the mode of production.

The point here is to suggest that thinkers living several centuries later, from a different civilization, may know and appreciate the works of their predecessors. This is rarely done in the field of sociology. Among the few exceptions are Becker and Barnes, who not only reserved a section in their work for Ibn Khaldūn, but also discussed the influence of his ideas on Europeans: that is, an instance of the intercivilizational encounter in sociology.[32] They suggest that Ibn Khaldūn's direct influence on sociology probably began in 1899, the year that Gumplowicz published his *Soziologische Essays* which included a chapter on Ibn Khaldūn. They also note the influence of Ibn Khaldūn on the conflict theory of Oppenheimer, who draws upon Ibn Khaldūn for his work on agrarian reform.[33]

More importantly, Barnes and Becker were able to recognize the "modern" aspects of Ibn Khaldūn's work without interpreting him out of context. They were perfectly aware of the fact that Ibn Khaldūn wrote in a time and place much unlike nineteenth century Europe. At the same time, they were able to understand those aspects of Ibn Khaldūn's work that are timeless and universal. They noted that his methodology was directed towards the critique of documentary history, which led him to formulate laws of society and social change. They also noted that while Ibn Khaldūn's approach was "secular", by which they probably meant "material", he did not have an empiricist mentality in that both experimental and supernatural elements were part of the same reality. Nevertheless, the supernatural elements refer to ultimate realities and are rarely brought in as explanations of social change.[34] More significantly, his importance as a social thinker lies not in his exhaustive treatment of a wide range of materials but rather in his peculiar treatment of this material. In that sense, he was much like Durkheim, Weber and others, "a human mind trying to *comprehend* rather than catalogue the specifically social factors in man's living and doing".[35]

The degree of recognition accorded to Ibn Khaldūn by Western scholars of the past, up to the early part of the twentieth century, was far greater than it is in contemporary teaching and the writing of the history of sociology. A contemporary or neo-Khaldūnian sociology has yet to be developed. Although Ibn Khaldūn developed theoretical tools and concepts that are valuable for the positive (as opposed to the normative) study of history, most students of Ibn Khaldūn have not been interested in building upon his ideas, combining them with concepts derived from modern sociology, and applying theoretical frameworks derived from his thought to historical and empirical realities. While Ibn Khaldūn's main empirical concern was with the Arab East and West, his theory of state formation and decline is of great relevance to the study of the Ottoman

Empire, the Safavid dynasty, the Mongol conquest of China and many other empirical fields.

Few studies have gone beyond the mere comparison of some ideas and concepts in Ibn Khaldūn with those of modern Western scholars, towards the theoretical integration of his theory into a framework that employs some of the tools of modern social science.[36] The reason for this state of affairs has to do with the continuing prevalence of Eurocentrism in the social sciences.

A definition of Eurocentrism

At this point, it should be said that it is not being claimed here that the topic of Eurocentrism has not been dealt with before. Although Eurocentrism has been discussed by a number of scholars, for example A. L. Tibawi, Anouar Abdel-Malek and Edward Said in the context of their systematic treatment of Orientalism, such concerns with Eurocentrism have not made their way into teaching in the social sciences. This is not to say that the topic of Eurocentrism is not raised in social science and humanities courses. However, the discussions are generally confined to courses on the Third World or on postcolonial topics. Rarely do we find that basic or foundational courses are informed by concerns raised by the critique of Eurocentrism. For example, while there is no dearth of literature on problems associated with Eurocentrism, courses on sociological theory generally do not attempt to correct that bias by introducing non-Western thinkers or by critiquing Eurocentric elements in the works of Western theorists such as Marx, Weber and Durkheim. Therefore, it is necessary to present a definition of Eurocentrism in order to demonstrate how it remains persistent as an orientation in the social sciences as they are taught in institutions of higher learning.

Eurocentrism is a particular instance of ethnocentrism. Ethnocentrism is generally defined as the regard of one's own ethnic group or society as superior to other groups. It involves the assessment and judgement of other groups in terms of the categories and standards of evaluation of one's own group. Eurocentrism, therefore, refers to the assessment and evaluation of non-European societies in terms of the cultural assumptions and biases of Europeans. In the modern world, Eurocentrism cannot be dissociated from the economic cultural domination of the United States, as a result of the settlement of America by Europeans and the subsequent rise to hegemony of the United States. We would therefore be more accurate to refer to the phenomenon under consideration as Euroamericocentrism.[37]

Having given this general definition, how can we understand the manifestation of Eurocentrism in the social sciences? Eurocentrism in the social sciences can be understood as the assessment and evaluation of European and other civilizations from a decidedly European point of view. For our purposes, it is crucial to define what is meant by the European point of view. This can be described as that which establishes and employs concepts derived from European philosophical traditions and popular discourse, which are applied to the empirical study of history, economy and society. The empirical field of investigation is selected according to European (for European read also American) criteria of relevance. As a result, any particular aspect of historical or social reality is constructed in terms of European categories, concepts as well as ideal and material interests. There is a failure to present the point of view of the other.[38]

The traits of Eurocentrism, particularly in historical and social scientific works on various topics relating to the grand macro questions such as the origins of modern civilization or the rise of modern capitalism, can be listed as (but not confined to) the following.

1 *The subject–object dichotomy*. Europeans are the knowing subjects or the narrators and protagonists, while non-Europeans remain as unheard objects whose points of view only get communicated to us as and when the narrators see fit. These objects are passive, non-participating, non-active, non-autonomous and non-sovereign.[39] Said spoke of Flaubert's meeting with an Egyptian courtesan who never spoke of or represented herself. Rather, it was Flaubert who spoke for and represented her.[40] The result of this "omniscience" was the problematic construction of things non-European. As noted by Wallerstein, these constructions came under attack at three levels – they do not fit empirical reality, they over-abstract, resulting in the erasure of empirical variety, and they are founded on European prejudices.[41]
2 *Europeans in the foreground*. There is a focus on Europeans in the foreground as opposed to intercivilizational encounters with non-Europeans. Modernity is seen as a specifically European creation and is due to European superiority, whether this is viewed in biological, cultural or sociological terms. Encounters with non-Europeans are often referred to but not assessed as contributing to any significant changes to the course of European history.
3 *Europeans as originators*. Europeans are consistently viewed as originators. As a result there is far less consideration of the multicultural origins of many aspects of our modern civilization. In works on the history of philosophy, for example, Islamic philosophy is often relegated to footnotes and regarded simply as having transmitted Greek thought to the European world of the Renaissance. Alfred Weber, the younger brother of Max Weber and author of a history of philosophy, noted that the Arabs were "apt pupils of the Greeks, Persians, and Hindoos in science. Their philosophy is the continuation of Peripateticism and Neo-Platonism. It is more learned than original, and consists mainly of exegesis, particularly of the exegesis of Aristotle's system".[42] Here, in a few lines, the entire contribution of Islamic philosophy to Renaissance thought was denied by claiming that it was utterly lacking in originality, despite the availability of the works of Muslim philosophers and scientists from the ninth to the fourteenth centuries that would show otherwise.
4 *The imposition of European categories and concepts*. Tibawi noted the "persistence in studying Islam and the Arabs through the application of Western European categories".[43] This was because of the basic fallacy of Eurocentrism, pointed out by Needham in 1955, that the universal nature of European science and technology meant that everything else European was universal too.[44] As Wallerstein noted, European social sciences were universalist in the

> sense that European achievements in the sixteenth to nineteenth centuries were regarded as replicable elsewhere not only because that was desirable but also because it was inevitable.[45] To the extent that this process was universal, so were the social scientific truths that explained it. European social science is seen as universal in the sense that it holds scientific truths that are applicable everywhere else in the world. If they are not, this has to do with specific problems in concept formation or empirical problems relating to observation or data collection, but not with social science itself. The result, then, is the imposition of European categories and concepts and the concomitant neglect of those of non-European origins. Things non-European are regarded as worthy as objects of analysis but rarely as cognizant subjects. For example, Ibn Khaldūn's fourteenth century theories of historical change and state formation have often been the objects of studies but rarely if ever developed and applied as theoretical perspectives to the study of empirical realities.

It should be clear that as long as these characteristics inform the social sciences it would be practically impossible to introduce the themes of intercivilizational encounters – the multicultural origins of modernity, and the variety of points of view – into social science education. In the next section I will show that this is indeed the case. The traits of Eurocentrism as outlined above are defining features of the social sciences as they are taught in universities around the world.

Ibn Khaldūn in the social science curriculum

In the teaching of both the history of sociological theory and sociological theory itself, four characteristics of Eurocentrism are evident.

The subject–object dichotomy

In the vast majority of sociological theory textbooks or works on the history of social theory, the subject–object dichotomy is a pervasive theme. Europeans are the knowing subjects, that is, the social theorists and social thinkers. To the extent that non-Europeans figure in these accounts they are objects of the observations and analyses of the European theorists, appearing as Marx's Indians and Algerians or Weber's Turks, Chinese and Jews, and not as sources of sociological concepts and ideas. In one historical account, "early social theories" in the so-called "simpler" or non-literate societies, as well as ancient Egypt, ancient Babylon, the Greek city-states, Japan and China, were covered under the category of religious theories.[46] This discussion is obviously founded on the old scientific–mythic dichotomy that is supposed to separate the West from the East. The fact that there existed, in parts of the Muslim world, India, Japan and China from the fourteenth century onwards, what would be considered positive, scientific thought that approximated to what was regarded as sociology in the West was not discussed even though the relevant works have been known to the Europeans since the nineteenth century.[47] In works on the history of social thought that chart the development of sociological theory, the focus is on European thinkers at the expense of thematizing intercivilizational encounters that possibly influenced social theory in Europe. Maus' *Short History of Sociology* does not refer to any non-European in his chapter on the antecedents of sociology.[48]

Most textbooks on classical social theory aim to introduce European classical theorists such as Marx, Weber, Simmel and Durkheim, but are not true to the definition of "classical" that they claim to adopt. I will later show that the logical implication of the definition of "classic" is the serious consideration of non-European thinkers in theory textbooks.

The absence of non-European thinkers in theory textbooks results in their absence in theory courses as well. The *Resource Book for Teaching Sociological Theory*, published in 1989 by the American Sociological Association, is very revealing on this point. It contains a number of course descriptions for sociological theory. The range of classical theorists whose works are taught include Montesquieu, Vico, Comte, Spencer, Marx, Weber, Durkheim, Simmel, Toennies, Sombart, Mannheim, Pareto, Sumner, Ward, Small and Wollstonecraft. No non-European thinkers are included, and women are by no means well represented.[49] Although Ibn Khaldūn may appear to be an exception to the rule because many Europeans had "discovered" and discussed his works since the nineteenth century, a quick review of these discussions would reveal that he is mainly of historical interest.[50]

Europeans in the foreground

The exclusive concern of the field of sociological theory with European and later North American scholars is the rule rather than the exception. Turning to the latter, it is interesting to note that Becker and Barnes, in their *Social Thought from Lore to Science*, first published in 1938, devote many pages to a discussion of the ideas of Ibn Khaldūn.[51] Referring to Ibn Khaldūn, they remark that the first writer after Polybius to apply modern-like ideas in historical sociology was not a European.[52] It is thanks to them, and others before them in the nineteenth and early twentieth centuries, that Ibn Khaldūn became known in the West.[53] Becker and Barnes not only reserved a section in their work for Ibn Khaldūn, they discussed the influence of his ideas on Europeans: that is, the intercivilizational encounter in sociology.[54] The topic of these links will be taken up in a later section. While these links have been recognized in a few early and relatively obscure works, they are not discussed in mainstream theory textbooks and other works.

Europeans as originators

As a result, Europeans are viewed as the sole originators of sociology and other social sciences, and there is little consideration of the multicultural origins of these disciplines. Early twentieth century accounts of the rise of social theory sometimes make mention of non-Western thinkers. Ibn Khaldūn is the most referred to in this respect. But Ibn Khaldūn was a pre-modern scholar, having died at the beginning of the fifteenth century. A host of other thinkers in India, China,

Japan, and Southeast Asia during the nineteenth and early twentieth centuries would qualify as modern social thinkers, but they are only briefly mentioned in the early histories of sociology (e.g. Maus, Becker and Barnes) or, in more recent works, totally ignored. It would not be an exaggeration to say that the generations after Gumplowicz, Oppenheimer, Becker and Barnes have erased non-European thinkers from the history books. For example, Becker and Barnes' reference to the influence of Ibn Khaldūn on Gumplowicz and Oppenheimer is a theme that was never taken up in later accounts of the history of social thought.

The dominance of European categories and concepts

A logical consequence of putting into practice the subject–object dichotomy – the foregrounding of Europeans and North Americans in sociological theory, and the sole contemplation of Europeans as founders and originators of sociology – is the dominance of European concepts and categories in social sciences at the expense of non-European ones. For example, it was mentioned above that interest in Ibn Khaldūn tends to be historical. There has always been little interest in developing his ideas, combining them with concepts derived from modern sociology, and applying theoretical frameworks derived from his thought to historical and empirical realities. While there are certainly exceptions, where attempts have been made to apply a Khaldūnian theory or model to social reality, these are few and marginal to mainstream social science teaching.[55] The dominance of European and North American derived concepts and theories in the teaching syllabi of sociology and the other social sciences translates into research. In the study of religion, for example, the bulk of concepts originate from Christianity. Concepts in the philosophical and sociological study of religion, such as church, sect, denomination and even religion itself, are not devoid of Christian connotations and do influence the social scientific reconstruction of non-Christian religions.[56] The field of the sociology of religion has yet to enrich itself by developing concepts and categories derived from other "religions" such as Islam, Hinduism, Judaism, and so on.

If the role, contributions, significance, values, passion and efforts of non-Europeans are largely ignored in teaching and research in the social sciences, the marginalization of such scholars will persist.

Obstacles to the development of Khaldūnian sociology

The treatment of Ibn Khaldūn as an object rather than a subject explains why Khaldūnian sociology remains undeveloped, because it has resulted in the lack of emphasis on the empirical application of his theoretical framework to historical and contemporary data. That Ibn Khaldūn continues to be marginal in the social sciences and in the discipline of sociology in particular has to do with the fact that there has been no development of what one might call neo-Khaldūnian sociology: that is, a Khaldūnian sociology of modern societies. Ibn Khaldūn himself was a product of pre-capitalist society and wrote on pre-capitalist society and state formation. Because he is marginal, his work does not receive that kind of attention that would lead to the development of a neo-Khaldūnian sociology. The kind of attention that I am referring to has seven aspects or levels.

1 History – by this I mean the history of social philosophy with particular emphasis on Ibn Khaldūn's life and thought.
2 Theory – this refers to the systematic exposition, analysis and critique of Ibn Khaldūn's theory, with reference to the main concepts utilized, the type of evidence marshalled, the assumptions about the subject matter, and empirical verification.
3 Meta-theory – this refers to the attention to, among other things, the epistemological and methodological dimensions underlying Ibn Khaldūn's theory.
4 Theory building – this refers to the abstraction from existing theory, in this case, that of Ibn Khaldūn, to generate what one might call neo-Khaldūnian theory and applying this to space-times other than his own.
5 Critical assessment of attempted applications of Ibn Khaldūn, such as the works of Gautier, Ortega, Gellner and Lacoste.
6 Dissemination via regular panels or papers at mainstream conferences in sociology on Ibn Khaldūn.
7 Teaching Ibn Khaldūn in mainstream sociology courses from mainstream sociology or sociological theory textbooks.

What is crucial for the development of neo-Khaldūnian sociology are levels 4 to 7 above. The basic historical and biographical information and the foundational theoretical and meta-theoretical literature on Ibn Khaldūn (levels 1 to 3) that provide the basis for building neo-Khaldūnian theory are available in abundance in several languages, the most important being Arabic, English and French, although there are also some important works in Persian, Turkish and German. In this section I will provide a very brief overview of the works on Ibn Khaldūn that have come out of the Arab and Muslim world, and discuss why they have not led to the development of neo-Khaldūnian theory. An idea of the nature of works that fall under levels 1 to 7 follows.[57]

The bulk of work on Ibn Khaldūn is theoretical and meta-theoretical.

Theory

As far as the area of theory is concerned, the works in existence are far too numerous to list here. Many of these fall into two categories. One category consists of works that attempt to reconcile Ibn Khaldūn with modern sociology. As noted by Aḥmad Zāyid, many Arab sociologists were committed to comparisons between Ibn Khaldūn and the modern founders of sociology in order to prove that it was the former who founded the discipline.[58] Ibn Khaldūn has been compared to Machiavelli,[59] Comte,[60] Marx[61] and Durkheim.[62] There are many studies of specific issues and concepts relating directly to Ibn Khaldūn's oeuvre that cannot be listed here. These studies cover topics such as state formation, *'aṣabiyyah* (solidarity), the city, sedentary and nomadic societies, production relations, and so on. (A glance at some bibliographies devoted to Ibn Khaldūn provide a good idea of the topical and linguistic range of such works.)[63]

Meta-theory

Analytical studies on the epistemological and methodological foundations of Ibn Khaldūn's work are not as numerous as those on theory discussed above. Nevertheless, several important works have been published during the last 50 years, one such being Muhsin Mahdi's *Ibn Khaldūn's Philosophy of History* (1957). Mahdi discussed Ibn Khaldūn's dialectical study of Muslim historiography in order to reveal its weaknesses and justify a new science of society, which has its own methods of demonstration based on the logic of Aristotle. Mahdi is critiqued by al-Wardī, who suggested that Ibn Khaldūn actually opposed the methods of the logicians and was instead influenced by al-Ghazāli and Ibn Taymiyyah.[64] Rabī', in his doctoral dissertation of 1967, provided a useful review of four trends in the study of Ibn Khaldūn's method. One trend is the exaggeration of Ibn Khaldūn's alleged secular thinking, suggesting that Ibn Khaldūn downplayed or denied the necessity of prophecy for culture. The second trend, represented by the renowned Orientalist H. A. R. Gibb, underestimates the originality of Ibn Khaldūn's method, suggesting that he did not do much more than adopt the methods of the Muslim jurists and social philosophers that preceded him. The third and fourth trends are represented by Mahdi and al-Wardī respectively.[65] In addition to these debates there are numerous works on other aspects of Ibn Khaldūn's methodology and epistemology.[66]

What is needed for the development of Khaldūnian sociology, however, are serious efforts to apply his theoretical framework to empirical situations, historical or contemporary. For this to happen, there have to be more critical assessments of existing applications. Furthermore, this must take place within an overall context of the promotion of Ibn Khaldūn in teaching and research.

Building a neo-Khaldūnian theory

Very few authors have attempted to integrate Ibn Khaldūn's theory of state formation with the theories and concepts of modern sociology.[67] An example of such an integration is the explanation of the rise and decline of the pre-modern Safavid dynasty of Iran in terms of Ibn Khaldūn's theory of state formation. According to such a historical political economy of Safavid Iran, the dynamic of historical change in Ibn Khaldūn's theory is applied to the Marxist concept of the mode of production. Safavid state formation is then explained in terms of the relationship between coexisting modes of production. Marxist and Weberian concepts may be integrated into a Khaldūnian framework of historical change and utilized to explain the decline in *'aṣabiyyah* (group feeling) and the rise of *mulk* and *khilāfah* authority.[68]

Critical assessment of applications of Ibn Khaldūn

If there is little in the area of building a neo-Khaldūnian theory, there is even less by way of the critical assessment of attempts to apply a Khaldūnian model to the study of periods and regions other than Ibn Khaldūn's own. Gellner, for example, advanced a theory of Muslim reform based on a fusion of the ideas of Ibn Khaldūn and David Hume. This was not taken up and engaged by others. The same is true of works by Ortega, Lacoste and others.

Regular panels or papers on Ibn Khaldūn at mainstream conferences in sociology

In the past, there have been several major conferences organized in the Arab world on Ibn Khaldūn. The more prominent ones include the Ibn Khaldūn Symposium in Cairo in 1962, the Colloque Internationale sur Ibn Khaldoun in Algiers in 1978, and the Ibn Khaldūn Seminar in Rabat in 1979.[69] There has been far less attention to Ibn Khaldūn at national or international scholarly meetings in the West or in other areas outside the Arab world.

Teaching Ibn Khaldūn in mainstream sociology courses from mainstream sociology or sociological theory textbooks

While a comprehensive study of Arabic as well as Western language sociology textbooks on space devoted to Ibn Khaldūn has yet to be attempted, it was noted by Zāyid that in the case of Egypt, the leading nation in the Arab world for sociology, Ibn Khaldūn was rarely mentioned in textbooks published after the 1960s, the heritage appeal having been lost.[70]

Defining the "marginalization" of Ibn Khaldūn

This begs the question of what we mean by the marginalization of non-European scholars. Let us consider the case of Ibn Khaldūn. While he is mentioned here and there and given some attention in courses, these are generally those in Middle Eastern, Arab or Islamic studies. But Ibn Khaldūn never appears on a par with Marx, Weber and Durkheim as a social theorist whose thought offers concepts and theories of universal relevance. This is because Ibn Khaldūn's sociological theory has not been developed over the centuries by theorists to make his work *qua* sociological theory, not only more accessible but also relevant to the study of modern societies. As a result, he is mentioned occasionally but not methodologically or theoretically encountered and reconstructed as a sociologist and then accepted as a sociologist. Because of the continuing Eurocentrism via the themes of the subject–object dichotomy, Europeans in the foreground, Europeans as originators, and the dominance of European concepts and categories, non-Western thinkers like Ibn Khaldūn remain marginal.

This brings us back to the four characteristics of Eurocentric social science: the subject–object dichotomy, Europeans in the foreground, Europeans as originators, and the dominance of European categories and concepts. The relegation of Ibn Khaldūn to Middle East, North African or Islamic studies is a manifestation of the presence of these characteristics in the social sciences. This relegation also reflects French colonial interest in Ibn Khaldūn. For example, Gautier, writing in the 1920s, interpreted Ibn Khaldūn in a manner that resonated with French colonial ideology. Gautier exaggerated the opposition between nomadic invading Arabs and sedentary Berbers in North Africa but attributed this view to Ibn Khaldūn and other Arab writers.[71] This fitted in with the intention of French colonial policy in Algeria and Morocco to create a hostile relationship between the Arab and Berber populations. This played a role in the French defeat of the Algerian revolutionary 'Abd al-Qādir in 1847. As noted by Lacoste, the French would not have been able to defeat 'Abd al-Qādir had the Berbers not remained neutral.[72] In this case, Ibn Khaldūn was not seen as a source of original ideas understood in terms of his context and concerns. Rather, his work was slotted within the French colonial definition of what was important. In this sense, any interest that the French had in Ibn Khaldūn in the nineteenth and early twentieth centuries existed in this larger context of exerting intellectual authority over the Orient.

To the extent that there had been interest in the pre-modern heritage, Ibn Khaldūn was noted as a founder. Today, however, that appeal to heritage has significantly declined, both in the Arab-Muslim world and in the West, as noted above. Even when there was a historical interest in Ibn Khaldūn, it was not for his work as a source of concepts and ideas to be brought into modern sociology. Even where Ibn Khaldūn is taken up more seriously in Islamic, Middle Eastern or North African studies or where he is referred to by Western scholars from without a colonial context, the type of work characterized by levels 4 to 7 (see above) is rarely engaged in and Ibn Khaldūn is not considered as a knowing subject and a source of concepts and categories in the social sciences. It is almost exclusively Western thought that continues to be the concern of teachers and students of social thought and theory.

As a result, work on Ibn Khaldūn that would lead to the development of a neo-Khaldūnian sociology that I suggest requires attention at seven levels, particularly levels 4 to 7, remains undeveloped.

I would argue that the emergence of neo-Khaldūnian theory would have to be preceded by a great deal of exposure to Ibn Khaldūn's life and thought, to systematic analysis and critique of his theory, and to the epistemological and methodological principles informing his work via the publication of scientific journals and sociological theory textbooks, international conferences and the teaching of courses. Now, there is an abundance of literature on Ibn Khaldūn, not just in Arabic but in English and French as well. These works are therefore accessible to social scientists who do not know Arabic. However, the reason for the neglect of Ibn Khaldūn, as far as the generation of Khaldūnian theory is concerned, is not a problem of language. The problem is that this exposure is lacking because of the general perception of the place of such works in sociology. Works on Ibn Khaldūn are often "relegated" to Middle East, North African or Islamic studies. One indication of this is that among the numerous works on Ibn Khaldūn that were published in the West, a negligible number appeared in sociology journals. This is as if to say that the universal and theoretical by default refers to Marx, Weber and Durkheim, while Ibn Khaldūn's work yields particular knowledge that is of more local relevance and, therefore, more suitable for area studies journals.

Islamization of knowledge as a response to Eurocentrism

The idea of "Islamic social science" was first expressed in terms of Islamic economics and later in the form of the Islamization of knowledge project. Islamic economics was conceived of in the 1930s, while the beginnings of the Islamization of knowledge project date from the 1970s. Islamic social science seeks to bring back religious experience and spirituality into knowledge by means of the sacralization of academic discourse. The process of secularization in the West is seen to have rendered Muslim scholars incapable of comprehending the causes of the problems that beset Muslim society.[73] The Islamization of knowledge project is still vaguely conceived as far as the social sciences are concerned, and it remains open to charges of nativism.

The expression "Islamization of knowledge" first made its appearance at a conference held in 1977 in Mecca, where Syed Muhammad al-Naquib al-Attas discussed the concept of education in Islam.[74] At the same conference, the late Ismail R. al-Faruqi presented a paper on the Islamization of the social sciences.[75] Nevertheless, the idea of Islamic science, and in particular Islamic methodology, emerged earlier in the late 1950s in the works of Seyyed Hossein Nasr,[76] who spoke of the need for all knowledge originating from without the Muslim world to be integrated into the Islamic world-view and "Islamicized".[77] The notion, couched in the new terminology of "Islamization of knowledge", was subsequently proselytized by al-Faruqi, through an institute that he established in the United States, the International Institute of Islamic Thought (IIIT). The activities of the institute are not restricted to the dissemination of the notion of Islamization of knowledge, but also encompass programmes aimed at the Islamization of the various disciplines in the social sciences.[78]

As far as the social sciences are concerned, what is meant by the Islamization of knowledge? In order to answer this question it is first necessary to know what is meant by the notion of Islamization of knowledge.

According to al-Attas, the sciences that originated in the West that have been disseminated throughout the world do not necessarily represent true knowledge, due to their being infused with Western elements and key concepts.[79] Islamization of knowledge requires, first of all, the isolation of the elements and key concepts in the human sciences that constitute Western culture and civilization, such as the dualistic vision of society, humanism, and the "emulation of the allegedly universal reality of drama and tragedy in the spiritual or transcendental, or inner life of man, making drama and tragedy real and dominant elements in human nature and existence".[80] Once knowledge is free of these Western elements and key concepts, it is then infused with Islamic elements and key concepts, thereby making it true knowledge: that is, in harmony with the essential nature (*fiṭrah*) of man.[81] The Islamization of knowledge is the liberation of knowledge from interpretations based on secular ideology.[82] The methodology of Islamized knowledge is to be based on the science of exegesis and commentary, which employs the interpretive techniques of *tafsīr* and *ta'wīl*. The first refers to the interpretation of the firm (*muḥkamah*) verses of the Qur'an. *Tafsīr* is based on the objective reading of the verses of the Qur'an, and there is "no room for interpretation based on subjective readings, or understandings based merely upon the idea of historical relativism".[83] *Ta'wīl*, on the other hand, is an intensive form of *tafsīr* and refers to the allegorical interpretation of the obscure and ambiguous (*mutashābihah*) verses of the Qur'an.[84]

In order to illustrate the differences between these two interpretive techniques, al-Attas gives an example of their application to the following verse: "He causeth the living to issue from the dead" (6, *al-An'ām*: 95). When this is interpreted to mean, for example, "He brings forth the bird from the egg", this is *tafsīr*. But if the same passage is interpreted to mean "He brings forth the believer from the unbeliever", for example, this is *ta'wīl* and it refers to the ultimate meaning of the verse.[85]

According to al-Attas, the world of phenomena consists of signs and symbols that are to be subjected to the interpretive techniques of *tafsīr* and *ta'wīl* in the same manner that the verses of the Qur'an are:

> What we have said above should make it clear to us that science according to Islam is ultimately a kind of *ta'wīl* or allegorical interpretation of the empirical things that constitute the world of nature. As such science must base itself firmly upon the *tafsīr* or interpretation of the apparent or obvious meanings of the things in nature.[86]

Islamic science is to interpret the facts of the phenomenal world in correspondence with the Qur'anic methods of interpretation.[87]

Al-Faruqi had called upon Muslim scholars to recast every discipline in modern knowledge "so as to embody the principles of Islam in its methodology, in its strategy, in what it regards as its data, its problems, its objectives, and its aspirations".[88] Each discipline has to be remoulded to incorporate the relevance of Islam along a triple axis constituting the concept of *tawḥīd* (unity of God): that is, the unity of knowledge, the unity of life, and the unity of history.[89] Knowledge, therefore, has to be framed in accordance with the vision of Islam.[90] The Islamization of knowledge refers to the redefinition and reordering of the data, the re-evaluation of the conclusions, and the re-projection of the goals of knowledge in such a way that it serves the cause of Islam.[91] The process of the Islamization of knowledge requires the subjection of the theory, method, principles, and goals of knowledge to the unity of Allah (*tawḥīd*), the unity of creation, the unity of truth, the unity of knowledge, the unity of life and the unity of humanity.[92]

Seyyed Hossein Nasr's notion of Islamized knowledge is best captured by the expression *scientia sacra* or sacred knowledge. This refers to knowledge that "lies at the heart of every revelation and is the center of that circle which encompasses and defines tradition".[93] The eclipse of sacred knowledge in the modern world, beginning with the desacralization of knowledge in the Occident among the ancient Greeks,[94] indicates that there is a need for a science that can "relate the various levels of knowledge once again to the sacred".[95] The problem with modern science is that its rejection of the several facets of a particular reality and its reduction of symbols to facts is partly responsible for the desacralization of knowing and being so characteristic of the modern world.[96]

For Nasr, there is an added emphasis on methodology. The definition of knowledge in Islam does not differ from the corresponding term in Latin, *scientia*. The Islamic sciences include the natural sciences (*al-'ulūm al-ṭabī'iyyah*), the mathematical sciences (*al-'ulūm al-riyāḍiyyah*), and the occult sciences (*al-'ulūm al-khafiyyah*).[97] What distinguishes the Islamic sciences from modern knowledge, which are for the most part based on observation and experimentation, is the fact that the former employs various methods "in accordance with the nature of the subject in question and modes of understanding that subject".[98] What defines the Islamic sciences as *Islamic* is its "paradigm", which is based on the Islamic worldview. The world or universe that was the object of study for the Muslim scientist was taken to be an Islamic cosmos. Furthermore, the minds and eyes of the scientists were Muslim minds and eyes transformed by the spirit and form of the Qur'an.[99] The Islamic theory of knowledge is based on a hierarchy of the means of access to knowledge ranging from revelation and illumination to ratiocination as well as empirical and sensual knowledge.[100] An important principle of Islamic science is that Islam defines a particular method or sets of methods for each discipline whether it is jurisprudence, physics or *taṣawwuf* (mysticism). These methods are not seen to be contradictory but complementary. The multiplicity of the various methods and sciences are integrated in Islam into a totality in accordance with the doctrine of unity (*tawḥīd*).[101]

Having glanced at the definitions of Islamization of knowledge and Islamic science as understood by three Muslim scholars, the problem of application arises. How is the notion of the Islamization of knowledge to be applied to the various disciplines in the social sciences? What is meant by the reformulation of the sciences so that they fall into harmony with the concept of *tawḥīd*? How are the interpretive methods of *tafsīr* and *ta'wīl* to be applied to the study of social phenomena and are they any different from what is known as hermeneutics or interpretive sociology?

It is obvious that the notion of Islamized knowledge or Islamic science as applied to the social sciences remains couched in vague terms. To date, no Islamized social scientific works have appeared. To be sure, the call to the Islamization of knowledge goes beyond the assertion that science is value-laden. The proponents of the Islamization of the social sciences do not refer merely to the value content of social scientific research activities but to the very principles, methods, theories and concepts in the social sciences that are to be Islamized. What are the ways in which a discipline or a field of knowledge that we call social science is defined by Islam such that this field takes on an Islamic or Islamized character?

Is it that the social sciences are to be defined by Islamic philosophy – that is, Islamic metaphysics and epistemology as they evolved among the Arabs, Persians, Turks, Berbers, Indians and Malays since the second century AH? But this is insufficient grounds to warrant our referring to such social science as Islamic. Islamic philosophy affirms the existence of an external world and the possibility of knowledge thereof, and it is this affirmation that makes social science possible. But such an affirmation is common to many philosophical systems, and their impression upon the social sciences is of a general nature, not leaving a peculiarly Indian, Greek or Islamic mark on the social sciences. To cite another example, if it is said that a rationalist basis for the social sciences is derived from Islamic philosophy, such a basis can be found in various non-Islamic philosophical systems. There is nothing peculiar in an Islamic epistemological stance that would define social science as Islamic. Although it cannot be denied that there is a relationship between Islamic philosophy and the social sciences, the nature of the impact of philosophy is not such that it can be said that the social sciences have been Islamized.

If by the Islamization of the social sciences is meant the application of the methods of *taṣawwuf*, that is, *tafsīr* and *ta'wīl*, this must be clarified. How can these methods be applied to the study of social phenomena? How does *ta'wīl* differ from hermeneutics of subjectivist interpretations, which have formed the basis of various theoretical perspectives in the West? Furthermore, the application of the methods of Islamic mysticism to the social arena no more renders the social sciences Islamic than the use of, say, materialist methods renders Marx's work Epicurean.

If by Islamized social science is meant a theocratic approach, then some insights may be drawn from discussions on Ibn Khaldūn. As discussed in Chapter 2, Ibn Khaldūn's approach was materialist, in the sense that he gave prominence to the role of economic, political and social factors in his sociology of the state and accounted for the differences between bedouin and sedentary society in terms of economic and geographical factors.[102] Historical change was explained in terms of the interaction between political and economic factors, and not spiritual factors such as divine intervention. In other words, Ibn Khaldūn's approach to the study of history was not a theocratic one. Some decades ago, H. A. R. Gibb raised this issue in response to discussions carried out by Ayad and Rosenthal. Ayad and Rosenthal tended to underemphasize the religious element in Ibn Khaldūn's science of society. According to Ayad, Ibn Khaldūn's doctrine of causality and natural law in history was contrary to any theological view of history as there was no place for God's intervention in Ibn Khaldūn's writing. Religion, according to Ayad, was regarded by Ibn Khaldūn as a social psychological factor in the process of change.[103] Rosenthal's view is similar. Although he saw Ibn Khaldūn to be a strong believer in Islam, he noted that he treated religion as simply one factor in the study of the state.[104] Gibb's view is more sophisticated. There was no contradiction between Ibn Khaldūn's mode of thought and the theological approach. His doctrine of causality and natural law can be restated in theological terms as the *sunnat Allāh* (the way of Allah).[105]

Therefore, while the call to an Islamic or "faithful" social science is being made, the province that it consists of is still *terra incognito*. As such, it would be problematic to view the Islamization of knowledge project as part of the call to the indigenization of the social sciences. This is especially so when it is considered that the Islamization of knowledge project falls under the threat of nativism. The trend of "going native" among both Western and indigenous scholars constitutes the elevation of the native's point of view to the status of the criterion by which descriptions and analyses are to be judged to the extent that the social sciences from the West are held to be irrelevant. Among the traits of nativism are the following:

1 The rejection of the social sciences of Western origin.
2 Shallow and superficial critiques of theoretical traditions in the West.
3 The neglect of various problems that *are* to be found in the contemporary social sciences.
4 The lack of attention to the classical Islamic tradition as the source and inspiration for a social science that is relevant to the Muslim world.

The first trait is evident in the thinking of some scholars. Consider the following view.

> The fact that concerns us here most is that all the social sciences of the West reflect social orders and have no relationship or relevance to Muslims, and even less to Islam. If we learn and apply Western social sciences, then we are not serious about Islam.[106]

Scholars with such views are undoubtedly of the opinion that Western and Islamic societies differ to such an extent that the concepts and theories that emerged in Western settings are of no relevance to Muslim or non-Western societies.[107]

With regard to the fourth trait, a good example comes from the case of the neglect towards Ibn Khaldūn. In general, those social scientists who are engaged in the Islamization of knowledge project have not taken much notice of the classical tradition of social thought and theory in Islam. For example, among those who are discussing the prospects of a neo-Khaldūnian sociology are French scholars.[108]

The neglect of Ibn Khaldūn as a source of an alternative sociology

For a variety of reasons, so-called Islamized social science is not the alternative to modernist discourse that it claims to be. The proponents of this orientation have in reality not paid much attention to Ibn Khaldūn.

The study of Ibn Khaldūn's theory can be divided into three aspects. One is the discovery of Ibn Khaldūn as the founder of a number of disciplines in the social sciences. Second, there are works that seek to draw comparisons between Ibn Khaldūn and several Western thinkers. Third, there are those who attempt to develop and apply Ibn Khaldūn's theory to specific problems in the historical and social sciences.

Regarding the discovery of Ibn Khaldūn, ever since European and American scholars proclaimed Ibn Khaldūn as the true founder of sociology, before Comte, as well as the precursor of ideas in many other fields such as economics, political science and anthropology,[109] there have been many descriptive treatments of his works in the light of his contribution to these various disciplines.

Apart from this, many studies also sought to draw comparisons between Ibn Khaldūn and the giants in modern Western thought. Some authors ignored or glossed over profound differences in the historical and philosophical contexts in which they wrote. The tendency has been to remain at the level of making comparisons to show that Ibn Khaldūn anticipated the ideas of modern thinkers in the humanities and social sciences.[110] Much of the work of Islamizers of sociology would fall within one of the above two categories.

Some authors, however, have gone beyond the mere comparison of selected ideas and concepts in Ibn Khaldūn with those of modern Western scholars, towards the theoretical integration of his theory into a framework that employs some of the tools of modern social science, although the field of application has been confined to North African and West Asian societies.[111] It is this kind of study on Ibn Khaldūn that must be supported and developed if there is to be more than a historical interest in him. What this requires, therefore, are works that apply Ibn Khaldūn's framework to the study of historical and contemporary states. Before moving on to examples of these in Chapters 5 to 8, I turn to a discussion of premodern applications of Ibn Khaldūn.

4 Pre-modern readings and applications of Ibn Khaldūn

This book argues for the possibility of non-Eurocentric and non-nativistic readings and applications of Ibn Khaldūn's work. A non-Eurocentric reading of Ibn Khaldūn is one that looks at his works as a source of theory with potential application to historical cases. Ibn Khaldūn is not relegated to a mere object of study but becomes a perspective from which to view both the historical and the contemporary development of states. Such a reading is a reversal of the trait of the imposition of European categories and concepts.

The application of Ibn Khaldūn would involve creative approaches to the study of various aspects of history and society, including the theoretical integration of Khaldūnian theory into a framework that employs concepts and theories from the modern social sciences. I do not argue that no non-Eurocentric readings and applications of Ibn Khaldūn exist in the literature. I do say, however, that these are few and far between.

The theme of this book is the application of Ibn Khaldūn's theory of state formation to both historical and contemporary cases. What I have in mind is combining Ibn Khaldūn's theoretical framework with concepts from modern sociology and applying the new formulation to specific cases such as those of Ottoman and Safavid history or the modern Syrian state. These will be taken up in later chapters. For now, however, it would be interesting to consider pre-modern readings and applications of Ibn Khaldūn.

For the purpose of the present study, the works that can be said to be illustrations of applications of Ibn Khaldūn fall into two broad categories. The first refers to works on Ibn Khaldūn by scholars who lived in periods and areas uninfluenced by the modern social sciences. The second refers to works by scholars writing in the postcolonial context where the modern social sciences make up the dominant discourse. The works of the first category are from the Muslim East and West and tend to be more descriptive of Ibn Khaldūn's theory as well as more normative in nature: that is, using Ibn Khaldūn to prescribe change of a certain nature. The works of the second category are positive and analytical, being applications of Khaldūnian theory to historical and contemporary cases of state formation. This chapter focuses on the first category of applications of Ibn Khaldūn.

In the modern period, Muslim reformers such as Jamāl al-Dīn al-Afghānī, Muḥammad ʻAbduh and Rashīd Riḍā were influenced by Ibn Khaldūn,[1] although this attention did not result in any sort of Khaldūnian social science theories. There is a widely accepted view that Ibn Khaldūn was first promoted by the Europeans after they "discovered" him. For example, Charles Issawi says that Ibn Khaldūn "remained for five centuries a prophet without honour in either his own country or abroad", and only attracted the interest of both Western and Arab scholars from the nineteenth century on.[2] Bernard Lewis was rather presumptuous in saying that the "discovery, evaluation, and appreciation of the *Muqaddima* of Ibn Khaldūn is an achievement of European scholarship".[3] This was not entirely the case. Several of Ibn Khaldūn's contemporaries in North Africa, as well as scholars after his time in the Muslim world, wrote what may be called Khaldūnian works. The most important follower of Ibn Khaldūn was Abū 'Abdallāh Muḥammad bin al-Azraq al-Andalusī (831–96 AH/1428–91 AD). His *Badā'i' al-Silk fī Ṭabā 'i' al-Mulk* (*The Wonders of State Conduct and the Nature of Kingship*) contains a detailed summary of Ibn Khaldūn's *Muqaddimah* which is discussed in connection with al-Azraq's concern with the relationship between ethics and royal authority (*mulk*).[4] Ibn Khaldūn is also said to have been influential over the fifteenth century historian al-Maqrīzī (d. 845/1441), who attended his lectures in Cairo.[5] Later on, seventeenth- and eighteenth-century Ottoman scholars developed an interest in Ibn Khaldūn, whose ideas they utilized in the discourse surrounding the Ottoman state.

It is fitting to begin the account of the application of Ibn Khaldūn with examples from al-Azraq and Ottoman scholarship as they differ in one very important respect from the examples that are being covered later in this chapter. The Arab and Ottoman interest in Ibn Khaldūn discussed here, which dates back to the fifteenth century, was independent of European influences and certainly did not arise as a result of their having learnt about him via European sources.

Al-Azraq, the commentator of Ibn Khaldūn

A work that demonstrates that Ibn Khaldūn was seriously read within decades of his death is that by al-Azraq. Al-Azraq was born in the city of Málaga, in what is today the Autonomous Community of Andalusia in Spain. He worked as a judge there and later in Granada. He tried to enlist the help of the Mamluk Sultan al-Ashraf Qāytbāy against the invading forces in Spain, but was not sucessful. He was also appointed as ambassador to Tunis and finally as Malikite judge in Jerusalem, a position to which he was nominated by the Mamluk sultan in 896/1491. He died in Jerusalem the same year.[6] Abdesselem notes that there had been a tendency among some to regard al-Azraq's work as superior to that of the *Muqaddimah* of Ibn Khaldūn. While Abdesselem sees this claim as pretentious, he says that the work of al-Azraq shows us a genial reading of the work of Ibn Khaldūn, informed by the trends of al-Azraq's own times.[7] In fact, it is quite interesting to note that although al-Azraq was a student and commentator of Ibn Khaldūn, his approach is generally un-Khaldūnian in the sense that it is more normative and descriptive rather than positive and empirical, as we shall see shortly.

The *Badā'i' al-Silk* is divided into two prefaces or introductions (*muqaddimāt*), four books and a conclusion. The first preface, entitled "An account of what leads to the rational theory of kingship", consists of 20 antecedent discussions (*sābiqah*). The aim of this preface is to establish the rational grounds for the existence of kingship.[8] It relies heavily on the *Muqaddimah* of Ibn Khaldūn and can be considered a restatement of the latter's views on the implications of the social nature of human beings for the development of kingship. Al-Azraq states that humans are civil (*madanī*) by nature and that it is thus inevitable that their coming together results in the emergence of a city. Humans come together to begin with in order to protect and sustain themselves collectively: that is, for the preservation of the species.[9] It is necessary for them to congregate in order to obtain the means of livelihood and organize their defence. Society is categorized into two basic types, that is, bedouin (*badawī*) and sedentary (*ḥaḍarī*). The bedouin live in fertile parts as well as the fringes of the desert and in mountainous areas. Their mode of living is such that they acquire only the bare essentials of life and live from grazing and cultivation. Sedentary people, however, live in towns and villages and acquire more than the essentials of life. Their mode of living is founded on luxury acquired through industry and trade.[10] While the bedouin are more or less engaged in subsistence living, the towns attract those bedouin who are more mild-tempered and given to luxury.

In this way, the sedentary life originates from bedouin life. The nature of sedentary life is such that the preoccupation with luxuries – that is, what is beyond subsistence requirements – results in leadership and defence being assigned to a minority.[11] The nature of rule can be seen to be of different kinds. First, there is rule by justice, which allows the bedouin qualities of bravery and courage to be maintained. When rule is established on the basis of coercion or despotism, the subjugation that arises therefrom results in the loss of courage. Then there is educational rule, which socializes humans into compliance.[12]

The bedouin have a greater degree of group feeling or *'aṣabiyyah* because of the agnatic ties that bind the members of their society.[13] Leadership can only exist through *'aṣabiyyah*, which means that the group with the strongest *'aṣabiyyah* rules.[14] Pure lineage only exists in the desert as it is protected from intermarriage with others.[15] But sedentary life results in the decline of *'aṣabiyyah* due to the sedentary lifestyle and the disappearance of lineage. The nobility of the group that ruled is therefore eroded and the ruling may disappear in four to six generations.[16]

The second preface, of 20 propositions (*al-fātiḥah*), has as its objective the establishment of the religious basis of kingship.[17] Having established the rational basis for the human need to congregate and live together and what that implies for the development of kingship and its types, while drawing heavily from Ibn Khaldūn's *Muqaddimah*, al-Azraq proceeds to discuss the foundations of kingship from the point of view of religious law or the shari'ah. The second preface consists of 20 openings or preambles. The natural tendency of humans towards competition and mutual destruction can only be curbed by adherence to the shari'ah. But, the implementation of the shari'ah can only be realized by an enforcer. People do not tend to preserve the traditions and practices (*sunnah*) of Islam without enforcement by a leader.[18] The need for such leadership in this regard is given by the shari'ah itself and not by reason and also agreed upon by the consensus of the scholars. The institution that is meant is that of the caliphate or imamate, which oversees both the affairs of religion (*al-dīn*) and the world (*al-dunyā*).[19] The preconditions that need to be satisfied by an imam are that he be a man, free, mature and rational. In addition, there are four other conditions, that he has courage, competence, perfection and ability.[20] Al-Azraq then raises an interesting point made by Ibn Khaldūn concerning the requirement that the imam be appointed from among the Quraysh. Ibn Khaldūn's opinion on this differed from that of other scholars. The hadith or tradition of the Prophet Muḥammad to the effect that the imam should be from the Quraysh had to be understood in terms of the social context of a particular time. The purpose of this condition was not religious, that is, for blessings, but for the practical ends of solving disputes. The Quraysh had this ability only during times when their *'aṣabiyyah* was intact and strong. After their *'aṣabiyyah* had declined and become weak, they were no longer able to play this role and it became unreasonable to insist that being Quraysh was a condition that had to be fulfilled to be the imam.[21] Caliphate or imamate rule, however, tends to give way to kingship, of which there are three types: religious, natural and rational. Religious kingship was founded on the application of the shari'ah, while natural and rational kingship were founded on unrestrained human purpose and desire on the one hand, and human reasoning without the benefit of revelation on the other.[22]

Despite the references to Ibn Khaldūn, al-Azraq's work belongs more to the genre of *naṣīhat al-mulūk* or advice to rulers, known in the Germanic areas in the Middle Ages as *Fürstenspiegel*. These works instruct rulers on various aspects of conduct befitting a ruler and the ethical basis of such conduct. These works may also deal with issues relating to state and society or with the history of past rulers in order to provide models for rulers to emulate. As noted by al-Azmeh, al-Azraq's work fits more within the genre of *Fürstenspiegel* rather than that of analytical or theoretical history as developed by his mentor, Ibn Khaldūn.[23] There is also another important difference between Ibn Khaldūn and al-Azraq. This has to do with the procedural aspect of justice, an issue discussed by Khadduri.[24] Ibn Khaldūn considered caliphate authority to be superior to kingship in that it functioned as a substitute for the authority of the Prophet, preserved religion and managed the political affairs of the world in a way that was consistent with the shari'ah.[25] Kingship, however, referred to the power to rule by force.[26] Kingship of the unbridled nature, that is, *mulk ṭabī'ī*, is distinguished from caliphate authority by the ability of the ruler to rule by force. Although the rulers of the dynasties following the *khilāfah* period continued to use the title of *khalīfah* (caliph), many of them were not *khulafā'* (sing. *khalīfah*) in the true sense of the term, as they ruled by force and not by allegiance to the shari'ah. Ibn Khaldūn resigned himself to the eternal repetition of the cycle that saw the rise and decline of dynasties founded on kingship. He did not foresee developments in the future that would lead to the elimination of the cycle. Al-Azraq seemed to have more faith in the ability of rulers to ensure the administration of justice if they were sufficiently inspired by religious values.[27]

It can be remarked that the lack of originality of al-Azraq's *Badā 'i' al-Silk* only serves to highlight the innovative character of Khaldūnian thought.[28] Al-Azraq may have been inspired by Ibn Khaldūn, but not by those aspects of Ibn Khaldūn's thought that distinguish him from his predecessors.

Ibn Khaldūn among Ottoman scholars and statesmen

The active interest of Ottoman scholars and statesmen in Ibn Khaldūn has to be contrasted with the relative absence of such interest among Arab, Iranian and other Muslims during the same period. The Ottomans had a practical interest in Ibn Khaldūn.

The first Ottoman scholar to systematically make use of Ibn Khaldūn was Kātib Çelebi (d. 1657), a prolific writer, having composed some 21 works covering history, biography and geography.[29] Kātib Çelebi listed the *Muqaddimah* in his bibliographical work, the *Kashf al-Ẓunūn*. In his treatise on reform, the *Düstūrül-Amel li-Islāh ıl-Halel* (*The Mode of Procedure for Rectifying the Damage*) he discusses the causes of state financial deficits and suggests remedies.[30] It is in this work that Ottoman history is thought of in terms of Ibn Khaldūn's cyclical stages of rise and decline.[31]

Following Kātib Çelebi was the Ottoman historian Muṣṭafā Na'īmā (d. 1716), who was greatly influenced by both Ibn Khaldūn and Kātib Çelebi. In his annalistic work of history, *Tārīkh-i Na'īmā*, he makes reference to Ibn Khaldūn's cyclical theory of the rise and decline of states, and the contradiction between nomadic and sedentary societies.[32] Na'īmā adopts the idea of the Circle of Equity, that is, the interconnected principles of good government. The Circle of Equity cited by Na'īmā is as follows:

1 There is no *mulk* and no *devlet* (state) without the military and without manpower.
2 Men are to be found only by means of wealth.
3 Wealth is only to be garnered from the peasantry.
4 The peasantry is to be maintained in prosperity only through justice,
5 And without *mulk* and *devlet* there can be no justice.

In other words, the closing of the circle implies that the military and manpower are essential to justice. As Thomas observed, the circle served to justify the necessity of the domestic reforms of the Ottoman *vezir*, Hüseyin Köprülü, in order to protect the empire from its European enemies.[33] Na'īmā adapted the idea of the Circle of Equity from Ḳınalızāde 'Alī Çelebi's well-known *Ahlāī-i 'Alā'ī* who Na'īmā says derived it from Ibn Khaldūn.[34] Fleischer says that there is no evidence to suggest that Ḳınalızāde had read Ibn Khaldūn and that the idea of the Circle of Equity was sufficiently known in other works that would have been available to Ḳınalızāde. To my mind, it is perhaps less important to know the source of Ḳınalızāde's reference to the Circle of Equity than to understand the different theoretical contexts in which the Circle of Equity has been understood by Ibn Khaldūn and the Ottoman scholars.

Ibn Khaldūn himself refers to eight sentences of political wisdom, arranged around the circumference of a circle, attributing this to the pseudo-Aristotelian *Book on Politics*.[35] The eight principles are:

1 There can be no royal authority without the military.
2 There can be no military without wealth.
3 The subjects produce the wealth.
4 Justice preserves the subjects' loyalty to the sovereign.
5 Justice requires harmony in the world.
6 The world is a garden, its walls are the state.
7 The Holy Law (shari'ah) orders the state.
8 There is no support for the shari'ah except through royal authority.[36]

But Ibn Khaldūn says that this topic in the *Book on Politics* is not dealt with exhaustively, nor is it treated in a thorough manner with all the necessary arguments.[37]

Ibn Khaldūn states:

> When our discussion in the section of kingship and dynasties has been studied and due critical attention given to it, it will be found to constitute an exhaustive, very clear, fully substantiated interpretation and detailed exposition of these sentences. We became aware of these things with God's help and without the instruction of Aristotle or the teaching of the Môbedhân.[38]

Indeed, the *Kitāb al-'Ibar Muqaddimah* is a detailed study of the rise and decline of states, understood in terms of the workings of three principal types of authority – caliphate, royal and kingship – and their interaction with the two major types of society and the principal ways of making a living that correspond to those societies. It differs from the works of Ḳınalızāde and Na'īmā who were more descriptive and prescriptive rather than theoretical and conceptual.

By the eighteenth century Ibn Khaldūn was well established in Ottoman circles as having provided a framework that explained the decay of the Ottoman state. The Ottoman Empire was said to be in Ibn Khaldūn's stage of "stasis and decline". As we saw in Chapter 2, the main concern in the *Muqaddimah* is the rise and decline of the various Muslim dynasties, particularly those of the North African states. Ibn Khaldūn focused on what he regarded as the essential differences in the social make-up between pastoral nomadic (*'umrān badawī*) and sedentary (*'umrān ḥaḍarī*) societies. After theorizing the differences in social organization between the two societal types, he distinguished between the types of authority and the nature of power that may take hold in sedentary societies. Pastoral nomadic and sedentary societies coexisted, but Ibn Khaldūn saw the former as naturally evolving towards the latter. This is not in the sense that the one gives way to the other but rather that the goal of bedouin life is the achievement of sedentary society and all that that entails such as its culture and luxury lifestyle.[39] Central to understanding these differences is the concept of *'aṣabiyyah*, often translated as group feeling or social cohesion. Ibn Khaldūn's thesis was that groups with strong *'aṣabiyyah* could establish political rule over those with weak *'aṣabiyyah*.[40] Ibn Khaldūn was, of course, referring to tribal groups for whom *'aṣabiyyah* has a specific meaning: the feeling of solidarity or cohesion among the members of a group that is derived from the knowledge that they share a common descent. The *'aṣabiyyah* of the bedouin was held to be stronger and this enabled them to militarily and morally defeat sedentary people, those settled in and around urban areas, and establish their own dynasties.

Because of superior *'aṣabiyyah* among the bedouin, they could defeat sedentary people in urban areas and establish their own dynasties. Having done so, they became set in the urban ways of life and experienced great diminution in their *'aṣabiyyah*. With this went their military strength and their ability to rule. This left them vulnerable to attack by fresh invasions of pre-urban bedouins with stronger *'aṣabiyyah* who replaced the weaker urbanized ones. But the relationship is not one of the domination of the city by the tribes. Rather it is a relationship of dominance in the other direction, of which there are two important aspects. First, the nature of the existence of the tribesmen makes them dependent on the cities for the basic necessities of life.[41] Second, the tribes are dependent on a religious leader or saint (*walī*) who interprets religion for them. The *walī* himself is motivated by the impiety that developed in the urban areas as a result of the luxurious life and political excesses committed by the townspeople.

And so the cycle repeats itself. A tribe conquers a dynasty, founds a new one and rules until it is overthrown by a reform-minded leader who has the support of tribes eager to cash in on the city. The luxury of city life is the chief cause of the rise of decadence, impiety and the loss of tribal solidarity:[42] hence the importance of a religious leader who is able to unite the pre-urban tribes.

Ottoman scholars like Kātib Çelebi and Na'īmā believed that the Ottoman state was at the stage of stasis and heading towards decline. They were concerned with institutional and administrative reforms that might serve to halt or reverse the decline.[43]

The appropriation of Ibn Khaldūn's ideas by the Ottomans is interesting because it provides us with a rare example of not only a non-Eurocentric but a pre-Eurocentric reading of Ibn Khaldūn. But it is also true that their reading of Ibn Khaldūn was generally normative and ideological. The so-called Circle of Equity was cited to justify reforms designed to strengthen royal authority. One of the mechanisms that did this was the *ḳānūn* or dynastic law by decree, which allowed for the suspension of laws derived from the shari'ah. This mechanism was used exclusively by Ottoman sultans to rule and undertake reforms that may have been blocked by the shari'ah in the absence of the *ḳānūn* mechanism. *Ḳānūn* law was seen as a way to implement laws needed for reform without violating the shari'ah.[44]

Ibn Khaldūn was also used by the Ottomans to justify their holding the caliphate. During the reign of Sultan Abdülhamid II (r. 1876–1909), some opposition to the Ottoman caliphate emerged among the British and Arabs.[45] Abdülhamid's claim to the caliphate was based on the three principles of divine will, hereditary rights and politico-military power. These justifications were traditionally recognized by the vast majority of Muslims, including leading Muslim scholars and jurists such as Ibn Khaldūn and Jalāl al-Dīn al-Dawwānī.[46] One objection that did emerge, however, was based on a disputed tradition of the Prophet, according to which the caliphate should remain in the hands of the tribe of the Prophet, that is, the Quraysh:

> Narrated by Muḥammad bin Jubayr bin Mut'im that while he was included in a delegation of Quraysh staying with Mu'āwiyyah, Mu'āwiyyah heard that 'Abdallāh bin 'Amr had said that there would be a king from the Qaḥṭān tribe, whereupon he became very angry. He stood up, and after glorifying and praising Allah as He deserved, said, "To proceed, I have come to know that some of you men are narrating things which are neither in Allah's Book, nor has [sic] been mentioned by Allah's Apostle. Such people are the ignorant among you. Beware of such vain desires that mislead those who have them. I have heard Allah's Apostle saying, 'This matter (of the caliphate) will remain with the Quraysh, and none will rebel against them, but Allah will throw him down on his face as long as they stick to the rules and regulations of the religion (Islam).'"[47]

In the late 1800s both British and Arab scholars and statesmen began to refer to what they claimed as the illegitimacy of the caliphate in Ottoman hands, a claim made on the basis of the above hadith.[48] In view of the circulation of such a view, that is, that the caliphate should be in the hands of Arabs, and specifically descendants of the tribe of the prophet Muḥammad, the Quraysh, there was an attempt on the part of the Ottomans to justify the Ottoman position regarding the caliphate. Even before the challenge to Abdülhamid, Pīrīzāde Meḥmed Ṣāḥib (1674–1749), who started the translation of Ibn Khaldūn's *Muqaddimah* into Ottoman Turkish and was greatly influenced by Ibn Khaldūn's ideas, sought to justify Ottoman claims to the caliphate by arguing that in their time the requirement that the caliph should come from the Quraysh was no longer relevant. This requirement held for the period of the Rightly Guided Caliphs (*khulafā' al-rashidūn*) only, while later Muslim rulers could assume the title of caliph as long as they fulfilled the functions of that office.[49] This function was in fact taken over by non-Quraysh, whose rule should be considered as legitimate. On the Quraysh themselves, Ibn Khaldūn noted:

> However, the power of the Quraysh weakened. Their group feeling vanished in consequence of the life of luxury and prosperity they led, and in consequence of the fact that the dynasty expended them all over the earth. (The Qurayshites) thus became too weak to fulfil the duties of the caliphate. The non-Arabs gained superiority over them, and the executive power fell into their hands. This caused much confusion among thorough scholars (with regard to Qurayshite origin as a condition of the caliphate).[50]

Despite this historical fact, the majority of scholars maintained that Qurayshite descent was a condition of the caliphate, even if the caliph was too weak to manage the affairs of the Muslims.[51] Ibn Khaldūn's argument was sociological and more rational than those who preceded him. He sought to understand the social contexts in which Qurayshite descent was a reasonable condition and those in which it was not.

> If it is established that Qurayshite (descent) as a condition (of the imamate) was intended to remove dissension with the help of (Qurayshite) group feeling and superiority, and if we know that the Lawgiver (Muḥammad) does not make special laws for any one generation, period, or nation, we also know that (Qurayshite descent) falls under (the heading of) competence. Thus, we have linked it up with (the condition of competence) and have established the overall purpose of (the condition of) Qurayshite (descent), which is the existence of group feeling. Therefore, we consider it a (necessary) condition for the person in charge of the affairs of the Muslims that he belong to people who possess a strong group feeling, superior to that of their contemporaries, so that they can force the others to follow them and the whole thing can be united for effective protection. (Such group feeling as a rule) does not comprise all areas and regions. Qurayshite (group feeling), however, was all-comprehensive, since the mission of Islam, which the Quraysh represented, was all-comprehensive, and the group feeling of the Arabs was adequate to that mission. Therefore, (the Arabs) overpowered all the other nations. At the present time, however, each region has people of its own who represent the superior group feeling (there).[52]

The argument of Ibn Khaldūn was in fact sociological, stating that the requirement of Qurayshite descent fell under the heading of competence. If it was considered a necessary condition that the caliph belonged to a group that possessed superior *'aṣabiyyah* or group feeling in order that other groups would follow them, the Quraysh may not always fulfil that condition.[53] This argument was later taken up by others in the nineteenth century, including Cevdet Paşa, who completed the Ottoman Turkish translation of the *Muqaddimah* that was begun by Pīrīzāde Meḥmed Ṣāḥib.[54]

Another issue surrounding the caliphate was that of the permissibility of having two caliphs. In 1726 the Afghans sent a delegation to Istanbul to ask the Ottoman Sultan to accept the coexistence of two caliphs. The Ottomans objected to this on the grounds of a hadith (saying of Muḥammad) which holds that it was not permissible for two caliphs to be appointed.[55] Furthermore, the Ottomans abided by a fatwa that declared coexisting caliphs as permissible only if they were separated by a great geographical barrier, such as the Indian Ocean, so that mutual interference in internal affairs would be difficult.[56] Again, Pīrīzāde drew from Ibn Khaldūn for his position against the idea of coexisting caliphs.

What is lacking in the Ottoman discourses that appropriate Ibn Khaldūn is a systematic application in the tradition of positive social science of his theory of the rise and decline of dynasties with reference to the historical facts of the Ottoman case. The application of Ibn Khaldūn's theory would result in the search for empirical manifestations of the consolidation of *'aṣabiyyah* among the Turkic tribes that formed the military force behind the rise of the Ottomans, and of the decline of *'aṣabiyyah* in terms of changes in land tenure systems. For example, it could be said that the assignment of *tīmār*s (benefices) to tribal chieftains had the effect of creating an economic and moral gap between the chieftains and the tribesmen, which in turn would affect *'aṣabiyyah*. In other words, the stages of growth and decay that a dynasty passes through in Ibn Khaldūn's scheme can be discussed in the context of the transition of the conquering tribesmen from the pastoral nomadic mode of production to the prebendal feudal mode of production – that is, one founded on the assignment of benefices. The next chapters discuss applications of Ibn Khaldūn that belong to the second category referred to above: applications of Ibn Khaldūn's theoretical framework to historical and contemporary cases of reform and state formation that are not prescriptive or normative but analytical.

5 A Khaldūnian theory of Muslim reform

A theory of Muslim revival

Muslim revival has been studied mainly as a modern phenomenon and as a reaction to Western imperialism and colonialism, and the modernization of the Muslim world. Muslim revival, however, is a much older phenomenon that dates back to the first century of Islam, which saw the first extremist groups to emerge in the Muslim world. An important theoretical resource for the study of Muslim revival is the work of Ibn Khaldūn. While Ibn Khaldūn is well known in both the Muslim world and the West, he has been seen more of a precursor of the various modern social sciences and as a source of historical data and information, rather than as a resource for the development of theoretical perspectives, as we have seen in Chapter 3. This chapter introduces Ibn Khaldūn's theory of state formation as a theory of Muslim revival founded on the concept of *taghyīr al-munkar* and makes some remarks concerning the relevance of this theory to the study of contemporary Muslim revival. Ibn Khaldūn's *Muqaddimah* has long been recognized as a pioneering work that theorizes the rise and decline of dynasties in the Arab East and West. The framework of the *Muqaddimah*, however, has not generally been seen as theorizing the phenomenon of Muslim revival.[1] At the same time, the traditionally trained *'ulamā'* were unlikely to take much interest in Ibn Khaldūn's theory of reform since he was not considered to be a historian on par with great historians like al-Ṭabarī, al-Mas'ūdī and al-Ya'qūbī, who were more accustomed to the more traditional methods[2] that Ibn Khaldūn critiqued.

Among the first to recognize that Ibn Khaldūn's theory of state formation was at one and the same time a theory of Muslim reform was probably the eminent Spanish philosopher José Ortega y Gasset (1883–1955). Ortega's account of Ibn Khaldūn's perspective is also an interesting early example of an attempt to incorporate Ibn Khaldūn into modern knowledge. In an essay that first appeared in 1934 entitled "Abenjaldún nos revela el secreto: pensamientos sobre Africa Menor" ("Ibn Khaldūn reveals his secrets to us: thoughts on North Africa"), Ortega presents, in a somewhat condescending manner, Ibn Khaldūn's as a mind struggling to be cosmopolitan and multicultural. Ortega makes the interesting distinction between ordinary curiosity and surprise. Something that arouses curiosity may merely be a novelty that could be soon forgotten. A curious person is not necessarily surprised by anything because he is simply attracted by the novelty of a thing. This is not true with something that evokes surprise. To be surprised is to discover a problem that requires an effort of the mind to solve. The thing that evokes surprise, however, contains a problem that requires an effort of the mind to unravel and master.[3] Ortega was contemplating the difference between curiosity and surprise with reference to Melilla, a North African town conquered by the Spaniards in 1497. Melilla presented a certain problem to Ortega. For the last 400 years the city and its countryside had existed in hostile opposition to one other, while at the same time there were practically no relations between the city and the countryside, with the latter remaining uninfluenced by the former.

To Ortega, this was a peculiarly African phenomenon which he was puzzled as to how to explain. Europeans would not be able to solve this problem as they had different conceptions of historical reality that were not appropriate for understanding Africa. It was necessary to ask a native, an African who was uninfluenced by Western ideas. This was no easy task in view of the fact that Africans generally were not thinkers. They did produce historical works but not conceptual frameworks for the study of history.[4]

An eminent exception to this was to be found in the philosopher of African history, Ibn Khaldūn. Ortega saw the work of Ibn Khaldūn as reducing the apparent chaos of North African events to the relationship between two modes of living, the nomadic and the sedentary.[5]

According to Ortega's reading of Ibn Khaldūn, there is a coexistence of two ways of life: the nomadic and the sedentary. The radically different types of humans from these societies interact to create the state and civilization in North Africa. These two great ways of life make the state and civilization, government and culture. Nomads create the state, but sedentary people create civilization. Although the city is where knowledge, jobs, riches and pleasures are found, it does not have the nerve of power. Power, which emerges from moral discipline and courage, is found among the nomads on account of the hard life they live. This inequality in strength and courage enables the nomads to conquer dynasties, take control of cities and even found new dynasties. Having done so, however, they fall prey to the civilizing process of the city and become vulnerable to conquest by new invading nomads. History is submitted to such a rhythm. Ortega was impressed that Ibn Khaldūn was even able to assign a figure to this rhythm, that is, three generations or 120 years.[6] Ortega regarded the *Muqaddimah* as the first ever philosophy of history to be elaborated, unlike the work of another African, St. Augustine, which was basically a theology of history. Ortega also recognized the *Muqaddimah* as the first work of sociology.[7]

Ortega insisted that Spaniards would not be able to understand their past, present and future if they did not understand North Africa. The same cultural influences that affected the northern part of Africa also passed through Spain. Ortega suggested that Ibn Khaldūn's theory of the rise and decline of states explains the emergence of the Saudi state and the role of Wahhabism. 'Abd al-'Āzīz Al Sa'ūd or Ibn Sa'ūd, the first monarch of Saudi Arabia, with the support of his family and tribe, and galvanized by the religious ideology of Wahhabism, was able to capture the city of Najd.

Ortega described Wahhabism as a form of puritanism – not a religion, "but a fanatic exaggeration of a religion".[8] But Ortega regarded Islam, which he referred to as Muhammadanism (Spanish *mahometismo*), as Puritanism. He delivered his damning verdict on Islam as follows:

> It is the only creed which starts with "no". The warlike efficiency that Muhammadanism had was not a coincidence, a chance. The Muhammadan faith is instrinsically polemic, warring. First of all, they believe that others have no right to believe what they believe not. Rather than monotheism the psychologically exact name of this religion should be "non-polytheism". Within Muhammadanism there are periodically new forms of archi-puritanism. One of them is Wahhabism: they hit children if they laugh and don't allow them to have toys.[9]

Although Ortega was not correct in reducing Islam to the Wahhabi phenomenon of his time, he was correct to see the relevance of Ibn Khaldūn's theory for explaining the role of religious reform in the formation of the Saudi state. As noted by Ansari, "Saudi Arabia … [was] the perfect candidate of Ibn Khaldūn's natural history model".[10]

Ibn Khaldūn's theory, therefore, is one of tribal-religious revolt,[11] ideologically founded on a theological rationalization that was ironically authored in the centres of learning, the cities. Such a theology viewed war against Muslims as a jihad against polytheists, requiring therefore the pronouncement of *takfīr* or the declaration of infidelity upon such Muslims. First adopted by the Kharijites in the first decades of the rise of Islam, *takfīr* is also practised during our times by some Wahhabis and so-called Salafis. For example, Sa'ūd bin 'Abd al-'Azīz sent a message to the Ottomans, accusing the caliphate of being in a state of unbelief, polytheism and apostasy and called on it to convert to Islam. Other messages were sent to the Ottomans calling on them to become Muslims.[12]

As we saw in Chapter 2, Ibn Khaldūn was very much aware of the role of religious leaders in the unification of the bedouin. He noted cases in history of religious personalities such as saints (sing. *walī*, pl. *awliyā'*) who had the capacity to rally the tribesmen around them, appealing to them to follow religious rulings and adopt praiseworthy qualities. Such leaders were able to unite the tribes around a religious ideology, uniting them as a social organization that would eventually participate in the founding of a state and kingship.[13] The solidarity implied by the concept of *'aṣabiyyah* is not wholly dependent on kinship ties. Religion may play a fundamental role in bringing about or consolidating tribal solidarity, a significant example being the rise of Islam itself. The following is one example cited by Ibn Khaldūn:

> It happened to the Sufi shaykh Ibn Qasī, the author of the *Kitāb Khal' al-Na'layn* on Sufism. He rose in revolt in Spain and made propaganda for

> the truth shortly before the time when the propaganda of the Mahdī (of the Almohads) started. His followers were called al-Murābiṭūn. (Ibn Qasī) had some success, because the Lamtūnah (Almoravids) were preoccupied with their own difficulties with the Almohads. (But) there were no groups and tribes there to defend him. When the Almohads took over control of the Maghrib, he soon obeyed them and participated in their cause. He took the oath of allegiance to them at his stronghold, the fortress of Arcos (de la Frontera). He handed his frontier province over to them and became their first missionary in Spain. His revolt was called the revolt of the Murābiṭūn.[14]

The Murābiṭūn or Almoravids was one of three important dynasties in North Africa that Ibn Khaldūn wrote about in terms of his thesis of rise and decline. These were case studies that empirically verified his theory and also illustrated the role of religion. The three dynasties – the Almoravids (al-Murābiṭūn) (1053–1147), the Almohads (al-Muwaḥḥidūn) (1147–1275) and the Marinids (1213–1524) – were each founded with the support of Berber tribes, the Ṣanhājah for the Almoravids, the Maṣmūdah for the Almohads, and the Zanātah for the Marinids, and declined generally according to the model suggested by Ibn Khaldūn.

The Almoravids established their state utilizing the power of the powerful Ṣanhājah Berber tribes; they enlarged and established cities, and then enlisted the help of the Ṣanhājahs to keep other possibly dissident tribes in the surrounding areas at bay. But the Almoravids were eventually overcome by the Almohads, which started as a religious reform movement under Ibn Tūmārt with the support of the Maṣmūdah Berber tribes. The Almohads themselves finally gave way to the Marinids who rode on the military support of the Zanātah Berber tribes.[15]

Therefore, the conflict between these two types of society, that is, pre-sedentary bedouins and sedentarized tribes, concerned more than the spoils of the city. At times, religious fervour and the will to bring about a return to the correct path of religion were a factor. The role of the religious leader was to reform society.

> Many religious people who follow the ways of religion come to revolt against unjust amirs. They call for a change in, and prohibition of, evil (practices) (*taghyīr al-munkar*) and for good practices. They hope for a divine reward for what they do. They gain many followers and sympathizers among the great mass of the people, but they risk being killed, and most of them actually do perish in consequence of their activities as sinners and unrewarded, because God had not destined them for such (activities as they undertake). He commands such activities to be undertaken only where there exists the power to bring them to a successful conclusion. Muḥammad said: "Should one among you see evil activities, he should change them with his hand. If he cannot do that, he should change them with his tongue. And if he cannot do that, he should change them with his heart."
>
> Rulers and dynasties are strongly entrenched. Their foundations can be undermined and destroyed only through strong efforts backed by the group feeling of tribes and families, as we have mentioned before. Similarly, prophets

> in their religious propaganda depended on groups and families, though they were the ones who could have been supported by God with anything in existence, if He had wished, but in His wisdom He permitted matters to take their customary course.[16]

As we have seen earlier, for Ibn Khaldūn the bedouin were not seeking merely the luxuries of sedentary life. They were driven by the will to reform, eager to abolish what was objectionable (*taghyīr al-munkar*).

The role of religion was essential but religion would not succeed without *'aṣabiyyah* or group feeling. Many examples were furnished by Ibn Khaldūn. For example:

> At the beginning of this century, a man of Sufi leanings, by the name of at-Tuwayzirī, appeared in al-Sūs. He went to the Mosque of Māssah on the shore of the Mediterranean and pretended to be the Expected Fatimid. He was taking advantage of the common people's firm belief in predictions to the effect that the Fatimid was about to appear and that his mission would originate at that mosque. A number of ordinary Berber groups were attracted to him like moths (to the flame). Their chiefs then feared that the revolt might spread. The leader of the Maṣmūdah at that time, 'Umar al-Saksīwī, secretly sent someone to him, who killed him in his bed.
>
> Also at the beginning of this century, a man known as al-'Abbās appeared among the Ghumārah. He made a similar claim. The lowest among the stupid and imbecile members of those tribes followed his blethering. He marched on Bādis, one of the (Ghumārah) cities, and entered it by force. He was then killed, forty days after the start of his mission. He perished like those before him.[17]

Ibn Khaldūn cites several such cases and notes that the mistake made by many aspiring revolutionaries was that they underestimated or ignored the significance of *'aṣabiyyah*. The combination of *'aṣabiyyah* and religion, however, was a potent one. It was the conquest of the dynasty by the more socially cohesive bedouin that effectively, albeit temporarily, abolished what is objectionable, that is, the excesses of sedentary life. In Ibn Khaldūn's world there was the cyclical change that rescued society from these excesses. The reform is cyclical. A tribe conquers a dynasty, founds a new one and rules until it is overthrown by a reform-minded leader who has the support of tribes eager to cash in on the city. The luxury of city life is the chief cause of the rise of impiety. In Ibn Khaldūn's world, ordinary folk were caught between the oppressive policies and conduct of a royal authority on one hand and the prospects of conquest by bloodthirsty tribesmen led by a religious leader bent on destruction of the existing order on the other. Ibn Khaldūn resigned himself to the eternal repetition of the cycle. He did not foresee developments that would lead to the elimination of the cycle. This happened with the Ottomans, the Qajar dynasty in Iran, and the state in the Yemen. The cycle ceased to be in operation when the basis of state power was no longer tribal.

Gellner on Ibn Khaldūn: an insufficiently sociological theory

Gellner's application of Ibn Khaldūn's theory by way of a merger with David Hume's oscillation theory of religion is well known. What is particularly interesting about Gellner's application of Ibn Khaldūn's model to North African history is not the above account in terms of circles of tribes, which does not add much to the original model, but Gellner's attempt to merge Ibn Khaldūn's sociology with David Hume's oscillation theory of religion. Hume rejected the unilineal theory of the development of religion from polytheism to monotheism in favour of an oscillation theory according to which there is a change from polytheism to monotheism and back again to polytheism. There is a flux and reflux in the human mind of polytheism and monotheism.[18] The swing from polytheism to monotheism is triggered by a competitive sycophancy. Devotees compete with each other in their adulation of one of the deities of a pantheon until that deity assumes the status of the one and only God. An example that Hume gives is the elevation of the God of Abraham, Isaac and Jacob to Jehovah and the creator of the world. Such a God, however, is then seen to be too distant and inaccessible. Demi-gods and middle beings are needed for mediation. But the pendulum swings back again to monotheism as "these idolatrous religions fall every day into grosser and more vulgar conceptions".[19]

As Gellner notes, Hume's theory was psychologistic. It is devoid of references to social factors, which were introduced in an ad hoc fashion as and when the system ran into difficulties.[20] Gellner considered that Ibn Khaldūn's model provided the social basis for Hume's pendulum swing theory of religion in that it explained how the urban setting provided for a scripturalist unitarian puritanism while the nomadic setting provided for a saint-mediated, hierarchical system.[21] The oscillation now had a social basis. While Gellner's work is probably the only serious attempt to look at Ibn Khaldūn's theory as a theory of Muslim reform, there are problems with it. Gellner noted that Hume's model was excessively psychological. Gellner's merger of Hume and Ibn Khaldūn does provide the social basis for a theory deemed too psychologistic. What it does not do, however, is introduce Ibn Khaldūn's concept of religious change or reform (*taghyīr al-munkar*) and elaborate on the social basis of such change. In fact, it is not merely that this religious change has a social basis. The relevance of the social goes beyond that. The process of religious change is part of a larger societal change that involves war and conflict, a change in the state elite and regime, and the ascendancy of a new ruling tribe. Furthermore, this change takes place within a certain political economic context that was not elaborated on, neither by Ibn Khaldūn nor by Gellner. In other words, Gellner's merger of Ibn Khaldūn and Hume lacks an economic base. In both Ibn Khaldūn's theory of the rise and decline of states and Gellner's version of it there is no conceptualization of the economy and no typology of economic systems. There is the prospect, therefore, of integrating a modes of production approach into the Khaldūnian model. The marrying of the Khaldūnian approach to a modes of production framework is discussed in the context of Ottoman and Safavid history in Chapters 6 and 7 respectively. In what remains of this chapter, I discuss examples from Ibn Khaldūn's own empirical cases and how these can be framed within a modes of production framework.

Ibn Khaldūn and the modes of production

Before proceeding, however, it might be interesting to note that while it appears that Marx and Engels were familiar with the work of Ibn Khaldūn, as we saw in Chapter 3, they had not thought in terms of integrating their own approach into that of Ibn Khaldūn. Consider Engels' classic Khaldūnian statement:

> Islam is a religion adapted to Orientals, especially Arabs, i.e., on one hand to townsmen engaged in trade and industry, on the other to nomadic Bedouins. Therein lies, however, the embryo of a periodically recurring collision. The townspeople grow rich, luxurious and lax in the observation of the "law". The Bedouins, poor and hence of strict morals, contemplate with envy and covetousness these riches and pleasures. Then they unite under a prophet, a Mahdi, to chastise the apostates and restore the observation of the ritual and the true faith and to appropriate in recompense the treasures of the renegades. In a hundred years they are naturally in the same position as the renegades were: a new purge of the faith is required, a new Mahdi arises and the game starts again from the beginning. That is what happened from the conquest campaigns of the African Almoravids and the Almohads in Spain to the last Mahdi of Khartoum who so successfully thwarted the English. It happened in the same way or similarly with the risings in Persia and other Mohammedan countries. All these movements are clothed in religion but they have their source in economic causes; and yet, even when they are victorious, they allow the old economic conditions to persist untouched. So the old situation remains unchanged and the collision recurs periodically.[22]

What is interesting here is that there is absolutely no reference to Ibn Khaldūn, although we can be quite certain that both Engels and his long-time collaborator Karl Marx knew of the work of Ibn Khaldūn. Even more astonishing is the fact that neither Marx nor Engels thought of integrating the cyclical theory of the rise and decline of state that Engels' seems to note in the passage above into their own modes of production framework.

North Africa or the Arab West (the Maghrib)[23] is fertile ground for the study of the history of state formation and its interaction with the prevailing modes of production. It is also the empirical field that Ibn Khaldūn knew best, having worked at the court of various rulers of the Maghrib and experienced the instabilities and uncertainties of political life. It is also the empirical field that we can consider for this preliminary attempt to merge the Khaldūnian model with a modes of production approach. Ibn Khaldūn's historical narrative of the Maghrib and the *Muqaddimah* in which he elaborated a historical sociology of the state must have been prompted and influenced by the intrigues, conflicts and conquests that he came uncomfortably close to. It is, therefore, rather strange that there has been no systematic assessment of his theoretical framework in the light of his empirical studies of the rise and decline of Maghribian dynasties.

This and the next sections of this chapter have two principal tasks. First, it briefly critiques Ibn Khaldūn's theory of state formation as detailed in the *Muqaddimah*. I argue that while Ibn Khaldūn's work does theorize the dynamics of state formation and the nature of social change that that entails, his work is silent on those aspects of political economy that have to do with the nature of the economic system. While there is a notion of political dynamics in Ibn Khaldūn's theory, there is no discussion in his works on the nature or types of economy that interact with political change. The second task, therefore, is to integrate a modes of production approach into Ibn Khaldūn's theory. This would bring us some way towards the elaboration of a general Khaldūnian historical sociology.

Empirically, the focus of this chapter is the westernmost region of North Africa, that is, *al-maghrib al-aqṣā*, or the Far West of the eleventh to sixteenth centuries, more or less corresponding to present-day Morocco. This was the period of the rise and decline of three dynasties: the Almoravids (1053–1147), the Almohads (1147–1275) and Marinids (1213–1524).

The next section of this chapter provides a Khaldūnian narrative of state formation in Morocco, for the period under consideration, pointing out the gaps and weaknesses in this account and suggesting the need for a modes of production approach that establishes the relationship between religion on the one hand and the political economy on the other. This is followed in the next section by discussions of Moroccan economy and society and a systematic reconstruction of the Moroccan modes of production for the period under consideration. I then turn to restating the original Khaldūnian dynamics presented earlier in terms of the modes of production framework just developed. The chapter concludes with some thoughts on the implications of this modified Khaldūnian theory for the development of a Muslim theory of reform as well as a more general Khaldūnian historical sociology of state formation.

Ibn Khaldūn and state formation in Morocco (1053–1524)

The Maghrib is a vast area populated by people of diverse origins, having been invaded by the Phoenicians, Romans, Vandals, Byzantines, Arabs, Ottomans and Europeans. For the period under consideration here, which comprises six centuries of the Muslim period in pre-modern times, the most important groups were the Berbers and the Arabs. Little is known about the origins of the Berbers. The Romans referred to those peoples who did not speak Latin or Greek as *barbaro* (barbarian), from which the English 'Berber' is derived.[24] A common theory is that the Berbers were of Canaanite or Himyarite origins and migrated to North Africa from Palestine or Yemen. Ibn Khaldūn himself cites numerous hypotheses regarding the origins of the Berbers but finally accepted that they were of Canaanite origin. According to this account, the Berbers were descendants of Noah through his son, Ham.[25] The learned among the genealogists say that all the Berber tribes derived from the two great branches of the Berbers, the Butr and Barānis, named after Madghīs al-Abtar and Barnas, the two sons of Bir, a descendant of Ham.[26] Of the three Berber tribes that concern us here, the Maṣmūdah and Ṣanhājah were Barānis tribes.[27]

Whatever their origins, the Berbers were likely to be a product of the admixture of the indigenous population and migrants to North Africa from West Asia. The generally accepted theory is that one Mediterranean group entered the Maghrib from the northeast and another from the southeast, via eastern Africa. This would account for the existence of physical distinctions and mutually incomprehensible dialects among the different Berber groups.[28] Prior to the coming of the Arabs, Phoenicians, Greeks, Romans, Vandals and Byzantines all entered North Africa. By the middle of the seventh century, however, Arab armies under the Umayyads in the east moved into North Africa, attacking Byzantine positions and facing strong resistance from the Berber tribes.[29] The Arabs conquered Carthage and effectively ended Byzantine power in the Maghrib in AD 698 and began the conquest of Spain a few years later. Umayyad control of Morocco was to remain precarious as a result of Berber resistance.

In AD 789 a member of the Umayyad royal family and a sharif,[30] Idrīs, after having fled for his life from Arabia to Morocco amid the collapse of the Umayyads and the takeover by the Abbasids, was accepted as the politico-religious leader of the locals. The Idrisid dynasty he founded lasted until AD 970. From 970 till 1053 Morocco was divided into petty warring states. After 1053, Morocco was ruled by successive dynasties until 1668 when the Alawite dynasty founded by a sharfian family from the east took control, and rule to this day.[31]

We are concerned in this chapter with the Almoravid, Almohad and Marinid dynasties. The Khaldūnian problematic in this context was discussed in detail in Chapter 2, as well as briefly in this chapter above. Among the well-known examples used by Ibn Khaldūn to illustrate the cyclical rise and decline of states as a consequence of the alternation between weak and strong *'aṣabiyyah* are those of these three dynasties. His study of these and other North African dynasties provided the empirical field on the basis of which he developed an original theory of state formation.

This theory of state formation is an abstraction from the empirical field of the history of the Maghrib that Ibn Khaldūn was only too familiar with. The theory of state formation and decline is elaborated in the *Muqaddimah*. In the latter, the formation and decline of North African states, including the three successive dynasties of Morocco – the Almoravids (1053–1147), the Almohads (1147–1275) and the Marinids (1213–1524) – are discussed in detail. Each of these dynasties were founded and upheld by Berber tribes, the Ṣanhājah for the Almoravids, the Maṣmūdah for the Almohads, and the Zanātah for the Marinids, and declined in terms suggested by Ibn Khaldūn's model.

The Almoravids established their state utilizing the power of the powerful Ṣanhājah Berber tribes; they enlarged and established cities, and then enlisted the

Ṣanhājahs' help to keep other possibly dissident tribes in the surrounding areas at bay. But the Almoravids were eventually overcome by the Almohads, which started as a religious reform movement under Ibn Tūmārt with the support of the Maṣmūdah Berber tribes. The Almohads themselves finally gave way to the Marinids who rode on the military support of the Zanātah Berber tribes.[32] The Almohad movement was started by Ibn Tūmart, who was a member of the Maṣmūdah, a Berber tribe of the Atlas Mountains. The son of a lamplighter in a mosque, he was known for his piety from a young age. When he performed the hajj while a young man he angered people in Mecca with his protests against what he saw as the laxity of other worshippers, and as a result he was expelled. He made his way to Baghdad where he studied religious sciences. Although Ibn Tūmart drew upon the Ash'arite school as well as al-Ghazālī, his reaction to what he observed of the religious practices around him was to uphold a form of unitarianism that went against the teachings of the dominant Sunni schools of his time.

He returned to Morocco at the age of 28, when it was under the Almoravids, and began preaching his ideas. His experience was not unlike that of Muḥammad ibn 'Abd al-Wahhāb several centuries later. The scholars of Fez were of the view that ibn Tūmart's views were extreme. Having been expelled on a number of occasions from many other towns, he finally found refuge among his tribesmen, the Maṣmūdah in the Atlas Mountains.[33] The *'aṣabiyyah* of the Maṣmūdah tribes was certainly a result of the kind of agnatic ties that are found in tribal social organizations. But religion also played a significant role in the group feeling of the Maṣmūdah, especially when there was a need for the tribe to be united on the basis of a larger rather than smaller unit. Religion, under the leadership of a prophet or saint, has the function of allowing individual aspirations to coincide, thereby creating a more socially cohesive unit.[34] Ibn Tūmart died in 1128 but his death was a kept a secret for two years by his principal disciple, a fellow Berber by the name of 'Abd al-Mu'min. This was a tactical move on the part of 'Abd al-Mu'min to keep the *'aṣabiyyah* forged by Ibn Tūmart alive while he consolidated his power.[35] Riding on this *'aṣabiyyah*, his campaigns eventually succeeded in overthrowing the Almoravids. The new Almohad dynasty was eventually to encompass all of northern Africa and Andalusia.

Ibn Tūmart's thought is characterized by the allegorical interpretation (*ta'wīl*) of the Ash'arite school of theology and the doctrine of the infallible Imam of the Shi'ah.[36] Ibn Tūmart lived in a region where *ta'wīl* and the study of *usūl al-fiqh* had been abandoned. *Fiqh* had been regarded as fixed and there were no longer efforts to explain the law in terms of the original sources. The dominant school of the region, Malikite, upheld the study of the *furū'* instead.[37] While this state of intellectual affairs was certainly problematic from the point of view of the prevailing consensus in the Muslim world of that time, Ibn Tūmart's reaction was extreme. He regarded the religious views of his contemporaries as *kufr*. He argued that the literal interpretation of the Qur'an inevitably led to *tajsīm* or anthropomorphism. Those who hold to such interpretations are *kāfir*s and should be expelled from society.[38] This justified war against the ruling dynasty, the Almoravids.

As Ibn Khaldūn says, it was by virtue of his religious knowledge that Ibn Tūmart could command a following among the Maṣmūdah. He noted that while the Zanātah were more deeply rooted in the desert and, therefore, more formidable as a fighting force, they lacked a religious call that the Maṣmūdah had under Ibn Tūmart.[39] The Maṣmūdah, however, were to be eventually defeated by the Zanātah. This was the fate of any tribe that came to power.

> As a result, the toughness of desert life is lost. Group feeling and courage weaken. Members of the tribe revel in the well-being that God has given them. Their children and offspring grow up too proud to look after themselves or to attend to their own needs. They have disdain also for all the other things that are necessary in connection with group feeling. This finally becomes a character trait and natural characteristic of theirs. Their group feeling and courage decrease in the next generations. Eventually, group feeling is altogether destroyed. They thus invite (their) own destruction. The greater their luxury and the easier the life they enjoy, the closer they are to extinction, not to mention (their lost chance of obtaining) royal authority. The things that go with luxury and submergence in a life of ease break the vigor of the group feeling, which alone produces superiority. When group feeling is destroyed, the tribe is no longer able to defend or protect itself, let alone press any claims. It will be swallowed up by other nations.[40]

Simplified versions of this Khaldūnian account are to found in modern works on Maghrib history. Gellner, for example, reconstructed the Khaldūnian model in terms of circles of tribes. Once a tribal group brings down a dynasty and establishes its own rule, it controls the *bilād al-makhzan* from which it is able to collect taxes. This is distinguished from the *bilād al-sība* or outlying regions that may be nominally under the ruler's control but which are populated by tribes that successfully evade tax collection. The pre-colonial history of Morocco was understood by Gellner as an oscillating system in which the *makhzan* and *sība* were in perpetual conflict. The *makhzan* was populated by the inner and middle circle of tribes, who extracted taxes and paid taxes respectively. The *sība* was populated by the outer circle of tribes who refused to pay taxes.[41] The *sība* was a permanent threat to the ruling dynasty, a breeding ground of potential conquerors and new dynasties.[42]

The dynasty based itself in a larger town such as Fez, Marrakesh, Meknes or Rabat. The ruling, tax-exempt tribe provided the military support to the ruler. Other tribes might swear allegiance to the ruler but there were also the dissident tribes of the *sība* who often refused to subject themselves to the fiscal authority of the ruler.[43]

As the state found it increasingly difficult to enforce laws, collect taxes and maintain a military force that kept the dissidents out but were not a threat to the dynasty itself, its ability to resist invasion from the *sība* declined. The nature of the oscillation was such that the weakened state was no longer able to control the dissident tribes because the political structure within the state evolved from one of tribal egalitarianism into an autocratic hierarchy. With the invasion of the *makhzan* by fresh supplies of more egalitarian and disciplined tribes from the *sība*, the system returned to its original egalitarian form every three generations or so.[44]

Wansborough and Brett draw attention to yet another Khaldūn-inspired model, this time based on a distorted reading of Ibn Khaldūn in the *Muqaddimah* and the *Kitāb al-'Ibar*. According to this deficiency model, North African society was intrinsically destructive owing to the pervasiveness of nomadic social patterns, and Oriental religion – that is, Islam, and nomadic Arab invasions – resulting in protracted Arab–Berber conflicts.[45] One account, for example, states that the religion of the Berbers was a combative Islam.[46]

As noted by Seddon, these Khaldūnian-inspired models combine the Orientalist image of a static, unchanging Muslim society with the anthropologists' image of a classless African tribal society.[47] The pre-colonial North African state was turbulent "but the turbulence affected only the personnel, not the structure itself".[48] Furthermore, these approaches, as well as that of Ibn Khaldūn, are largely innocent of political economy. The *Kitāb al-'Ibar* itself is full of references to political personalities, tribal chieftains, rulers and religious reformers. The volumes covering the various Berber dynasties such as the Almoravids, Almohads and Marinids narrate struggles, plots and intrigues, revolts and invasions. But the conflict between the *makhzan* and *sība* seems to take place in an economic vacuum. The relationship between the economic system and political change, that is, the rise and decline of dynasties, is not specified.

Despite these weaknesses, however, the very attempt to develop a Khaldūnian model of the state in North Africa leads us to begin to identify the structure and dynamics of the state, economy and society in a more systematic manner. Gellner observed that pre-colonial Morocco was neither a feudal nor an "Oriental society" founded on the establishment and maintenance of an irrigation system.[49] What is implied here is the need to specify the nature of the economic system of pre-colonial Morocco and its corresponding social and political structures. However, Marxist or Marxist-inspired attempts to do this, by way of the concept of mode of production, have also proven problematic.

For example, Mourad, in his brief discussion of what he called the feudal state in pre-colonial Morocco, refers to the tribe as a political and economic entity corresponding to a mode of production.[50] But the understanding of the Moroccan modes of production is confused. Mourad understood that the fundamental contradiction in pre-colonial Morocco was between tribal interests of pastoral and agricultural producers and the ruling dynasty. This he saw as a typically feudal society.[51] The inappropriateness of applying the concept of feudalism to pre-colonial Morocco or the possibility of the existence of other modes of production was not entertained.

The approach of Lacoste focuses on political economy and brings attention to trade, landownership and tenure, and the mode of production, in his discussion of the Khaldūnian dynamics of North African history.[52] There are, however, problems with Lacoste's characterization of the North African pre-colonial economy in terms of the Asiatic mode of production. First of all, he tends to use the term as a residual category referring to different modes of production that cannot be identified with either slavery or feudalism.[53] Second, his attempt to conceptualize North African economy in terms of one mode of production tends to oversimplify what was in reality a complex interaction of several coexisting modes of production.

The next section provides a brief overview of Moroccan economy and society in order that the variety of Moroccan modes of production can be abstracted.

Moroccan economy and society: reconstructing the Moroccan modes of production

For our description of the pre-colonial Moroccan economy and society and its conceptualization in terms of modes of production, we begin with Ibn Khaldūn. Ibn Khaldūn lists the principal modes of making a living (*wujūh al-ma'āsh*) as *falḥan*, by which he means the cultivation of crops as well as the herding of animals, crafts or the expenditure of human labour on specific materials, and trade.[54] The mode of making a living is defined as the desire for and the effort to obtain both sustenance as well as surplus.[55] If we were to reformulate Ibn Khaldūn's modes of making a living in terms of modes of production,[56] we would be able to list four modes of production. Corresponding to the *falḥan* mode of making a living are three modes of production: the Asiatic, prebendal feudal and pastoral modes of production. Corresponding to crafts is the petty commodity mode of production. Trade is a not a mode of production in itself but a means by which different modes of production are linked.[57]

Most works on pre-colonial Moroccan economy and society tend to describe the system in terms of unitary modes of production. As mentioned above, Lacoste characterized the North African pre-colonial economy in terms of the Asiatic mode of production and Mourad in terms of feudalism. My approach, following Amin and Wolf, is to argue that pre-colonial Moroccan society was organized along the lines of three modes of production: that is, the tributary, petty commodity and pastoral nomadic.[58]

The tributary mode of production itself has its centralized and decentralized variants. An example of the centralized variant is the Asiatic mode of production, where power is centralized in the state, which appropriates the entire economic surplus. The state is the owner of agricultural and manufacturing property.[59] The state is also both landlord and sovereign. Taxes coincide with rent in the sense that there is no tax that differs from ground-rent.[60] However, unlike Asiatic modes to be found in China and Southeast Asia, the power of Moroccan dynasties did not derive from the control of large-scale irrigation or other public works. Rather, the centralized tributary mode of production here was based on the control by the state of superior tribal military capabilities provided by pastoral nomads such as the Ṣanhājah, the Maṣmūdah and the Zanātah. The state was a major owner of land, denoted by the term *jazā'* or *makhzan*, which was often either rented out to cultivators or cultivated through crop-sharing or wage labour arrangements with the state.[61] The state also owned rent and tax-paying establishments such as workshops, public bath houses, houses, inns and others in the cities.[62]

But, centralization was not the only feature of the tributary mode of production that existed in Morocco of the period under consideration. Not all rural and urban land was owned by the state or administered directly by the state. There was a category of land called *iqṭāʿ*, a term for a form of an administrative or military grant or benefice. It is possibly due to the identification of the *iqṭāʿ* with the European fief that some scholars have described the mode of production in pre-colonial North Africa in terms of feudalism. But the similarities between the *iqṭāʿ* and the fief are superficial. Unlike the European fief, the granting of *iqṭāʿ* did not involve a contract of personal fealty, but rather fiscal considerations. Benefices were granted largely in return for military and administrative services. The differences between the European feudal system and that based on the granting of benefices were sufficiently great and led Weber to conceptualize the latter as prebendal feudalism.[63] Prebendal feudalism can be said to be a decentralized or fragmented variation of the tributary mode of production.

The beneficiaries of *iqṭāʿ* in pre-colonial Morocco included members of the political elite, and Arab and Berber tribal shaykhs.[64] In Marinid Morocco, for example, tribal chieftains received landed *iqṭāʿ* worth up to 20 gold *mithqāl* in taxes and in kind.[65] Sometimes an entire village would have been granted as an *iqṭāʿ*. There was a tendency for *iqṭāʿ* holders to gain a degree of independence from the ruler to the extent that it became his private property. It often happened that tribal chieftains became rulers of their own smaller-scale *makhzan*s, which contained within them towns, villages and tribal populations.[66]

The second mode of production to be found in pre-colonial Morocco was the petty commodity mode of production, in which production for the market is carried out by producers who own their own means of production. It often involves private owners who hire craftsmen as wage labour on a small scale as well.[67] Unlike the tributary mode of production, in the petty commodity mode the producer does not live directly on the products of his labour. This mode of production was found in both rural and urban areas; in the rural areas, it was found where peasants owned land.

Many of the large cities of medieval Morocco under the Almoravids, Almohads and Marinids were important centres of manufacturing. Fez, for example, was well known for its artisans and craftsmen. During the reigns of the Marinids, Abū al-Ḥasan (1331–51) and his son, Abū ʿInān (1351–58), the most important industry in Fez was weaving, which employed about 20,000 persons.[68] Other industries typically found in the Maghrib included carpentry, tailoring, shoe production, leather production, silk weaving, goldsmiths and others. Wage labour was common within these industries and this involved both men and women. Work in the urban areas in this mode of production that involved wage labour of women included flax spinning, silk weaving and hairdressing.[69] In rural areas there was private ownership of medium and smallholdings and the land was often cultivated on a share-cropping basis.[70] Producers would include free cultivators (*fallāḥīn*), quasi-indentured share-croppers (*khamāmisah*) or clients (*mawālī*).[71]

In the pastoral nomadic mode of production, the absence of permanent habitation, determined by geographical factors, defined the means of production. These consisted of domesticated animals and land incapable of cultivation. Animals such as sheep, camels and goats provided basic needs such as butter, cheese, meat, milk, clothing, fuel (from dung) and means of transportation. While animals, tools and dwellings were often owned on an individual basis, grazing land was considered as belonging to the tribe. In the Maghrib, the ruling tribes lived in the *makhzan* while the non-tax-paying tribes, both nomadic and sedentary, populated the *sība*.[72]

The Khaldūnian dynamics of Moroccan state formation from a modes of production perspective

The key to understanding the decline of a dynasty such as those of the Almoravids, Almohads and Marinids is the phenomenon of *'aṣabiyyah*. A decline in *'aṣabiyyah* means that the tribal chieftain, now the ruler, is no longer able to command the military support of the tribe that brought him to power in the first place, by appealing to kinship ties. This is effectively a decline in social cohesion that results, according to Ibn Khaldūn, from luxurious urban life. As *'aṣabiyyah* declines, the ability of the ruler to maintain his hold over the *makhzan* decreases until the dynasty is overrun by another tribal group with a superior or stronger *'aṣabiyyah*. This cycle repeats itself. The mechanisms by which this happens can be restated in terms of a modes of production approach. In this section, I discuss the relationship between the pastoral nomadic mode of production on the one hand, and the centralized and decentralized tributary modes of production on the other, in terms of Ibn Khaldūn's theory.

Ibn Khaldūn's theory provides an explanation for the basis of the centralized tributary mode of production in Morocco. According to the popular variant of the Asiatic mode of production, the basis of power of the state is derived from its control over large-scale public works. Ibn Khaldūn's theory and the case of precolonial Morocco provide the argument and historical data for understanding the basis of another type of centralized tributary mode of production, one in which the power of the state is derived from its control of tribal military support. Once the state is formed, however, the basis for the gradual decentralization of the mode of production is established. It is this decentralization that provides the context for the erosion of *'aṣabiyyah*.

Ibn Khaldūn notes that once the dynasty was established, the supporting tribes were absorbed into the sedentary life of the *makhzan*. This fact can be restated to mean that these tribes were absorbed into the prebendal feudal mode of production, whereas they were previously organized in terms of the pastoral nomadic mode of production. After the dynasty was established, the problem of remunerating members of the tribal elites and their armies arose. The initial tribal force that eventually helped in the establishment of a dynasty had seniority (*sābiqah*) and was entitled to higher salaries and greater benefits in terms of offices, land, tax exemptions and patronage.[73] In addition to this core group of fighting manpower, there was also the main army consisting of military tribes, the *jaysh*. They provided military services on a more systematic basis and were paid in terms of tax exemptions and the right to collect taxes, *iqṭā'*, and so on, and constituted a kind of nomadic aristocracy.[74]

According to Schatzmiller, the state in Morocco never lacked the funds to pay salaries in return for military services.[75] Lacoste, citing Marçais, states that the granting of *iqṭā'* was more prevalent during times of economic downturn.[76] The first grants of *iqṭā'* were made in the second part of the twelfth century and became more popular in the fourteenth century. The logic of this is that in periods of lesser prosperity, rulers had to resort to the granting of *iqṭā'* as a means of paying members of the tribal elite. But as Schatzmiller notes, while *iqṭā'* land was supposed to revert back to the state after the services were granted, when the government was weaker the *iqṭā'* land remained in the possession of its holders and eventually became *mulk* or private property, *makhzan*s on a smaller scale than that of the ruling dynasty. The tribal elite then attained an independence of sorts from the ruler. When Ibn Khaldūn said that the tribesmen lose their discipline and experience a diminishing of their *'aṣabiyyah* as a result of becoming set in the ways of luxurious city life, he was possibly referring to the *iqṭā'* holders. In any case, the phenomenon of *iqṭā'* holding is one means by which *'aṣabiyyah* diminishes.

This negative effect on *'aṣabiyyah* of the incorporation into the prebendal feudal mode of production is exacerbated by a tactic that was resorted to by the ruler. Ibn Khaldūn observed that the ruler often tried to become less reliant on the ruling tribe by granting positions and salaries to clients and followers from groups and tribes other than those on whose power the dynasty was established.

> (The rulers) maintain their hold over the government and their own dynasty with the help, then, either of clients and followers who grew up in the shadow and power of group feeling, or (with that) of tribal groups of a different descent who have become their clients …
>
> The same happened to the Ṣinhājah in the Maghrib. Their group feeling was destroyed in the fifth [eleventh] century, or before that. Dynastic (power), but of decreasing importance, was maintained by them in al-Mahdiyyah, in Bougie, in al-Qal'ah, and in the other frontier cities of Ifrīqiyā. Frequently, some rival aspirant to royal authority would attack these frontier cities and entrench himself in them. Yet, they retained government and royal authority until God permitted their dynasty to be wiped out. Then the Almohads came, fortified by the strong group feeling among the Maṣmūdah, and obliterated all traces of the (Ṣinhājah dynasty).
>
> The same happened to the Umayyad dynasty in Spain. When its Arab group feeling was destroyed, the *reyes de taïfas* (small princes) seized power and divided the territory among themselves. In competition with each other, they distributed among themselves the realm of the (Umayyad) dynasty. Each one of them seized the territory under his control and aggrandized himself. (These rulers) learned of the relations that existed between the non-Arabs (in the East) and the Abbasids. (Imitating them,) they adopted

> royal surnames and used royal trappings. There was no danger that anyone would take (the prerogatives they claimed) away from them or alter (the situation in this respect), because Spain was no (longer the) home of groups and tribes ...[77]

We will see examples of this from the Ottoman and Safavid cases as well.[78] The reason for this was that the tribe that brought the ruler to power constituted a potential ruling class.[79]

The impact of the absorption of the ruling tribe into the prebendal feudal mode of production had, therefore, two consequences. First, the tribal elite were alienated from the ruler, formerly a tribal chieftain himself. This happened either because they attained some independence as a result of the grants of *iqṭā'* land or because the ruler himself attempted to dispense with their support by relying on new clients. Second, the tribesmen themselves, after having become sedentary as a result of either being *iqṭā'* holders or wage earners, also experienced diminishing *'aṣabiyyah* and could not provide that level of military support that could stave off an attack from fresh supplies of hostile tribes from the *sība*.

In Ibn Khaldūn's theory of reform, *'aṣabiyyah* combines with religion to create a strong sense of cohesion among the group that is already related through blood ties. The primary force forging the ties is kinship, upon which religion is dependent. As Ibn Khaldūn says:

> This is because, as we have mentioned before, every mass (political) undertaking by necessity requires group feeling. This is indicated in the aforementioned tradition: "God sent no prophet who did not enjoy the protection of his people." If this was the case with the prophets, who are among human beings those most likely to perform wonders, one would (expect it to apply) all the more so to others. One cannot expect them to be able to work the wonder of achieving superiority without group feeling.[80]

As *'aṣabiyyah* diminishes, religion also loses its ability to unite. Furthermore, *'aṣabiyyah* itself erodes in a specific political economic context that can be understood in terms of the modes of production.

The relevance of the Khaldūnian model

While there is no such cyclical logic today, general lessons from Ibn Khaldūn's theory of Muslim reform and state formation can be stated as follows:

1. Religious reform takes place within the context of regime change, the coming of a new ruling class and, therefore, a realignment of loyalties.
2. Religious reform functions as an overarching *'aṣabiyyah* that transcends tribalism, class and ethnicity and yet is immanent in them. For example, an Islamic *'aṣabiyyah* transcends all tribes, but is at the same time dependent on the *'aṣabiyyah* of the strongest tribe, which appealed to religion as

a galvanizing force. The same logic of interacting *'aṣabiyyah* can be applied to non-tribal forms of solidarity and their relationship to religion.
3 The source of religious change or revival originates from societal groups characterized by simpler modes of making a living and less luxurious lifestyles.
4 Religious revival is the outcome of conflict between a lesser institutionalized religion-based solidarity (*'aṣabiyyah*) and an urban-based religiosity regulated by institutions.[81]
5 Religious zeal and religion-based solidarity are positively correlated.
6 The religious experience can be understood beyond its individual and psychological manifestations as a sociological phenomenon to the extent that it is a function of a type of *'aṣabiyyah*. As noted by Spickard, the Khaldūnian approach is not grounded in individuals.[82]

The weakness of Ibn Khaldūn's model is that it treats the changes in religiosity and *'aṣabiyyah* without a sophisticated account of the political economic context in which these changes take place. The decline in *'aṣabiyyah* and the erosion of religiosity in the Khaldūnian model take place in sedentary society. But, it is not merely city life and its luxuries as general factors that cause this decline. The nature of the sedentary political economy was such that the three modes of production – the Asiatic, prebendal feudal and petty commodity – each provided different contexts within which *'aṣabiyyah* and religiosity functioned and underwent changes. The political economic system, however, is not described or conceptualized in Ibn Khaldūn's model.

This chapter has tried to show how a modes of production approach contextualizes the rise and decline of the state and the role of *'aṣabiyyah* and religion in that. The merging of a modes of production approach with the Khaldūnian theory of state formation is further discussed in the contexts of Ottoman and Safavid history in the next two chapters.

6 Ibn Khaldūn and the Ottoman modes of production

In the previous chapter it was suggested that the political economy of *'umrān ḥaḍarī* consisted of three modes of production, that is, the Asiatic, prebendal feudal and petty commodity. Each of these modes of production formed the context within which *'aṣabiyyah* functioned and changed. Ibn Khaldūn, however, did not provide a conceptualization of the political economy of the states he was discussing. The idea of modes of production had to be introduced in the Khaldūnian model. In doing so, I have tried to show how the modes of production provide the political economic background for understanding the rise and decline of the state and the role of *'aṣabiyyah* and religion in that. In this and the next chapter, I further discuss the merging of the Khaldūnian theory of state formation with the modes of production approach, with specific reference to Ottoman and Safavid history.

In order to assess the potential application of Ibn Khaldūn's theory of state formation to the case of the rise of the Ottoman Empire, at least two relevant questions have to be asked. The first addresses the issue of what factors explain the emergence and growth of the Ottoman Empire from its humble beginnings as a Turcoman *beylik* (principality). The second question has to do with the role of Islam in the rise and development of the Ottoman state. In view of the paucity of fourteenth century sources,[1] how can the Khaldūnian theoretical framework help us to identify the key factors and formulate an alternative explanation for Ottoman state formation? Before directly answering this question, it will be useful to examine existing approaches in order to see possible conflicts or convergences with a Khaldūnian perspective. We will then be in a position to assess if the facts and conditions discussed in these theories can be reformulated in Khaldūnian terms and if this reformulation results in a different and more plausible reading of Ottoman history.

The chapter proceeds as follows. The first section discusses the various perspectives on the emergence of the Ottoman Empire. The section that follows introduces the Ottoman political economy in terms of its modes of production. I then turn to a discussion of the dynamics of the Ottoman political economy in terms of a combination of the Khaldūnian and modes of production approaches. Drawing from Marxism as well as Max Weber, I discuss four distinct modes of production as characterizing Ottoman society. These are the Asiatic, prebendal feudal, petty commodity and pastoral nomadic modes of production. The relationship between these modes of production in the formative period of the Ottoman state is discussed in terms of the theoretical framework derived from Ibn Khaldūn.

Approaches to the rise of the Ottoman Empire

The first approach to this question, at least from the point of view of the modern social sciences, was set forth in Herbert Gibbons' *Foundation of the Ottoman Empire*.[2] In this 1916 work, Gibbons proposed that a new Ottoman "race of swordbearers" was founded from the co-mingling of Greek and Balkan converts to Islam and Turks. The domination of the Christian element in this new race meant that Byzantine administrative practices could be transferred to the state that was to be founded by the Ottomans.[3] Lowry remarks that Gibbons possibly held the opinion that the Ottoman Empire could not have achieved its stature had it been a purely Turco-Muslim affair and that its Byzantine-Christian origins had to take the credit for the emergence and subsequent development of the empire.[4]

Gibbons' views were rejected by the Turkish scholar M. Fuat Köprülü, who argued in 1922 that Ottoman administrative practices were derived from the Seljuks and Ilkhanids rather than from the Byzantine Christians.[5] Köprülü's view was that the role of the Turcomans in the rise of the Ottoman Empire was due to their success in providing to the leaders of the formative state the human and material resources needed.[6] The work of the German scholar Friedrich Giese supported Köprülü's argument as he demonstrated the role played by Anatolian merchants and craftsmen in the transferring of administrative practices to the emerging Ottoman state.[7] Twelve years after his first intervention, Köprülü asserted the purely Turkish nature of the Ottoman state and put forward his thesis that it was the result of the co-mingling of Anatolian tribes rather than Greek and Balkan peoples. He also reiterated that the Anatolian administrative practices were inherited from the Seljuks and Ilhanids.[8] Also disagreeing with Gibbons but giving more weight to the Islamic factor was Paul Wittek, who put forward an argument that was to become known as the Gazi Thesis, advanced in a series of lectures in London in 1937. According to this thesis, the early Ottomans were Anatolian Muslims who were united by a *gāzī* or warrior ethos, devoted to fighting Christians. Wittek suggests that the foundation of the Ottoman Empire was not tribal based because of the contradictory nature of the evidence regarding the tribal tradition, which itself was invented only in the fifteenth century.[9]

According to the tribal tradition, the Ottomans were nomadic Turks who had been forced to move into Anatolia as a result of the Mongol invasions of the thirteenth century. They were led by the grandfather of Osman, the eponymous founder of the Ottoman state. The tradition would have us believe that it was this tribe that eventually created a world empire. For Wittek, it would have been something of a miracle for a nomadic tribe to have founded an empire of the duration of the Ottomans.[10] The official Ottoman tradition says that the Oghuz, to which Osman belonged, were divided into 24 tribes. Wittek assumes that this cannot be considered to be a historical reality but should be treated as "a systematizing legend, attributing to Oghuz Khan, 6 sons, and to each of them, 4 sons, the 24 grandsons of Oghuz Khan".[11] Wittek casts the tribal tradition in doubt because of what he regards as inconsistencies in the genealogical account of the Oghuz. Elswehere, Wittek argued that 31 out of 52 names in the Ottoman family tree were introduced later into the genealogy of Osman, speculating that this was done in order to remove certain chronological inconsistencies in the genealogy.[12] These and other contradictions led him to the curious conclusion that if historians in the fifteenth century felt free to invent a tribal tradition, that is proof that a tribal tradition and tribal feeling did not exist.[13]

For Wittek, the Ottoman state was founded instead on the basis of a *gāzī* or warrior tradition. The Ottomans were "a community of *Ghāzīs*, of champions of the Mohammedan religion; a community of Moslem march-warriors, devoted to the struggle with the infidels in their neighbourhood".[14] Wittek noted that the fact that the *gazāh* or holy war was a crucial element, and the *raison d'être* of the Ottoman state, was generally recognized. Sultan Meḥmed had proved this by reclaiming the area of Constantinople on the Asian shore and by conducting extensive *gāzī* raids into Hungary and Styria.[15]

Lowry's critique of the Wittek thesis deserves mention as it raises an important question as to how to deal with tradition as a historical source. Lowry's essential point is that the main work that Wittek utilized as a source of evidence for his Gazi Thesis was not a chronicle or history but rather a work of advice, or *naṣīhatnāme*, directed to the early Ottoman rulers. The source in question is the fifteenth century epic poem, the *İskendernāme* of Tacüddin İbrahim bin Hidr, also known by his pen name, Ahmedī. Appended to this work are 334 couplets that Ahmedī called the *Destān-i Tevārīh-i Mülūk-i Āl-i 'Uthmān* (*The Epic Chronicles of the Ottoman Rulers*).[16] Since Wittek regarded the verses of the *İskendernāme* and specifically the *Destān* as a versified chronicle rather than versified council for the Ottoman rulers, he was inclined to accept the contents as an empirical description of the *gazāh* and *gāzīs* of the early formative period of the Ottoman dynasty.[17] Wittek believed that Ahmedī provided a very accurate understanding of what the Ottomans felt about themselves and their state – that they were a community of *gāzīs* in a state of struggle against the neighbouring Christian infidels.[18]

To my mind, Lowry's critique is not up to the mark. That Ahmedī's *İskendernāme* might be a *naṣīhatnāme* in no way precludes historical facts as being a part of its content. It cannot be assumed that every statement derived from a *naṣīhatnāme* did not refer to historical facts, particularly his account of Osman and Orhan as *gāzīs*, which he regarded as inspirational for Sultan Bayezid I (1389–1402) and his son, Süleyman Çelebi. The view that the idea of the early Ottomans as *gāzīs* was merely a construction dreamt up some decades later by popular tradition and canonized in versified chronicles implies that the Ottomans freely circulated myths and nothing more about themselves. If we accept the possibility that the early Ottomans such as Osman and Orhan were indeed *gāzīs* and that their motivations were founded on some form of religious piety, this would not be inconsistent with their secular or worldly quest for empire and the spoils of war. Lowry too easily dismisses the *gazāh* factor when he notes that the prime objectives of the Oghuz Turks were spoils and booty rather than religious conversion.[19] The duality between the this-worldly and the other-worldly that Lowry seems to insist upon in reality often does not exist in the minds and experiences of actors in history. For example, Bayezid II's so-called secular edict promising booty and land grants to *gāzīs* who offered their services in the holy war or *cihad* in the defence of Islam[20] does not contradict the idea of the *gazāh* as religious, as noted by İnalcik.[21] In fact, for Ibn Khaldūn it was the three elements of kinship ties, the social cohesion provided by Islam and the strength of the leader derived from trade, booty and pillage, that made for a strong *'aṣabiyyah*. Any raiding party consisted of men with a variety of convictions and motivations that were this-worldly as well as other-worldly.

Lowry's alternative to the Gazi Thesis is that the Ottoman Empire was founded on the basis of a predatory confederacy of people of various ethnic and religious backgrounds.[22] He cites as evidence against the Gazi Thesis examples of Byzantine Christians who converted to Islam and pledged their loyalties to the Ottomans. The motivation for conversion and participation in the predatory confederacy were the spoils of conquest.[23] In response to this, it might be said that a predatory confederacy motivated by pecuniary benefits does not preclude it from being a *gazāh*, for the reasons stated earlier. In Jennings' critique of the Gazi Thesis, he refers to what he cites as Islamic legal prerequisites of the *cihad*. These include Islamization as the motivation for conquest, submission of non-Muslims to Muslim rule and the exclusively Muslim composition of the army.[24] Even if we were not to consider Lowry's predatory confederacy as a *gazāh* in the technical or legist sense, it is still reasonable to hypothesize, based on the available evidence, that the multi-ethnic, multi-religious confederacy that Lowry refers to was not devoid of an overarching Islamic ethic that the Muslims believed in and that the motivation for participation in the raids and wars was not purely mercenary or material. The latter point is perfectly in line with what is known of the tribal confederacies that Ibn Khaldūn wrote about or which appeared after his lifetime, such as the *qizilbāsh* of the Safavid Empire (see Chapter 7). There is no reason to assume that it was otherwise for the Oghuz clans.

The opposition between worldly concerns and a religious rationality implied by Lowry[25] is textual and theoretical and is often not found in the empirical world. Even in the time of Prophet Muḥammad the two came together. The Prophet was as much concerned with the building of a polity, the establishment of economic institutions and other-worldly affairs as he was with salvation in the afterlife. The Prophet also worked with non-Muslims even as he was consolidating authority over the Muslims. For example, he entered into an agreement known as the *ṣahīfah* with the Jews of Medina. The *ṣahīfah* defined relations of mutual aid between the Muslims and Jews and specified punitive measures to be applied to those who broke treaties.[26] According to the *ṣahīfah*:

> This is a dictation from Muḥammad, the unlettered prophet, between the believers and the Muslims from Quraysh and Yathrib and those who comply

with them and adhere to them and strive with them; they are one single *ummah*, with the exclusion of the rest.[27]

According to the agreements made between the Prophet and the Jews of Medina, the Jews were obliged to aid the Muslims in war by fighting alongside them and sharing in the expenses of war. In return, they were accorded complete religious freedom and autonomy over their fiscal affairs.

After the prophetic period, many conquests were carried out throughout Muslim history with a variety of motivations that included neither purely religious nor secular ones. This is simply in the nature of things. It is therefore reasonable to suggest that the *gāzī* element cited in the fifteenth century chronicles and by the scholars that interpreted these chronicles cannot be dismissed.

Lowry's critique of Wittek's Gazi Thesis does not amount to a denial of religious factors in the rise of the Ottoman dynasty but rather places them alongside economic and other material factors. This, as we shall see later, fits perfectly well within a Khaldūnian framework which emphasizes the role of both religious factors and material interests under the concept of *'aṣabiyyah*.

So, the role of the *gāzī* element in Ottoman state formation is certainly plausible, despite the critique of Lowry and others before him of Wittek's Gazi Thesis. The presence of the *gāzī* element does not preclude other factors such as the desire of booty and the spoils of war. Nevertheless, Wittek's argument against the tribal tradition is a weak one. Even if the Ottomans' genealogies were various, contradictory and later creations, it does not follow that in reality there was no tribal feeling, or what Ibn Khaldūn called *'aṣabiyyah*, among the Oghuz. Furthermore, the idea of a community of *gāzīs* is not incompatible with the existence of tribal feeling among the *gāzīs*. Wittek says that the *gāzī* emirates of western Anatolia had no tribal consciousness, although each had a ruler as its chief who founded a dynasty,[28] the Ottoman being one of them. It was the *gāzī* emirate of Osman that triumphed over the other *gāzī* emirates and founded a great dynasty. By denying the element of tribal feeling based on circumstantial evidence rather than direct proof, Wittek is forced to offer a weaker explanation for the rise of the Ottoman state, citing factors such as resistance from the Byzantines, aid from unemployed warriors from other emirates, the decline of Mongol rule and the inciting of the "fanatical darvishes" of Islam.[29] But all of these factors are not incompatible with, indeed are essential to, a Khaldūnian theory that emphasizes the role of tribal *'aṣabiyyah* in state formation. As we saw in Chapter 2, religion alone was insufficient in disciplining tribes and subordinating them to a leader.

The Gazi Thesis was dominant among the generation of scholars after Wittek, particularly in the West. Within Turkey, it was the prominent Turkish historian of the Ottoman Empire, Halil İnalcık, who held a similar view of Ottoman history, that the predominant factor in the rise of the Ottomans was the *gāzī* or warrior ethos dedicated to the struggle against Christian Byzantium.[30] In a later work, Inalcik looked at the problem of Ottoman state formation with reference to an early source, Aşıkpaşazāde's *menākıbnāme*, the *History of the House of Osman*, written in the 1480s. İnalcık affirmed the *gāzī* nature of the Ottoman state but emphasized that they fought both for *cihad* as well as for making a living. The bond of companionship tied the *gāzī*s to each other.[31]

An important difference between Wittek on the one hand and Köprülü and Inalcık on the other has to do with the role of tribes in Ottoman state formation. Both Köprülü and İnalcık stress the tribal factor, while Wittek does not.[32] We could say, therefore, that the Gazi Thesis has two dimensions to it, one of which emphasizes the tribal element in Ottoman state formation. The tribal dimension of the Gazi Thesis, if we could still label the perspective in this way, was influenced by Köprülü and developed by İnalcık. It is the combination of Wittek's *gāzī* factor with Inalcık's stress on the religious nature of the Turcoman tribes that brings us closer to a Khaldūnian approach to Ottoman state formation.

According to İnalcık's reading, the situation in Anatolia during the first decades of the fourteenth century was that there were 16 Turcoman principalities, which could mobilize between a quarter and half a million cavalrymen. The migration to Anatolia was a process that had begun much earlier. The migration of Turcoman nomads from what is today called Outer Mongolia to West Asia was represented in part by the Oghuz, a nomadic band of warriors also known as the Seljuks, during the tenth century.[33] By the eleventh century, when the Seljuk Empire was centred at Isfahan, various Turcoman tribes, which were autonomous from the Seljuks, were trying to establish themselves in Anatolia. The Seljuk Empire disintegrated in the midst of Turcoman nomadic opposition, giving way to the establishment of the Great Mongol Empire in the thirteenth century.[34] The Mongol Empire itself broke up into several parts, divided among the relatives of the Great Han. One of these parts, constituting Iran, Iraq and Anatolia, became the Ilhan Empire founded by Hulagu. However, several Turkmen tribes were able to establish independent principalities as the Seljuks and the Mongols weakened.[35]

One of these was the Ottoman (Osmanli) principality established by Osman of the Kayı tribe.[36] The question of theoretical as well as historical importance is how a pastoral nomadic clan could rise to subordinate other Turcoman principalities, conquer the "infidel" and establish an empire. The idea that only a society with a strong *'aṣabiyyah* can establish an empire is operative in the case of the Ottomans. İnalcık's description of the *cihad* raids (*gazāh*),[37] is really that of the form of an *'aṣabiyyah* that united the Turcoman tribes under Osman and his descendants.

The demographic potential created by the migrations was heightened by a *gāzī* or holy war ideology, supported by dervishes, among the Turcomans, who developed a sense of social cohesion around the person of Osman. Furthermore, the opportunities for material gain as well as war against the neighbouring Christians were altogether considered as part of the "pious" act.[38] Jennings' argument against the Gazi Thesis, that a real *gāzī* army that included Christians was inconceivable, misses the mark.[39] It is true that in theory this was and is inconceivable. In practice, however, the fact that the Turcoman armies included Christians did not mean that the Turcomans did not regard themselves as *gāzī*s involved in *cihad*. Also, this point is not inconsistent with the fact that the early Ottoman state did not crush the Byzantine state, nor entered into marriage alliances with Christians.

All this means that worldly considerations were often combined with those of the hereafter. To think otherwise would be to give a textualist reading of Ottoman history by reading into history what was expected in the text regarding the conditions and requirement of *cihad*.

That being the case, in what way can a Khaldūnian framework be utilized to explain the early rise of the Ottoman state?

Ibn Khaldūn and Ottoman state formation

The basic ingredients for a Khaldūnian approach to Ottoman state formation have been given in a number of the existing accounts of the rise of the Ottoman Empire discussed above. In the theoretical scheme derived from historical facts from North Africa and the Arab East, Ibn Khaldūn highlighted the following as essential to state formation.

Only houses with the attribute of nobility (*sharaf*) were able to found a dynasty. Various dominant group feelings may compete until one emerged victorious. Were there several competing groups, the one with the greatest degree of *'aṣabiyyah* or social cohesion would eventually lead the rest to found a dynasty. The groups with the strongest *'aṣabiyyah* were tribal groups because it was cohesion based on agnatic ties that were strongest. Agnatic ties tended to be strongest in tribal groups that were nomadic as opposed to those that were sedentarized. Nomadic groups with stronger *'aṣabiyyah* were also physically and militarily stronger. This is due to the fact that such groups, bound as they were by kinship ties, functioned more effectively as self-help groups. There is a positive correlation between *'aṣabiyyah* and the degree of mutual support and aid. The fact that the *'aṣabiyyah* among the bedouin was relatively more intact than that in settled tribes made for greater fortitude and a higher degree of mutual support among them. However, bedouin groups, after founding a new dynasty and becoming sedentarized, would experience a diminishing in their *'aṣabiyyah*, for reasons that have to do with the nature of sedentary life. This led to the weakening of the dynasty in both military and political terms, leaving it vulnerable to attack and conquest by pre-sedentary tribes with their *'aṣabiyyah* intact. Characteristic of the Khaldūnian cycle, therefore, was the circulation of tribal elites with the rise and fall of dynasties, with the system remaining stable.

In the context of the Ottoman Empire, what are the factors that are crucial from the point of view of the Khaldūnian perspective? Some of these factors have been indicated in the works of Wittek, Köprülü, İnalcık and others cited above. It was Osman's clan that became the most respected among the Turcoman tribes of western Anatolia. This became the clan that was able to garner the support of other Turcoman tribes and eventually found a dynasty. It is unanimously agreed by all the sources and scholars that the Ottoman family originated from the Oghuz Turcomans who had settled in Anatolia with the first Seljuk conquerors. The branch of the Oghuz to which the Ottoman family belonged was the Kayı tribe, as attested to in several chronicles and *menākıbnāme*. These works also refer to the nobility and illustriousness of the Kayı over the other Oghuz clans.[40] Apart from the ties of kinship that obviously bound Osman's clan together and commanded the respect of other Turcoman groups, the cohesion of the Turcomans was further buttressed by the religion of Islam, which socialized them into a common orientation that functioned to legitimize Osman's and later Orhan's power and authority. At the same time, the strength of these leaders was boosted by their material standing, which was derived from trade, booty and pillage.

It is important to stress a point made by İnalcık. Even if the traditional sources, such as hagiographies of the Ottomans or the early chronicles, are not to be regarded as true historical accounts, they do shed light on how "in a Turcoman clan of pastoral nomads, a *ghazi* can emerge to create a subordinate band of mounted warriors and comrades (*nöker* and *yoldash*) constantly occupied with raiding the lands of the 'infidels'".[41] The reason for trusting these sources, Inalcık explains, is partly because the pattern of change described by them was a very old one among the Central Asian Turks.[42]

Gellner remarks in his *Muslim Society* that the early period of Ottoman state formation exemplified the Khaldūnian pattern. In fact, Ibn Khaldūn himself seems to have sensed something of the greatness of the Ottomans, as he was reported by Ibn Ḥajar to have said that "there was no one to fear with regard to Egypt but the sons of Osman".[43]

But Gellner also notes that the Ottoman Empire contradicted the Khaldūnian model in other ways, mostly because it was stale and long-lived.[44] When it did end, it was not so much a natural decline according to the laws discovered by Ibn Khaldūn, but an outcome of military defeat by an alliance of Western and Arab powers. What needs to be explained, then, is why the Ottomans were not subject to the fate of the Khaldūnian cycle. In order to answer this question, it is necessary to bring in a missing element from the above account. What is missing is the political economy context. How can the Khaldūnian account of the rise of the Ottoman dynasty be reformulated to take into account the Ottoman political economy – specifically, the modes of production that characterized Ottoman society? Providing the political economy context will allow us to explain the dynamics of change that characterized the formative Ottoman state and the means by which the Khaldūnian cycle was avoided.

The Ottoman modes of production

The three areas of surplus appropriation were agriculture, industry and trade. The ruling class consisted of the state and military bureaucracy, and the religious institution. The following account of the sources and recipients of surplus is largely based on the situation in the sixteenth and early seventeenth centuries.

In the area of agriculture, land was generally owned by the state. In Ottoman Turkey, peasants were allowed to work either individually or communally on state land in exchange for paying a regular tax called the *mīrī*. However, the prime consideration was not always the maximization of revenue. In Anatolia, where it was necessary to maintain an army, land was awarded as *tīmār*s or *ziamet*s (benefices) to Turkish Muslim cavalrymen, *sipāhī*s, who in return provided military services to the state. The taxes that the *sipāhīs* collected were utilized for the purpose of local security as well as for the maintenance of troops for service in the Ottoman army.[45] The rest of the land was kept as imperial estates, from which revenue was collected by tax-farmers (*mültezims*) or it was used to provide support for provincial governors. Also, religious endowments or *evkāf* (sing. *vakf*) were maintained for the upkeep of mosques and other religious institutions. In the Egyptian part of the Ottoman Empire, on the other hand, where a local Egyptian army was maintained, the Ottoman state maximized revenue by collecting the *mīrī* directly. Occasionally, the sultan would grant state land to individuals and then it would become *mulk* or private property.

The next source of revenue was the urban surplus obtained by means of taxes and duties imposed on craft industry and trade. In the Ottoman Empire, the craft industry was subject to rigid state control and lost a lot of the surplus. Members of craft guilds (*eṣnāf*, sing. *ṣinif*) paid high taxes.[46] As far as trade was concerned, merchants were relatively free from state control. In addition to profits from international trade and the marketing of the rural surplus, these merchants benefited from their role as creditors to tax-farmers.[47]

Apart from the sultan and his bureaucracy which collected the surplus, there were also the *'ulamā'* (religious clerics) who formed part of the ruling class. The *evkāf* were an independent source of revenue for the *'ulamā'* and represented a source of economic power for them.[48] The religious institution or the *ilmiye* of the Ottoman Empire controlled law, justice, religion and education. The head of the religious institution was the *şeyḥülislām* who presided over the cadis and muftis of the empire.[49] The *'ulamā'* were critical of and antagonistic towards the state, this antagonism increasing as financial problems of the state emerged. Nevertheless, in Turkey the *'ulamā'* were unified into a religious institution and became incorporated into the Ottoman state.

Thus, the picture we have of the Ottoman state in the sixteenth century is one of a strong ruling elite consisting of civil, military and religious classes extracting surplus from peasantry, craftsmen and merchants.

There is one more element of the class structure of this society that we need to mention before we proceed. This is the tribal population. For our purposes, two important aspects of the tribal population must be understood. One is that they have played key roles in the establishment of the Ottoman dynasty.[50] Beyond this, various tribes continued to exert an influence on the state. In the Ottoman Empire they served as a reservoir for the ruling elite[51] and continued to be a threat to the central authority of the state.[52] Together with the *'ulamā'* they constituted the main opposition to the state.

Having thus presented a brief account of the Ottoman economic system, we are now in a position to examine the modes of production that accurately portray this economic system. I begin with a definition of the concept of mode of production. This is derived from an oft-quoted statement of Marx, that as humans engage in their social production, they "inevitably enter into definite relations, which are independent of their will, namely relations of production appropriate to a given stage in the development of their material forces of production".[53]

The mode of production, then, consists of the relations of production and the forces of production. The relations of production refer to the mode of appropriation of the economic surplus and the economic ownership of the forces of production that correspond to that mode of appropriation of the economic surplus.[54] The forces of production are the means of production and the labour process. It refers to the labour process involved in the transformation of the raw natural material into products by means of the tools, skills, organization and knowledge of the worker.[55] For example, in the capitalist mode of production the economic surplus is appropriated in the form of surplus value by a class of non-producers, the capitalists, who own the means of production. Workers are forced to sell their labour-power for wages in order to buy commodities for personal consumption, as they do not own the means of production. Every mode of production has a determinate form of the relations of production and the forces of production. Thus, in order to identify a particular mode of production it is necessary to specify both the relations and forces of production.

Hitherto, works on Ottoman society have tended to describe its economic system in terms of unitary modes of production. Attempts have been made to characterize this economic system in terms of the feudal mode of production.[56] Others have characterized this system in terms of the Asiatic mode of production.[57] Islamoğlu and Keyder speak of the coexistence of two or more modes of production; nevertheless, overwhelming emphasis is placed on the analysis of one mode of production. Little mention is made of the relationship between the various modes of production. In addition to this, the various characterizations of Ottoman society as feudal or Asiatic tend to stretch the meaning of the terms Asiatic and feudal too far and also amount to obscuring the true nature of the relations and forces of production that operated in this society.

In what follows, I discuss what I consider to be the four modes of production that existed in Ottoman Turkey. These are the Asiatic, prebendal feudal, petty commodity, and pastoral nomadic modes of production. I argue that these modes of production coexisted in Ottoman Turkey. The theoretical antecedence for this approach arises from debates in development studies on modes of production. Andre Gunder Frank, who popularized the works of the Latin American dependency school during the 1960s, argued that the capitalist mode of production embraces the entire economies of capitalist countries in Latin America. He was, therefore, denying that capitalist and feudal modes of production coexist in the same economic system.[58] This view was criticized by Ernesto Laclau, who called into question Frank's usage of the term capitalism. According to Laclau, Frank could subsume feudalism under the capitalist mode of production because he excluded the relations of production in his definitions of capitalism and feudalism. As a result, the nature of the exploitation of such diverse groups as the Peruvian peasantry, Chilean tenants, Ecuadorian share-croppers, West Indian sugar plantation slaves, and textile workers in Manchester comes under the banner of capitalism.[59] Laclau's point is that if the relations of production are taken into account, then it can be seen that both capitalist and feudal modes of production exist in Latin America.[60] During the last 20 years there have been numerous contributions to the conceptualization of modes of production that stress the coexistence of modes of production in an economic system.[61]

In what follows I evaluate previous attempts to characterize Ottoman modes of production, and present my own argument as to how the Asiatic, prebendal feudal, petty commodity and pastoral nomadic modes of production accurately describe the Ottoman economic system.

The Asiatic mode of production

In 1853 the charter of the British East India Company was renewed by Parliament. This was also the time when Marx turned his attention to the problem of "oriental" societies.[62] In his studies on the development of capitalism in Europe, Marx made brief excursions into the history of India and other "oriental" societies in order to discover what he regarded as the barriers to capitalist development in these societies. Marx conceptualized the economic systems of these societies in terms of the Asiatic mode of production.

In the Asiatic mode of production, power is centralized in the state. The entire economic surplus is appropriated by the state and the state is the legal owner of landed and manufacturing property.[63] Such a state is extremely strong when it controls a strategic element in the production process, such as irrigation works or an army of superior military ability.[64] In addition to the centralization of power in the state, the Asiatic mode of production is defined in terms of the absence of private property in land[65] and the combination of agriculture and manufacturing within the self-sustaining small community.[66] The basic ingredient of historical progression – class struggle – is missing. As a result, Asiatic societies were stagnant.[67]

The Ottoman system was not Asiatic in the sense that it controlled major large-scale public works. Neither was it Asiatic in the sense of being a classless society. The Ottoman state was a centralized system that derived its power, at least in its inception and formative period, from the superior military capability provided by the Turcoman pastoral nomads. The tribute paid by tribal members to the tribal chieftain was the forerunner of the Asiatic tax/rent.[68] This is the trait of the Asiatic mode of production that existed in Ottoman Turkey.

Another trait concerns the extraction of surplus directly from the dominated classes. In the Asiatic mode of production the state is both landlord and sovereign. Taxes and rent coincide in the sense that there is no tax that differs from ground-rent.[69] The tax/rent is a result of the "coupling of political sovereignty and land-ownership in the state which appropriates the surplus-product through taxation which is simultaneously a land-rent".[70]

In the theory of the Asiatic mode of production the state is the legal owner of landed and manufacturing property and appropriates the economic surplus directly from the populace. The Ottoman economic system cannot be characterized by this mode of production alone. In the Ottoman Empire, it was only from certain areas that a revenue, known as the *sālyāne*, was remitted directly to the central government. The *sālyāne* provinces were found in Egypt, Baghdad, Basra, Abyssinia, Lahsa, in some areas of eastern Anatolia and various areas of Christian,

Cossack and subject Muslim principalities.[71] However, not all revenues went directly to the ruler or the state. There were other forms of surplus appropriation pertaining to different modes of production other than the Asiatic mode, to which we now turn.

The prebendal feudal mode of production

In a typical Ottoman province it was the *tīmār* system that was in operation, in which land was awarded as benefices to *sipāhīs* who became entitled to the revenue. This is what can be called the prebendal feudal mode of production, which differs from the feudal mode of production as it was found in Europe.

Like the Asiatic mode of production, feudalism is one in which land is the dominant means of production. The fragmented nature of sovereignty is due to the independence of the landed nobility and the urban crafts from the state: that is, there is private property in both land and urban manufactories. The central feature of the feudal mode of production as it was found in Europe is the fief. The fief was granted by the lord to a vassal in return for military services.[72] The lord–vassal contract was based on a free relation of personal fealty which "involves reciprocal obligations of loyalty, to be sure, on a legally unequal basis".[73]

The lord–vassal relationship is one aspect of the feudal relations of production. Another relation is that between the vassal and his dependents, the serfs, which is denoted by the term *seigneurie*.[74] The economic surplus is paid by the serfs to the knightly vassals in the form of a rent. Based on this understanding of feudalism, there have been attempts by scholars of Ottoman history to identify the institutions of the *tīmār* and the *iqṭā'* with the European fief, and to assert, therefore, that the Ottoman economic system was a feudal one.[75] *Iqṭā'* is a term for a form of administrative or military grant.[76] It is an institution that became regularized during the Seljuk Empire (1087–1157).[77] In Ottoman Turkey it was known as the *tīmār*. The *tīmār* referred to grants of land that were assigned to a *tīmār* holder who, in return, provided a military contingent for the sultan in times of need. He was also entrusted with the administration of the land.

There are superficial similarities between the institutions of the *tīmār* on the one hand and the fief on the other. These include the grant of land in return for military service, the grant of land in lieu of salary, the grant of immunities, the high status of the military, and the existence of an exploited peasantry.[78] However, there is a fundamental difference between the fief on the one hand and the Ottoman institution on the other. The granting of a fief was based on a contract of fealty that established a solidary, fraternal relationship between lord and vassal, involving reciprocal obligations of loyalty. This is in contrast to the granting of *tīmārs*, which generally did not involve a contract of personal fealty carrying reciprocal obligations of loyalty. Rather they were granted mainly out of fiscal considerations and existed in the general context of a despotic state. In the feudal mode of production as it existed in Europe, rule at the apex of the system was relatively fragile and weak. Power was held mainly by local lords. In Ottoman Turkey, however, rule at the apex of the system was strong. In the case of European feudalism land was owned by local lords, but it was the property of the state in the case of Ottoman Turkey. This difference is not trivial and led Weber to characterize the Turkish situation as belonging to the system of prebendal feudalism.[79] The relations of production in prebendal feudalism are sufficiently different from those of "occidental" feudalism to warrant referring to the former as a distinct mode of production. The prebendal feudal mode of production existed in Ottoman Turkey and was based on the granting of benefices (*tīmār*), generally in return for military and administrative services. In the agricultural sector, the Ottoman economic system consisted of Asiatic relations of production, in which the state appropriated the surplus directly from the populace and the state was the owner of landed and manufacturing property. The economy also consisted of prebendal feudal relations of production, in which the surplus was collected by assignees to land grants (*sipāhīs*) who did not legally own land but nevertheless exerted control over it. Thus, there were two main types of relations of production: two distinct modes of production that characterized the agricultural sector.

The petty commodity mode of production

In the simple or petty commodity mode of production, production for the market is carried out by producers who own their means of production.[80] It differs from other pre-capitalist modes of production, such as the Asiatic or prebendal feudal modes, in that in those cases it is use-values that are created for the purpose of consumption in the home or the community, whether the community is a family, tribe, village or a whole empire. The producer lives on the products of his labour. In the petty commodity mode of production, however, production is for the purpose of exchange; it is exchange-values that are important and the producer does not live solely or directly on the products of his own labour. Petty commodity production is found in both rural and urban areas. In the rural sector it exists when peasants are free owners of land. Production is in the form of both use- and exchange-values. Whatever is not consumed by the peasants themselves is sold as a commodity on the market. Such commodity production may not encompass the whole of rural society, however; not all peasants become petty commodity producers. The development of independent crafts, in its initial stages, consists of the peasant-craftsman bringing to the market only the surplus of his production. In this case, craft production, trade and the division of labour are not well developed.[81] When the whole production of craftsmen consists of exchange-values, however, petty commodity production encompasses the whole of a society. This happens when towns have reached the stage of development where extensive markets are created.

Petty commodity production existed in both rural and urban areas of Ottoman Turkey but it reached its highest expression in the urban sector in craft guild production. We can, therefore, speak of a petty commodity mode of production that was especially developed in the towns.

The Ottoman craft guild was a well-established institution by the beginning of the sixteenth century.[82] The guildmaster (*usta*) and his apprentice (*şagirt*) owned the means of production, such as tools and working space. In addition to the masters and their apprentices, there were also workers (*ecir*) who were employed in the craft guilds, under a master, for wages.[83] In this sense, one can speak of capitalist production in Ottoman society, although strictly speaking this cannot be understood in terms of the existence of a capitalist mode of production. In the capitalist mode of production, commodity production – the production of exchange-values – is generalized. All objects of economic life are commodities and there is a mass of property-less people who are compelled to sell their labour-power in order to survive.[84] These conditions were not met in Ottoman Turkey. Instead we find capitalist production restricted to the production of luxury goods.

Furthermore, production in craft industries as a whole, while based on the creation of exchange-values, did not have as its main object of production "*enrichment or exchange-value as exchange-value,* but the *subsistence of man as an artisan, as a master-craftsman,* and consequently use-value" (original italics).[85] So, while capitalist production did exist in Ottoman Turkey, it was clearly subordinate to the petty commodity mode of production and did not constitute a mode of production of its own.[86]

The pastoral nomadic mode of production

Of interest to us are the Turcomans of Anatolia, a pastoral nomadic people that made up the military force by which Osman founded a dynasty. The form of pastoral nomadism found among the Turcomans was that of multi-animal pastoralists who bred sheep, goats, cattle and camels, but above all horses.[87] The horse was a vital means of production as it facilitated the procurement of booty through raids and conquest.

In the pastoral nomadic mode, the means of production consists of certain species of domestic animals and land unsuitable for cultivation.[88] The term nomadic pertains to the absence of permanent habitation, while the term pastoral refers to subsistence by the products of domesticated animals.[89] These animals provide nomadic society with its basic needs in food (butter, cheese, meat, yoghurt), drink (milk), clothing (hides, wool), fuel (dung) and means of transportation (camels, donkeys, horses, oxen).[90] Animals, tools and dwelling items are owned on an individual basis, while grazing land is the collective property of the tribe. The system of property relations can be understood in terms of kinship. Property is transferred from one individual to another through mechanisms such as inheritance by sons, marriage agreements and redistribution through the agency of tribal chiefs.[91] In the pastoral nomadic mode of production, there is production of both use-values and exchange-values. Exchange arises out of the need for nomads to obtain from sedentary societies goods that they do not produce for themselves.

A form of stratification does exist in the pastoral nomadic mode of production. Among the Turkic and Mongol pastoralists, the principle of kinship in the "bone" is elaborated in terms of the division into nobles and commoners.[92] The bone refers to kin in the paternal line; this is contrasted with the idea of kin in the flesh which is in the maternal line.[93] Noble origin is expressed through the paternal line by white bone and commoner origins by black bone. The occurrence of classes, white bone versus black, is not found in all pastoral nomadic societies. For example, it did not exist among the Turcoman people, who directly concern us in this chapter; nevertheless, hereditary tribal chiefs were found among these people.[94]

The study of the various types of social units to be found among pastoral nomadic societies has been plagued by uncertainties and inconsistencies in terminology. In an attempt at systematization of the nomenclature, Radloff believed that *ulus* designated the largest unit, which he translated as people. Each *ulus* was in turn divided into *il* or *al*, that is, a clan; each clan was divided into *aimak* or tribes; each tribe into *boi*, or sub-tribes; and each *boi* into *uruk*, or families.[95] However, this terminology was not rigidly employed by the pastoralists themselves.[96] The tribe was also referred to as *oba*, which was led by a war chief whose title was inherited through the paternal line but whose real authority was derived from his talent and success. An aggregation of several *oba* generally engaged in raids: pillage, or conquest in enemy territory. The Turcoman *oba*, then, is a horde,[97] a political-military organization, in addition to being a socio-economic one. The function of the hereditary tribal chief was, therefore, both military and economic. Surplus acquisition was at once an economic and a military operation.

Having discussed the existence of four distinct modes of production in Ottoman Turkey, the question of how they relate to each other inevitably arises. Various relations between the different modes of production have been discussed thus far. Rather than discuss each of these relations I will confine myself to those that pertain specifically to the interaction between nomadic and sedentary societies, for it is these relations that are relevant to the topic of applying Ibn Khaldūn. It is this interaction that constituted a great part of the dynamics of Ottoman society. The Ottoman Empire was established as a result of the interaction between nomadic and sedentary societies and it is in this area that Ibn Khaldūn is relevant. Therefore, in the next section I discuss the relations between the pastoral nomadic mode of production on the one hand and the Asiatic and prebendal feudal modes of production on the other. The theoretical framework for doing so comes from Ibn Khaldūn.

Ibn Khaldūn, Marx and the Asiatic mode of production

Ibn Khaldūn's theory has been used to both reject and support the theory of the Asiatic mode of production. In describing the Asiatic mode of production, Marx spoke of the stagnation of Asiatic societies such as India, which has "no history at all, at least no known history. What we call its history is but the history of successive intruders who founded their empires on the passive basin of that unresisting and unchanging society".[98] Andreski says that the theory of the Asiatic mode of production (or Oriental Despotism) is contradicted by the fact that "oriental" societies were characterized by change on by no means a small scale, as indicated by Ibn Khaldūn's theory of dynastic succession.[99] However, reference to this dynamism in itself does not constitute a critique of the theory of the Asiatic mode of production. It is important to make the distinction between stagnation on the one hand and the absence of barriers to capitalist development on the other. Marx's point was to reveal the absence of certain prerequisites to capitalism in "oriental" societies. I do not think that he meant "oriental" society was literally stagnant, just that it lacked the dynamism in the direction of capitalist development of the European sort.

On the other hand, Ibn Khaldūn has also been used in support of the theory of the Asiatic mode of production. The Asiatic mode claims that the "oriental" despot derives his power from the fragmented nature of his society. The stratification of Asiatic society into clans, tribes and ethnic groups and the consequent lack of unity among them along class lines enable the ruler to keep a firm hand over his subjects. Ibn Khaldūn's theory of dynastic succession, it is said, provides one component of the orientalist view of despotism in that it stresses the lack of urban and social integration and thereby supports the view of the insignificance of class as a prime mover of history.[100] Although Turner is critical of this version of the theory of the Asiatic mode of production, he has not addressed the issue of Ibn Khaldūn being used to support this theory. I believe that Ibn Khaldūn's theory can be used in support of Marx's theory of the Asiatic mode of production, but not in the sense referred to above.

How does Ibn Khaldūn's theory support the theory of the Asiatic mode of production? It provides a reason for the despotic nature of the state – that is, for the theory of bureaucratic despotism (one variant of the theory of the Asiatic mode of production). While Marx attributed the power of the state to the control of public works, Ibn Khaldūn referred to tribal military power as a source of state power. This situation particularly fits the case of Ottoman Turkey, which did not have large-scale centralized irrigation works, but did derive its power from the tribes. The periodic conquest of dynasties by tribes does not violate the Asiatic mode of production model, for the basic structure of society remains unchanged and the state remains despotic, merely going through periods of conquest, rise and decline. We have already seen, in Chapter 2, how it was possible that Marx and Engels were aware of Ibn Khaldūn's work, a conclusion that we may arrive at after reading Engels' account of the periodic rise and fall of dynasties through successive tribal conquests.

Ibn Khaldūn's theory provides the basis for the despotic nature of the Ottoman state. This was an Asiatic state that can be characterized by the theory of the Asiatic mode of production in which state power derived not from the control of large-scale irrigation works but rather from tribal support. The Ottoman Empire was founded with the aid of tribal groups. We have already made reference to the tribal origins of the Ottomans.

Two types of Asiatic states have been recognized – one based on large-scale public works and the other on pastoral nomadism.[101] The Ottoman Empire is an example of the latter, in which there was a "non-hydraulic" genesis of the Asiatic mode of production which can be explained by Ibn Khaldūn's theory concerning tribal *'aṣabiyyah*, religious fervour and military superiority.

There is another variant of the theory of the Asiatic mode of production to be considered. This is the theory of fragmented society, which stresses the fragmented nature of "oriental" societies into clans, tribes, ethnic groups and villages as a source of state power. When it is said that Ibn Khaldūn's theory of elite circulation is in harmony with the theory of fragmented society, this is to say that the tribes, by their very presence as tribes, are an element in a fragmented society that precludes unity along class lines, thereby bestowing power to the state. The main objection to this is that Ibn Khaldūn's theory is not a theory of fragmented society. In the theory of fragmented society, the tribes play a different role from that in Ibn Khaldūn's theory.

Ibn Khaldūn's theory does not provide support for the theory of the Asiatic mode of production in the sense of the theory of fragmented society. In his theory the tribe does not play the role, side by side with the village and ethnicity, of fragmenting society. That is to say, his is not a theory of fragmented society. The circulation of tribal elites neither radically alters nor reinforces the Asiatic state. All it does is cause it to swing back and forth between periods of centralization and decentralization. Why has Ibn Khaldūn's theory of elite circulation been seen as support for the theory of fragmented society, when it seems clear that the role of tribes in the two theories is vastly different? To my mind, this question can be answered by recourse to Durkheim's concept of mechanical solidarity. Some have referred to the similarity between Ibn Khaldūn's tribal *'aṣabiyyah* and Durkheim's mechanical solidarity.[102] It is true that tribal *'aṣabiyyah* and mechanical solidarity both refer to solidarity that arises out of similar states of conscience, duties and responsibilities: that is, a low level of division of labour.[103] In this sense, both Ibn Khaldūn and Durkheim speak of mechanical solidarity. If we stay at this level of comparison, then it is easy to proceed to the next step, to say that mechanical solidarity/tribal *'aṣabiyyah* is exemplified by the fragmentary/segmentary nature of society in which there is a very low level of division of labour and, therefore, no social classes. Ibn Khaldūn's theory, therefore, supposedly supports the theory of fragmented society because it is a theory of fragmented society based on tribal *'aṣabiyyah* or mechanical solidarity. This is opposed to more complex societies, of organic solidarity, based on a complex division of labour and, therefore, social classes. All this may be an accurate portrayal of the similarity between tribal *'aṣabiyyah* and mechanical solidarity when both are considered in the abstract; when considered in their proper historical contexts, however, the comparison is unfounded. Ibn Khaldūn, unlike Durkheim, was looking at the conflict between tribal and urban societies. Ibn Khaldūn described the role of tribal *'aṣabiyyah* as not fragmenting society but as weakening the state.

Ibn Khaldūn and the prebendal feudal mode of production

In the foregoing section I discussed Ibn Khaldūn in connection with the relationship between the pastoral nomadic and Asiatic modes of production. The former provided the basis for the establishment of the latter. Once the empire was established, however, the supporting tribes were absorbed into the sedentary life of the empire by means of the prebendal feudal mode of production. The pastoral nomadic and prebendal feudal modes of production interacted in the sense that the latter more or less derived its existence from the former. In the event of the establishment of a dynasty through tribal support there arose the problem of providing adequate remuneration to tribal elites and their armies who by now aspired towards an urban, more luxurious life. The granting of benefices to tribal chieftains achieved the aim of such remuneration. But, as we shall see, the absorption of tribal society into the prebendal feudal mode of production also had the effect of diminishing the *'aṣabiyyah* of the dominant tribes upon whose power the dynasties rode. The problem has been neatly summarized by Cafadar. Referring to the early Ottomans, he observes:

> But they soon faced the quintessential Ibn Khaldunian predicament of tribal war-band leaders-turned-state builders: namely, the loosening of bonds of solidarity among members of the war band as the administrative mechanisms and stately pomp of imperial polities are adopted by the leaders of the successful enterprise. In other words, as the House of Osman was being transformed into a dynasty at the head of an emerging administrative network of controls, the relatively egalitarian community of gāzī commanders was giving way to a widening hierarchical space between central power and subordinate begs; not all of the latter were content with this role.[104]

When the Ottoman Empire was established, benefices were granted to tribal chieftains. Generally, the old Seljuk *iqṭā'* system was applied. Conquered territories were divided into *muqāṭa'as* and were named *tīmārs* (benefices).[105] These assignments were made in return for military services provided by the *tīmār* holders, the *sipāhīs*. There were moves to restrict the power of the tribes by doing away with the *tīmār* system altogether. *Tīmārs* were converted into crown lands and leased out as *iltizāms* (tax-farms) to tax-farmers. This led to the decline of the *sipāhīs* as a class.[106] Nevertheless, the prebendal feudal mode of production remained intact as the prebendal feudal organization involving the "assignment to officials of rent payments deriving from material goods … in compensation for the fulfillment of real or fictitious duties of office" survived.[107] The absorption of tribal society into the prebendal feudal mode of production, by way of assigning benefices to tribal chieftains and other tribal members, achieved the dual goal of paying them and reducing their ability to maintain superior *'aṣabiyyah*. As we saw in Chapter 2, Ibn Khaldūn notes that the nature of sedentary society was such that it eventually led to the erosion of the nomadic traits of an austere lifestyle, morality, courage, fortitude, and intact group feeling or *'aṣabiyyah*. As the tribesmen became sedentary these traits gradually declined. Although it is difficult for us to observe the decline in *'aṣabiyyah* – that is, to provide empirical examples of it – the fact is that the *gāzī* ideology, and the sense of cohesion that accompanied it, on which the early Ottomans rode to power, no longer had such a transformational role once the empire was established. Ibn Khaldūn does not discuss the economic system within which this process takes place. In the case of the Ottoman Empire, it would have taken place within the context of the prebendal feudal mode of production.

The effect of incorporation into the prebendal feudal mode of production on *'aṣabiyyah* was exacerbated by another tactic described by Ibn Khaldūn and resorted to by the Ottoman rulers. As mentioned above, according to Ibn Khaldūn, once a dynasty is established with the aid of tribal military power, the ruler attempts to dispense with *'aṣabiyyah*. The form that this took in the Ottoman state differs from that described by Ibn Khaldūn. In Ibn Khaldūn, the ruler attempts to blunt the aspirations of the people who shared in his *'aṣabiyyah* by relying on clients and followers who were nurtured in the shadow of *'aṣabiyyah*, or on tribal groups of a different descent who have become his clients.[108] Among the Ottomans, however, the rulers attempted to dispense with tribal military support altogether. The Turks invented the *devşirme* system. This refers to the conversion and conscription of non-Muslim youth to the sultan's army. While the tribes were a source of military and state power, they also constituted a potential ruling class.[109] The Turks were able to blunt tribal aspirations through the invention of the *devşirme* system. In fact, the tribes ceased to be a factor in Ottoman political economy, representing the close of Ibn Khaldūn's system.

This is reflected in the way the *gazāh* ideology was interpreted by the sedentary *'ulamā'* of the Empire. Cafadar notes that although they supported this ideology, they gave a different interpretation to it by distancing it from its frontier traditions. In their versions of Ottoman history, the focus is on the early success of the *gāzīs*, ultimately leading to a sophisticated centralized Ottoman state. Underlying such a narrative is the "waning of *'aṣabiyya* (group solidarity), as Ibn Khaldūn would have said, in the anonymous chronicles and in Apz".[110]

Conclusion

This chapter has attempted to apply both Ibn Khaldūn's theory of dynastic succession and a modes of production framework to Ottoman history. Having described four distinct modes of production in Ottoman Turkey, I explained the interactions between the pastoral nomadic mode of production on the one hand and the Asiatic and prebendal feudal modes of production on the other. While these various economic systems have been couched in terms of the Marxian concept of mode of production, their interactions have been described in terms of Ibn Khaldūn's theory of dynastic succession. The weakness of the argument presented is partly due to the paucity of materials regarding the kinship ties of the Oghuz, and the Kayı in particular. However, the fact that later traditions refer to nobility of birth, warriorship and the importance of Islam, point to the importance of the cementing role of kinship and religion. Even if kinship was less of a factor in the rise and consolidation of the Ottoman state, why this happened also needs to be explained. The explanation from Ibn Khaldūn would be that the group feeling derived from kinship was replaced with one derived from religion. If we accept that social cohesion was a necessary element and that the formative Ottoman society we are referring to was tribal, then that cohesion had to be based on agnatic kinship ties or something that replaced it, such as religion, or a combination of the two.

7 The rise and fall of the Safavid state in a Khaldūnian framework

This chapter, like the previous one, marries Khaldūnian theory to a modes of production approach, with reference to the case of the rise and decline of the Safavid dynasty in pre-modern Iran. The history of the Safavid dynasty provides empirical material for the study of the interaction of modes of production within the context of Khaldūnian dynamics.

From what is known of the facts of early Safavid history, the rise and decline of the state conforms to the general pattern delineated by Ibn Khaldūn in the *Muqaddimah*. The main purpose of this chapter is to present a Khaldūnian perspective of the rise and decline of the Safavid state. As in the case of the Khaldūnian account of the Ottoman Empire, a Khaldūnian interpretation of the Safavid state requires the reconstruction of the Safavid economy, which I will do in terms of its modes of production. The rise and decline of the Safavid state can then be understood in terms of developments in the modes of production of Safavid Iran. The chapter proceeds as follows. In the next section, I discuss the application of Ibn Khaldūn to the rise of the Safavid state. I then introduce the Safavid economy and its modes of production. This is followed by a discussion of the decline of the Safavid state. Existing approaches explaining the fall are discussed and a Khaldūnian alternative is presented.

A Khaldūnian account of the rise of the Safavid state

Unlike the case of the Ottoman Empire, there is surprisingly little controversy surrounding the issue of the rise of the Safavid state. Contemporaneous with the emergence of the Ottoman Empire in the fourteenth century was the founding of the Safavid Sufi movement by Shaykh Ṣafī al-Dīn. His descendant, Ismā‘īl (905–30 AH/1499–1524 AD), based in Azerbaijan, was the founder of the Safavid dynasty. In the mid-tenth century, during Ottoman attempts to centralize their control in Eastern Anatolia, Ismā‘īl took advantage of the turmoil and attempted to make inroads there.[1] Pastoral nomadic tribes played key roles in the establishment of the Safavid dynasty.[2] Ismā‘īl's tribal support came from a number of Turcoman tribes, the Ustajlu, Shamlu, Taqalu, Baharlu, Zulqadar, Qajar and Afshar, collectively known as the *qizilbāsh*.[3] What held these tribes together was an *‘aṣabiyyah* based on the Safavid mystical order to which the *qizilbāsh* owed allegiance. Unsuccessful in Anatolia and on the defensive, Ismā'īl and his followers retreated to Iran and established the Safavid state in 907/1501. By 909/1503 he had control over Azerbaijan, western Iran and the Tigris-Euphrates basin.

The account by Savory, generally accepted as the standard narrative, begins with the story of the emergence of the Safavid sufi order in Ardabīl in eastern Azerbaijan in north-western Iran, and its emergence into a movement and its founding of a state. The Safavids rose to power on the basis of a dynamic ideology. The main components of this ideology were that (1) the Safavid shahs were "the shadows of God upon earth" (*ẓill Allāh fī al-arḍ*); (2) they were also the representative of the Mahdī, the twelfth Imam of the Ithnā 'Asharī Shi'ah; and (3) they were the perfect spiritual directors (sing. *murshid-i kāmil*) of the Ṣafaviyya order.[4] The Safavid family claimed descent from the the seventh Imam, Mūsā al-Kāẓim (d. 183 AH/799 AD). The most important ancestor of the Safavid shahs was Shaykh Ṣafī al-Dīn (b. 1252/53), founder of the order of the Ṣafaviyya.[5] Shaykh Ṣafī was succeeded as spiritual head of the order by his son, Ṣadr al-Dīn Mūsā (1304/05–91/92). During his time the order spread among the tribes of eastern Anatolia and Syria, particularly among the pastoral Turcoman nomads.[6] It was also during Shaykh Ṣadr al-Dīn's time that the Ilkhanid Empire in Iran disintegrated and gave way to numerous Turcoman and Persian principalities. The Chubadin amir in Azerbaijan, Mālik Ashraf, had Shaykh Ṣadr al-Dīn imprisoned in Tabriz, probably out of fear of the growing influence of the Ṣafaviyyih order which was turning into a political movement.[7] Many members of the order fled north and found refuge with the Jānī Beg Maḥmūd, a descendant of Chingiz Khan and the ruler of the western Qipchāq (1340–57).[8] Jānī Beg took the side of the refugees, captured Mālik Ashraf and had him executed. Shayhkh Ṣadr al-Dīn was able to return to Ardabīl. Shortly before Shaykh Ṣadr al-Dīn's death, the Qarā Quyūnlū federation of Turcoman tribes conquered Azerbaijan.

Shaykh Ṣadr al-Dīn was succeeded by his son, Khvājah 'Alī, who led the order until he died in 1427. According to Safavid tradition, the great Mongol conqueror Timur met Khvājah 'Alī on a trip through Ardabīl. During this meeting Timur gave him a poisoned drink. The poison, however, was not able to do its work because the rhythmic chanting of *dhikr* of the dervishes present caused Khvājah 'Alī to engage in a spiritual dance so physically taxing that he sweated the poison out of his body. Timur, upon witnessing this wonder, became Khvājah 'Alī's disciple.[9] During the vicegerency of Khvājah 'Alī's successor, his son Ibrāhīm, the Safavid order spread more extensively in Anatolia. The structure of the order was such that below the *murshid-i kāmil* came the *khalīfat al-khulafā'* who oversaw the *pīra* or leaders of the order.[10] The quest for temporal and not just spiritual power among the Safavids began to manifest itself during the vicegerency of Ibrāhīm's son, Junayd. He aroused his disciples to engage in a holy war against the infidels, that is, the Christians of Circassia, Georgia and Shirvān.[11] Alarmed at this development, the Qarā Quyūnlū leader Jahānshāh expelled Junayd, who found refuge with Jahānshāh's enemy, the Āq Quyūnlū leader, Ūzūn Ḥasan. The quest for temporal power was further manifested in the marriage of

Junayd's son Ḥaydar to the daughter of Ūzūn Ḥasan, 'Ālamshāh Begum. Ḥaydar also engaged in battle against the Christians of Circassia and Dāghistān. It was now the turn of the Āq Quyūnlū to be alarmed. Their leader, Sultan Ya'qūb, sent an army to aid the ruler of Shirvān, Farrukhyasār, who was being attacked by Ḥaydar. At this battle, Ḥaydar was defeated and killed on 9 July 1488.[12] It was during Ḥaydar's time that the followers donned the scarlet headgear with gores symbolizing the Twelve Imams. This became a symbol of the Safavids and the supporters were called the *qizilbāsh*, or redheads.[13] The term generally applied to the Turcoman tribes of eastern Anatolia, northern Syria and the Armenian highlands, but also referred to those non-Turcoman tribes that supported the Safavid cause.[14]

Ḥaydar's place was taken by his son, 'Alī, who adopted the title *pādishāh* (king) and was subsequently arrested by the anxious Sultan Ya'qūb.[15] As the Āq Quyūnlū disintegrated due to civil war, one of the claimants to the throne, Rustam, released 'Alī with the aim of enlisting his help. But after helping him to defeat his enemies, Rustam issued orders for 'Alī to be rearrested.[16] 'Alī attempted to escape to Ardabīl but he was intercepted by the Āq Quyūnlū forces and killed, but not before designating his son, Ismā'īl, as his successor.[17] Ismā'īl was pursued by the Āq Quyūnlū and spent nearly five years in hiding at Lāhījān, all this while keeping close contact with his *qizilbāsh* supporters.[18] In 1501, after battling the Āq Quyūnlū, Ismā'īl was crowned shah in Tabriz.[19] Here he announced that the official religion of the new Safavid state was to be Ithnā 'Asharī Shi'ism.[20] He conquered the rest of Iran within ten years.[21] It can be seen from the above account that the establishment of the Safavid state took place in three stages: the development of the order (*ṭarīqat*), the establishment of relations with political powers, and the founding of a state with a new Shi'i orientation.[22]

How can this narrative be restated in Khaldūnian terms? According to Ibn Khaldūn, only houses with the attribute of nobility (*sharaf*) were able to found a dynasty. In tribal-based societies with competing *'aṣabiyyah*s or group feelings, competition ensues until one group is victorious. The possibility of victory is determined by the degree of social cohesion or *'aṣabiyyah* of the group. Tribal groups had the strongest *'aṣabiyyah* as their ties were agnatic. Furthermore, agnatic ties were stronger in nomadic than in sedentarized tribal groups. Stronger *'aṣabiyyah* also implied physical and military strength. To the extent that such groups were bound by kinship ties, they functioned more effectively as mutual support groups. *'aṣabiyyah* was more effective if there was an overarching religion that functioned to pull the competing groups together, to subordinate the *'aṣabiyyah* of individual groups to the cause of a larger entity.

In the case of the Safavid shahs, they had all these characteristics. First, they were able to claim nobility by claiming descent from the seventh Imam, Mūsā al-Kāẓim. Among the works in which these claims are made are the poems of Shah Ismā'īl:

> My name is Shah Ismā'īl. I am God's mystery. I am leader of all these ghāzīs.

My mother is Fāṭima, my father is 'Alī; and I am the *pīr* of the Twelve Imāms.
I have recovered my father's blood from Yazīd. Be sure that I am of Ḥahdarian essence.
I am the living Khiḍr and Jesus, son of Mary. I am the Alexander of (my) contemporaries.
Look you, Yazīd, polytheist and the adept of the Accursed one, I am free from the Ka'ba of hypocrites.
In me is Prophethood (and) the mystery of Holiness. I follow the path of Muḥammad Muṣṭafā.
I have conquered the world at the point of (my) sword. I am the Qanbar of Murtaḍā 'Alī.
My sire is Ṣafī, my father Ḥaydar. Truly I am the Ja'afar of the audacious.
I am a Husaynid and have curses for Yazīd. I am Khatā'ī, a servant of the Shāh's.[23]

In this poem, Shah Ismā'īl, the founder of the Safavid state, claims descent from the Prophet Muḥammad, through his daughter Fāṭimah and cousin 'Alī. He asserts his moral pedigree by declaring to be free of the evil and hypocrisy of Yazīd, and a true follower of the way of his ancestors Muḥammad, 'Alī, Ḥusayn, Shaykh Ṣafī, and his father Ḥaydar. The Islamic character of the Safavid ideology was also conditioned by the Anatolian craftsmen warriors or *akhī*. These Anatolian fraternities of the fifteenth century created a culture of chivalry by promoting the prestige of the *sayyid*s by engaging in the veneration of 'Alī and his progeny, and by recounting the story of Ḥusayn at Karbala. It is from these circles that the *qizilbāsh* were recruited by the Safavids a century later.[24]

There has been much controversy surrounding these claims. Several scholars, both Iranian and Western, have insisted that the Safavid genealogy is a fabrication. Savory says that the Safavids falsified evidence of their origins.[25] Kasravi, Togan, Mazzaoui and Bello seem certain that the genealogy is fabricated.[26] I do not intend to take this discussion further, beyond saying that the Safavid claims cannot be dismissed so easily. More relevant to the topic of this study, however, is the fact that the strength of the Safavid propaganda does not lie in the truth of their genealogical claims but in the belief that the groups who shared in their group feeling had in their claims.

The Safavids also forged a religious orientation by claiming to be the "the shadows of God upon earth" as well as the representative of the Mahdī.[27] Strengthening these claims were dreams that Shaykh Ṣafī al-Dīn was said to have, recorded by numerous chroniclers over a period of 200 years. The earliest version of these was recorded by Ibn Bazzāz's hagiography of Shaykh Ṣafī, the *Ṣafvat al-Ṣafā*. It is related how Shaykh Ṣafī dreamt that one night he was on the dome of the congregational mosque of Ardabīl. When a sun rose to illuminate the land, he realized that sun was his own face. Recounting the dream to his mother, she interpreted it to mean that Ṣafī would in future become a great shaykh.[28] More than a century later, the Safavid historian Ibrāhīm Amīnī wrote the first official Safavid chronicle, which has Shaykh Ṣafī's mother give a different interpretation of her son's dream. She says that Ṣafī would become a person whose splendour of guidance would light up the world.[29]

The nature of this overarching ideology is given in Arjomand's *Shadow of God and the Hidden Imam*, in which he discusses how the Shi'i doctrine of the occultation of the Imam led to the development of millenarian extremist movements in Islamic history. The emergence of the Safavid movement and state is to be understood in this context.[30]

What of the groups that shared in the *'aṣabiyyah* of the Safavids? They were the pastoral nomadic *qizilbāsh* tribes or *ūymāq*. As noted by Savory, the great fighting spirit of the *qizilbāsh* was derived from their intense tribal loyalty (*ta'aṣṣub-i uymāqīyat* or *ta'aṣṣub-i qizilbāshīyat*).[31] The role of the tribes in the founding of the Safavid state was merely one episode among many in which tribes formed the main military force of the emergent dynasty. Commenting on Iran, Sha'bānī and Sarī'al-Qalam note that her political history is in fact the history of the rise and fall of tribal groups (*'ashāyir*) such as the Ghaznavids, Seljuks, Ilkhanids, Afshar, Zand and Qajar.[32] The characteristics of the tribes include kinship solidarity (*khvīshavandī*), a propensity to war, and survival through booty and pillage. The idea of personal security through attachment to the tribe has important social, cultural and political consequences.[33] The tribes were generally conscious of their own tribal structure and were not only familiar with their tribal (*īlī*) hierarchy but were fiercely loyal (*ta'aṣṣub*) to it.[34] If the tribe shared in the group feeling of another house, loyalty to the tribe meant loyalty to that house as well. The extent of loyalty of the *qizilbāsh* to Shah Ismā'īl can be gauged from the interesting case of cannibalism in early Safavid Iran. This is discussed in a study by Shahzad Bashir, who cites the earliest report of cannibalism from the *Tārīkh-i Shāh Ismā'īl va Shāh Ṭahmāsb-i Ṣafavī* of Amīr Maḥmūd Khvāndamīr, written about 1550. It relates the story of the desecration of the body of the Uzbek leader Shaybanī Khan near the city of Merv. Shaybanī Khan was killed in a battle with Shah Ismā'īl's *qizilbāsh* forces. His severed head was brought to the shah. Not satisfied, Shah Ismā'īl demanded to see Shaybanī Khan's whole body, after which he said: "whoever among our sincere soldiers [*qūrchiyān-i kathīr al-iklāṣ*] and special servants [*malāzimān kathīr al-ikhtiṣāṣ*] loves our imperial head [*sar-i navvāb-i humāyūn-i mā*] should partake of the flesh of this enemy".[35] Bashir notes that the subsequent feasting was an act of love for and loyalty to Shah Ismā'īl.[36]

Iran was ruled by the Safavid dynasty during the years 907–1134 AH/1501–1722 AD. The Safavid Sufi order upon which the dynasty was founded was established some 200 years before the state itself emerged. In the next section, the nature of the Safavid political economy is discussed, in order to assess how a state of nomadic tribal origins presided over a sedentary based system. Safavid Iran is an example of a tributary state in which there was a "non-hydraulic" genesis of its mode of production. This genesis was explained above in terms of Ibn Khaldūn's theory concerning tribal *'aṣabiyyah*, religious fervour and military superiority.

I now turn to the nature of Safavid Iran's tributary mode of production and what that implies for our understanding of the fall of the Safavid dynasty.

The Safavid economy and its modes of production

The Safavid empire was made up of two great societal types, nomadic (*al-'umrān al-badawī*) and sedentary society (*al-'umrān al-ḥaḍarī*). The main areas of surplus appropriation in sedentary society were agriculture, industry and trade. The ruling class consisted of the state and military bureaucracy, and the religious institution. The following account on the sources and recipients of surplus is largely based on the situation in the sixteenth and early seventeenth centuries.[37]

In the area of agriculture, land was generally owned by the state. Land tenure was based on the contract of *muzāra'ah*, a share of the crop being the rent.[38] All categories of land, state, *mulk*, *tuyūl/suyūrghāl* (benefice) and *vaqf* (religious endowment) lands were worked by peasants.[39] Tribal khans who were granted *tuyūl/suyūrghāl* land in return for their military services to the state[40] had the right to collect tax revenue from these lands.

The next source of revenue was the urban surplus obtained by means of taxes and duties imposed on craft industry and trade. In Safavid Iran craft guilds (*aṣnāf*, sing. *ṣinf*) were subject to various taxes, as well as to corvées, but the rations, pay and fringe benefits they received were substantial.[41] As far as trade was concerned, in Safavi Iran merchants were relatively free from state control. Apart from the shah and the sultan and their bureaucracies which collected the surplus, there was also the *'ulamā'* (religious clerics), some of whom formed part of the ruling class. The *'ulamā'* had sources of wealth and economic power such as *vaqf* land. The *ṣadr* administered the *arbāb-i 'amā'im* (religious institution) and *vaqf* property.[42] In addition to this, the Iranian Shi'i *'ulamā'* derived economic power by virtue of being the direct recipients of a tax called the *khums*, unlike their Sunni counterparts in the rest of the Muslim world. In addition to this, a poor tax, the *zakāt* was also paid directly to the *'ulamā'*. The *'ulamā'* were often critical of and antagonistic towards the state, this antagonism increasing as financial problems of the state emerged. The *'ulamā'* were not unified into a religious institution and were able to avoid being totally incorporated into the Safavid state. A distinction could also be made between the local Persian *'ulamā'* and the imported Arab *'ulamā'* who were patronized by the Safavid shahs.[43] Thus, the picture that we have of the Safavid political economy is that of a ruling elite consisting of civil, military and religious factions extracting surplus from the peasantry, craftsmen and merchants.

Nomadic society formed a crucial part of Safavid society. Between the twelfth and nineteenth centuries the various tribes constituted approximately one-quarter of the population of Iran. These tribes were divided into five major ethnic groups: Turcoman, Iranian, Kurdish, Arab and Baluch.[44] Of particular importance, as far as the rise of the Safavid state is concerned, were the Turcoman tribes. As early as the eleventh century the administrative, economic and social systems of Iran came under the influence of the Turcoman tribal institution. After the Safavid state was established with the aid of tribal military support, vast territories of Iran came under the administration of *uymāqs*. The *uymāq* in Safavid times referred to a concept of a tribe that was constituted by economic, administrative and military ties between groups that were not necessarily related by ties of kinship, although succession to the rule of the *uymāq* was based on kinship. Tribal chieftains or khans controlled the various *uymāqs* in Iran which oversaw both rural and urban production.[45] The *uymāq* was the means by which the tribal population became integrated with sedentary society and participated in the administration of the state.

In Ibn Khaldūn's understanding of society, there were two main types, distinguished in terms of their social structure and ways of making a living (*naḥlat min al-ma'āsh*).[46] Ibn Khaldūn, however, did not conceptualize or characterize these societal types in terms of the relations between their social, economic and political aspects in the way that, for example, Marx did with the concept of modes of production. How can the Safavid political economy be characterized in terms of modes of production?

As discussed in Chapter 6, the mode of production consists of two basic elements: the relations of production and the forces of production. Forces of production refers to the means of production – that is, the non-human inputs such as raw materials, machines and tools used in the process of production. It also refers to the labour process or the manner in which work is organized. This involves the transformation of the raw natural material into products by means of the tools, skills, organization and knowledge of the worker. Relations of production refers to the mode of appropriation of the economic surplus and the economic ownership and control of the forces of production that correspond to that mode of appropriation of the economic surplus. Every mode of production has a specific form of the forces of production and relations of production. Thus, in order to identify a particular mode of production it is necessary to specify both the forces and relations of production.

What was the dominant mode of production in the sedentary society of Safavid Iran? Hitherto, works on Safavid society have tended to describe its economic system in terms of unitary modes of production. Attempts have been made to characterize the economic system in terms of the feudal mode of production.[47] Others have characterized the system in terms of the Asiatic mode of production.[48] The various characterizations of Safavid Iran as feudal or Asiatic tend to stretch the meaning of the terms Asiatic and feudal too far and also amount to obscuring the nature of the relations and forces of production that operated there. Foran's article on the modes of production in seventeenth century Iran is a significant improvement on previous works, in that he views Safavid society as having been made up of three distinct modes of production. The three discussed by Foran are the pastoral nomadic, peasant crop-sharing, and petty commodity modes of production.[49]

Following Amin and Wolf,[50] my approach will be to view various pre-capitalist systems that are based on political coercion in the relations of production as tributary modes of production. Thus, the feudal and Asiatic systems would be examples of tributary modes of production, the former being less centralized than the latter. Clearly, the Safavid mode of production was a tributary one. But was it a tributary mode of production of the feudal, Asiatic or some other variety?

Some scholars have taken the view that it is the Asiatic mode of production that aptly characterizes Safavid society. The basic characteristics of the Asiatic mode of production have been discussed in Chapter 6 and will not be repeated here. Abrahamian, in his discussion of the Asiatic mode of production in Qajar Iran, refers to two separate explanations for the power of the Asiatic state in the writings of Marx and Engels. According to the first explanation, "the public works were the business of the central government". The strength of the state, therefore, is derived from of its having a large bureaucracy to administer public works. According to the second explanation, "the whole empire, not counting the few larger towns, was divided into villages, which possessed a completely separate organization and formed a little world in themselves".[51] In this case, the state is strong by virtue of the existence of a weak and fragmented society. The first explanation is a theory of bureaucratic despotism and the second a theory of fragmented society.[52] Abrahamian opts for the theory of fragmented society as the key to understanding oriental despotism in Iran. Although his work is on Qajar Iran, it would be reasonable to assume, as suggested by Foran, that he would have applied the theory of the Asiatic mode of production to Safavid Iran as well, as capitalism was more extensive in nineteenth century Iran than in earlier times.[53] For Abrahamian, it was Qajar Iran's "complicated mosaic", its diversity in terms of religious, sectarian, tribal, linguistic and ecological terms, that created communal rivalry and a fragmented state.[54]

Abrahamian's work has internal contradictions. While he claims that the Qajar state was despotic due to its high level of diversity, he also states that the Qajars were despots "without the instruments of despotism", were not effective in enforcing their power, and were often forced to retreat in the face of dangerous opposition.[55] The logic of the theory of fragmentation is that the diversity was such that it precluded the transformation of socio-economic interests into collective behaviour.[56] Yet, Abrahamian cites an example of how a Qajar shah's appointment of a provincial governor to Kashan proved to be so unpopular with the city notables there that he was forced to recall the appointee.[57] Savory makes an interesting point about the nature of Safavid rule. Noting that European observers were unanimous in asserting the absolute nature of power of the Safavid shahs, Savory draws attention to the relatively high degree of individual freedom and personal security in Safavid Iran.[58] The arbitrary use of despotic power was rarely wielded against the lower classes. It was more often directed against court officials, members of the nobility, or other ranks within the Safavid administrative system.[59]

At any rate, the theory of fragmented society does not seem to be applicable to the case of Safavid Iran. In fact, as we shall see later, it was precisely the rulers' use of diversity that served to make the administration ineffective and the military weak. The theory of bureaucratic despotism is also to be rejected. The centralized despotic Safavid state did not derive its power from the administration of large-scale public irrigation works. Although irrigation was crucial to Iranian agriculture because of the semi-arid nature of the land, and the regulation of water distribution was an important concern of the government, the subterraneous irrigation channels called *qanāt* were managed by local officials.[60] What, then, was the basis of the power of this state? It was derived from the control by the state, at least in the sixteenth and seventeenth centuries, of the superior military capability provided by pastoral nomads. Invading nomads aided in the establishment of a centralized state. As in the case of the Ottoman Empire, the tribute paid by tribal members to the tribal chieftain was the forerunner of the Asiatic tax/rent.[61] Ibn Khaldūn's theory provides the basis for the despotic nature of the Safavid Asiatic state.[62] This was a tributary mode of production in which state power derived not from the control of large-scale irrigation works but rather from tribal support.

Another trait of the Asiatic mode of production, also discussed in Chapter 6 in connection with the Ottoman Empire, is the direct extraction of surplus from the dominated classes where the state is landlord and sovereign, and taxes and rent coincide.[63] If we understand the Asiatic mode of production to be one in which the state, as the legal owner of landed and manufacturing property, appropriates the economic surplus directly from the populace, then it will be clear that the Safavid economic system cannot be characterized by "Asiatic" forms of surplus appropriation alone. In Safavid Iran there was the distinction between *divānī* (state) and *khāṣṣah* (imperial estate) land.[64] It was revenue from the latter that accrued directly to the ruler and his household.[65] However, not all revenues went directly to the ruler or the state. Other forms of surplus appropriation were to be found in the tributary mode of production in Safavid Iran. Benefices (*tuyūl* and *suyūrghāl*) were also granted, in which cases revenues accrued to the holders of such benefices. In fact, superficial similarities between certain Safavid institutions and those found in European feudalism may explain why some glossed over the differences and chose to designate the Safavid system as feudal. This was true of Marxist scholarship on Iran.[66]

Nomani, defining feudalism essentially as a mode of production in which there is an "exploitative relation between the landlords and the dependent peasants, based on the extraction of surplus product by means of three types of rent: labor, kind or money", refers to the enserfment of Iranian communes since the Sassanian period and traces the development of what he calls feudal servile obligation from then until 1600 AD.[67] He cites as evidence the development of the *iqtā'* (benefice), along with the increase in large holdings and the greater dependence of peasants on the lords.[68] Shaugannik is more critical of the tendency to read feudalism into the Iranian pre-capitalist mode of production without qualification. He does see features of the Asiatic mode of production in pre-capitalist Iran, such as scattered and self-sufficient villages, and the ownership of the means of production in communal or state hands.[69] Furthermore, he does not equate the *iqtā'* with any European feudal institution, recognizing that it inhibits the emergence of an independent feudal class.[70] However, he also says that it would be wrong to contrast the Iranian system with feudalism in too stark terms when it is considered that there was private property in land (*mulk*) and there was such a thing as personal *iqtā'*.[71] He also notes that in Safavid times, the *iqtā'* gave way to the *tuyūl* and *suyūrghāl* systems that were closer to their feudal counterparts.[72] Shaugannik opts to characterize the "medieval" Iranian society in terms of a variant of feudalism that is quite different from the European variety. Features of the Iranian economy such as the existence of three types of ownership – tribal, communal/state and estate – and subsistence level production, were not characteristic of European feudalism.[73]

Lambton's remark on the *iqtā'* system is relevant and also applies to the *tuyūl* and *suyūrghāl* institutions:

> The *iqtā'* system is sometimes spoken of as feudalism, but the circumstances in which the *iqtā'* system became established and the causes which gave rise to it were different from those which prevailed in Western Europe when feudalism developed. The results were dissimilar, and it is misleading to talk of feudalism in the lands of the Eastern Caliphate, including Persia, unless it is first made clear that Islamic feudalism does not correspond to any of the various types of feudalism found in Western Europe. The element of mutual obligation inherent in the nexus of feudal tenure in Western Europe is notably absent.[74]

Iqtā' means a form of administrative or military grant.[75] It was an institution that became regularized during the period of the Seljuk Empire (1087–1157).[76] In Safavid Iran, two kinds of benefices were widely granted, the *tuyūl* and *suyūrghāl*, and the *iqtā'* was replaced by the *tuyūl* and *suyūrghāl*. *Tuyūl* referred to grants of land that were not hereditary and were made mostly in outlying areas, resembling provincial governments. In return, the *tuyūldār* (*tuyūl* holder) provided a military contingent for the shah in times of need. He was also entrusted with the administration of the land.[77] The term *tuyūl* was also used to designate land assigned in lieu of salary.[78] Other uses of the term referred to grants of immunity of property and grants of *khāṣṣah* (imperial estate) land to the army.[79] The term *suyūrghāl* was used mainly to denote hereditary or life grants of *khāṣṣah* and *vaqf* land, and usufructory property, and often included a grant of immunity.[80]

There are superficial similarities between the institutions of the *tuyūl/suyūrghāl* and the fief. These include the grant of land in return for military service, the grant of land in lieu of salary, the grant of immunities, the high status of the military, and the existence of an exploited peasantry.[81] However, there is a fundamental difference between the fief on the one hand and the Safavid institutions on the other. The granting of a fief was based on a contract of fealty that established a solidary, fraternal relationship between lord and vassal involving reciprocal obligations of loyalty. In contrast, the granting of *tuyūl/suyūrghāl* generally did not involve a contract of personal fealty carrying reciprocal obligations of loyalty. Rather they were granted mainly out of fiscal considerations and existed in the general context of a despotic state. In the feudal mode of production as it existed in Europe, rule at the apex of the system was relatively fragile and weak. Power was held mainly by local lords. In Safavid Iran, however, rule at the apex of the system was strong. In European feudalism, land was owned by local lords, but it was the property of the state in the case of Safavid Iran. It would, therefore, not be accurate to characterize the Safavid system in terms of the feudal mode of production.

To my mind, the differences between the *tuyūl/suyūrghāl* institutions on the one hand and the European fief on the other warrant our referring to the Safavid political economy in terms of a separate mode of production that is neither feudal nor Asiatic. The prebendal feudal mode of production, as I have named it, is one possibility.

The prebendal feudal mode of production can be defined as one based on the granting of benefices, which is what *tuyūl/suyūrghāl* are. Unlike the European feudal system, the prebendal feudal mode of production was more centralized as far as the ownership of land by the state was concerned. Furthermore, the European fief differed from the Safavid prebend in many ways. For example, there was no contract of fealty between the shah and the holder of the *tuyūl/suyūrghāl*. The relationship was mainly a fiscal one. We discussed in Chapter 6 that the differences between European feudalism and the Ottoman system were not minor, leading Weber to characterize the Ottoman system as belonging to the system of prebendal feudalism.[82] The relations of production in prebendal feudalism are sufficiently different from those of "occidental" feudalism to warrant our referring to the former as a distinct mode of production. The prebendal feudal mode of production existed in Safavid Iran as well and was based on the granting of benefices (*tuyūl/suyūrghāl*) in return for military and administrative services.

Another system, it has been suggested, that characterizes the agricultural sector of Safavid Iran is the peasant crop-sharing mode of production. This mode of production was advanced by Foran as an alternative to feudalism. According to Foran, the economic surplus of the agrarian sector was appropriated in the form of a share of the crop, regardless of what the dominant class was – private landlords, the shah or *tuyūl* holders. While this is an interesting possibility there are possible objections to it. Share-cropping was also found in England and France in feudal times, where it was known as "farming to halves" and "*metayage*" respectively.[83] Reducing a mode of production to the mode of surplus appropriation, for example, crop-sharing, could result in our designating European feudalism as a crop-sharing mode of production. More importantly, in different systems where crop-sharing is present the relations of production and ideological conditions may be so varied as to warrant our distinguishing between different modes of production, that is, among systems that involve crop-sharing.

The petty commodity mode of production

The petty commodity mode of production made up primarily the urban sector. In this mode of production, the producers were artisans who not only owned their means of production but also performed the labour and produced for the market. In other words, it was characterized by the unity of labour and capital.[84] Petty commodity production was found in the agricultural as well as urban sectors in Safavid Iran. In the rural sector, however, petty commodity production did not encompass the whole of society and was subordinate to the prebendal feudal mode of production. It reached a higher level of development in the towns in the form of the royal workshops, and craft guilds (*aṣnāf*, sing. *ṣinf*). The dominant classes included the shah, the state *'ulamā'*, with the merchants, bazaar *'ulamā'* and artisans making up the intermediate classes. The day labourers constituted the dominated class.[85]

The pastoral nomadic mode of production

Any discussion on the Safavid modes of production cannot ignore the presence of nomadic tribes. The pastoral mode of production was the sole mode of production to be found in nomadic society (*al-'umrān al-badawī*). The term nomad (*badū*) pertains to temporary habitation or the absence of permanent habitation. The term pastoral refers to domesticated animals as the principal means of production.[86] Through these animals the basic needs of the pastoralists – food (butter, cheese, meat, yoghurt), drink (milk), clothing (hides, wool), fuel (dung) and means of transportation (camel, donkey, horses, oxen) – are procured.[87] As in the Ottoman case, animals, tools and dwelling items were owned on an individual basis while grazing land was the communal property of the tribe.[88] Individually owned property did move from owner to owner, this movement taking place within the system of kinship (for example, marriage and inheritance) rather than market relations.[89] The dominated class consisted of the rest of the tribespeople, who owned on an individual basis their animals, tools and dwelling items. Those who had insufficient animals with which to subsist constituted the underclass of the pastoral nomadic mode of production and sold their labour to those higher up in the system.[90]

The Turcoman tribes of Anatolia are a pastoral nomadic people that are of direct concern to us because it was the various Turcoman tribes that played a significant role in the founding, development and fall of the Safavid Empire. Of the various types of pastoral nomadism, only one is found among the Turcoman tribes. These were multi-animal pastoralists who bred sheep, goats, cattle and camels. But the most important animal among the Turcomans was the horse.[91] This is due to the fact that very often the means of subsistence were procured through conquest or raids, for which horses were indispensable.

It is necessary to mention at this point that what is meant by tribe is inexact. Tapper has noted that there is little consensus among scholars regarding the levels that the term tribe or confederation refers to. Adding to the confusion are the indigenous terms such as *īl*, *'ashīrah*, *qabīlah*, *ṭā'ifah*, *tīrah*, *uymāq* and *ulūs*. These terms have multiple meanings, are often used interchangeably and lack precision with regard to the levels or segments they refer to.[92]

Approaches to the decline of the Safavid state and the prebendal feudal mode of production: a Khaldūnian perspective

Most of the Safavid rulers after Shah 'Abbās I were weak and ineffective. 'Abbās II (1642–66) was an exception. Two of the shahs, Sulaymān and Sultan Ḥusayn, were disinterested in state affairs and proved to be the weakest of the Safavid shahs, ruling from 1666 to 1722. It was during this period of ineffectual rule that the *mujtahids* asserted their independence from the shah and claimed themselves to be the only legitimate representatives of the Imam and, therefore, the only source of legitimate authority.[93] From here on the country became more unstable due to both internal and external factors.

Externally, there were frequent raids conducted on the frontiers by the Baluchis, Afghans and Arabs. In fact, when the Baluchis raided Kerman, Shah Sultan Ḥusayn turned to a visiting Georgian prince, Giorgi XI, for help. He appointed Giorgi Governor of Kerman in 1699, who successfully repelled the invaders.[94] Ten years later, the Ghilzay Afghans under Mir Vays killed Giorgi and took Kandahar from the Safavids. In 1722 Mir Vays' son Maḥmūd besieged Isfahan until Shah Sultan Ḥusayn abdicated, and crowned himself Shah of Persia. When Ashraf succeeded Maḥmūd in 1725, the Afghans controlled the main urban centres of central and southern Iran. The Afghans' further expansion was checked by the Safavid military leader Nādir Khan, who was actually a member of the Afshar tribe, one of the tribes that made up the *qizilbāsh*. Allying himself with Ṭahmāsp II, he fought and drove out the Afghans from Iran by 1730 and placed Ṭahmāsp II on the throne. He then deposed Ṭahmāsp II, ruled as regent under the infant Shah 'Abbās III, and finally had himself crowned as Nādir Shah, the first ruler of the Afshar dynasty.[95] The place of the Afshar dynasty was taken by the Zand, who initially ruled under the name of Safavid Ismā'īl III. After the death of Ismā'īl III in 1773, fighting between the Zand in the south and the Qajars in the north ensued. The Qajar leader, Āqā Muḥammad Khan, succeeded in disposing of the Zand, established Tehran as the new capital and was crowned Shah in the spring of 1796.[96]

A few perspectives have emerged concerning the causes of the decline of the Safavids. The standard reference is Minorsky's discussion on the causes of decline, which he lists as:

(a) The disappearance of the theocratic basis of the state that was established by Shah Ismā'īl I, with no substitute ideology taking its place.
(b) Opposition within the Persian military establishment.
(c) Upset of the equilibrium between *mamālik* and *khāṣṣah* land.
(d) The irresponsible role of the harem, Queen Mother and eunuchs who formed something of a "shadow government".
(e) The ineptitude of rulers who were brought up in the confines of the harem and were consequently ignorant of the outside world.[97]

The principal Safavid period scholars that followed, Lockhart and Savory, did not depart from this assessment, with Lockhart stressing the personal failing of the shahs and Savory concentrating on the structural factors listed by Minorsky.[98] Lockhart's views have been said to be Eurocentric: for example, he gives much attention to the role of factors from European commercial and diplomatic history in his account of the fall of the Safavids.[99] He describes with adulation Peter the Great's invasion of Iran:

> An excellent trait in Peter's character was his wish to champion the cause of the Christian minorities in Persia, of whose trials and tribulations he had doubtless heard much from Alexander Archilovich and other Georgians, as well as from Armenians; it is probable that this desire did not take definite shape until early in the eighteenth century.[100]

Foran, in his valuable study, follows up on the discussion of the role of structural factors by drawing attention to the economic problems confronted by the late Safavid state, looking at the balance of trade deficit, fiscal crisis, inflation, tax exploitation and corruption.[101] The most recent and comprehensive study is by Matthee, who makes a strong case by bringing in several factors that contributed to the decline of the Safavid state. Arguing that an empire such as the Safavids' could only be held together through negotiated arrangement of mutual benefit with the various vested interest groups, such as tribal chieftains and the *'ulamā'*, the factors that worked against this model are discussed. Matthee concludes that in the seventeenth century, leadership at all levels – political, military and administrative – was inadequate and failed to solve pressing economic problems. The decline is blamed on leadership.[102]

The accounts of the decline and fall of the Safavid state referred to above have uncovered important facts and provided strong arguments to explain the reasons as to why the light of the Safavids was eventually extinguished. But, for the most part, these studies enumerate factors rather than present a theoretical framework for the analysis of the fall. I am not citing that as a weakness of the above studies. However, it is my intention to examine whether a Khaldūnian theoretical framework can add anything to the account of the fall of the Safavids.

When Minorsky cited the lack of a substituting ideology for the theocratic ideas established by Shah Ismā'īl, that begged the question of what the material base of that ideology could have been. The Khaldūnian question here is: what solidary group was available that could have been the recipient of this ideology, which could have taken up the role of the group with the strongest *'aṣabiyyah* after decades of alienation of the *qizilbāsh*, the carriers of the former ideology? There must also be a substitute group to be the carrier of the substitute ideology. The logic of the system was that either another group from the same lineage with a weakened *'aṣabiyyah* and ideology would rule, or a new group from a different lineage would establish a new dynasty. In either case, it is not just a matter of the historical convergence of external and internal factors that leads to decline, as implied in the above accounts. The manner in which the Safavid state emerged set in place a logic of decline. The very fact of tribal support for the formative state and their sedentarization via the prebendal feudal mode of production set in motion a process by which the tribesmen become less effective as a fighting force and are perceived as a threat to the ruling elite that they helped bring to power.

There are then attempts by the ruling house to marginalize them. The alienation of the tribesmen from the ruling house constitutes what Ibn Khaldūn refers to as the loss of *'aṣabiyyah*. An alternative ideology "proposed" by Minorsky would not prevent or slow down the decline were there no group that shared in the *'aṣabiyyah* of the ruling house, and which would provide military support. Indeed, there was a new *'aṣabiyyah* in the Qajar family, which no longer shared in the *'aṣabiyyah* of the Safavids but created their own dynasty. In other words, there was an alternative ideology but it resided in alternative family that contributed to bringing down the Safavids.

At the outset of the chapter, I discussed Ibn Khaldūn in connection with the support of the tributary Safavid state by tribal military power. Once the Safavid Empire was established, however, there were attempts to absorb the supporting tribes into the sedentary life of the empire, or in Khaldūnian terms, to dispense with *'aṣabiyyah*. The very forces behind state formation eventually become a source of instability for the new state. The stability of the new state rested on its ability to destroy its own nomadic foundations. The dominant mode in sedentary society in the Safavid Empire was the prebendal feudal mode of production, not the petty commodity mode of production, because the majority of the population lived outside the towns.[103] But it was the petty commodity mode of production that produced the goods coveted by the pastoral nomads. Once they conquered a state and founded a new dynasty, however, they became absorbed into the prebendal feudal mode of production. In the event of the establishment of a dynasty through tribal support there arose the problem of providing adequate remuneration to tribal elites and their armies, who by now aspired towards a sedentary and luxurious life. The granting of benefices (*tuyūl, suyūrghāl*) to tribal chieftains achieved the aim of such remuneration. But in the eyes of the ruler, the chieftains of the dominant tribes upon whose power the dynasties rode posed a threat to the rulers once the dynasty was founded. The rulers marginalized them by instruments that were features of the prebendal feudal mode of production. This marginalization and subsequent alienation of the tribesmen constituted in Khaldūnian terms the erosion of *'aṣabiyyah* or group feeling that the *qizilbāsh* shared with the Safavid rulers.

When the Safavid Empire was established, benefices were granted to tribal chieftains. In Iran, benefices known as *tuyūl* were granted to *qizilbāsh* tribal chieftains.

The *tuyūl* were non-hereditary, unlike the *suyūrghāl*.[104] As Fragner notes, the "reason for avoiding *suyūrghāl* grants in such cases was the intention to restrict, at least formally, the autonomy of the high amirs in the provinces".[105] Indeed, this is a case of the ruler attempting to dispense with *'aṣabiyyah* for fear that the tribesmen, with whose help he came to power, were potential usurpers. Their fears were well founded, as there were many cases of tribal chieftains making efforts to consolidate their positions as governors and landowners through, for example, intermarriage. The marriages of Muḥammad Ḥassan Khan Qajar illustrate this very well. Some of his marriages were to non-Qajar women; marrying outside of the tribe was a way of reinforcing his economic and political position beyond the tribe and strengthened his claim to the throne.[106]

Attempts to marginalize the *qizilbāsh* by Safavid rulers began as early as the period of Ismā'īl I. It was during his reign that the trend of reducing the influence of the *qizilbāsh* was started. From 1508 onwards Shah Ismā'īl did not appoint a *qizilbāsh* chief to the position of the *vakīl*, the vicegerent of the shah. Another tactic resorted to was replacing the tribal district chiefs in order to reduce their influence. For example, Ismā'īl appointed an Ustājlū, Muḥammad Beg, to the office of the *amīr al-umarā'* or commander-in-chief and also put him in charge of the tribal district of a Shāmlū, Ḥusayn Beg. An Ustājlu *amīr al-umarā'* would not be able to gain the same level of support from Shāmlū tribesmen as a Shāmlū *amīr al-umarā'* would.[107]

The attempt to control the *qizilbāsh* was not successful, and there was a period in which the *qizilbāsh* actually ruled Iran (1524–33).[108] However, Shah 'Abbās (1588–1629) continued with attempts to reduce the influence of the *qizilbāsh*. Reducing the influence of the *qizilbāsh* was necessary for rulers who did not want their power to be usurped, but at the same time they were dependent on the *qizilbāsh* for their military services. It was necessary to lessen this dependency. The solution that Shah 'Abbās came up with was the creation of the *ghulām* (slaves of the royal household) regiment. The *ghulām* were former prisoners from campaigns that the shahs conducted in Georgia and Armenia. Many were converted to Islam and trained to serve as cavalrymen in the standing army.[109] In order to solve the problem of paying the *ghulām*, Shah 'Abbās converted *mamālik* land, from which *tuyūl* were granted to the *qizilbāsh* chiefs, to *khāṣṣah* or crown provinces and appointed the *ghulām* as their administrators.[110] The intention was to reduce the power and influence of the *qizilbāsh* but the policy was not successful. The *ghulām* were militarily weak and the policy of appointing them as administrators of converted lands led to the weakening of the state militarily. In times of crisis, the *qizilbāsh* were reappointed to their former positions, as they were better able to defend the crown lands.[111] Shah 'Abbās also applied the tactic of transferring groups of *qizilbāsh* of one tribe to *ulkā* or tribal districts held by another tribe, with the hope of weakening tribal bonds.[112] In addition, Shah 'Abbās appointed Georgians, Armenians and Circassians, that is, non-Muslims, to the highest offices of the state.[113] In the long run the shahs' policy of marginalizing the *qizilbāsh* weakened the state militarily and economically but did not actually succeed in marginalizing the *qizilbāsh*. Hurewitz notes that at the end of 'Abbās' reign, five out of six provincial governors were still *qizilbāsh* chiefs.[114]

The assignment of benefices to tribal chieftains was strategic in that it paid them and at the same time contributed to the erosion of their *'aṣabiyyah*. In fact, there were signs of decline in *'aṣabiyyah* in Safavid Iran, as indicated by the difficulty tribal chieftains had raising sufficient troops.[115] This account can be restated at a theoretical level in terms of the relationship between the pastoral nomadic and prebendal feudal modes of production. It is within the context of the prebendal feudal mode of production, therefore, that the *'aṣabiyyah* of the ruling tribes experiences a decline.

The effect on *'aṣabiyyah* of incorporation into the state was exacerbated by another tactic described by Ibn Khaldūn and resorted to by the Safavid rulers, as discussed above. As stated before, according to Ibn Khaldūn, once a dynasty is established with the aid of tribal military power, the ruler attempts to dispense with the support of that group. The form that this took in Safavid Iran differs from that described by Ibn Khaldūn. In Ibn Khaldūn, the ruler attempts to blunt the aspirations of the people who shared in his *'aṣabiyyah* by relying on clients and followers who were nurtured in the shadow of that *'aṣabiyyah*, or on tribal groups of a different descent who have become his clients.[116] In Safavid Iran, however, the rulers attempted to dispense with tribal military support altogether. Shah 'Abbās tried to reduce the power of the *qizilbāsh* elite by creating a *ghulām* regiment.[117]

According to the Khaldūnian model, once a house declines, another house from among the same descent may replace it, riding on the *'aṣabiyyah* of the larger descent group. The tribe that represents the group with the superior group feeling may attain kingship either by acquiring actual and direct control of the state or providing assistance to the ruling dynasty. In the Safavid case, it was the former that happened. As the state declined militarily and economically, it gave way to rule by the same ruling tribes that had supported its rise, that is the Afshars, Zand and Qajars. Kingship was transferred from one branch, or one tribe (*īl*), of the confederation of *qizilbāsh* tribes to another and continued within that particular *ummah* until the force of the *'aṣabiyyah* of that nation was completely eroded, or until the various groups making up that nation no longer existed.[118]

The last of the *qizilbāsh* tribes that were able to establish superiority over other *qizilbāsh* tribes and then take the place of the ruling Safavid dynasty was the Qajar. The military force of the Qajars was drawn from their tribal population. The shahs would ask the tribal leaders to mobilize their own men for assembly in the spring. The army would usually be disbanded as winter approached.[119]

Nevertheless, we must assume that the *'aṣabiyyah* of the Qajar was relatively weak compared to that of the Safavids during their peak. This is indicated by the early Qajar rulers' attempts to create a sense of legitimacy of their rule and authority. Unlike the Safavids, the Qajars could not claim descent from the Hidden Imam. They did, however, utilize many of the forms of address used by the Safavid shahs to refer to their sacred origins. For example, they arrogated to themselves the title of Shadow of God Upon Earth.[120] It is significant that they had to resort to borrowing forms of address from the Safavids rather than create their own.

The Safavid Empire was established as a result of the migration of nomadic peoples. The rulers attempted to defuse the power of tribal groups once they (the rulers) were firmly established in power. Nevertheless, for centuries up until the twentieth, tribal military power was essential in bringing dynasties to power. What accounts for the prevalence of tribal power in Iran? One reason has to do with geography. In the case of Iran, the topography is such that centralization was more difficult than in other regions, such as the Ottoman Empire. The mountainous terrain made it much more difficult to control the tribes. Another reason is the location of the various tribal groups. In Iran the population of the tribes (estimated at half of the total Iranian population at the beginning of the nineteenth century)[121] occupied large geographical areas of the empire.[122] Third, in Iran the *tuyūldār* consisted of a great number of tribal khans (chiefs): that is, they were drawn by and large from the tribal population. Another reason is that apart from the fact that there were a larger number of independent and armed nomadic tribes in Iran, the Iranian states were very dependent on the tribes for their military force.[123] The proximity of tribal groups to the central state in Iran, coupled with the fact that they were superior warriors, made them a constant threat to the state.

Conclusion

An immediate concern of this chapter has been to make an argument for the cogency of the Khaldūnian theory of state formation in debates surrounding the nature of the Safavid political economy or mode of production. I have indicated an avenue for the integration of a modes of production framework into Ibn Khaldūn's theory of state formation, the field of application being Iranian history. While the economic system of Safavid Iran has been couched in terms of Marxist concepts, their dynamics have been described in terms of Ibn Khaldūn's theory of state formation. As mentioned at the outset, the Safavid political economy can be characterized in terms of the prebendal feudal mode of production. Ibn Khaldūn's work provides a theoretical framework with which to understand the rise and dynamics of the Safavid Empire.

Ibn Khaldūn said that the goal of nomadic society was sedentary society: an organized collectivity of nomads aspire to attain the lifestyle of sedentary people. The interaction between the two types is continuous, involving the conquest of the latter by the former, who then are gradually absorbed into the sedentary culture and institutions. Restated in terms of the modes of production framework, the establishment of a new dynasty on the basis of tribal military support is the political dimension of the interaction between the pastoral nomadic on the one hand and the prebendal feudal and petty commodity modes of production on the other. In order for the Khaldūnian cycle to perpetuate, the nomads of the new dynasty, now settled in towns, hamlets and villages, have to be absorbed into the prebendal feudal mode of production, lose their nomadic characteristics and fighting spirit, and undergo the erosion of their *'aṣabiyyah*: that is, their sense of solidarity with the ruling elite that they helped bring to power. It is only when this happens that the cycle can continue, with the ruling dynasty giving way to fresh new supplies of pre-sedentary nomads enviously eyeing the spoils of the towns. A prerequisite for this to happen is that the earlier generation of nomads, now sedentarized, must undergo change until they no longer constitute a force to be feared by the pre-sedentary nomads. The mechanisms by which this takes place can be understood by knowing how pastoral nomads are absorbed into sedentary society via the offices provided in the prebendal feudal mode of production and the commodities made available by the petty commodity mode of production. I end this chapter with a quotation from Matthee on the relevance of Ibn Khaldūn to Iranian history:

> The trajectory of the Safavid state in some ways exemplifies Ibn Khaldūn's famous paradigm about the flux and reflux of premodern Middle Eastern states.

> It does so better than the Ottoman Empire in the shortness of its life span and the abruptness of its collapse, and more closely than the Mughal state in the religious inspiration that fueled its rise and the sloth that hastened its fall – from the charismatic warrior Shah Isma'il I to the feeble, palace-bound Shah Sultan Husayn, from the Qizilbāsh fighters who helped the former conquer a land and turn it into a state in the name of a millenarian faith, to a sedentary court elite which, preferring the cushions of the palace to the rigors of the saddle, gave up on war and exposed the country to attack by a new cohort of vigorous tribesmen. The decline and fall of the Safavids may be seen as the natural fate of a regime precariously ruling over hardscrabble lands, one case in a long sequence stretching from the Archaemenids to the Qajars. A feeble entity that, like all premodern states, hardly inspired any inherent loyalty and that faced greater obstacles to control than most, the Safavid state was held together as much by inertia as by design. Its longevity thus is more remarkable than its sudden demise is puzzling, and only the association of the Safavid polity with Twelver Shi'ism, the overlapping religious and territorial boundaries it produced, and its (questionable) status as the first Iranian nation-state, sets it apart from all other Iran's dynastic regimes until the twentieth century.[124]

Matthee's endorsement of the Khaldūnian model is encouraging, but also somewhat puzzling in that he does not seem to read Safavid history in *Persia in Crisis* from a Khaldūnian vantage point. A Khaldūnian reading would have suggested that the Safavid decline and eclipse was in the nature of things and inevitable, and that their defeat "at the hand of a rag-tag bunch of tribesmen"[125] was not something surprising.

8 A Khaldūnian perspective on modern Arab states

Saudi Arabia and Syria

One of the most challenging aspects of the development of Khaldūnian sociology lies in the area of application to the modern state. Here there is the realization that not only does the use of Ibn Khaldūn extend beyond claiming that he is a precursor of the modern social sciences or that his works are applicable to the study of the rise and fall of pre-modern states, but that his framework also provides an alternative to contemporary modern state theories.

Here it is important to note that although various perspectives on the modern state have been discussed with reference to Arab states, there have been hardly any attempts to bring Ibn Khaldūn into these discussions. The more established theories and concepts that have been used to discuss the Arab state include the following:[1]

1 The constitutional law school, with its stress on the "moral personality" of the state, sovereignty and public interest.
2 The Gramscian view of the hegemony of the state, with its emphasis on the ideological domination of the state rather than coercion.
3 The theory of the relative autonomy of the state, with its stress on the mediating role of the state between the landowning class, indigenous capital and metropolitan capital.
4 The derivation theory of the state, based on the classical Marxist view of the state as the executive that manages the affairs of the bourgeoisie.
5 The theory of the bureaucratic-authoritarian state, which links economic strategies adopted by the state with changing political coalitions such as populism, corporatism and bureaucratic-authoritarianism.

In this chapter I provide a critical assessment of the relevance of Ibn Khaldūn to the study of the modern state. I consider the application of Ibn Khaldūn to two cases of state formation and decline in the modern world: those of Saudi Arabia and Syria. This topic has become all the more relevant in view of the phenomenon of the "Arab Spring", no doubt an unfinished project that has yielded much data for those interested in scenario development and analysis.

The rise of the Wahhabi state

While the Ottoman Empire exerted authority over the Hijaz and eastern Arabia, it was not able to do so in the interior of the Arabian peninsula, in the region known as Najd. As a result, the towns and oases there were ruled by their own amirs and the tribal population remained independent and autonomous.[2] The key actors in the eventual rise of the Saudi state, Muḥammad ibn Sa'ūd and Muḥammad ibn 'Abd al-Wahhāb (1703–92), formed an alliance that has endured to this day.

The Āl Sa'ūd, a sedentary clan of the Banū Wā'il, founded the small settlement of Dir'iyyah. Muḥammad ibn Sa'ūd (d. 1765) himself was a chieftain, landowner and broker. Because of an apparent lack of tribal origins and the absence of any great economic surplus, the Āl Sa'ūd's authority was limited to Dir'iyyah. Their role in the Arabian peninsula, however, was to expand greatly as a result of the alliance between the Āl Sa'ūd and the founder of the al-Muwāḥidūn movement, Muḥammad ibn 'Abd al-Wahhāb, a member of the Banū Tamīm, a sedentary tribe spread across several oases in Najd. After having pursued a religious education in Medina, Basra and Hasa, Ibn 'Abd al-Wahhāb returned to his native village of 'Uyaynah and began preaching his ideas.[3]

Muḥammad ibn 'Abd al-Wahhāb and his followers referred to themselves as the Muwāḥidūn or the Ahl al-Tawḥīd: the Unitarians or the People of Unity.[4] Ibn 'Abd al-Wahhāb saw himself as returning the Arabs to the true monotheistic teachings of Islam. In his time, the veneration not only of saints but also of trees and other objects was common. These were all manifestations of unbelief (*kufr*) and polytheism (*shirk*), and Ibn 'Abd al-Wahhāb saw his role as rooting out these practices by emphasizing the unity of God and returning the people to the true beliefs and practices of Islam.

He enforced rules and punishments considered excessive by the people of 'Uyaynah. These included the public stoning to death of women accused of adultery. He was eventually expelled and went to Dir'iyyah, where he was enthusiastically received by Muḥammad ibn Sa'ūd.[5] By 1744, Ibn 'Abd al-Wahhāb, allied with Muḥammad ibn Sa'ūd, undertook preaching, raids and the demolition of shrines and tombstones. These activities led to the founding of the first Wahhabi emirate in central Arabia. This gradually expanded beyond Dir'iyyah to encompass Riyadh, al-Kharj and Qāsim under the leadership of the son of Muḥammad ibn Sa'ūd, 'Abd al-'Azīz (1765–1803), and Mecca and Medina under Sa'ūd ibn 'Abd al-'Azīz (1803–14).[6]

While the fighting forces at their disposal derived from the quasi-tribal confederation of both nomadic and sedentary elements of the population, united by Wahhabi utopian ideas, the overall dependence was on the townsmen for a fighting force. At a political level, the Wahhabi movement took the form of opposition to the ruling Ottoman Empire which defeated it in 1818.[7]

The Khaldūnian nature of the Saudi–Wahhabi alliance as a politico-religious phenomenon drawing upon the nomadic or *badawī* population began to emerge with the appearance of the Ikhwān. Up until the first decade of the twentieth century, the founder of the kingdom of Saudi Arabia, 'Abd al-'Azīz ibn 'Abd al-Raḥmān Āl Sa'ūd (1880–1953), known usually as Ibn Sa'ūd, relied mainly on townsmen to make up his army. Although the townspeople who had supported him continued to remain loyal to him, Ibn Sa'ūd realized that he could not rely on them for his operations that began to take place further and further away from Riyadh. They were unable to leave their fields and homes to go to war in distant areas. What Ibn Sa'ūd needed was the mobility, loyalty and bravery of the bedouin.[8] Adding to his problem was rebellion from within his own family. He therefore turned to the tribesmen for military support.[9] From among various tribal confederations of Arabia, Ibn Sa'ūd founded a tribal military force known collectively as the Ikhwān, which between 1917 and 1930 played a crucial role in the military and political events of the sultanate of Najd, what was later to become Saudi Arabia.[10]

The Ikhwān was a movement that emerged in Najd and consisted of several nomadic tribes that were encouraged to become sedentarized by incentives provided by Ibn Sa'ūd such as money, seed and equipment. They lived in various settlements or *hijrahs*, located near wells or in oases, and engaged in agriculture. The major tribes of the Ikhwān included the Muṭayr, 'Utaybah, Ḥarb and Shammar.[11] Like the nomadic tribes of the *Muqaddimah*, the various tribes that made up the Ikhwān were bound together by Islam as well as kinship. As far as Islam was concerned, what united the various tribesmen that made up the Ikhwān was a trans-tribal ideology founded on an understanding of Islam via the Hanbalite school as preached by Muḥammad ibn 'Abd al-Wahhāb.[12] At the same time, they constituted groups of mutual aid that rallied around each other to provide moral as well as material assistance.[13] The Ikhwān can be defined as those nomadic tribesmen who gave up their nomadic way of life, migrated (*hajara*) to settlements (*hijrah*), as the Prophet Muḥammad did from Mecca to Medina, and adopted a strictly Islamic way of life. In these *hujar* (sing. *hijrah*) they were trained by a special team of instructors called the *muṭawwa'ah*.[14] The physical migration symbolized leaving behind unbelief and moving to the realm of Islam.[15] In fact, the Ikhwān were zealots who considered those who did not follow their teachings and interpretation of Islam as polytheists and committed acts of atrocity against them.[16]

The Ikhwān provided the military support that Ibn Sa'ūd needed to conquer that part of the Arabian peninsula that was to become Saudi Arabia, which included Mecca, Medina and Jeddah by the end of 1924. However, once this vast area was under his control, Ibn Sa'ūd was faced with the difficult task of governing it in the midst of declining Ikhwān allegiance. The Ikhwān were against the modernization efforts of Ibn Sa'ūd and in 1927 began a rebellion; this that was put down in 1930 with the help of men from the Najdī oases and the British.[17] The assistance rendered by the British was considerable, for they wished to maintain close relations with Ibn Sa'ūd. Although oil had not yet been discovered in the Najd region, Ibn Sa'ūd's friendship was important to the British as his territory was located near the rich oil fields of Persia and Iraq, which were under British control.[18] Ibn Sa'ūd did not proceed to destroy the Ikhwān, however. Instead, he forgave them and gave them a share and vested interests in the regime.[19] In other words, ultimately it was contestation rather than war that neutralized the Ikhwān.[20]

The history of the rise and consolidation of the Saudi state, and the role of the Ikhwān in it, can be restated in Khaldūnian terms. As we have seen in previous chapters, according to Ibn Khaldūn, strong *'aṣabiyyah* or group feeling is a necessary requirement for a group to found a house with the attribute of nobility (*sharaf*), which may then found a dynasty. The superiority of a leader derives from his coming from the group with the strongest *'aṣabiyyah*. The formula is that leadership (*al-ri'āsah*) is derived from superiority (*al-ghulub*), which in turn is derived from group feeling.[21] Furthermore, "each individual group feeling that becomes aware of the superiority of the group feeling of the leader is ready to obey and follow (that leader)".[22] But:

> if an individual tribe has different "houses" and many diverse group feelings, still, there must exist a group feeling that is stronger than all the other group feelings combined, that is superior to them all and makes them subservient, and in which all the diverse group feelings coalesce, as it were, to become one greater group feeling.[23]

The Ikhwān consisted of many houses and diverse group feelings. Their coalescence, or *iltiḥām*, was brought about by Wahhabi ideology. *Iltiḥām* is a form of hegemony that integrates the larger group around the ideology of the ruling *'aṣabiyyah*.[24] It is through the instrumentality of an *'aṣabiyyah* buttressed by Wahhabi teachings that Ibn Sa'ūd was able to unite the tribes under the Ikhwān. According to the Khaldūnian model, once the dynasty was established and its members assumed the various positions of the ruling class, the conditions for the decline in *'aṣabiyyah* are in place. As noted earlier in this book, there are at least two general ways in which this takes place. One is where the second generation of tribesmen who founded the dynasty experience a change

> from the desert attitude to sedentary culture, from privation to luxury, from a state in which everybody shared in the glory to one in which one man claims all the glory for himself while the others are too lazy to strive for (glory), and from proud superiority to humble subservience. Thus, the vigour of group feeling is broken to some extent.

By the third generation *'aṣabiyyah* disappears completely.[25]

Another distinct way in which *'aṣabiyyah* declines is when the "ruler gains complete control over his people, claims royal authority all for himself, excluding them, and prevents them from trying to have a share in it".[26] In other words, when a tribal group establishes a dynasty and its authority becomes legitimate, the ruler can dispense with *'aṣabiyyah*. The ascendant ruler then rules with the help of not his own people but rather that of other tribal groups who have become his clients. The ruler attempts to exclude the supporting tribe from power. Under these circumstances, the ability of a tribal chieftain to maintain *'aṣabiyyah* is diminished.

When we speak of diminishing *'aṣabiyyah*, then, we refer to the circumstances under which a chieftain is no longer able to command tribal support, that is: (1) by appealing to kinship and/or other ties; (2) due to the corrosion in social cohesion that results from either luxurious urban life or from attempts by the ruler to dispense with *'aṣabiyyah*.

The decline in *'aṣabiyyah* took place in Saudi Arabia via the second mode. Ibn Sa'ūd claimed authority for himself and was faced with a rebellious Ikhwān. The very tribal groups that aided the cause of Saudi state formation became threats to the state and had to be marginalized. Their *'aṣabiyyah* had to be dispensed with. This Ibn Sa'ūd did by enlisting the support of the Najdī oases settlers and the British.[27] The *'aṣabiyyah* of the Ikhwān was further diminished when Ibn Sa'ūd gave them political and administrative positions in the regime.

There are virtually no works that have attempted to explain the rise of the Saudi state in Khaldūnian terms. Exceptions are the Spanish philosopher, Ortega y Gasset, who claimed that the development of that state followed the letter of the historical laws of Ibn Khaldūn, and Ghassan Salame, who produced a Khaldūnian account of the rise of the Saudi state.[28]

We now turn to a Khaldūnian account in relation to the question of the fall of the Saudi state. Relevant to this discussion is the work of Peter Turchin.[29] Turchin uses a reconstructed version of Ibn Khaldūn's theory of the state in order to gauge the possibility of state collapse in Saudi Arabia. Following Goldstone, he calls this reformulation the demographic-structural theory. Writing about northern Eurasia in the seventeenth century, Goldstone's theory discusses population growth in large agrarian states that outstripped productivity gains and resulted in poverty, price inflation and other problems. Rulers attempted to compensate for this by expanding taxation. This was resisted by elites and the masses alike. Elites, in particular, who vied for positions formed rival networks of patronage, while rural poverty led to the migration of rural artisans to the towns where they joined urban workers in riots and protests against the state. The combination of elite fragmentation, mass protests and fiscal crisis led to the breakdown of the state.[30]

In Turchin's synthesis between Ibn Khaldūn and Goldstone, the emphasis is on the role of luxury in the decline of the state. In the early stages of the dynasty, economic prosperity results in population growth and an increase in spending and luxury. As the taste for luxury increases, there are greater demands from state and military officials for higher pay. In order to meet this demand, the state raises taxes and confiscates property. At some point, elites find ways to channel tax revenues to themselves. When the incomes of the elite are no longer sufficient for them to maintain expenditure levels and lifestyle, they abandon the state. At the same time poverty, political unrest and other economic problems leave the dynasty vulnerable to conquest.[31] The elite that are being referred to are the grandchildren of the original beneficiaries of the flow of oil wealth since 1946. The development of Saudi Arabia as an oil-rich state since 1946, the modernization programme instituted by King Faysal since 1958, and the rise of a new, Western-educated middle class of bureaucrats, professionals and businessmen, have all helped to define the commitments of the current elite.[32]

Although not discussed by Turchin in his reformulation of the Khaldūnian model, the role of *'aṣabiyyah* is crucial. The decline in *'aṣabiyyah* between the ruler and the conquering tribal elite also contributes, because of the marginalization of the latter by the former, to state collapse. In fact, the decline in *'aṣabiyyah* is due to the inability of state policies to satisfy the consumption needs of the elite. Turchin formalizes the theory with a mathematical version of the Khaldūnian model.[33]

Turchin's findings are that the Saudi state is on the track postulated by the demographic-structural theory that the connection between the price of oil and total revenues is such that a boom and bust cycle can be observed in the three decades following 1970. The impact on the material interests of the elites can be gauged from facts such as more intensive competition for higher level jobs and higher unemployment rates for university graduates.[34] Going by a simple mathematical model that does not take into account various sources of uncertainty, bankruptcy of the state was predicted to happen in 2014. In view of the complex nature of the real world, however, such a forecast cannot be made. But, such empirical testing as attempted by Turchin can enable us to distinguish between predictions of rival theories by looking at the actual trajectory of the Saudi state and economy (that is, as it happened, rather than as it is forecasted to happen). Turchin discusses the "IMF theory" as an alternative to the demographic-structural theory; by this Turchin means a model that adopts a market oriented economic approach and a democratic political system. A policy of reform, if implemented successfully, would increase revenues and enable the Saudi state to avoid or postpone state collapse to the extent that it would allow the elites to maintain their positions and lifestyles.[35]

Both the Khaldūnian and IMF alternatives are based on the assumptions of endogenous development.[36] In the real world, however, the Saudi state exists in the context of regional powers, the United States as a superpower and external forces. These external forces may, as Turchin put it, "spoil the experiment". Potential scenarios mentioned by him include United States military intervention in Saudi Arabia and a Shi'i revolt in Saudi Arabia. This refers to the exogenous alternative. The logic of the experiment is as follows. The endogenous models – that is, the demographic-structural theory and the IMF alternative – can predict the endogenous development of the Saudi political economy. The test is predicated on the exogenous intervention not happening. If the external environment allows the endogenous development to take its course, then the experiment can be done and it would be possible to adjudicate between the demographic-structural theory and the IMF alternative. However, if the exogenous variable were to intervene, the experiment would be spoiled and it would not be possible to test for the Khaldūnian and IMF theories.[37]

What are the possible outcomes? If Saudi Arabia is allowed to develop without the intervention of external forces, either the Ibn Khaldūn inspired demographic-structural theory or the IMF alternative would be proven right. But if we assume, as Turchin does, that there will be some degree of exogenous intervention, what is more likely to happen is a mixed scenario – there would be some economic reforms undertaken by King Abdullah; there would be modest economic growth; some decrease in state subsidies would be palatable to the public, etc. – and these may be able to head off a fiscal and political collapse. Turchin makes a compelling case for the need for an explicit model that would make such questions answerable.[38]

It is interesting to note that the latter-day al-Muwāḥḥidūn state did not suffer the fate of its twelfth century predecessor in Morocco, and even became a global phenomenon in terms of its ideological reach. This was due in a large part to the historical accident of Saudi Arabia having vast oil reserves. It is the presence of oil above all that enabled the Saudis to dispense with tribal military power: that is, to avoid the fate of the Khaldūnian cycle and to push for the global spread of Wahhabi ideas in a way that may not have been possible had they not had access to such wealth. The Saudis were able to do this because they found alternative bases of state strength that allowed them to dispense with tribal support. These alternatives were British support, oil and integration into the world economy.

With regard to the application of Khaldūnian theory to the question of the survival of the Saudi state, if the demographic-structural theory proves to be correct and the Saudi state does collapse due to fiscal and then political crisis, this collapse would actually not be due to the dynamics of state formation described in the Khaldūnian model. First, it would not be because of incoming tribes with their *'aṣabiyyah*s intact, ready to move in and prop up a new dynasty. Second, there is no new house that may vie for royal authority. Ibn Khaldūn's theory explains the rise of the Saudi state, but it does not explain its decline, for the Saudis, like the Ottomans, were able to break the Khaldūnian cycle. While this does not make them immune to collapse, it would be a non-Khaldūnian collapse.

Alawite *'aṣabiyyah* and the future of Syria

Syria, more than other Arab states, has been the focus of some scholars interested in applying a Khaldūnian framework. My account in this section draws upon their works and assesses the relevance of the Khaldūnian model to the Syrian case.[39]

With reference to the Syria of the 1970s, Michaud describes the state in terms of the relations of primary and secondary *'aṣabiyyah*. Power is held by the minority Alawite community. At the head of the state is President Hafiz al-Asad. Down the hierarchy are family members of the president such as his brother, Rifaat, but also others who occupy the highest positions in the intelligence services (*mukhabarāt*), army, air force and interior ministry. Power is constituted not just by membership in the Alawite community but by clientele, alliances and blood ties (*nasab*), the key to *'aṣabiyyah*. Michaud notes that according to Ibn Khaldūn, *'aṣabiyyah* does not exclude hierarchy but, as a result of the integration of several *'aṣabiyyah*, implies it.[40] The significance of blood ties explains why a commandant may have greater power than a general in the Syrian army.

Following his coming to power in 1970, Hafiz al-Asad strove to exert greater control over the Alawite community. He had some of the chiefs of the secondary *'aṣabiyyah* eliminated for maintaining too close extra-community relations with the Sunnis of Damascus. This suggests that the Khaldūnian scheme of a dominant *'aṣabiyyah* of tribal origin persists in the city.[41]

Legitimation is provided through its preaching of Arab progressivism. The Syrian Ba'thist state, unable to rely on a long tradition of centralized power or on a traditional system of allegiance, had to justify its existence by claiming to defend the honour of the Arab nation in the face of Zionism and imperialist aggression.[42]

The state abandoned the civil façade of its relations with society, what Ibn Khaldūn referred to as *siyāsī* (politics that leads to the adoption of laws for the common interest), in favour of primitive power (*mulk ṭabī'ī*) – that is, power through simple violence.[43]

While Michaud's article amounts to little more than a description of the Syrian state and the nature of political power there, it has to be admitted that this is an advance in the development of Khaldūnian sociology, or what Carré calls neo-Khaldūnian sociology,[44] because it is an attempt to apply Khaldūnian concepts. A more successful attempt in this regard is to be found in Carré's work, in which he develops a typology of the exercise of power. This is based on three major divisions in Ibn Khaldūn's thought on the state: ideal versus rational systems, internal versus external repression, and the interests of the governed versus the interests of the government.[45] In the resulting typology, there are six possible forms of the exercise of power.[46]

1 Rational power with external oppression, functioning in the interests of the public. Repression is externally applied through enforcement of norms and codes, with the basis of solidarity being tribal. Examples are the types of Ba'th regimes advocated by Syria and Iraq under Saddam Hussein.
2 Rational power with external repression, functioning in the interests of the government. Examples are the same Ba'thist regimes as in (1) above, this time not as advocated by their leaders but as actually existing systems that act to preserve their power by leveraging on tribal agnatic ties.
3 Rational power with external repression inspired religiously, that functions in theory in the interests of the governed and is founded on the solidarity that is partly tribal, partly professional in the urban milieu. Examples are Nasserism and the Muslim Brotherhood.
4 Rational power with external repression inspired religiously, but functioning to advance the interests of the governing group and dependent on military solidarity. An example is the Nasserist regime in actuality.
5 The ideal power of the utopian city, with internal control and repression founded on faith in the virtue of social egalitarianism but also on legal repression in the context of military solidarity and a flourishing urban milieu. An example is South Yemen.
6 The ideal power of the Medinan community around the Prophet Muḥammad, founded on purely internal control.

What Carré has done here is reflect on Khaldūnian concepts such as *'aṣabiyyah*, as well as Ibn Khaldūn's distinctions between the ideal and rational, internal and external, and the interests of the governed and those of the government, in the light of the realities of contemporary Middle Eastern politics. He develops a typology that has potential applicability to actually existing politics. This line of analysis is extended in what follows.

Michaud discusses what he calls the Khaldūnian triad of *'aṣabiyyah*, *da'wah* (call, invitation) and *mulk* (absolute power) in the context of the modern Syrian state.[47] The tightly knit tribal kinship group are the Alawites, led by then President Hafiz al-Asad. The Alawite *'aṣabiyyah* was based not only on tribal affiliation of the Alawites but also the religion of the Alawite sect and the Ba'thist ideology superimposed upon that. What held the Syrian state together was the *'aṣabiyyah* of the military establishment, which constituted a kinship group. President Hafiz al-Asad and several of his blood relations together dominated the power structure of the Syrian regime. Asad himself was president as well as commander-in-chief of the armed forces. His brothers, Rifaat and Jamil al-Asad, were commanders of the Sarāyā al-Difā' (Defence Units) and a special unit of the Sarāyā al-Difā' respectively. His cousin, 'Adnan al-Asad, commanded the Sarāyā al-Ṣirā' (Struggle Companies). Two nephews of Hafiz al-Asad also had important posts in the Sarāyā al-Difā'. The task of the Sarāyā al-Difā' was to protect the Asad regime, while the special unit of the Sarāyā al-Difā' was tasked with protecting the Alawite community.[48] That there was a special unit to protect the Alawite community, the group representing the dominant *'aṣabiyyah* of the state, is significant.

The Alawites are a tribe that are divided into four major groups: al-Matāwirah, al-Ḥaddādīn, al-Khayyāṭīn and al-Kalbiyyah. The Asad family belongs to the Matāwirah group, as did many other leading figures of the regime at that time, such as Brigadier Muhammad al-Khawli, adviser to the president, Chief of Air Intelligence and Chairman of the Presidential Intelligence Committee; Brigadier Ali Dubah, the head of Military Intelligence; Brigadier Ali Aslan, the Deputy Chief of Staff and the Chief of the Bureau of Military Operations and Training; and Major General Ali Salih, Commander of the Air Defence Forces and the Missile Corps.[49] The reliance of the Asad family on the Alawite tribes cannot be overstated. In addition to those mentioned above, many other appointments to crucial positions in the military service were made that indicate the extent of this reliance.

As a minority branch of the Shi'i schools of thought, the Alawites were marginalized for centuries, working the land under exploitative conditions for Christian and Sunni landowners.[50] The question is, of course, how was it possible for a group that had been on the social and political margins for centuries, that constitutes less than one-eighth of the population of the country, rise to form a state in the modern period? According to Batatu, the question resolves itself into the issue of understanding what made it possible for the Alawites to rise to control the military.[51]

One important factor was the economic position of the Alawites. In Syria, men could avoid military service by making a payment known as the *badal* or financial substitute. The *badal* amounted to 500 Syrian pounds in the 1950s but was progressively raised to US$3,000 in the 1970s. Even when the *badal* was as low as 500 or 600 pounds, many Alawite peasants were unable to come up with the money. They were therefore disproportionately represented among the rank and file draftees of the military.[52] What needs explanation, however, is why the Alawites came to control the officer corps of the armed forces. Batatu notes that the Alawites were a homogeneous group, being mainly of peasant origins and of the Ba'thist ideological orientation. Sunni officers, on the other hand, were divided along class, ideological and regional lines.

> Sunni officers were hopelessly divided in political, regional and class terms. Thus, the Sunni officers were clearly differentiated into urban and rural officers. Among the urbanites the most active and the most politically distinguishable were the Damascenes and the Ḥamawīs, among the country officers the groups of Dayr al-Zūr and the Ḥawrān. The Damascenes were in part Nāṣirites but identified themselves mostly with the Secessionists, who represented a maze of discordant elements, ranging from groups with roots in the affluent landed, commercial and industrialist parts of society, to Muslim Brethren, socialists and independent leftists from the middle and lower middle classes. The Ḥamāwīs largely sympathized with socialist-minded Akram Ḥurānī and partly with the old elite. Some of the officers from Dayr al-Zūr and the Ḥawrān were Nāṣirites, but most threw in their lot with the Ba'ath Party.[53]

In-fighting and multiple alliances among the Sunnis led to purges within the officer corps and eventually a decrease in their numbers and importance.[54] In addition, the fact that the Alawites dominated the Ba'thist section of the military[55] added to their influence. This domination came about because the Alawite officers formed the core of the Ba'th Secret Military Committee which was established in Cairo in 1959. This committee attracted dissident Syrian officers and was to play a prominent role in the military coup of March 1963 that brought the Ba'th party to power.[56] Batatu makes an important point that the Alawite officers did not always consciously act as Alawites, and there were other dimensions of their identity such as their being of rural peasant background. Nevertheless, their control of the Ba'th Military Section meant that they were able to oversee admission into the military academies and determine the commands of military units. Alawites were in the officer corps as a group with a particular tribal and sectarian identity, unlike the Sunnis who were there more as individuals rather than as a group.[57]

During the first generation of the Asad dynasty, Alawite *'aṣabiyyah* was founded not just on tribal affiliation, sectarian identity and the Ba'th ideology, but also on the hope for social and material improvements in their lives. President Hafiz al-Asad's rural development programmes, involving the building of roads and supply of water and electricity, greatly benefited the Alawites, who were predominantly rural.[58] They also supported Hafiz al-Asad against the Muslim Brotherhood, who branded the Alawites as infidels (*kuffār*).[59]

During the second generation of the Asad dynasty, we see more Khaldūnian dynamics at play. As we have seen in the case of the Ottoman and Safavid Empires, and as noted by Ibn Khaldūn in the *Muqaddimah*, the second generation of rulers of a dynasty attempt to distance themselves from their own people, from the very group with whose aid they rose to power. This is because the rulers consider members of this group as potential usurpers of power. For their part, the Alawites imagined that Hafiz al-Asad's son, Bashar al-Asad, would continue the policies of his father, and they would continue to experience improvements in their social and economic lives.[60] In fact, however, the regime did regard certain elements among the Alawites as potential usurpers. An indication of this was the mysterious death of the Minister of the Interior, and Alawite patron, Ghazi Kanaan.[61] Economic reforms put in place by Bashar al-Asad, such as privatization and the encouragement of foreign investment, have served to marginalize the Alawites who were employed in the state bureaucracy.[62] In reality, the reforms instituted by Bashar al-Asad not only ran counter to the interests of the Alawites in general, but also enriched those close to the president through the "corporatization of corruption".[63] The beneficiaries of corruption were the close family members of the president, including his brother Mahir al-Asad, his sister Bushra al-Asad and her husband Asif Shawkat, and the cousins of the president from the Makhluf and Shalish families.[64]

The alienation of the Alawites in Syria has taken a toll on Alawite *'aṣabiyyah*. The source of solidarity with the rulers has eroded. Many Alawites no longer see the Asad dynasty as representing them.[65] In the classical Khaldūnian model, the rulers start to rely on clients instead of their own people. This has proved to be the case during the second generation of the Asad dynasty, when the regime began to rely on outside forces such as Iran, Hizballah, Hamas and other groups, instead of the Alawites.[66] But there is an interesting contradiction here. There seems to have been an increase in support among the Alawites in recent times for the Asad regime, when it was thought that the regime was in danger. Goldsmith refers to this as the fortification of Alawite *'aṣabiyyah*.[67] In contrast, I am inclined to read this as an increase in support for the Asad regime for instrumental reasons, due to the Alawite sectarian insecurity cited by Goldsmith. This insecurity was particularly felt after the Alawites began to be marginalized after Bashar al-Asad came to power. Furthermore, the Alawites also feared revenge against their community should the Asad regime fall. For example, they feared retaliation against them as a result of their having taken up arms as troops in the Syrian army on the side of Hafiz al-Asad against the Muslim Brotherhood in the massacre of Hama in 1982 in which thousands were killed.[68] It is the fear of retaliation rather than genuine solidarity or *'aṣabiyyah* that accounts for continuing Alawite support for the Asad dynasty.

According to the Khaldūnian model, during the next two to three generations the regime would collapse due to declining *'aṣabiyyah* and the consequential loss of Alawite support in the military as well as in society in general. During this time, the clients that the regime had come to rely on would continue to support the regime to the extent that the rewards that accrued to them were forthcoming.

The clients, however, would not be as cohesive as the group that shared in the lineage, *'aṣabiyyah* and ideology of the regime.

What are the possibilities for Syria? What is likely to be the outcome of the current uprising? One possibility is that the regime will survive if it can successfully bring about economic and political reforms and win over the Sunni majority. In this case the regime may experience a natural Khaldūnian lifespan of four to five generations, or even break the Khaldūnian cycle to last longer than that, if there are exogenous forces great enough to allow for this. The extent to which the regime can survive depends greatly on whether the tensions between the Sunni majority and Alawite minority can be managed by the regime.[69] Another possibility is that the Alawites will withdraw their support for the regime, the Asad dynasty will collapse and the state will be taken over by the Sunni majority. This will spell an end to the Khaldūnian cycle, which would be broken because no new kinship-based groups with alternative *'aṣabiyyah* are available to found a new dynasty and take over the state. Yet another possibility is that the Asad regime will fall but the state will continue to be in hands of the Alawites, through clients of the Asad family.

As we saw in Chapter 2, Ibn Khaldūn discussed three types of relationships that constitute *'aṣabiyyah*: blood ties (*ṣilat al-raḥim*), clientship (*walā'*), and alliance (*ḥilf*).[70] While *'aṣabiyyah* based on blood ties may have been more important for Hafiz and Bashar al-Asad, it may be *'aṣabiyyah* based on clientship and alliance that become dominant in a post-Asad Alawite state. This is a realistic scenario in view of the fact that the Alawites still dominate the Syrian economy. For example, it was reported in the *Financial Times* that Rami Makhluf, a maternal first cousin of Bashar al-Asad, controls up to 60 per cent of the Syrian economy through a web of holding companies,[71] and has a significant presence in the finance, telecommunications and oil sectors as well as in the media, tourism, restaurants, real estate and duty free shops.[72]

The way that the opposing trends – the ruling group alienating the Alawites versus enriching a circle of family members and clients – resolve themselves will determine how far *'aṣabiyyah* and, therefore, the social cohesion and survival of the ruling group remains intact.

9 Towards a Khaldūnian sociology of the state

The dangerous state

What we understand as the state in the modern sense – that is, as a political association through which the power of various groups is exercised – is captured in the classical Islamic tradition by the term *dawlah*. The term "state", as understood in modern political science and sociology,[1] owes its birth in large part to Machiavelli's "*stato*".[2] This corresponds somewhat to the Arabic *dawlah*. The *dawlah* for Ibn Khaldūn, however, referred both to what we understand as state and to "dynasty". In Ibn Khaldūn's world the only kind of political association that he knew was the dynasty. The ideal state in the Islamic tradition was founded upon what Ibn Khaldūn called caliphate authority.

We referred in Chapter 2 to the distinction Ibn Khaldūn made between caliphate authority (*khilāfah*) and kingship as an important sociological contribution. Caliphate authority referred to the ability of the ruler to get the masses to act in a manner that was harmonious with religious law. In this sense, the caliph was a substitute for the Prophet Muḥammad in terms of his temporal role.[3]

Kingship, on the other hand, refers to authority that is founded on a non-religious rationalization of power. There are two types of kingship: *mulk siyāsī*, or royal authority, and *mulk ṭabī'ī*, or unbridled kingship.[4] Royal authority is kingship that results in behaviour that is guided by rational insight and functions to maximize worldly interests.[5] Under royal authority life is not regulated in an arbitrary manner according to the whimsicalities of the ruler.[6] Royal authority is founded on the legitimacy of the ruler and is buttressed by a strong *'aṣabiyyah*. With the disintegration of *'aṣabiyyah*, however, the element of kinship is replaced by alliance and clientship, and royal authority is replaced by *mulk ṭabī'ī* or unbridled kingship. Under such authority, life is regulated by the purpose and desires of the rulers.[7]

For Ibn Khaldūn, caliphate authority was historically brief in its appearance, and unlikely to emerge after the period of the rightly guided caliphs or the *khulafā' al-rāshidūn*. The greater part of the history of rulership was characterized by injustice. "Government decisions are as a rule unjust, because pure justice is found only in the legal caliphate that lasted only a short while. Muḥammad said: 'The caliphate after me will last thirty years; then, it will revert to being tyrannical royal authority'".[8] This injustice is to be understood in a more general sense than as the confiscation of property and money. It includes measures undertaken by the state that do not conform to Islamic law, such as forced labour, the imposition of duties and the collection of unjustified taxes.

> Injustice should not be understood to imply only the confiscation of money or other property from the owners, without compensation and without cause. It is commonly understood in that way, but it is something more general than that. Whoever takes someone's property, or uses him for forced labor, or presses an unjustified claim against him, or imposes upon him a duty not required by the religious law, does an injustice to that particular person. People who collect unjustified taxes commit an injustice. Those who infringe upon property (rights) commit an injustice. Those who take away property commit an injustice. Those who deny people their rights commit an injustice. Those who, in general, take property by force, commit an injustice. It is the dynasty that suffers from all these acts, in as much as civilization, which is the substance of the dynasty, is ruined when people have lost all incentive.[9]

Writing more than 500 years later, Ortega, whose views on Ibn Khaldūn we assessed earlier, put forward the idea, in a chapter entitled "The Greatest Danger, the State", that state intervention is "the greatest danger that threatens civilization".[10] At the end of the eighteenth century the state was a very small affair and weak in terms of its ability to manage public order and tend to the administration of the land. However, the disproportion between state and social power was developed by the nineteenth century, when the state became a formidable machine and the threat to civilization became state intervention, the enslavement of society, and the bureaucratization of human existence.[11] With the creation of a new type of man, the industrial worker, an increase in criminality in Europe led to the rise of the strengthening of public authority. Ortega warned:

> But it is foolish for the party of "law and order" to imagine that these "forces of public authority" created to preserve order are always going to be content to preserve the order that the party desires. Inevitably they will end by themselves defining and deciding on the order they are going to impose – which, naturally, will be that which suits them best.[12]

Dangerous states founded on *mulk ṭabīʿī* type authority are empirically exaggerated in the historical cases of fascism and communism, but can also be found in capitalist postcolonial states of both democratic and authoritarian varieties.

In political sociology and political science there is a tendency to be obsessed with the question of the legitimacy of the state in a way that overrides consideration of the dangers posed by the state due to the presence of criminal elements. Even Marxist and neo-Marxist theories of the state operate on the assumption of the legitimacy, and more importantly the legality, of the state.

When it comes to criminality, the focus is generally on crimes against the state, including white-collar abuses and corruption. Crimes committed by government agencies and personnel that victimize thousands, even millions, of citizens often go unreported, their perpetrators are not prosecuted, and they remain unresearched.

The extent to which the state is not dangerous depends to some degree on how the distinction between the public and the private is put into practice. In both classical Islam and medieval Europe there was the notion of the higher good of the people (*ummah*, *patria*), as opposed to private interests. In Islam, this had come across very clearly in the hadith (sayings) of the Prophet as well as those of Sayyidinā 'Ali ibn abī Ṭālib regarding the impropriety of receiving gifts in return for official duties performed and nepotism.[13] In Cicero, the higher good of the *patria* superseded private interests and those based on familial bonds.[14] It is quite obvious to most that the private/public distinction is an ideal that is far from realized in much of the Third World, as is indicated by the prevalence of patronage, cronyism, presidential families, royal capitalists and rent-seeking. A theory of the postcolonial state, therefore, is as much a criminology as it is a political sociology of the state. This is because political independence from colonial rule had set the stage for kleptocracy as a result of the sudden acquisition of political power, the rapid growth of bureaucracy and the opening up of opportunities for corruption in the context of the international division of labour.

In Ibn Khaldūn's world, he only knew of the eternal cycle of the rise and fall of dynasties. Strictly speaking, he was not aware of historical cases of great empires that had avoided the cyclical development. Gellner made an interesting point when he said that Ibn Khaldūn's ignorance about other types of societies, other than those conceptualized in the *Muqaddimah*, was a mark of his genius. The works of Western classical theorists such as Max Weber could ask questions about the specificity of the West because they were able to compare it with other societies. Ibn Khaldūn, on the other hand, was able to provide a theoretical account of one type of society, without the benefit of a comparative perspective.[15] Probably for this reason, and also because he dealt with the nomadic origins of states, his theory was seen to be of limited application, the limits being defined by ecology and period. We have seen that few works have systematically applied the Khaldūnian framework, whether to geographies and times closer to his own or to the modern state.

Applying Ibn Khaldūn

That Ibn Khaldūn was the founder of sociology has been recognized by certain prominent sociologists since the nineteenth century.[16] Becker and Barnes, in their 1938 classic and important history of sociology entitled *Social Thought from Lore to Science*, discuss the ideas of Ibn Khaldūn over several pages and recognize him as the first to apply modern-like ideas in historical sociology.[17]

Nevertheless, such recognition is reflected neither in the contemporary teaching of sociology in universities and colleges throughout the world, nor in the writing of the history of sociology. The idea of developing Khaldūnian concepts, combining them with those of modern sociology and applying the resultant theoretical approaches to a variety of empirical and historical fields outside his own, remains marginal. This book is an exercise in such application.

However original Ibn Khaldūn may have been, he did write seven centuries ago, and many theoretical and empirical developments have taken place in the social sciences, particularly during the last 200 years. Therefore, the formulation of a modern Khaldūnian sociology requires assimilating to his theory concepts and theories of the modern social sciences. But few have been interested in undertaking this task. It would require going beyond merely comparing some concepts in Ibn Khaldūn's works with those of modern social sciences. Systematic attempts are needed to integrate his theory into the approaches of the modern social sciences. Examples of such attempts have been provided in preceding chapters. This then raises the question as to what Khaldūnian sociology is.

Khaldūnian sociology is a historical sociology of state formation. It is applicable to a wide range of societies, including North Africa, West and Central Asia, Northern India, China, and the American West: that is, societies for which kin-based solidary groups were important in state formation. A Khaldūnian approach, however, would have to assimilate concepts and theories from modern sociology and the other social sciences. For example, Ibn Khaldūn's theory provides a means of understanding the dynamics of many pre-modern states. Ibn Khaldūn's account of the rise and decline of dynasties is decidedly sociological in the sense that he speaks of social groups such as tribes and the state or ruling dynasty, and relations between them. The central concept of *'aṣabiyyah* is also sociological as it refers to a type of social cohesion founded on the knowledge of common kinship or descent. But Ibn Khaldūn's explanation of the mechanisms according to which *'aṣabiyyah* declines and the ruling dynasty is deprived of the source of its power, is offered without any reference to the mode of organization of economic life. His theory lacks a concept of the economic system. What I have attempted in this book is to provide an economic basis for Ibn Khaldūn's theory of state formation by integrating into his theory a modes of production framework.

Many of the societies that Ibn Khaldūn's theory can be applied to were characterized by the coexistence of four modes of production: pastoral nomadic, Asiatic, prebendal feudal and petty commodity. While the Khaldūnian model lacks a concept of the economy, existing modes of production approaches would gain from viewing the relationship between modes of production and the dynamics of the system in terms of Ibn Khaldūn's theory of state formation. The same type of theoretical integration can be considered for Weber and Ibn Khaldūn, Durkheim and Ibn Khaldūn, and others.

Some historical cases can also be used to merge Khaldūnian and world-systems theory. According to this approach, the historical development of, say, the Safavid state can be viewed in terms of the notion of a core–periphery hierarchy.[18] The dynamics of state formation and decline elaborated in the Khaldūnian modes of production framework can also be restated in terms of historical timeframes of what Turchin calls the Ibn Khaldūn cycle.[19] According to Turchin and Hall, this is a secular wave "that tends to affect societies with elites drawn from adjacent nomadic groups" and which operates on a timescale of about four generations or a century.[20] They discuss four Chinggisid dynasties that fit the Khaldūnian theory of the cyclical rise and fall of states: the Yuan dynasty in China, the Jagataids in Turkestan, the Ilkhanids in Iran, and the Juchids in the Kipchak Steppe. All these dynasties went through the typical Khaldūnian cycle of about 100 years.

The originality that the Khaldūnian approach brings to this is the focus on the unit of analysis that encompasses the set of social relations that are central to the rise of nomadic origin states: that is, those of nomadic and sedentary societies. This transcends the usual association of civilizations with settled peoples organized around states with fixed boundaries.[21]

Previous studies that have applied the Khaldūnian model have not systematically attempted to integrate other models into the Khaldūnian approach. For example, a study by Khatibi presents the Khaldūnian as one among three models, the other two being Marxist and segmentary models. But he implies that they are theoretically incompatible, owing to the distinctive logics upon which they are founded – respectively, the Aristotelian, the dialectical and the Kantian.[22] While that may be the case at the meta level of analysis, at the theoretical and empirical levels it is certainly possible to bring in new concepts, such as the mode of production, to Ibn Khaldūn's theory of state formation and attempt an explanation of the very same phenomena that he dealt with, but with the added approaches provided by newly introduced concepts.

Here I wish to point out the sense in which the applications undertaken in this book are theoretical. The integration of aspects of Ibn Khaldūn's theory into a modes of production framework is not merely at the substantive level, where certain historical facts arising from the application of Ibn Khaldūn's theory are combined with other historical facts arising from the application of the concept of modes of production, with a resulting picture of the past. Although this level of integration is itself important, because it highlights the explanatory value of Ibn Khaldūn's theory and his relevance to more modern theories, there is also a theoretical level at which this integration can be appreciated.

The object of the field of theoretical history is the "bridging of the gap that divides the cautiously objective technique employed to ascertain the isolated facts of history, and the arbitrarily subjective method by which these facts are assembled into a picture of the past".[23] As such, the territory of theoretical history has a number of provinces, two of which are: (1) the study of the pattern and rhythm of history, and (2) the study of driving forces in history.[24] It is these two concerns of theoretical history that have been brought together in the integration that I have attempted. It can be said that Ibn Khaldūn's work was a study of the pattern and rhythm of history, while the modes of production framework emphasizes the modes of production in the study of the driving forces of history. The period that I selected for study – the sixteenth to early seventeenth centuries – was one in which the Ottoman and Safavid modes of production reached their classic expressions, the period before they began to experience fundamental changes in their economic systems as a result of gradual incorporation into the expanding European world economy. Thus, Ibn Khaldūn's theory, which established a pattern and rhythm in history, was applied to Ottoman and Safavid political economy, conceptualized in terms of modes of production. A few points can be made regarding this exercise in application.

First of all, although Ibn Khaldūn's work was exclusively about pre-modern states, this is not to say that it has no bearing upon the study of modern state formation, as I have tried to show in the discussion on the cases of the Saudi and Syrian states.

Second, Ibn Khaldūn's theory of state formation is at one and the same time a theory of religious reform. It is a macro theory of religious reform that is informed by certain ideas not found in modern theories of religious reform. As discussed in Chapter 5, these include the idea that religious reform takes place within the context of the emergence of a new ruling group and the realignment of loyalties; that it functions as an overarching *'aṣabiyyah* that transcends tribalism and other loyalties; that it is founded on groups characterized by simpler modes of making a living; that religious reform is the outcome of conflict between two religious types, these differences based on the degree of institutionalization; and that there is a positive correlation between religious zeal and religion-based solidarity. What the macro approach suggests is that the religious experience can be understood beyond its individual and psychological manifestations as a sociological phenomenon, to the extent that it is a function of a type of solidarity, known to Ibn Khaldūn as *'aṣabiyyah*.

Third, it is necessary here to state how the application of Ibn Khaldūn in this book can be claimed to be theoretical application as opposed to a mere rephrasing of the known and available data in Khaldūnian terms. A theoretical application of a particular perspective should either suggest the need for new data or lead us to a new way of organizing the data such that it yields an alternative construction of a social phenomenon. The Khaldūnian explanation attempted in this book furnishes both types of applications. The study of Muslim reform is an example of the first type, in which our attention is drawn to the macro dimensions of religious reform. This is also true of the application of the Khaldūnian framework to the Syrian state, which suggested the need to examine, for example, indicators of *'aṣabiyyah* in the Alawite community. On the other hand, the application of the Khaldūnian framework to the rise and decline of the Ottoman and Safavid states are examples of the second type of application. Here, the Khaldūnian application "transcends" the same historical facts that were discussed in existing explanations by explaining those facts in terms of a different set of underlying concepts and ideas. In fact, the existing explanations discussed in the chapters on Ottoman and Safavid history were generally observational rather than theoretical statements that universally generalized the facts. The Khaldūnian application, on the other hand, generally "transcends" the facts (or *khabar* in Ibn Khaldūn's terminology) by explaining them in terms of an underlying, causal and theoretical scheme made up of notions such as *'aṣabiyyah* or the contradiction between nomadic and sedentary ways of life.

Finally, an obvious question concerns Ibn Khaldūn's own application of his theory of state formation in his history, the *Kitāb al-'Ibar*. As noted by Talbi, Ibn Khaldūn has been accused of not fulfilling promises made in the *Muqaddimah* in the *Kitāb al-'Ibar*. Talbi's defence of Ibn Khaldūn, that this is obvious but that it could not have been otherwise as no one person could alone write a universal history according to the framework established by the *Muqaddimah*, is inadequate and misses the mark.[25] The *Kitāb al-'Ibar*, far from being uninfluenced by the *Muqaddimah*, is in fact arranged in a way that is determined by it. Ibn Khaldūn says of the entire work:

> In (this book) I lifted the veil from conditions as they arise in the various generations. I arranged it in an orderly way in chapters dealing with historical facts and reflections. In it I showed how and why dynasties and civilization originate. I based the work on the history of the two races that constitute the population of the Maghrib at this time and people its various regions and cities, and on that of their ruling houses, both long- and short-lived, including the rulers and allies they had in the past. These two races are the Arabs and the Berbers. They are the two races known to have resided in the Maghrib for such a long time that one can hardly imagine they ever lived elsewhere, for its inhabitants know no other human races.
>
> I corrected the contents of the work carefully and presented it to the judgment of scholars and the elite. I followed an unusual method of arrangement and division into chapters. From the various possibilities, I chose a remarkable and original method. In the work, I commented on civilization, on urbanization, and on the essential characteristics of human social organization, in a way that explains to the reader how and why things are as they are, and shows him how the men who constituted a dynasty first came upon the historical scene. As a result, he will wash his hands of any blind trust in tradition. He will become aware of the conditions of periods and races that were before his time and that will be after it.[26]

Ibn Khaldūn also says that on the surface, "history is no more than information about political events, dynasties, and occurrences of the remote past, elegantly presented and spiced with proverbs".[27] This is history at the level of appearances (*ẓāhir*). This is to be distinguished from the inner meaning (*bāṭin*) of history, which is arrived at through "speculation and an attempt to get at the truth, subtle explanations of the causes and origins of existing things, and deep knowledge of the how and why of events".[28]

If we imposed a modern social scientific standard on Ibn Khaldūn, then it could be said that he did not apply the theoretical framework that he developed in the *Muqaddimah* to the historical facts reported in the rest of the *Kitāb al-'Ibar*. In the field of historical sociology or theoretical history the facts of the past are reconstructed according to a specific scheme that may be defined by particular theoretical traditions, such as Marxism or Weberian sociology. Such works aspire to be more than mere chronological enumerations of facts. Rather, the facts would be reconstructed in such a manner that a particular view of history would be expressed, a specific epistemology applied, definite concepts deployed and facts selectively arranged so as to answer a particular set of questions or deal with a problem. If this is what characterizes the science history, then it could be said that Ibn Khaldūn failed to put into practice what he outlined in the *Muqaddimah*. If, on the other hand, we were to assess Ibn Khaldūn in terms of the objectives he set for himself – that is, speculation (*naẓar*) and inquiry (*taḥqīq*) regarding the underlying causes of existing things[29] – we would then reach a different verdict.

As Ibn Khaldūn himself stated, he structured the *Kitāb al-'Ibar* according to the scheme developed in the *Muqaddimah*. The *Muqaddimah* discusses the basic premises (*muqaddimāt*) for the study of history and the theoretical framework that establishes the central concepts used in the study. The *Muqaddimah* as a whole discusses the underlying structure (*bāṭin*) of history while the rest of the *Kitāb al-'Ibar* supplies the historical facts (*akhbār*) that represent the surface phenomena (*ẓāhir*) of history, from which the scheme elaborated in the *Muqaddimah* was extracted.[30]

In this sense, the "application" of the theory set out in the *Muqaddimah* to the facts of history was fulfilled. For example, details regarding the founder of the Almohad movement, Ibn Tūmart, a member of the Maṣmūdah, a Berber tribe of the Atlas Mountains, are provided in the *Kitāb al-'Ibar*.[31] More importantly, the chapters of the *Kitāb al-'Ibar* are arranged in such a manner as to impose the explanatory scheme developed in the *Muqaddimah*. Among the dynasties of North Africa that Ibn Khaldūn discusses are the Almoravids (al-Murābiṭūn) (AD 1053–1147), Almohads (al-Muwāḥḥidūn) (1147–1275) and Marinids (1213–1524), each of which were founded with the support of Berber tribes: the Ṣanhājah for the Almoravids, the Maṣmūdah for the Almohads, and the Zanātah for the Marinids. The history of the rise and decline of these dynasties conforms to the model given by Ibn Khaldūn. In the *Kitāb al-'Ibar* the facts of these dynasties are discussed in chronological order, one after the other, detailing the rulers, their successors, the alliances they entered into and the support they received and lost.[32] The explanatory scheme is only apparent if one reads the *Muqaddimah*. Without reading the *Muqaddimah*, the facts reported in the rest of the *Kitāb al-'Ibar* appear to be just that: a collection of reports about rulers and events.

The exercise in the application of Ibn Khaldūn in this book has implications for Khaldūnian theory in two basic ways. First, the applications undertaken above provide alternative explanations of social phenomena in the sense that they suggest new ways of organizing known data as well as new questions to ask about the facts of history and society. On the other hand, there is also an impact in the other direction, that is, on Khaldūnian theory. The events and conditions of history and society to which Khaldūnian theory is being applied help to further develop and refine the theory. For example, conceptualizing Ottoman and Safavid economies in terms of prebendalism shows the mechanisms by which nomadic tribesmen become sedentarized and socialized into the lifestyle of the *'umrān ḥaḍarī*.

Non-Eurocentric readings and applications of Ibn Khaldūn

In Chapter 3, I argued that it was the Eurocentric orientation that was at least partly responsible for the neglect of Ibn Khaldūn as a source of modern theory in the social sciences. The project of applying Ibn Khaldūn can also be seen as one of developing non-Eurocentric readings of Ibn Khaldūn. Here, I would like to make a few remarks on this project.

First of all, the above account or selective survey of non-Eurocentric applications of Ibn Khaldūn's theory of state formation was intended to demonstrate how the contributions of a social thinker may be approached, not just as an object of study in which his theories and concepts are repeatedly described or in which his work is looked upon as a source of historical data, but as a source of theory that is potentially applicable to historical and contemporary phenomena. The point regarding Ibn Khaldūn was made years ago by a small number of Arab scholars, such as Lilia ben Salem who proposed a Khaldūnian theory of the Maghribine state.[33] I have suggested that Eurocentrism, which maintains the subject–object dichotomy and therefore perpetuates the dominance of European categories and concepts in the social sciences, is at least partly responsible for the lack of interest in Ibn Khaldūn as a knowing subject, as a source of theories and concepts that may be utilized to interpret and construct realities. The examples of non-Eurocentric readings and applications of Ibn Khaldūn that I have presented above do not exhaust the list. Nevertheless, the list is not very long, considering that Ibn Khaldūn's works have been known for 600 years.[34]

Second, such a project should be undertaken not for the purpose of replacing European categories and concepts with Arab and Muslim ones but with the intention of enriching the social sciences by making available a greater variety of ideas and perspectives. The idea is not to replace one ethnocentrism with another. As Djeghloul puts it, being true to Ibn Khaldūn is to explain why and how things are as they are in the world that we live in,[35] and it is in this spirit that we must make his ideas available to us.

Third, it should be noted that a non-Eurocentric reading of Ibn Khaldūn is not to be equated with a non-European reading. The examples from Chapter 8 show that there are non-Eurocentric readings of Ibn Khaldūn undertaken in European languages by Europeans. The Eurocentric/non-Eurocentric divide does not correspond to the European/non-European divide. In fact, the bulk of work in Arabic, Persian and Turkish on Ibn Khaldūn are descriptive writings on his theory, comparative studies between Ibn Khaldūn and the modern sociologists that are often designed to prove that Ibn Khaldūn was the founder of the discipline, and discussions of the epistemological and methodological foundations of his work. It would not be an exaggeration to say that there is a dearth of non-Eurocentric readings of Ibn Khaldūn in those languages, if by non-Eurocentric is meant the presentation of Ibn Khaldūn as a knowing subject, a source of theories and concepts with applicability to historical and contemporary realities. I note, for example, that many Persian-language works on Ibn Khaldūn fail to discuss the possible relevance of Ibn Khaldūn to the study of Iranian history and society.[36]

It should be stressed that the politics of knowledge does not simply determine the hegemony of certain paradigms in the social sciences within the Western tradition, but affects the elision of other civilizational discourses, and that this elision is noted despite the fact that Ibn Khaldūn is often referred to in the literature. The problem is not the omission of references to Ibn Khaldūn but the lack of consideration of Ibn Khaldūn in a non-Eurocentric manner, that is, as a knowing subject and as a founder of concepts and categories for the social sciences. To a great extent, Eurocentrism remains a dominant orientation because of the nature of the sociology curriculum.

Ibn Khaldūn in the sociology curriculum

While Ibn Khaldūn began to be taken seriously by European scholars in the nineteenth and early twentieth centuries, this interest did not continue among scholars who were not in Middle Eastern or Islamic studies. This was possibly due to the consolidation of the sociological canon after World War Two. It was really then that the notion of what constituted classical sociology developed, particularly in the United States. Marx, Weber and Durkheim were identified as integral to classical sociology according to the canonical view of the field.[37] It is this view of the discipline that "generates distorted pictures of the history of sociology, and of the scope and value of sociology".[38] The narrower scope defined by the canonical view left out non-Western progenitors and contributors to social thought and theory.

A more multicultural approach to the teaching of sociology is therefore in order. Multiculturalism – that is, the celebration of cultural variety and diversity – is juxtaposed to Eurocentrism. While Eurocentrism in the social sciences has long been identified and criticized in the literature, the attention that it has received in research and writing is not paralleled in teaching in the social sciences. The topic of Eurocentrism is often raised in social science and humanities courses in universities throughout the world, but the discussions are generally confined to courses on the Third World or on postcolonial topics. Basic or foundational courses, such as introductory courses to social theory, are rarely informed by concerns raised by the critique of Eurocentrism. For example, courses on sociological theory generally do not attempt to correct the Eurocentric bias by introducing non-Western thinkers or by critiquing Eurocentric elements in the works of European theorists such as Marx, Weber and Durkheim. Using the example of Ibn Khaldūn, I have shown how Eurocentrism and the resulting marginalization of non-Western ideas in the history and teaching of sociology obstruct the emergence of a more multicultural social theory and suggest what conditions must be fulfilled in order that multiculturalism in the teaching of the social sciences can be realized.

Multiculturalism, or the celebration of cultural variety and diversity in the social sciences, would require that at least three themes inform social science education. These themes are intercivilizational encounters, the multicultural origins of modernity, and the variety of points of view. If these themes are applied to teaching in the social sciences it would lead to a more multicultural approach in teaching in the following ways. First, the focus on intercivilizational encounters in the teaching of the history of the social sciences would reveal the extent to which European and American scholars have borrowed ideas from non-Western sources. Second, stressing the multicultural origins of modernity, or modern social science as an aspect of modernity, would serve to highlight the non-Western sources of and contributions to modern thought. Third, taking seriously the idea of varieties of points of view in the teaching of the social sciences would mean being open to the possibility of theories and concepts of non-Western origins.

Having understood multiculturalism in the social sciences in this way, I suggest that a serious obstacle to the inculcation of the multicultural imagination among our students and the generations after us is the Eurocentric nature of education in much of Asia and Africa. This is because Eurocentrism defines the content of education in such a way that intercivilizational encounters, the origins of modernity and the question of points of view are not thematized. It is this lack of thematization that does not allow for the implantation and cultivation of a broader approach and perspective that is characterized by multiculturalism.

Many sociology course syllabi do not facilitate the development of a multicultural social science, resulting in the neglect or marginalization of non-Western thinkers and ideas. In this book, I have discussed a specific case of such marginalization, that of Ibn Khaldūn. How can this marginalization be addressed? One way is to bring in a multicultural sensibility in the teaching of the social sciences. This is a central feature of several courses I teach at the National University of Singapore, including one entitled "Social Thought and Social Theory" that I co-taught for many years with my colleague Vineeta Sinha. This is a compulsory final year module for sociology majors at the university that covers classical sociological theory. After having taught the course the conventional way for a couple of semesters, we decided to make some radical changes to the syllabi. The conventional classical sociological theory course typically features Comte, Marx, Weber, Durkheim, de Tocqueville and other white males of the nineteenth and early twentieth centuries. We put into practice an alternative way of teaching classical sociological theory. Our experience and findings were reported in the journal *Teaching Sociology*.[39] The revamping of the course syllabus to take these themes into account corrects the Eurocentric bias in social science teaching by bringing into focus non-Western thinkers and ideas in a way that can facilitate the instilling of a more multicultural outlook in the social science community: an outlook informed by concern with intercivilizational encounters, the multicultural origins of modernity, and the variety of points of view.

While we retained the focus on Marx, Weber and Durkheim, we brought to the foreground those topics pertaining to non-European societies that are generally ignored or given little attention in the conventional versions of the course. For example, more attention was devoted to Marx's Asiatic mode of production, his and Engels' writings on India and Algeria, and Weber's writings on Islam, Hinduism, Confucianism and Taoism.

Also, we attempted to eliminate the subject–object dichotomy by bringing in non-Europeans as well as women as subjects – that is, as theorists and social thinkers. These include Ibn Khaldūn, Jose Rizal, Rammohun Roy, Benoy Kumar Sarkar and Harriet Martineau. In the future we intend to introduce Chinese and Japanese thinkers. Doing this, of course, requires our redefining classical sociological theory.

Furthermore, the course stresses the multicultural origins of sociological theory. Given that a sociology of sorts was being done outside of Europe in pre-modern as well as modern times, a case for the multicultural origins for sociology can be made. This would require a redefinition of classical sociology. Sociology has been defined as the "product of modernity, born of the great intellectual and social upheavals that destroyed the medieval European world".[40] What is often not realized is that the same intellectual and social upheavals that destroyed the European medieval world also destroyed the pre-capitalist political economies of other parts of the world, and that these transformations resulted in bodies of sociological literature attempting to make sense of such changes, urging for reform or revolution, and charting a new social order. The same forces that caused the decline of feudalism and the rise of capitalism in Europe were behind the colonization and social transformation of the rest of the world. It is in this context that we may view the emergence of thinkers like Roy, Rizal and Sarkar. The vast majority of sociologists, however, tend to have a more parochial view of the history and origins of sociology.

Finally, we raised the question of alternative categories and concepts with the aim of enriching and universalizing the social sciences. There is a variety of points of view, in this case, of theoretical perspectives that have multicultural origins. Ibn Khaldūn's work, for example, contains concepts and theoretical explanations that emerge from his own period and cultural setting and suggest interesting ways in which they can be applied to the study of social phenomena both within and outside his own time and milieu. A case in point would be the use of Ibn Khaldūn's theory of state formation to explain the rise and decline of the Safavid and Ottoman states. A variety of theoretical perspectives derived from the works of Marx and Weber have been applied to the study of these histories. Why should an obvious candidate like Ibn Khaldūn be excluded?

The various changes we made to our course on classical sociological theory, described above, are meant to prompt us to ask ourselves why some founders of sociology are not taught in textbooks and classrooms. It is not simply a question of setting the record straight, which is itself very important, but also one of opening ourselves up to other sources of knowledge.

Talbi, Lawrence and others say that Ibn Khaldūn had no successor in the Muslim world and that he was discovered in Europe. He was a product of Orientalism.[41] This is true only to an extent. As discussed in Chapter 4, Ibn Khaldūn did have intellectual followers, including al-Azraq al-Andalusī and al-Maqrīzī. What is true, however, is that no Khaldūnian school of social historical thought developed. But Lawrence's view that Ibn Khaldūn cannot be assessed apart from Orientalist interest in him is an overstatement.[42] This book has tried to show that Ibn Khaldūn can, and indeed should, be assessed apart from the Orientalist interest evoked by him, moving from pre-modern readings of Ibn Khaldūn to modern applications of Khaldūnian theory to history and the contemporary state.

10 Bibliographic remarks and further reading

This chapter discusses a selection of the literature on Ibn Khaldūn, which is indeed vast. Countless works have been published on Ibn Khaldūn in the modern period, particularly from the nineteenth century onwards. This chapter lists and discusses only the ones I consider to be helpful to those who wish to acquaint themselves with Ibn Khaldūn studies and who wish to develop a more social scientific approach to Ibn Khaldūn. The selection of works on Ibn Khaldūn here has two purposes. One is to orient the reader to the various types of works on Ibn Khaldūn. The other is to introduce the reader to the few works that attempt applications of the Khaldūnian model to empirical cases. The discussion that follows covers a number of categories of works pertaining to Ibn Khaldūn studies.[1] These are:

1 Ibn Khaldūn's works in the Arabic and in translation;
2 Biographies;
3 Works on Ibn Khaldūn as a forerunner of social sciences;
4 Comparative studies between Ibn Khaldūn and seminal Western thinkers;
5 Reviews and descriptions of the ideas contained in the *Muqaddimah;*
6 Discussions of Ibn Khaldūn's methodology;
7 Analysis and critique of Ibn Khaldūn's theory;
8 Applications of Ibn Khaldūn's theoretical framework.

A listing of works cited in this book can be found in the Bibliography.

Ibn Khaldūn's works in the Arabic and in translation

The great number of published editions of the *Muqaddimah* makes it difficult for students and researchers to decide which ones to adopt in their work. Adding to the problem is the fact that many contain errors and are incomplete. Among the few complete and edited versions that have been published, the best is that by 'Abd al-Salām al-Shaddādī (Abdesselam Cheddadi). Cheddadi's edition of five volumes presents the Arabic text in a readable form. The *Muqaddimah* is printed in three of the volumes, with numerous footnotes providing citations of works that

Ibn Khaldūn refers to and explaining technical terms. The other two volumes are appendices dealing with manuscripts found in Great Britain and the Netherlands. A work on the manuscripts of the *Muqaddimah* that is worthwhile consulting is Nathaniel Schmidt's 1926 publication, "The Manuscripts of Ibn Khaldun".

The *Muqaddimah* was first translated in a European language by William MacGuckin de Slane in 1862–68. Charles Issawi's abridged English translation, under the title *An Arab Philosophy of History*, appeared in 1950. Issawi's edition is useful as a quick introduction to the *Muqaddimah* as it is organized according to a number of themes, such as method, geography, economics, public finance, religion and politics. The standard reference, as far as an English translation goes, however, is Franz Rosenthal's *The Muqaddimah: An Introduction to History*, in three volumes. Rosenthal's translation first appeared in 1958, and is useful for researchers as it includes a valuable discussion in the translator's introduction on Ibn Khaldūn's life, some remarks on various aspects of the *Muqaddimah* and some details of the history of the text of the *Muqaddimah*. For those not wishing to plough through all three volumes of Rosenthal's translation, with their numerous footnotes providing explanations of technical terms and citations of works referred to by Ibn Khaldūn, there is the abridged and edited version of Rosenthal's translation by N. J. Dawood. An excellent French translation of the *Muqaddimah* was undertaken by Vincent Monteil and appeared as *Discours sur l'histoire universelle* in 1967–68. A very useful feature of Monteil's translation, in comparison to that of Rosenthal, is that it frequently provides the original Arabic technical terms in parenthesis.

No complete translation of the *Kitāb al-'Ibar* is available in any language. De Slane's French translation, *Histoire des Berbères et des dynasties musulmanes de l'Afrique septentrionale*, deals with the parts of the *Kitāb al-'Ibar* that cover the history of the Arabs and Berbers, and comprises four volumes. There is also an English translation of the section of the *Kitāb al-'Ibar* on the dynasties of Yemen by Henry Cassels Kay (*Yaman, its early medieval history by Najm ad-Din Omarah Al-Hakami. Also the abridged history of its dynasties by Ibn Khaldun*). Of greater value are French translations of extracts of the *Kitāb al-'Ibar* undertaken by Abdesselam Cheddadi covering aspects of the Maghrib and Mashriq, appearing in two volumes.[2] For those interested in the problems of translation and transmission of ideas in the context of Orientalism, an article that would be of interest is Abdelmajid Hannoum's "Translation and the Colonial Imaginary: Ibn Khaldūn Orientalist", which discusses the extent to which the translation, *Histoire des Berbères*, is the production of a new text.

Biographies

The best source on Ibn Khaldūn's life is his autobiography. An excellent edition with beautiful illustrations and a French translation appearing on opposite pages has been published by Cheddadi (Ibn Khaldoun, *Autobiographie*). An early biography of Ibn Khaldūn was penned by Ibn al-Khaṭīb and can be found in his *al-Iḥāṭah fī Akhbār Gharnāṭah* (*A Comprehensive History of Granada*). Among the few modern biographies of Ibn Khaldūn, it is the one by the Egyptian scholar Muhammad Abdullah Enan (Muḥammad 'Abdallāh 'Inān) that is most well known and has been published in both the Arabic original and English translation. The first biography of Ibn Khaldūn to be published in the West appeared in the *Bibliothèque Orientale* of d'Herbelot in Paris in 1697. Mention must also be made of Walter Fischel's writings on Ibn Khaldūn's Egyptian period (Fischel, *Ibn Khaldūn in Egypt*; *Ibn Khaldūn and Tamerlane*). More recently, there appeared the historical novel, *The Polymath*, written by Bensalem Himmich.

Works on Ibn Khaldūn as a forerunner of the social sciences

Apart from biographies, there are numerous works that provide overviews of the *Muqaddimah*. Many of these works seek to present Ibn Khaldūn as the precursor of the various disciplines of the social sciences. Indeed, two generations of scholars across the Muslim and Western worlds have written books and articles on him as the founder of one social science or another. This is symptomatic of what Rosenthal refers to as the forerunner syndrome – that is, the tendency to view Ibn Khaldūn as a forerunner of later, usually modern intellectual developments.[3] Sometimes, the desire to find in Ibn Khaldūn a forerunner of disciplines in the modern social sciences runs the risk of interpreting the *Muqaddimah* out of context and anachronistically attributing to it modern meanings that distort the intent of the author. Among some of the earlier works that present Ibn Khaldūn as a forerunner are 'Abd al-'Azīz 'Izzat's thesis of 1932, *Ibn Khaldun et sa science sociale*, supervised by Fauconnier and René Maunier in France;[4] a well-known piece by 'Ali 'Abd al-Wāḥid Wāfī on him as the founder of sociology, "Ibn Khaldūn, Awwal Mu'assis"; Astre on Ibn Khaldūn as a precursor of sociology, "Un précurseur de la sociologie"; Conyers on him as the father of sociology, "Ibn Khaldun: The Father of Sociology?"; and an article by Syed Hussein Alatas, the Malaysian sociologist who considered Ibn Khaldūn to have established the principles of modern sociology, "Objectivity and the Writing of History".

As noted by some, such as Roussillon and Abaza, writing on Ibn Khaldūn became something of a rite of passage in the field of sociology.[5] Other works in this category include the following articles: Dhaouadi, "Ibn Khaldun: The Founding Father of Eastern Sociology"; Qadir, "The Social and Political Ideas of Ibn Khaldūn"; Ben Salem, "Ibn Khaldoun, père de la sociologie?"; and Turner, "Sociological Founders and Precursors: The Theories of Religion of Emile Durkheim, Fustel de Coulanges and Ibn Khaldûn".

Similar claims about Ibn Khaldūn's forerunner status have also been made for the discipline of economics. Of particular interest are articles by Spengler ("Economic Thought of Islam: Ibn Khaldun"), Boulakia ("Ibn Khaldûn: A Fourteenth Century Economist"), Soofi ("Economics of Ibn Khaldūn Revisited") and Oweiss ("Ibn Khaldūn, the Father of Economics").

Comparative studies between Ibn Khaldūn and seminal Western thinkers

Partly as a result of seeing Ibn Khaldūn as a forerunner of many ideas in the modern social sciences and also attributing to him, often erroneously, modern ideas, there was a drive to compare Ibn Khaldūn to the giants of Western thought. This is not to say that those who carried out such studies had anachronistic interpretations of Ibn Khaldūn or were afflicted by the forerunner syndrome.

The Egyptian sociologist Aḥmad Zāyid noted that many Arab sociologists made comparisons between Ibn Khaldūn and Western scholars in order to prove that it was the former who founded sociology.[6] Western scholars also undertook such comparative studies, impressed by what many considered to be a lone, towering figure in pre-modern Muslim scholarship. While many of these studies are not of high quality and make spurious comparisons that are often founded on decontextualized, anachronistic readings of Ibn Khaldūn, some deserve attention. In various works Ibn Khaldūn has been compared to Durkheim, Machiavelli, Comte, Marx and Engels, and Thucydides.[7]

Reviews and descriptions of the ideas in the *Muqaddimah*

In view of the vast literature that surveys and describes Ibn Khaldūn's writings on virtually all the topics that are covered by the *Muqaddimah*, it is unnecessary to provide an extensive list here. There are a few works that should be mentioned, however, that are useful in terms of providing readable introductions to his thoughts. A more recent work that provides an excellent account of Ibn Khaldūn's life and thought is Cheddadi's *Ibn Khaldûn: L'homme et le theoretician de la civilization*. Earlier works of interest include Alfred von Kremer's "Ibn Chaldun und seine Kulturgeschichte der Islamischen Reiche" of 1879.[8] Enan provides us with a good account of Ibn Khaldūn's social thought and how he had been received both in his time and by modern scholars (*Ibn Khaldūn*, particularly Section Two). Rabī', in his excellent *Political Theory of Ibn Khaldūn*, undertook a systematic study of Ibn Khaldūn's political theory. Published in 1967, it continues to be one of the best treatments of Ibn Khaldūn's political thought. For a short and readable orientation to Ibn Khaldūn, Baali's *Social Institutions: Ibn Khaldūn's Social Thought* is useful. Also useful is his more in-depth study, *Society, State, and Urbanism: Ibn Khaldun's Sociological Thought*. Heinrich Simon's *Ibn Khaldun's Science of Human Culture*, originally published in German as *Ibn Khaldūns Wissenschaft Vonder Menschlichen Kultur* in 1959, is also accessible, as is Syed Farid Alatas' *Ibn Khaldun*. Other works that are worth reading for introductions to Ibn Khaldūn include the following articles: Erwin Rosenthal, "Ibn Khaldūn as a Political Thinker"; Monteil, "Introduction à la sociologie religieuse d'Ibn Khaldûn"; Richard Walzer, "Aspects of Islamic Political Thought: Al-Fārābī and Ibn Khaldūn"; and Hamès, "La filiation généalogique (*nasab*) dans !a société d'Ibn Khaldūn".

Apart from the above works, encyclopaedic entries are useful as orientations to Ibn Khaldūn's life and thought. The standard reference is Talbi's entry in *The Encyclopaedia of Islam*. The entry in the *Encyclopaedia Iranica* by Franz Rosenthal is useful in that it assesses Ibn Khaldūn's views on Persia.[9] Riaz Hassan provides a sociological account of Ibn Khaldūn in his entry on the sociology of Islam in the *Encyclopaedia of Sociology*.[10] There is also Yūsuf Raḥīmlū's entry on Ibn Khaldūn in the *Dā'irat al-Ma'ārif-i Buzurg-i Islāmī*, published in Tehran in 1990.

There are many studies on Ibn Khaldūn's theory of dynastic succession and state formation that cover his ideas on the rise and fall of states, group feeling, the city, sedentary and nomadic societies, production relations and other subjects. These are too numerous to refer to here but have been cited in various chapters in this book.

Discussions of Ibn Khaldūn's methodology

Analytical studies on the epistemological and methodological aspects of Ibn Khaldūn's work are not nearly as numerous as those that describe his theory or survey his works. Nevertheless, a few serious studies have appeared. A short but useful orientation can be found in George F. Hourani's "Ibn Khaldūn's Historical Methodology". Also useful in this respect is Ferial Ghazoul's "The Metaphors of Historiography", which discusses Ibn Khaldūn's use of tropes and figures.[11] An important work focusing on the epistemological and methodological issues of the *Muqaddimah* is Muhsin Mahdi's *Ibn Khaldun's Philosophy of History*. Mahdi discusses Ibn Khaldūn's use of dialectics to critique Muslim historiography and his use of the method of demonstration derived from Aristotle in order to construct the new science of society. Mahdi was critiqued by Al-Wardī, who disagreed about the Aristotelian origins of Ibn Khaldūn's methods.[12] Rabī' reviewed four trends in the study of Ibn Khaldūn's method.[13] These are his alleged secular thinking, the unoriginality of his methods, his indebtedness to Aristotle and his rootedness in Islamic tradition. Relevant to this discussion are Ali Oumlil's *L'histoire et son discours* and Muḥammad 'Ābid al-Jābirī's *al-'Aṣabiyyah wa-l-Dawlah* (*Group Feeling and the State*), which deal with the historicization of Ibn Khaldūn's discourse.

Relevant to the debate about Ibn Khaldūn's method and its origins are several papers. An excellent article by Stephen Frederic Dale, "Ibn Khaldūn: The Last Greek and the First Annaliste Historian", discusses the meaning of historical explanation and Ibn Khaldūn's roots in Aristotelian logic. Nurullah Ardıç's "Beyond 'Science as a Vocation': Civilisational Epistemology in Weber and Ibn Khaldun" looks at the extent to which Ibn Khaldūn was influenced by Islamic espistemological ideas. James Winston Morris's discussion in "An Arab Machiavelli? Rhetoric, Philosophy and Politics in Ibn Khaldun's Critique of Sufims" shifts our attention to Ibn Khaldūn's use of rhetoric. Meuleman's "La causalité dans la *Muqaddimah* d'Ibn Khaldūn" centres the discussion of Ibn Khaldūn's new science around the all-important issue of causality. Also of interest are Abu Yaareb al-Marzouki's "Ibn

Khaldun's Epistemological and Axiological Paradoxes" and Hans P. van Ditsmarsch's "Logical Fragments in Ibn Khaldūn's *Muqaddimah*". A helpful overview of Ibn Khaldūn's epistemology can be found in Zaid Ahmad's *The Epistemology of Ibn Khaldūn*.

A very important contribution to debates on the place of rationality in Islam with reference to Ibn Khaldūn was made by the late Moroccan scholar Mohammed 'Abed Al-Jabri (Muḥammad 'Ābid al-Jābirī). Writing in Arabic and French, one of his themes is the continuity between Ibn Ḥazm and Ibn Rushd as representatives of the beginnings of Arab rationalism, and the innovative work of Ibn Khaldūn.[14] Other contributions to discussions on Ibn Khaldūn's methodology and epistemology in Arabic are those of 'Afīfī, Badawī, al-Marzūqī, al-Sā'ātī, Ṭāhā and al-Ṭālbī.[15] In connection with methodology is the issue of sources. This has been discussed in a comprehensive manner by Fischel in "Ibn Khaldun's Use of Jewish and Christian Sources" and "Ibn Khaldūn's Use of Historical Sources".

Analysis and critique of Ibn Khaldūn's theory

Another category of works on Ibn Khaldūn goes beyond descriptive accounts of his thoughts. Three kinds of critique can be discerned in the literature. The first deals with his overall theory or thought on philosophical grounds that relate to methodological or theological or other issues. The second is the critique of specific concepts, and the third of his biases and prejudices.

Regarding the first, Brett provides a brief but excellent account of the main positions in a critique and assessment of Ibn Khaldūn's thought.[16] Orientalist H. A. R. Gibb's view is that belief took precedence over reason in Ibn Khaldūn's thought,[17] while Mahdi maintains that Ibn Khaldūn's thought is a product of rationalist philosophical tradition.[18] Gibb's and Mahdi's assessments were based on the dichotomy between faith and reason. Al-Azmeh, while not seeing a conflict between faith and reason, finds Ibn Khaldūn's nominalism to be a problem, not allowing for the derivation of the particular from the general.[19] As a result, he finds the promise of the *Muqaddimah* to reinterpret history not fulfilled in the *Kitāb al-'Ibar*. Then there is the position of Cheddadi, who holds the opposite view. He feels that the *Kitāb al-'Ibar* does deliver on the promise of the *Muqaddimah*, and that the particular is related to the general in the way that the *Muqaddimah* determines the arrangement of the *akhbār* or event in the *Kitāb al-'Ibar*.[20] For a critique of the idea of "applying" Ibn Khaldūn, readers should look at Al-Azmeh's "The *Muqaddima* and *Kitāb Al'Ibar*: Perspectives from a Common Formula".

On the analysis and critique of specific concepts in the *Muqaddimah,* several works are important, a few of which are mentioned here. An excellent account of Ibn Khaldūn's thought dealing with various methodological and conceptual issues, and also disagreeing with some dominant views, is to be found in Cheddadi's *Actualité d'Ibn Khaldûn*. Helmut Ritter's "Irrational Solidarity Groups: A Socio-Psychological Study in Connection with Ibn Khaldûn" carries an extensive study from a socio-psychological point of view of Ibn Khaldūn's concept of *'aṣabiyyah*, while Cheddadi's "Le système du pouvoir en Islam d'après Ibn Khaldun" discusses his concepts of rank (*jāh*) and royal authority (*mulk*). A critical paper of a more general nature regarding Ibn Khaldūn's theory is Peter von Sivers' "Back to Nature: The Agrarian Foundations of Society According to Ibn Khaldūn".

Applications of Ibn Khaldūn's framework

Systematic applications of Ibn Khaldūn's theory of the rise and decline of states to historical data are few, although some have appeared recently. Furthermore, few works have attempted to integrate Ibn Khaldūn's theory of state formation with the theories and concepts of the modern social sciences. Attempts at these applications may be divided into three categories. The first are works that are guided by Ibn Khaldūn in a general manner without linking the details of historical or contemporary events to specific concepts and ideas in his theory. Examples of such works include Ortega's attempt to understand the history of Melilla in Khaldunian terms ("Abenjaldún nos revela el secreto") and Gellner's application, in his well-known paper "Flux and Reflux in the Faith of Men", of Ibn Khaldūn's cyclical theory to understand changes in faith over time.[21] Also relevant are Abdallah Laroui's *L'état dans le monde Arabe contemporain*, Gordon N. Newby's "Ibn Khaldun and Frederick Jackson Turner: Islam and the Frontier Experience", the articles by Bruce Lawrence and Warren Fusfeld on Islamic reform, which appeared in a special issue of the *Journal of Asian and African Studies* on Ibn Khaldūn in 1983, and Abdelkabir's Khatibi's "Hierarchies pre-coloniales: les théories".

In the second category are works that are direct applications to specific empirical cases. Examples in this category include applications of Ibn Khaldūn's theory to the modern state as well as to historical cases. On the modern state, two French scholars have made important contributions to such works. Gerard Michaud, in "Caste, confession et société en Syrie: Ibn Khaldoun au chevet du 'Progessisme Arabe", discusses what he calls the Khaldūnian triad of *'aṣabiyyah, da'wah* (call, invitation) and *mulk* (absolute power) in the context of the modern Syrian state. Olivier Carré, in two important essays – "Ethique et politique chez Ibn Khaldûn, juriste musulman: actualité de sa typologie des systèmes politique" and "A propos de vues néo-Khalduniennes sur quelques systèmes politiques Arabes actuels" – also critically assesses the relevance of Ibn Khaldūn to the understanding of the contemporary Arab state. Gabriel Martinez-Gros' *Ibn Khaldûn et les sept vies de l'Islam* is a very important contribution in that it assesses the relevance of Ibn Khaldūn's theory not only to the Arab East and West but also to Hellenistic civilization and the Roman Empire. Messier critically appraises Ibn Khaldūn's theory in the light of Almoravid history.[22]

The third category consists of works that attempt to integrate the theory of Ibn Khaldūn with the modern social sciences. Yves Lacoste, in *Ibn Khaldun: The Birth of History and the Past of the Third World*, played an important role in suggesting that research apply to Ibn Khaldūn with modern concepts in mind. As argued in this book, Ibn Khaldūn's theory of the dynamics of tribal state formation could be applied to the Ottoman Empire and Safavid Iran, combining his idea of cyclical change with the concept of modes of production; change in Ottoman and Safavid history can be understood in terms of a modes of production framework, while the dynamics of this change can be captured by the Khaldūnian model.[23] Other examples of Khaldūnian applications are discussed in my article "The Historical Sociology of Muslim Societies: Khaldunian Applications", as well as in this book.

Such dynamics of the rise and decline of states can also be restated in terms of historical timeframes, or what Turchin calls the Ibn Khaldūn cycle.[24] Turchin and Hall define this as a secular wave "that tends to affect societies with elites drawn from adjacent nomadic groups" and that operates on a timescale of about four generations or a century.[25] They apply this to the rise and fall of four Chinggisid dynasties.

While there have been few works that apply Ibn Khaldūn to historical cases, more such studies are beginning to appear and are necessary attempts in the direction of systematic applications of his works. They include Stephen Cory's "Breaking the Khaldunian Cycle? The Rise of Sharifianism as the Basis for Political Legitimacy in Early Modern Morocco", and Diana Wylie's "Decadence? The Khaldunian Cycle in Algeria and South Africa", both of which were published in a special issue of the *Journal of North African Studies* in 2008.

The lack of applications of Ibn Khaldūn's theory to historical and contemporary empirical cases has partly to do with the fact that a Khaldūnian school of historiography or sociology never developed. Some insight as to why a Khaldūnian school did not emerge may be derived from reading about how Ibn Khaldūn was received in the Muslim world. For this, readers are referred to Enan's *Ibn Khaldūn*, which discusses the reception of Ibn Khaldūn among Egyptian scholars, and Cengiz Tomar's "Between Myth and Reality: Approaches to Ibn Khaldun in the Arab World", which discusses the Khaldūnian legacy before and during the nineteenth century. Ahmed Abdesselem discusses the place of Ibn Khaldūn in both the Arab world of Ibn Khaldūn's time as well as among later Orientalists.[26] Also important is Claude Horrut's *Ibn Khaldûn, un islam des <<Lumières>>*, which critically discusses Ibn Khaldūn's reception in the West.

Notes

Introduction

1 Alatas, *Alternative Discourses*, 26–31.
2 Alatas and Sinha, "Teaching Classical Sociological Theory", 318, n.4.
3 Ibn Khaldoun, *L'Autobiographie*, 17.
4 Rosenthal, "Translator's Introduction", xxxiii–xxxiv.
5 Ibn Khaldoun, *Autobiographie*, 18.
6 Ibn Khaldoun, *Autobiographie*, 22; Enan, *Ibn Khaldūn*, 7.
7 Ibn Khaldoun, *Autobiographie*, 23.
8 Ibn Khaldoun, *Autobiographie*, 23–4.
9 Ibn Khaldoun, *Autobiographie*, 24.
10 Ibn Khaldoun, *Autobiographie*, 25–6.
11 See Merad, "L'Autobiographie", 54; Talbi, "Ibn Khaldūn", 825; and Talbi, *Ibn Khaldūn et l'histoire*, 6.
12 Ibn Khaldoun, *Autobiographie*, 27, 31.
13 Ibn Khaldoun, *Autobiographie*, 26, 34, 42, 44, 60.
14 Ibn Khaldoun, *Autobiographie*, 61.
15 Ibn Khaldoun, *Autobiographie*, 61–2.
16 Ibn Khaldoun, *Autobiographie*, 62, 64.
17 Ibn Khaldoun, *Autobiographie*, 80.
18 Ibn Khaldoun, *Autobiographie*, 92; Enan, *Ibn Khaldūn*, 31.
19 Ibn Khaldoun, *Autobiographie*, 92.
20 Ibn Khaldoun, *Autobiographie*, 93, 95.
21 Ibn Khaldoun, *Autobiographie*, 145.
22 *Kitāb al-Manhal al-Ṣāfī*, manuscript cited in Enan, *Ibn Khaldūn*, 52.
23 *Kitāb al-Ḍaw' al-Lāmi'*, manuscript cited in Enan, *Ibn Khaldūn*, 52–3.
24 Enan, *Ibn Khaldūn*, 53.
25 See Abdesselem, *Ibn Khaldun et ses lecteurs*, 14–15.
26 Ibn Khaldoun, *Autobiographie*, 239, 242.
27 Fischel, *Ibn Khaldūn and Tamerlane*, 68.
28 Ibn Khaldoun, *Autobiographie*, 242–3.
29 Talbi, "Ibn Khaldūn", 827–8. See also Ibn Khaldoun, *L'Autobiographie*, 244–5.
30 Ibn Khaldūn, *Autobiographie*, 246.
31 Al-Maqrīzī, *Al-Sulūk fī Duwal al-Mulūk*, cited in Enan, *Ibn Khaldūn*, 67–8.
32 Ibn Iyās, *Tārīkh Miṣr*, cited in Enan, *Ibn Khaldūn*, 68.
33 Enan, *Ibn Khaldūn*, 68.
34 Ibn Khaldoun, *Autobiographie*, 244–5.
35 Talbi, *Ibn Khaldūn*, 827–8.
36 Other works of Ibn Khaldūn that are of lesser relevance to sociology and the social sciences include the *Lubāb al-Muḥaṣṣal fī Uṣūl al-Dīn* (*The Resumé of the Compendium in the*

Fundamentals of Religion), being his summary of Fakhr al-Dīn al-Rāzī's Compendium of the Sciences of the Ancients and Moderns, and the *Shifa' al-Sā'il* (*The Healing of the Seekers*), a work on Sufism. In addition to the above works, Ibn Khaldūn is also said to have produced five other works: a commentary on the Burda of al-Būsīrī, an outline of logic, a treatise on arithmetic, resumés of works by Ibn Rushd, and a commentary on a poem by Ibn al-Khatīb. See Talbi, "Ibn Khaldūn", 828. These works, which have not come down to us, were mentioned by Ibn al-Khaṭīb, a close friend of Ibn Khaldūn and his biographer.

37 Roussillon, "La représentation de l'identité", 56, n.48.
38 'Izzat, *Etude comparée d'Ibn Khaldun et Durkheim*.
39 Wāfī, *Al-Falsafah al-Ijtimā'iyyah li Ibn Khaldūn wa Aujust Kumt*; Wāfī, "Ibn Khaldūn, awwal mu'assis li 'ilm al-ijtimā".
40 Alatas, "Objectivity and the Writing of History", 2.
41 Roussillon, "Durkheimisme et réformisme", 5; Abaza, *Debates on Islam and Knowledge in Malaysia and Egypt*, 146.
42 Hussein, *La philosophie sociale d'Ibn-Khaldoun*, 75.
43 von Kremer, "Ibn Chaldun und seine Kulturgeschichte der Islamischen Reiche" ("Ibn Khaldûn and His History of Islamic Civilization"); Bombaci, "La Dottrina Storiografica di Ibn Haldûn"; Talbi, "Ibn Kaldun et le sens de l'histoire"; Talbi, *Ibn Khaldūn et l'histoire*.
44 Michaud, "Caste, confession et société en Syrie"; Lacoste, *Ibn Khaldūn*; Carré, "A propos de vues néo-Khalduniennes"; Alatas, "A Khaldunian Perspective on the Dynamics of Asiatic Societies".
45 Al-Azmeh, *Ibn Khaldun in Modern Scholarship*; Al-Azmeh, *Ibn Khaldūn*.
46 Lacoste, *Ibn Khaldūn*, 92–4.

1 The errors of history and the new science: Introduction to the *Muqaddimah*

1 Ibn Khaldoun, *Autobiographie*, 17.
2 Ibn Khaldūn, *Al-Muqaddimah*, I, 5–6 [I, 6]. Page numbers in square brackets refer to Franz Rosenthal's English translation, from which the English quotations are taken (see Ibn Khaldūn, *The Muqaddimah*).
3 Ibn Khaldūn, *Al-Muqaddimah*, I, 7 [I, 7].
4 Ibn Khaldūn, *Al-Muqaddimah*, I, 8 [I, 9–10].
5 Ibn Khaldūn, *Al-Muqaddimah*, I, 13–14 [I, 15–16].
6 Ibn Khaldūn, *Al-Muqaddimah*, I, 14–16 [I, 16–18].
7 Ibn Khaldūn, *Al-Muqaddimah*, I, 17–20 [I, 21–4].
8 Ibn Khaldūn, *Al-Muqaddimah*, I, 30–32 [I, 41–4].
9 Ibn Khaldūn, *Al-Muqaddimah*, I, 33–34 [I, 45–6].
10 Ibn Khaldūn, *Al-Muqaddimah*, II, 368 [II, 449].
11 Ibn Khaldūn, *Al-Muqaddimah*, I, 42–44 [I, 58, 60–2].
12 Ibn Khaldūn, *Al-Muqaddimah*, I, 51–53 [I, 71–2].
13 Ibn Khaldūn, *Al-Muqaddimah*, I, 53 [I, 72–3].
14 Ibn Khaldūn, *Al-Muqaddimah*, I, 53–4 [I, 73–4].
15 Ibn Khaldūn, *Al-Muqaddimah*, I, 54–5 [I, 74–5].
16 Ibn Khaldūn, *Al-Muqaddimah*, I, 55 [I, 76].
17 Ibn Khaldūn, *Al-Muqaddimah*, I, 56 [I, 76–7].
18 Ibn Khaldūn, *Al-Muqaddimah*, I, 40–1 [I, 55–6].
19 Ibn Khaldūn, *Al-Muqaddimah*, I, 9 [I, 10].
20 Ibn Khaldūn, *Al-Muqaddimah*, I, 45–6 [I, 63–4].
21 Ibn Khaldūn, *Al-Muqaddimah*, I, 46 [I, 65].
22 Ibn Khaldūn, *Al-Muqaddimah*, I, 56 [I, 77].
23 Ibn Khaldūn, *Al-Muqaddimah*, I, 5–6 [I, 6].

24 Mahdi, *Ibn Khaldūn's Philosophy of History*, 234–5, 253–4, 261.
25 Ibn Khaldūn, *Al-Muqaddimah*, I, 10 [I, 11–12].
26 El-Azmeh, "The *Muqaddima* and *Kitab Al-'Ibar*", 17.
27 Ibn Khaldūn, *Al-Muqaddimah*, I, 56 [I, 77].
28 Ibn Khaldūn, *Al-Muqaddimah*, I, 63 [I, 85].
29 Ibn Khaldūn, *Al-Muqaddimah*, I, 11 [I, 12].
30 Ibn Khaldūn, *Al-Muqaddimah*, I, 56 [I, 78].
31 Ibn Khaldūn, *Al-Muqaddimah*, I, 11 [I, 14].
32 Ibn Khaldūn, *Al-Muqaddimah*, I, 56 [I, 77].
33 Ibn Khaldūn, *Al-Muqaddimah*, I, 46 [I, 65].
34 Ibn Khaldūn, *Al-Muqaddimah*, I, 226, 259 [I, 284, 313].
35 El-Azmeh, "The *Muqaddima* and *Kitab Al-'Ibar*", 19.
36 El-Azmeh, "The *Muqaddima* and *Kitab Al-'Ibar*", 19.

2 Ibn Khaldūn's theory of state formation

1 Mahdi, *Ibn Khaldûn's Philosophy of History*, 172.
2 Ibn Khaldūn, *Al-Muqaddimah*, I, 67 [I, 89].
3 Ibn Khaldūn, *Al-Muqaddimah*, I, 62 [I, 84].
4 Ibn Khaldūn, *Al-Muqaddimah*, I, 71, 132, 138, 140 [I, 94, 167, 174, 177].
5 Hodgson, *The Venture of Islam*, Vol. 2, 479–80.
6 Mahdi, *Ibn Khaldûn's Philosophy of History*, 160.
7 Ibn Khaldūn, *Al-Muqaddimah*, III, 91 [III, 137].
8 Ibn Khaldūn, *Al-Muqaddimah*, III, 92 [III, 138–9].
9 Ibn Khaldūn, *Al-Muqaddimah*, III, 94 [III, 142].
10 Ibn Khaldūn, *Al-Muqaddimah*, I, 53 [I, 72–3].
11 Ibn Khaldūn, *Al-Muqaddimah*, III, 93–4 [III, 140–1].
12 Ibn Khaldūn, *Al-Muqaddimah*, I, 56 [I, 78].
13 Ibn Khaldūn, *Al-Muqaddimah*, I, 191–2 [I, 249–50].
14 Ibn Khaldūn, *Al-Muqaddimah*, I, 193–4 [I, 251–2].
15 Ibn Khaldūn, *Al-Muqaddimah*, I, 196 [I, 253].
16 Ibn Khaldūn, *Al-Muqaddimah*, I, 197 [I, 253–4].
17 Ibn Khaldūn, *Al-Muqaddimah*, I, 200–1 [I, 257–8].
18 Ibn Khaldūn, *Al-Muqaddimah*, I, 226 [I, 284].
19 Ibn Khaldūn, *Al-Muqaddimah*, I, 203 [I, 259–60].
20 Ibn Khaldūn, *Al-Muqaddimah*, I, 206 [I, 262–3].
21 Rabī', *The Political Theory of Ibn Khaldūn*, 49; von Sivers, "Back to Nature", 80.
22 Ritter, "Irrational Solidarity Groups", 3.
23 Ibn Khaldūn, *Al-Muqaddimah*, I, 207 [I, 264].
24 Ibn Khaldūn, *Al-Muqaddimah*, I, 207–8 [I, 264–5].
25 Ibn Khaldūn, *Al-Muqaddimah*, I, 213 [I, 269].
26 Ibn Khaldūn, *Al-Muqaddimah*, I, 216 [I, 273].
27 Ibn Khaldūn, *Al-Muqaddimah*, I, 216–17 [I, 273–4].
28 Ibn Khaldūn, *Al-Muqaddimah*, I, 219–20 [I, 277–8].
29 Ibn Khaldūn, *Al-Muqaddimah*, I, 219–20 [I, 277–8].
30 Ibn Khaldūn, *Al-Muqaddimah*, I, 221–2 [I, 279–80].
31 Ibn Khaldūn, *Al-Muqaddimah*, I, 222 [I, 280–1].
32 Ibn Khaldūn, *Al-Muqaddimah*, I, 240 [I, 297].
33 Ibn Khaldūn, *Al-Muqaddimah*, I, 240–1 [I, 298–9].
34 Ibn Khaldūn, *Al-Muqaddimah*, I, 227 [I, 285].
35 Ibn Khaldūn, *Al-Muqaddimah*, I, 261–2 [I, 314–15].
36 Ibn Khaldūn, *Al-Muqaddimah*, I, 312–13 [I, 372–3].
37 Ibn Khaldūn, *Al-Muqaddimah*, I, 288 [I, 344].
38 Ibn Khaldūn, *Al-Muqaddimah*, I, 228 [I, 286].

39 Ibn Khaldūn, *Al-Muqaddimah*, I, 296 [I, 353].
40 Ibn Khaldūn, *Al-Muqaddimah*, I, 267 [I, 320].
41 Ibn Khaldūn, *Al-Muqaddimah*, I, 269 [I, 322].
42 Ibn Khaldūn, *Al-Muqaddimah*, I, 250 [I, 305].
43 Ibn Khaldūn, *Al-Muqaddimah*, I, 198 [I, 255].
44 Ibn Khaldūn, *Al-Muqaddimah*, II, 92 [II, 117].
45 Ibn Khaldūn, *Al-Muqaddimah*, II, 94–5 [II, 119–20].
46 Ibn Khaldūn, *Al-Muqaddimah*, II, 95 [II, 120].
47 Ibn Khaldūn, *Al-Muqaddimah*, II, 95–6 [II, 121].
48 Ibn Khaldūn, *Al-Muqaddimah*, II, 103–4 [II, 129–30].
49 Ibn Khaldūn, *Al-Muqaddimah*, I, 328 [I, 387–8].
50 Ibn Khaldūn, *Al-Muqaddimah*, I, 226 [I, 284].
51 Ibn Khaldūn, *Al-Muqaddimah*, I, 69 [I, 91–2].
52 Rabī‘, *The Political Theory of Ibn Khaldūn*, 141.
53 Ibn Khaldūn, *Al-Muqaddimah*, I, 327–8 [I, 387].
54 Ben Salem, "La notion de pouvoir", 309.
55 Ibn Khaldūn, *Al-Muqaddimah*, I, 327 [I, 387].
56 Ben Salem, "La notion de pouvoir", 310.
57 Gellner, *Muslim Society*, 34.
58 Ibn Khaldūn, *Al-Muqaddimah*, II, 79 [II, 102–3].
59 Ibn Khaldūn, *Al-Muqaddimah*, II, 67–8 [II, 89–90].
60 Ibn Khaldūn, *Al-Muqaddimah*, II, 68 [II, 90–1].
61 Ibn Khaldūn, *Al-Muqaddimah*, I, 97–8 [122–4].
62 Ben Salem, "Interêt des analyses d'Ibn Khaldoun", 5–6.
63 Newby, "Ibn Khaldun and Frederick Jackson Turner", 275.
64 Djeghloul, "Ibn Khaldoun: Mode d'emploi", 38.

3 Ibn Khaldūn and modern sociology: An aborted tradition

1 Simon, *Ibn Khaldun's Science*, 51.
2 D'Herbelot, "Khaledoun", II, 418.
3 de Sacy, "Extraits de Prolégomènes d'Ebn Khaldoun".
4 Baali, *Ilm al-Umran and Sociology*, 32–3.
5 Ibn Khaldoun, *Histoire des Berbères*.
6 von Kremer, "Ibn Chaldun und seine Kulturgeschichte der Islamischen Reiche"; Flint, *History of the Philosophy of History*, 158ff.; Gumplowicz, *Soziologische Essays*, 90–114; Maunier, "Les idées économiques d'un philosophe arabe", Oppenheimer, *System der Soziologie*, vol. II: 173ff.; vol. IV, 251ff.; Ortega, "Abenjaldún nos revela el secreto".
7 Becker and Barnes, *Social Thought from Lore to Science*, 721–6.
8 Becker and Barnes, *Social Thought from Lore to Science*, 706–8.
9 Becker and Barnes, *Social Thought from Lore to Science*, 266.
10 Ortega, "Abenjaldún nos revela el secreto", 95.
11 Ortega, "Abenjaldún nos revela el secreto", 97.
12 Ortega, "Abenjaldún nos revela el secreto", 98.
13 Ortega, "Abenjaldún nos revela el secreto", 99.
14 Ortega, "Abenjaldún nos revela el secreto", 100.
15 Ortega, "Abenjaldún nos revela el secreto", 101.
16 Ortega, "Abenjaldún nos revela el secreto", 108.
17 Ortega, "Abenjaldún nos revela el secreto", 112.
18 Ortega, "Abenjaldún nos revela el secreto", 112.
19 Lacoste, *Ibn Khaldun*; Gellner, *Muslim Society*.
20 Abdesselem, *Ibn Khaldun et ses lectures*, 60ff.
21 Al-Jābirī, "Ibistīmūlūjiyā al-Ma‘qūl"; Oumlil, *L'Histoire et son discours*.

22 Becker and Barnes, *Social Thought from Lore to Science*, vol. I: 266–79.
23 Barnes, "Ancient and Medieval Social Philosophy", 25–6.
24 Baali, *Ilm al-Umran and Sociology*, 17.
25 Baali, *Ilm al-Umran and Sociology*, 29–32.
26 This connection was made first of all by Bousquet, "Marx et Engels se sont-ils intéressés aux questions Islamiques", 119–30; Gellner, *Muslim Society*; and later by Hopkins, "Engels and Ibn Khaldun", 9–18.
27 Hopkins, "Engels and Ibn Khaldūn", 12.
28 Engels, "On the History of Early Christianity", 276.
29 Hopkins, "Engels and Ibn Khaldūn", 12.
30 Ibn Khaldūn, *Al-Muqaddimah*, I, 71, 132, 138, 140 [I, 94, 167, 174, 177].
31 Bousquet, "Marx et Engels se sont-ils intéressés aux questions Islamiques?", 124–5.
32 Becker and Barnes, *Social Thought from Lore to Science*, Vol. I: 266–79.
33 Becker and Barnes, *Social Thought from Lore to Science*, Vol. I: 267.
34 Becker and Barnes, *Social Thought from Lore to Science*, Vol. I: 269.
35 Becker and Barnes, *Social Thought from Lore to Science*, Vol. I: 269.
36 Cheddadi, "Le système du pouvoir en Islam d`après Ibn Khaldun"; Gellner, *Muslim Society*; Lacoste, *Ibn Khaldūn*; Carré, "A propos de vues néo-Khalduniennes"; Alatas; "A Khaldūnian Perspective".
37 For other accounts of Eurocentrism see Amin, *Eurocentrism*; and Wallerstein, "Eurocentrism and its Avatars".
38 Tibawi, "English Speaking Orientalists", 191, 196; Tibawi, "Second Critique of English-Speaking Orientalists", 5, 13, 16–17.
39 Abdel-Malek, "Orientalism in Crisis", 107–8.
40 Said, *Orientalism*, 6.
41 Wallerstein, "Eurocentrism and its Avatars", 8.
42 Weber, *History of Philosophy*, 164n.
43 Tibawi, "Second Critique of English-Speaking Orientalists", 37.
44 Needham, "The Dialogue of East and West", 26.
45 Wallerstein, "Eurocentrism and its Avatars", 5.
46 Fletcher, *The Making of Sociology*, Ch. 2.
47 For example, Sarkar notes that the overemphasis of Orientalist scholarship on metaphysics and religion in Hindu culture and stressed the positive and secular aspects. See his *The Positive Background of Hindu Sociology*, 351.
48 Maus, *A Short History of Sociology*, Ch. 1.
49 Moodey, *Resource Book for Teaching Sociological Theory*.
50 Ritzer acknowledged Ibn Khaldūn as an example of a sociologist that predated the Western classical thinkers but he was not able to do more than provide a brief biographical sketch of Ibn Khaldūn in his textbook, *Classical Sociological Theory*.
51 Becker and Barnes, *Social Thought from Lore to Science*, Vol. I: 266–79. Barnes suggested in 1917 that it was Ibn Khaldūn rather than Vico who "has the best claim to the honor of having founded the philosophy of history", and his view of the factors involved in the historical process was sounder and more modern than that of the Italian of three centuries later (Barnes, "Ancient and Medieval Social Philosophy", 3–28).
52 Becker and Barnes, *Social Thought from Lore to Science*, Vol. I: 266.
53 Examples are von Kremer, "Ibn Chaldun und seine Kulturgeschichte der Islamischen Reiche", 93: 581–634; Flint, *History of the Philosophy of History in France, Belgium, and Switzerland*, 158ff., Gumplowicz, *Soziologische Essays*, 90–114; Maunier, "Les idées sociologiques d'un philosophie arabe au XIVe siècle"; Oppenheimer, *System der Soziologie*, Vol. II, 173ff.; Vol. IV, 251ff.; Schmidt, *Ibn Khaldun*; Ortega, "Abenjaldún nos revela el secreto", 95–114; Ritter, "Irrational Solidarity Groups", 1–44.
54 Becker and Barnes, *Social Thought from Lore to Science*, Vol. I: 267.
55 For these exceptions see Gellner, *Muslim Society*, Ch. 1; Michaud, "Caste, confession et société en Syrie", 119–30; Lacoste, *Ibn Khaldun*; Carré, "A propos de vues

néo-Khalduniennes”, 368–87; and Alatas, “A Khaldunian Perspective on the Dynamics of Asiatic Societies”, 29–51.

56 Matthes, “Religion in the Social Sciences”.

57 References are mainly to works in Arabic, French and English published out of the Arab and Muslim world.

58 Zāyid, “Saba‘ūn ‘Āmā li-l-‘Ilm al-Ijtimā‘ fī Misr”, 14.

59 Al-‘Arawī, “Ibn Khaldūn wa Mākyāfīlī”; Laroui, *Islam et modernité.*

60 Wāfī, *Al-falsafah al-Ijtimā‘iyyah li Ibn Khaldūn wa Aujust Kumt*; Baali, *Ilm al-Umran and Sociology*; Faghirzadeh, *Sociology of Sociology*; Khayrī, “Tā’sīs ‘Ilm al-Ijtimā‘”.

61 Baali and Price, “Ibn Khaldun and Karl Marx”.

62 Faghirzadeh, *Sociology of Sociology*; ‘Izzat, *Etude comparée d'Ibn Khaldun et Durkheim*; Khayrī, “Tā’sīs ‘Ilm al-Ijtimā‘”.

63 *Al-Hayāt al-Thaqāfiyyah*; Tixier-Wieczorkiewicz, *L'œuvre d'Ibn Khaldun dans la recherché contemporaine depuis 1965.*

64 Al-Wardī, *Manṭiq Ibn Khaldūn*, cited in Rabī‘, *The Political Theory of Ibn Khaldūn*, 26.

65 Rabī‘, *The Political Theory of Ibn Khaldūn*, 24–6.

66 Badawī, “Ibn Khaldūn wa Arastū”, and “Al-Mūrfūlūjiyā al-Ijtimā‘iyyah wa Asasuhā al-Minhajiyyah ‘inda Ibn Khaldūn”; ‘Afīfī, “Mawqif Ibn Khaldūn min al-Falsafah wa al-Taṣawwuf”; Al-Sā‘ātī, “Al-Minhaj al-‘Ilmī fī Muqaddimah Ibn Khaldūn”; ‘Ṭāhā (1979); Al-Jābirī, “Ibistīmūlūjiyā al-Ma’qūl fī Muqaddimah Ibn Khaldūn”; Al-Ṭālbī, “Minhajiyyah Ibn Khaldūn al-Tārīkhiyyah wa Atharuhā fī Diwān <<Al-‘Ibar>>”; and Al-Marzūqī, “Minhajiyyah Ibn Khaldūn wa Ijtimā‘ahu al-Naẓarī”.

67 Ortega, “Abenjaldún nos revela el secreto”; Laroui, *L'état dans le monde Arabe contemporain*; Cheddadi, “Le système du pouvoir en Islam d`après Ibn Khaldun”; Gellner, *Muslim Society*; Michaud, “Caste, confession et société en Syrie”; Lacoste, *Ibn Khaldun*; Carrē, “A propos de vues néo-Khalduniennes”; Alatas, “A Khaldunian Perspective on the Dynamics of Asiatic Societies”.

68 Alatas, “A Khaldunian Perspective on the Dynamics of Asiatic Societies”.

69 National Centre for Social and Criminological Research (1962); Centre National d'ētudes Historiques (1978); Faculty of Letters and Human Sciences (1979).

70 Zāyid, “Saba‘ūn ‘Āmā li-l-‘Ilm al-Ijtimā‘ fī Misr”, 16.

71 Gautier, *Le Passé de l'Afrique du Nord*, 72, 374.

72 Lacoste, *Ibn Khaldun*, 75.

73 Al-Attas, *Islam and Secularism*, 16, 91.

74 Al-Attas, “Preliminary Thoughts on the Nature of Knowledge and the Definition and Aims of Education”. For the proceedings of this conference see Al-Attas, *Aims and Objectives of Islamic Education.* See also Al-Attas, *Islam and Secularism*, Ch. 5; and *The Concept of Education in Islam.*

75 Al-Faruqi, “Islamizing the Social Sciences”, 8–20.

76 See Nasr, *Science and Civilization in Islam*; *Islamic Science*; “Reflections on Methodology in the Islamic Sciences”; *Knowledge and the Sacred*; *The Need for a Sacred Science.*

77 Personal correspondence with Professor Seyyed Hossein Nasr, 10 April 1995.

78 Al-Faruqi, *Islamization of Knowledge: General Principles and Work Plan.*

79 Al-Attas, *Islam and Secularism*, 131.

80 Al-Attas, *Islam and Secularism*, 131–2, 155.

81 Al-Attas, *Islam and Secularism*, 156; *The Concept of Education in Islam*, 43.

82 Al-Attas, *The Concept of Education in Islam*, 43.

83 Al-Attas, *The Concept of Education in Islam*, 4.

84 Al-Attas, *Islam and the Philosophy of Science*, 30.

85 Al-Attas, *The Concept of Education in Islam*, 5.

86 Al-Attas, *Islam and the Philosophy of Science*, 31.
87 Al-Attas, *Islam and the Philosophy of Science*, 35.
88 Al-Faruqi, "Islamization of Knowledge", 16–17.
89 Al-Faruqi, "Islamization of Knowledge", 17.
90 Al-Faruqi, "Islamization of Knowledge", 31.
91 Al-Faruqi, "Islamization of Knowledge", 32.
92 Al-Faruqi, "Islamization of Knowledge", 38–53.
93 Nasr, *Knowledge and the Sacred*, 130.
94 Nasr, *Knowledge and the Sacred*, 34.
95 Nasr, *The Need for a Sacred Science*, 173.
96 Nasr, *Knowledge and the Sacred*, 212.
97 Nasr, "Reflections on Methodology in the Islamic Sciences", 4.
98 Nasr, "Reflections on Methodology in the Islamic Sciences", 7.
99 Nasr, "Reflections on Methodology in the Islamic Sciences", 8.
100 Nasr, "Reflections on Methodology in the Islamic Sciences", 8–9.
101 Nasr, "Reflections on Methodology in the Islamic Sciences", 9. Nasr's ideas and the intepretive methods of *tafsīr* and *ta'wīl* are discussed by Osman Bakar, "The Question of Methodology in Islamic Science", 91–109.
102 Dale, "Ibn Khaldun: The Last Greek", 440.
103 Ayad, *Die geschichts*, 51–3, 143, cited in Gibb, "The Islamic Background", 27.
104 Rosenthal, *Ibn Khalduns Gedanken*, 58, cited in Gibb, "The Islamic Background", 27.
105 Gibb, "The Islamic Background", 29.
106 Siddiqui, *The Islamic Movement: A Systems Approach.*
107 For a discussion on such views see Abaza and Stauth, "Occidental Reason, Orientalism, Islamic Fundamentalism", 218–20; Turner, "From Orientalism to Global Sociology", 629–38.
108 Carré, "A propos de vues néo-Khalduniennes", 368–87 ; Michaud, "Caste, confession et société en Syrie", 119–30.
109 Gumplowicz, *The Outlines of Sociology*; Barnes, "Sociology before Comte", 197–8; Toynbee, *A Study History*, 321–8.
110 Baali and Price, "Ibn Khaldun and Karl Marx: On Socio-Historic Change", 17–36; Faghirzadeh, *Sociology of Sociology*; Laroui, "Ibn Khaldun et Machiavel"; Newby, "Ibn Khaldun and Frederick Jackson Turner"; Stowasser, *Religion and Political Developmenti*; Turner, "Sociological Founders and Precursors", 32–48.
111 S. F. Alatas, "Ibn Khaldun and the Ottoman Modes of Production", 45–63; "A Khaldunian Perspective on the Dynamics of Asiatic Societies", 29–51; Carré, "A propos de vues néo-Khalduniennes", 368–87; Cheddadi, "Le système du pouvoir en Islam d'après Ibn Khaldun"; Gellner, *Muslim Society*; Laroui, *L'état dans le monde Arabe Contemporain*; Lacoste, *Ibn Khaldun*; Michaud, "Caste, confession et société en Syrie", 119–30.

4 Pre-modern readings and applications of Ibn Khaldūn

1 Abdesselem, *Ibn Khaldun et ses lectures*, 60ff.
2 Issawi, "Introduction", 25.
3 Lewis, *Islam in History*, 233.
4 Al-Azraq, *Badā'i' al-Silk*; Abdesselem, *Ibn Khaldun et ses lecteurs*, 19.
5 Issawi, "Introduction", 24; Abdesselem, *Ibn Khaldun et ses lecteurs*, 14.
6 Abdesselem, *Ibn Khaldun et ses lectures*, 17.
7 Abdesselem, *Ibn Khaldun et ses lectures*, 18.
8 Abdesselem, *Ibn Khaldun et ses lectures*, 19; Aldila, *Ibn al-Azraq's Political Thought*, 9.
9 Al-Azraq, *Badā'i' al-Silk*, I, 71 [173]. Page numbers in brackets refer to the English translation of the First and Second Prefaces by Aldila in *Ibn al-Azraq's Political Thought*, 173–94.
10 Al-Azraq, *Badā'i' al-Silk*, I, 71–2 [173–4].

11 Al-Azraq, *Badā'i' al-Silk*, I, 73 [174].
12 Al-Azraq, *Badā'i' al-Silk*, I, 74 [175].
13 Al-Azraq, *Badā'i' al-Silk*, I, 75–6 [176].
14 Al-Azraq, *Badā'i' al-Silk*, I, 77 [177].
15 Al-Azraq, *Badā'i' al-Silk*, I, 87 [183].
16 Al-Azraq, *Badā'i' al-Silk*, I, 78–81 [178–80].
17 Abdesselem, *Ibn Khaldun et ses lecteurs*, 20; Aldila, *Ibn al-Azraq's Political Thought*, 45.
18 Al-Azraq, *Badā'i' al-Silk*, I, 91–2 [186–7].
19 Al-Azraq, *Badā'i' al-Silk*, I, 93 [187].
20 Al-Azraq, *Badā'i' al-Silk*, I, 94–5 [188].
21 Al-Azraq, *Badā'i' al-Silk*, I, 97 [189].
22 Al-Azraq, *Badā'i' al-Silk*, I, 93 [188].
23 Al-Azmeh, *Muslim Kingship*, 95–6.
24 Khadduri, *The Islamic Conception of Justice*.
25 Ibn Khaldūn, *Al-Muqaddimah*, I, 328 [I, 387–8].
26 Ibn Khaldūn, *Al-Muqaddimah*, I, 226 [I, 284].
27 Al-Azraq, *Badā'i' al-Silk*, I, 232–9; Khadduri, *The Islamic Conception of Justice*, 191.
28 Abdesselem, *Ibn Khaldun et ses lecteurs*, 36.
29 Gökyay, "Kâtib Celebi".
30 Kâtib Çelebi (Kātib Çelebī), *Düstūrü'l-amel li-ıslāhı'l-halel.*
31 Fleischer, "Royal Authority, Dynastic Cyclism, and 'Ibn Khaldunism'", 199.
32 Fleischer, "Royal Authority, Dynastic Cyclism, and 'Ibn Khaldunism'", 200.
33 Thomas, *A Study of Naima*, 78.
34 Thomas, *A Study of Naima*, 78.
35 Ibn Khaldūn, *Al-Muqaddimah*, I, 58–9 [I, 81–2].
36 Ḳınalızāde, *Ahlāḳ-i 'Alā'ī*, Book III, 49, cited in Fleischer, "Royal Authority, Dynastic Cyclism, and 'Ibn Khaldunism'", 201.
37 Ibn Khaldūn, *Al-Muqaddimah*, I, 58 [I, 81].
38 Ibn Khaldūn, *Al-Muqaddimah*, I, 59 [I, 82].
39 Ibn Khaldūn, *Al-Muqaddimah*, II, 226 [II, 291].
40 Ibn Khaldūn, *Al-Muqaddimah*, I, 226, 259 [I, 284, 313].
41 Ibn Khaldūn, *Al-Muqaddimah*, I, 253–4 [I, 308–9].
42 Ibn Khaldūn, *Al-Muqaddimah*, I, 226–7, 290–3 [I, 284–5, 347–51].
43 Fleischer, "Royal Authority, Dynastic Cyclism, and 'Ibn Khaldunism'", 200.
44 Fleischer, "Royal Authority, Dynastic Cyclism, and 'Ibn Khaldunism'", 202.
45 Buzpınar, "Opposition to the Ottoman Caliphate".
46 Buzpınar, "Opposition to the Ottoman Caliphate", 59–61, 63.
47 Al-Bukhārī, *Ṣaḥīḥ al-Bukhārī*, Hadith 9.253, 190–1.
48 Buzpınar, "Opposition to the Ottoman Caliphate", 56–66, 69–72.
49 Buzpınar, "The Question of Caliphate", 29.
50 Ibn Khaldūn, *Al-Muqaddimah*, I, 334 [I, 397].
51 Ibn Khaldūn, *Al-Muqaddimah*, I, 335 [I, 399].
52 Ibn Khaldūn, *Al-Muqaddimah*, I, 336–7 [I, 401].
53 Ibn Khaldūn, *Al-Muqaddimah*, I, 336–7 [I, 401].
54 Buzpınar, "The Question of Caliphate", 29.
55 Ibn Khaldūn, *Al-Muqaddimah*, I, 332 [I, 392]; Buzpınar, "Osmanlı Hilâfet", 4. I would like to thank Tufan Ş. Buzpınar for translating the relevant passages from his article during our meeting in Istanbul on 22 February 2006.
56 Buzpınar, "Osmanlı Hilâfet", 4.

5 A Khaldūnian theory of Muslim reform

1 A work that is related to our theme is Spickard's "Tribes and Cities", although it is more concerned with elaborating an alternative sociology of religion rather than a theory of reform.

2 Lawrence, "Ibn Khaldun and Islamic Reform", 230–1.
3 Ortega, "Abenjaldún nos revela el secreto", 95–6. I have used an unpublished English translation of this alongside the original Spanish, made available to me in April 2000. The translator was Saida del Moral Llobat, who was a PhD student at the International Institute of Islamic Thought and Civilization (ISTAC) in Kuala Lumpur. I am grateful to Syed Muhammad al-Naquib Al-Attas for having organized the translation of Ortega's essay.
4 Ortega, "Ibn Khaldūn reveals his secret to us", 97. We shall bracket any concerns with Ortega's Orientalist orientation for now.
5 Ortega, "Abenjaldún nos revela el secreto", 98.
6 Ortega, "Abenjaldún nos revela el secreto", 99–100.
7 Ortega, "Abenjaldún nos revela el secreto", 100–1.
8 Ortega, "Abenjaldún nos revela el secreto", 111.
9 Ortega, "Abenjaldún nos revela el secreto", 112.
10 Ansari, "Civilization and its Enemy", 85.
11 Ruthven, "The Eleventh of September and the Sudanese Mahdiya", 344.
12 Al-Sa'ūd, *Rasa'il a'immah da'wah al-tawḥīd*, 79, cited in Moussalli, *Wahhabism, Salafism and Islamism*, 7.
13 Ibn Khaldūn, *Al-Muqaddimah*, I, 250 [I, 305–6].
14 Ibn Khaldūn, *Al-Muqaddimah*, I, 269–70 [I, 322–3].
15 Montagne, *The Berbers*, 14–15.
16 Ibn Khaldūn, *Al-Muqaddimah*, I, 270 [I, 323–4].
17 Ibn Khaldūn, *Al-Muqaddimah*, I, 272 [I, 326–7].
18 Hume, *The Natural History of Religion*, cited in Gellner, *Muslim Society*, 9.
19 Hume, *The Natural History of Religion*, cited in Gellner, *Muslim Society*, 10.
20 Gellner, *Muslim Society*, 16.
21 Gellner, *Muslim Society*, 41–2.
22 Engels, "On the History of Early Christianity", 276.
23 Al-Maghrib is a term used by Arab scholars to refer to the region that today consists of Morocco, Algeria, Tunisia and Libya. Arab historians and geographers used the term Ifrīqiyā to refer to what is now Tunisia. The region consisting of modern Tunisia, Algeria and Libya formed an administrative province (*vilayat*) of the Ottoman Empire, the basis of present borders of the three countries. The pre-Islamic kingdom of Mauritania, later to become a Roman protectorate, more or less corresponds to present-day Morocco.
24 Abun-Nasr, *A History of the Maghrib*, 7.
25 Ibn Khaldūn, *Tārīkh*, VI, 97 [I, 184]. Page numbers in brackets refer to de Slane's French translation of the *Tārīkh* of Ibn Khaldūn, the original title of which is the *Kitāb al-'Ibar*.
26 Ibn Khaldūn, *Tārīkh*, VI, 89 [I, 168].
27 Ibn Khaldūn, *Tārīkh*, VI, 90–1 [I, 169, 172].
28 Laroui, *The History of the Maghrib*, 17; Abun-Nasr, *A History of the Maghrib*, 7–8.
29 Abun-Nasr, *A History of the Maghrib*, 67–8.
30 Idrīs bin 'Abdallāh was an Alawite sharīf, a descendant of the Prophet Muḥammad through the fourth Caliph 'Alī ibn abī Ṭālib, who was married to the daughter of the Prophet, Faṭimah. See Abun-Nasr, *A History of the Maghrib*, 78 n.1.
31 Landau, *Islam and the Arabs*, 100.
32 Montagne, *The Berbers*, 14–15.
33 Shatzmiller, M. (1992) "Al-Muwaḥḥidūn".
34 Ibn Khaldūn, *Al-Muqaddimah*, I, 250 [I, 305].
35 Ibn Khaldūn, *Tārīkh*, VI, 228–9 [II, 174].
36 Ibn Khaldūn, *Tārīkh*, VI, 226, 228 [II, 164, 173]; Urvoy, "La pensée d'Ibn Tūmart".
37 Bel,"Almohades".
38 Bel,"Almohades".

39 Ibn Khaldūn, *Al-Muqaddimah*, I, 268 [I, 322].
40 Ibn Khaldūn, *Al-Muqaddimah*, I, 228 [I, 287].
41 Gellner, *Saints of the Atlas*, 3–5.
42 Gellner, *Saints of the Atlas*, 5.
43 Waterbury, *Commander of the Faithful*, 16–17.
44 Gellner, *Saints of the Atlas*, 3; Gellner, *Muslim Society*, 16–34.
45 Wansborough, "The Decolonization of North African History"; Brett, "Ibn Khaldūn and the Dynastic Approach to Local History"; both cited in Shatzmiller, *The Berbers and the Islamic State*, xiv.
46 Marçais, *La Berbérie Musulmane*, 235.
47 Seddon, "Tribe and State", 28. See also Burke III, "The Image of the Moroccan State".
48 Gellner, *Saints of the Atlas*, 5.
49 Gellner, *Saints of the Atlas*, 6.
50 Mourad, *Le Maroc à la Recherche d'une Revolution*, 35.
51 Mourad, *Le Maroc à la Recherche d'une Revolution*, 36.
52 Lacoste, *Ibn Khaldūn*.
53 Lacoste, *Ibn Khaldūn*, 30.
54 Ibn Khaldūn, *Al-Muqaddimah*, II, 249–50 [II, 315–17]. Ibn Khaldūn also refers to hunting as a mode of making a living but this was not a principal mode of making a living in the Morocco of our period.
55 Ibn Khaldūn, *Al-Muqaddimah*, II, 249 [II, 315].
56 The mode of production is defined as a political economic system consisting of the relations and forces of production. The relations of production refer to the mode of the appropriation of the economic surplus and the economic ownership of the forces of production that correspond to it. The forces of production are the means of production and the labour process. It refers to the labour process involved in the transformation of the raw materials of nature into products by means of the tools, skills, organization and knowledge of the worker (Bottomore, *A Dictionary of Marxist Thought*, 178; Hindess and Hirst, *Pre-Capitalist Modes of Production*, 9–10; Wolf, *Europe and the People Without History*, 75).
57 For a discussion on trade in the context of Ibn Khaldūn's world, see Bedford, "Parasitism and Equality"; and Khazanov, *Nomads and the Outside World*, 202–3.
58 Amin, *Eurocentrism*; Wolf, *Europe and the People Without History*.
59 Marx, *Capital*, Vol. 3, 791; Marx and Engels, *On Colonialism*, 77–80; Akat, "Proposal for a Radical Reinterpretation of the Asiatic Versus the European Social Formation", 70.
60 Marx, *Capital*, Vol. 3, 791.
61 Shatzmiller, *The Berbers and the Islamic State*, 121–2; 124–5.
62 Shatzmiller, *The Berbers and the Islamic State*, 130.
63 Weber, *Economy and Society*, I, 255.
64 Shatzmiller, "Unity and Variety of Land Tenure", 25.
65 Shatzmiller, *The Berbers and the Islamic State*, 126.
66 Cook, *The Hundred Years War for Morocco*, 81.
67 Shatzmiller, "Women and Wage Labour", 197.
68 Abun-Nasr, *A History of the Maghrib*, 136.
69 Shatzmiller, "Women and Wage Labour", 189–96.
70 Shatzmiller, "Unity and Variety of Land Tenure", 25.
71 Cook, *The Hundred Years War for Morocco*, 71.
72 Lacoste, *Ibn Khaldūn*, 35, 73.
73 Cook, *The Hundred Years War for Morocco*, 79.
74 Cook, *The Hundred Years War for Morocco*, 80–1.
75 Shatzmiller, "Unity and Variety of Land Tenure", 25.
76 Lacoste, *Ibn Khaldūn*, 82.
77 Ibn Khaldūn, *Al-Muqaddimah*, I, 262 [I, 315].

78 See Chapters 6 and 7.
79 Gellner, *Muslim Society*, 76.
80 Ibn Khaldūn, *Al-Muqaddimah*, I, 269 [I, 322].
81 Spickard, "Tribes and Cities", 109.
82 Spickard, "Tribes and Cities", 108.

6 Ibn Khaldūn and the Ottoman modes of production

1 Lowry, *The Nature of the Early Ottoman State*, 1.
2 For this as well as other approaches discussed in this section, I draw from Lowry's *The Nature of the Early Ottoman State*, Ch. 1.
3 Gibbons, *The Foundation of the Ottoman Empire*, 27; Lowry, *The Nature of the Early Ottoman State*, 5.
4 Lowry, *The Nature of the Early Ottoman State*, 5; Gibbons, *The Foundation of the Ottoman Empire*, 55.
5 Köprülü, "Anadolu'da Islamiyet"; Köprülü, *Islam in Anatolia*.
6 Ersanlı, "The Empire in the Historiography of the Kemalist Era", 131.
7 Giese, "Das Problem der Enstehung".
8 Köprülü, *The Origins of the Ottoman Empire*.
9 Wittek, *The Rise of the Ottoman Empire*, 13.
10 Wittek, *The Rise of the Ottoman Empire*, 6.
11 Wittek, *The Rise of the Ottoman Empire*, 8.
12 Wittek, *The Rise of the Ottoman Empire*, 8; Wittek, "Der Stammbaum der Osmanen".
13 Wittek, *The Rise of the Ottoman Empire*, 9, 13.
14 Wittek, *The Rise of the Ottoman Empire*, 14.
15 Wittek, "De la défaite d'Ankara", 28.
16 Lowry, *The Nature of the Early Ottoman State*, 15.
17 Lowry, *The Nature of the Early Ottoman State*, 30, 33.
18 Wittek, *The Rise of the Ottoman Empire*, 14.
19 Lowry, *The Nature of the Early Ottoman State*, 69.
20 Lowry, *The Nature of the Early Ottoman State*, 48.
21 İnalcık, *The Ottoman Empire*, 6–7.
22 Lowry, *The Nature of the Early Ottoman State*, 56–7.
23 Lowry, *The Nature of the Early Ottoman State*, 66.
24 Jennings, "Some Thoughts on the Gazi-Thesis", 152.
25 Lowry, *The Nature of the Early Ottoman State*, 69.
26 Hashmi, *Kitābu'r-Rasūl*; Serjeant, "The 'Constitution of Medina'".
27 Hashmi, *Kitābu'r-Rasūl*, 106.
28 Wittek, *The Rise of the Ottoman Empire*, 34.
29 Wittek, *The Rise of the Ottoman Empire*, 40–3.
30 İnalcık, *The Ottoman Empire*, 6–7, cited in Lowry, *The Nature of the Early Ottoman State*, 6.
31 İnalcık, "The Problem of the Foundation of the Ottoman State" (in Turkish). I am grateful to M. Fatih Calisir of Bilkent University for having brought this article to my attention and translated relevant passages for me.
32 Lowry, *The Nature of the Early Ottoman State*, 7.
33 Shaw, *History of the Ottoman Empire*, Vol. 1, 4.
34 Shaw, *History of the Ottoman Empire*, Vol. 1, 8–9.
35 Shaw, *History of the Ottoman Empire*, Vol. 1, 9.
36 Shaw, *History of the Ottoman Empire*, Vol. 1, 10, 13.
37 İnalcık, "The Question of the Emergence of the Ottoman State", 73–6.
38 İnalcık, "The Question of the Emergence of the Ottoman State", 74–6.
39 Jennings, "Some Thoughts on the Gazi-Thesis", 152, 154.
40 Köprülü, *The Origins of the Ottoman Empire*, 72.

41 İnalcık, "The Question of the Emergence of the Ottoman State", 75; İnalcık, "The Khan and the Tribal Aristocracy".
42 İnalcık, "The Question of the Emergence of the Ottoman State", 76. On the Central Asian Turks, see Barthold, *Turkestan down to the Mongol Invasion*.
43 İnalcık, "Ibn Hacer'de Osmanlılara Dair Haberler", 351, 356, cited in Cafadar, *Between Two Worlds*, 182, n.142.
44 Gellner, *Muslim Society*, 73.
45 Owen, *The Middle East in the World Economy*, 11.
46 Shaw, *History of the Ottoman Empire,* Vol. I, 158.
47 Owen, *The Middle East in the World Economy*, 22–3.
48 Shaw, *History of the Ottoman Empire,* Vol. I, 161–2.
49 Lewis, *The Emergence of Modern Turkey*, 445–6.
50 Wittek, "Le role de tribus Turques dans l'Empire Ottoman", 666.
51 Lewis, *The Emergence of Modern Turkey*, 9.
52 Wittek, "Le role de tribus Turques dans l'Empire Ottoman", 671.
53 Marx, *A Contribution to the Critique of Political Economy*, 20.
54 Bottomore, *A Dictionary of Marxist Thought*, 178; Hindess and Hirst, *Pre-Capitalist Modes of Production*, 9–10.
55 Hindess and Hirst, *Pre-Capitalist Modes of Production*, 10–11; Wolf, *Europe and the People Without History*, 75.
56 Lewis, *The Emergence of Modern Turkey*, 43, 90–2, 384–5.
57 See Divitçioğlu, *Asya Üretim Tarzı ve Osmanlı Toplumu*; Islamoglu and Keyder, "Agenda for Ottoman History", 37–44; Keyder, "The Dissolution of the Asiatic Mode of Production".
58 Frank, *Capitalism and Underdevelopment.*
59 Laclau, "Feudalism and Capitalism in Latin America", 25.
60 Laclau, "Feudalism and Capitalism in Latin America", 31.
61 See, for example, Asad and Wolpe, "Concepts of Modes of Production"; and Forster-Carter, "The Modes of Production Controversy".
62 Tokei, "Le mode de production Asiatique", 7.
63 Marx, *Capital,* Vol. 3, 791; Marx and Engels, *On Colonialism*, 77–80; Akat, "Proposal for a Radical Reinterpretation", 69–71; Keyder, "The Dissolution of the Asiatic Mode of Production", 179.
64 Wolf, *Europe and the People Without History*, 80.
65 Marx, *Pre-Capitalist Economic Formations*, 82.
66 Marx, *Pre-Capitalist Economic Formations*, 70.
67 Marx and Engels, *On Colonialism*, 81.
68 Akat, "Proposal for a Radical Reinterpretation", 75.
69 Marx, *Capital*, Vol. 3, 791.
70 Turner, *Marx and the End of Orientalism*, 45–6.
71 İnalcık, *The Ottoman Empire*, 105, 107.
72 Weber, *Economy and Society*, Vol. I, 255; Poggi, *The Development of the Modern State*, 21–2.
73 Weber, *Economy and Society*, Vol. I, 255.
74 Poggi, *The Development of the Modern State*, 23.
75 Barkan, "Turkiye' de Sarvaj var mi idi?"; Lewis, *The Emergence of Modern Turkey*; Poliak, "La féodalité Islamique."
76 For a description of the *iqṭā*‘ see Cahen, "Ikta‘".
77 Lambton, "The Evolution of the Iqta‘", 41.
78 Lambton, "Reflections on the Iqta‘", 358.
79 Weber, *Economy and Society*, Vol. I, 259–61. In the context of Ottoman Turkey, I have seen only one which discusses prebendal feudalism as a system of production. See Matuz, "The Nature and Stages of Ottoman Feudalism", 283–4. This contains a more detailed discussion of Ottoman prebendal feudalism than the present account.

80 Marx, *Capital*, Vol. I, 761; Mandel, *Marxist Economic Theory*, 65–6.
81 Mandel, *Marxist Economic Theory*, 58.
82 Baer, "The Administrative, Economic and Social Functions of Turkish Guilds", 28–9.
83 İnalcık, "Capital Formation in the Ottoman Empire", 115.
84 Mandel, *Marxist Economic Theory*, 125–6.
85 Lambton, "The Evolution of the Iqta'", 41.
86 See Baer, "The Administrative, Economic and Social Functions of Turkish Guilds"; and İnalcık, "Capital Formation in the Ottoman Empire".
87 Bacon, "Types of Pastoral Nomadism", 46.
88 Coon, "Badw".
89 Spooner, "Towards a Generative Model of Nomadism", 198–9.
90 Krader, *Social Organisation in Mongol-Turkic Pastoral Nomads*, 317.
91 Irons, "Variation in Economic Organisation", 92–4.
92 Krader, *Social Organisation in Mongol-Turkic Pastoral Nomads*, 134–7.
93 Krader, *Social Organisation in Mongol-Turkic Pastoral Nomads*, 134.
94 Krader, *Social Organisation in Mongol-Turkic Pastoral Nomads*, 325.
95 Radloff, *Ethnographische Ubersicht der Turkenstamme Sibiriens*, 1696–7.
96 Cuisenier, "Kinship and Social Organization", 206.
97 Cuisenier, "Kinship and Social Organization", 205.
98 Marx and Engels, *On Colonialism*, 81.
99 Andreski, *The Uses of Comparative Sociology*, 172–3.
100 Turner, *Marx and the End of Orientalism*, 41–3.
101 Akat, "Proposal for a Radical Reinterpretation", 74.
102 Baali and Wardi, *Ibn Khaldun and Islamic Thought-Styles*, 81.
103 Durkheim, *The Division of Labour in Society*, 109, 130.
104 Cafadar, *Between Two Worlds*, 16–17.
105 Shaw, *History of the Ottoman Empire,* Vol. I, 25.
106 Lewis, *The Emergence of Modern Turkey*, 91.
107 Weber, *Economy and Society*, Vol. II, 966–7.
108 Ibn Khaldūn, *Al-Muqaddimah*, I, 261 [I, 314].
109 Gellner, *Muslim Society*, 81.
110 Apz refers to Aşıkpaşazade. See Cafadar, *Between Two Worlds*, 113–14.

7 The rise and fall of the Safavid state in a Khaldūnian framework

1 Shaw, *History of the Ottoman Empire,* Vol. I, 77.
2 Minorsky, *Tadhkirat al-Mulūk*, 12–14.
3 Falsafi, *Zindigānī-yi Shāh 'Abbās*, 165; Farmayan, *The Beginning of Modernization in Iran*, 6–7.
4 Savory, *Iran Under the Safavids*, 2–3.
5 Savory, *Iran Under the Safavids*, 5.
6 Savory, *Iran Under the Safavids*, 10.
7 Savory, *Iran Under the Safavids*, 11.
8 Savory, *Iran Under the Safavids*, 12.
9 Savory, *Iran Under the Safavids*, 13–14; Shukrī, *'Ālam Ārā-yi Ṣafavī*, 19.
10 Savory, *Iran Under the Safavids*, 16.
11 Savory, *Iran Under the Safavids*, 17.
12 Savory, *Iran Under the Safavids*, 18.
13 Shukrī, *'Ālam Ārā-yi Ṣafavī*, 20. For the history and sociology of the gores see Floor, *The Persian Textile Industry*.
14 Savory, *Iran Under the Safavids*, 19–20.
15 Savory, *Iran Under the Safavids*, 20.
16 Shukrī, *'Ālam Ārā-yi Ṣafavī*, 33.
17 Savory, *Iran Under the Safavids*, 20–1.

18 Savory, *Iran Under the Safavids*, 22.
19 Shukrī, *'Ālam Ārā-yi Ṣafavī*, 63-65.
20 Ja'fariyān, *Dīn va Siyāsat*, 77; Savory, *Iran Under the Safavids*, 26.
21 Savory, *Iran Under the Safavids*, 35.
22 Hinz, *Tashkīl-i Daulat-i Mellī dar Irān*, 14.
23 Minorsky, "The Poetry of Shāh Ismā'īl", 1042a–3a.
24 Babayan, *Mystics, Monarchs and Messiahs*, 173–4.
25 Savory, *Iran Under the Safavids*, 2.
26 Kasravi, "Najhād va Tabār-i Ṣafaviyyah"; Togan, "Sur l'origine des Safavides"; Mazzaoui, *The Origins of the Ṣafawids*. See also the discussion by Marcinkowski, *Mīrzā Rafī'ā's Dastūr al-Mulūk*, 12–14.
27 On Islam and the state in the Safavid period see Mirahmadi, *Dīn va Daulat dar 'Asr-i Safavī*.
28 Quinn, "The Dreams of Shaykh Ṣafī- al-Dīn", 133–4.
29 Quinn, "The Dreams of Shaykh Ṣafī- al-Dīn", 134.
30 Arjomand, *The Shadow of God*, 234.
31 Savory, *Iran Under the Safavids*, 50, 81.
32 Sha'bānī, *Mabāni-yi Tārīkh-i Ijtimā'ī-yi Irān*, 67–8; Sarī' al-Qalam, *Farhang-i Siyāsī-yi Irān*, 55.
33 Sarī' al-Qalam, *Farhang-i Siyāsī-yi Irān*, 57.
34 Sarī' al-Qalam, *Farhang-i Siyāsī-yi Irān*, 60.
35 Khvāndamīr, *Tārīkh-i Shāh Ismā'īl*, 71, cited in Bashir, "Shah Ismā'il and the Qizilbash", 243. The translation is Bashir's.
36 Bashir, "Shah Ismā'il and the Qizilbash", 244.
37 See Sha'bānī, *Mabāni-yi Tārīkh-i Ijtimā'ī-yi Irān*, 106ff.
38 Nomani, "Notes on the Economic Obligations of Peasants", 63.
39 Nomani, "Notes on the Economic Obligations of Peasants", 63.
40 Banani, "Reflections on the Social and Economic Structure of Safavid Persia", 95; Lambton, *Landlord and Peasant in Persia*, 107–8.
41 Savory, *Iran Under the Safavids*, 188–9.
42 Savory, *Iran Under the Safavids*, 30.
43 Arjomand, "The Clerical Estate and the Emergence of a Shi'ite Hierocracy", 175. See also Newman, "The Myth of the Clerical Migration to Safawid Iran".
44 Helfgott, "Tribalism as a Socioeconomic Formation in Iranian History", 36.
45 Reid, "Comments on 'Tribalism as a Socioeconomic Formation'", 276–7; Reid, "The Qajar Uymaq in the Safavid Period", 120–1.
46 Ibn Khaldūn, *Al-Muqaddimah*, I, 191–2 [I, 249–50].
47 Petruchevsky, "The Socio-economic Condition of Iran", 514; Ivanov, *Tārīkh-i Nuvīn-i Irān*, 6; Pigulevskaya *et al.*, *Tārīkh-i Irān*, 525–31; Shaugannik, "Mode of Production in Medieval Iran", 85; Turner, *Capitalism and Class in the Middle East*, 154, 165.
48 See Abrahamian, "Oriental Despotism"; and "European Feudalism and Middle Eastern Despotisms". See also Ashraf's discussion on Asiatic patrimonialism which draws on Weber, "Historical Obstacles to the Development of a Bourgeoisie in Iran".
49 Foran, "The Modes of Production Approach to Seventeenth Century Iran", 351.
50 Amin, *Unequal Development*; Wolf, *Europe and the People Without History*.
51 Abrahamian, "Oriental Despotism", 6. The relevant citation is Marx's letter to Engels in Torr, *The Correspondence of Marx and Engels*, 70.
52 Abrahamian, "Oriental Despotism", 6–7.
53 Foran, "The Modes of Production Approach to Seventeenth Century Iran", 348–9.
54 Abrahamian, "Oriental Despotism", 16.
55 Abrahamian, "Oriental Despotism", 11–13.
56 Abrahamian, "European Feudalism and Middle Eastern Despotisms", 138.
57 Abrahamian, "Oriental Despotism", 12.
58 Savory, "Notes on the Safavid State", 98.

59 Savory, "Notes on the Safavid State", 99.
60 Floor, *The Economy of Safavid Persia*, 295–6; Akhavi, "State Formation and Consolidation", 203.
61 Akat, "Proposal for a Radical Reinterpretation", 75.
62 Although I have retained the use of the term "Asiatic" here, I have selected only some traits of the Asiatic mode of production discussed by Marx and am not referring to the Orientalist connotations of the term such as the view that Islam is a fake religion and that the Turks were only a little more civilized than nomadic peoples. For these views see Marx and Engels, *Selected Correspondence*, 96; and Marx and Engels, *The Russian Menace to Europe*, 137–8.
63 Marx, *Capital*, Vol. 3, 791.
64 Lambton, *Landlord and Peasant in Persia*, 108.
65 Minorsky, *Tadhkirat al-Mulūk*, 25–6.
66 See Ivanov, *Tārīkh-i Nuvīn-i Irān*, 6; Pigulevskaya *et al.*, *Tārīkh-i Irān*, 525–31.
67 Nomani, "Notes on the Origins and Development", 122, 132.
68 Nomani, "Notes on the Origins and Development", 132.
69 Shaugannik, "Mode of Production in Medieval Iran", 78.
70 Shaugannik, "Mode of Production in Medieval Iran", 81.
71 Shaugannik, "Mode of Production in Medieval Iran", 82.
72 Shaugannik, "Mode of Production in Medieval Iran", 83.
73 Shaugannik, "Mode of Production in Medieval Iran", 87.
74 Lambton, *Landlord and Peasant in Persia*, 53, cited in Shaugannik, "Mode of Production in Medieval Iran", 81–2.
75 See Cahen, "Ikta‘".
76 Lambton, "The Evolution of the Iqta‘ in Medieval Iran", 41.
77 Lambton, "Reflections on the Iqta‘", 374.
78 Lambton, "Reflections on the Iqta‘", 374.
79 Lambton, "Reflections on the Iqta‘", 374.
80 Lambton, "Reflections on the Iqta‘", 374.
81 Lambton, "Reflections on the Iqta‘", 358.
82 Weber, *Economy and Society*, Vol. I, 259–61.
83 Moore, *Social Origins of Dictatorship and Democracy*, 55–6; Griffiths, "Farming to Halves", 5.
84 Afshari, "The Pīshivarān and Merchants", 135.
85 Foran, "The Modes of Production Approach to Seventeenth Century Iran", 353.
86 Coon, "Badw"; Spooner, "Towards a Generative Model of Nomadism", 198–9.
87 Krader, *Social Organization in the Mongol-Turkic Pastoral Nomads*, 317.
88 Foran, "The Modes of Production Approach to Seventeenth Century Iran", 351.
89 Helfgott, "Tribalism as a Socioeconomic Formation", 42.
90 Foran, "The Modes of Production Approach to Seventeenth Century Iran", 352.
91 Bacon, "Types of Pastoral Nomadism in Central and Southwest Asia", 46.
92 Tapper, "Confederations, Tribal".
93 Savory, *Iran Under the Safavids*, 238.
94 Savory, *Iran Under the Safavids*, 241.
95 Savory, *Iran Under the Safavids*, 253.
96 Lambton, *Qajar Persia*, 11–12.
97 Minorsky, *Tadhkirat al-Mulūk*, 23–4.
98 Foran, "The Long Fall of the Safavid Dynasty", 282.
99 Dickson, "The Fall of the Ṣafavi Dynasty", 511.
100 Lockhart, *The Fall of the Ṣafavī Dynasty*, 60, cited in Dickson, "The Fall of the Ṣafavi Dynasty", 511.
101 Foran, "The Long Fall of the Safavid Dynasty".
102 Matthee, *Persia in Crisis*, 243–4.

103 Floor, *The Economy of Safavid Persia*, 3–4.
104 Fragner, "Social and Internal Economic Affairs", 509.
105 Fragner, "Social and Internal Economic Affairs", 513–14.
106 Helfgott, "Tribalism as a Socioeconomic Formation", 51.
107 Savory, *Iran Under the Safavids*, 50–1.
108 Savory, *Iran Under the Safavids*, 51, 56.
109 Savory, *Iran Under the Safavids*, 78–9.
110 Savory, *Iran Under the Safavids*, 80.
111 Savory, *Iran Under the Safavids*, 80–1.
112 Savory, *Iran Under the Safavids*, 81.
113 Savory, *Iran Under the Safavids*, 81.
114 Hurewitz, "Military Politics in the Muslim Dynastic State", 103.
115 Reid, *Tribalism and Society in Islamic Iran*, 129.
116 Ibn Khaldūn, *Al-Muqaddimah*, I, 261 [I, 314].
117 Savory, "The Safavid State and Polity", 195–6.
118 Ibn Khaldūn, *Al-Muqaddimah*, I, 240 [I, 297]; Sarī' al-Qalam, *Farhang-i Siyāsī-yi Irān*, 73.
119 "Army vii. *Qajar* Period", *Encyclopædia Iranica*, online at: www.iranicaonline.org/articles/army-vii-qajar#pt1 (accessed 19 April 2012).
120 Meredith, "Early Qajar Administration", 60.
121 Issawi, *The Economic History of Iran, 1800–1914*, 20.
122 Keddie, "Class Structure and Political Power", 306.
123 Lambton, *Qajar Persia*, 47, 97.
124 Matthee, *Persia in Crisis*, 243.
125 Matthee, *Persia in Crisis*, 244.

8 A Khaldūnian perspective on modern Arab states: Saudi Arabia and Syria

1 For these theories I rely on Ayubi, *Over-Stating the Arab State*, Ch. 1.
2 Al-Rasheed, *A History of Saudi Arabia*, 14.
3 Al-Rasheed, *A History of Saudi Arabia*, 16.
4 Habib, *Ibn Sa'ud's Warriors of Islam*, 3–4.
5 Al-Rasheed, *A History of Saudi Arabia*, 17.
6 Al-Rasheed, *A History of Saudi Arabia*, 21.
7 Al-Rasheed, *A History of Saudi Arabia*, 23.
8 Habib, *Ibn Sa'ud's Warriors of Islam*, 15.
9 Habib, *Ibn Sa'ud's Warriors of Islam*, 15; Al-Rasheed, *A History of Saudi Arabia*, 59.
10 Kostiner, "On Instruments and their Designers", 298–9.
11 Vassiliev, *The History of Saudi Arabia*, 227–8.
12 Habib, *Ibn Sa'ud's Warriors of Islam*, 16.
13 Vassiliev, *The History of Saudi Arabia*, 228.
14 Kostiner, "On Instruments and their Designers", 298.
15 Al-Rayḥāni, *Najd wa-l-Mulḥaqātihā*, 261, cited in Habib, *Ibn Sa'ud's Warriors of Islam*, 17.
16 Vassiliev, *The History of Saudi Arabia*, 230–1.
17 Al-Rasheed, *A History of Saudi Arabia*, 69. See Kostiner for more on the conflict betwern Ibn Sa'ūd and the Ikhwān: "On Instruments and their Designers", 309f.
18 Silverfarb, "Great Britain, Iraq, and Saudi Arabia", 243.
19 Habib, *Ibn Sa'ud's Warriors of Islam*, 154.
20 Bandar bin Sultan, *al-Watan*, 1 June 2004, cited in Teitelbaum, "Terrorist Challenges to Saudi Arabian Internal Security".
21 Ibn Khaldūn, *Al-Muqaddimah*, I, 213 [I, 269].

22 Ibn Khaldūn, *Al-Muqaddimah*, I, 213 [I, 269].
23 Ibn Khaldūn, *Al-Muqaddimah*, I, 226–7 [I, 284–5].
24 Salame, "'Strong' and 'Weak' States", 32.
25 Ibn Khaldūn, *Al-Muqaddimah*, I, 288 [I, 344–5].
26 Ibn Khaldūn, *Al-Muqaddimah*, I, 296 [I, 353].
27 Vassiliev, *The History of Saudi Arabia*, 280.
28 Salame, "'Strong' and 'Weak' States".
29 Turchin, "Scientific Prediction in Historical Sociology".
30 Goldstone, *Revolution and Rebellion in the Early Modern World*, 24–5; Turchin, "Scientific Prediction in Historical Sociology", 6.
31 Turchin, "Scientific Prediction in Historical Sociology", 7.
32 Abir, "The Consolidation of the Ruling Class", 159.
33 Turchin, "Scientific Prediction in Historical Sociology", 6. See also Turchin, *Historical Dynamics*, Section 7.2.3.
34 Turchin, "Scientific Prediction in Historical Sociology", 12.
35 Turchin, "Scientific Prediction in Historical Sociology", 15.
36 Turchin, "Scientific Prediction in Historical Sociology", 15.
37 Turchin, "Scientific Prediction in Historical Sociology", 15.
38 Turchin, "Scientific Prediction in Historical Sociology", 18.
39 Michaud, "Caste, confession et société en Syrie"; Carré, "A propos de vues néo-Khalduniennes"; Carré, "Ethique et politique chez Ibn Khaldûn"; Goldsmith, "Syria's Alawites".
40 Michaud, "Caste, confession et société en Syrie", 120.
41 Michaud, "Caste, confession et société en Syrie", 123.
42 Michaud, "Caste, confession et société en Syrie", 125.
43 Ibn Khaldūn, *Al-Muqaddimah*, II, 103–4 [II, 111–12]; Michaud, "Caste, confession et société en Syrie", 123.
44 Carré, "A propos de vues néo-Khalduniennes".
45 Carré, "Ethique et politique chez Ibn Khaldûn", 118–19.
46 Carré, "Ethique et politique chez Ibn Khaldûn", 121–4.
47 Michaud, "Caste, confession et société en Syrie", 168.
48 Batatu, "Some Observations on the Social Roots of Syria's Ruling", 331.
49 Batatu, "Some Observations on the Social Roots of Syria's Ruling", 331–2.
50 Batatu, "Some Observations on the Social Roots of Syria's Ruling", 333–4.
51 Batatu, "Some Observations on the Social Roots of Syria's Ruling", 340.
52 Batatu, "Some Observations on the Social Roots of Syria's Ruling", 342.
53 Batatu, "Some Observations on the Social Roots of Syria's Ruling", 342.
54 Batatu, "Some Observations on the Social Roots of Syria's Ruling", 342–3.
55 Batatu, "Some Observations on the Social Roots of Syria's Ruling", 343.
56 Batatu, "Some Observations on the Social Roots of Syria's Ruling", 343.
57 Batatu, "Some Observations on the Social Roots of Syria's Ruling", 343.
58 Batatu, *Syria's Peasantry*, 63–9. Cited in Goldsmith, "Syria's Alawites", 41.
59 Goldsmith, "Syria's Alawites", 42.
60 Goldsmith, "Syria's Alawites", 43.
61 CNN, "Syria: Minister commits suicide", online at: www.edition.cnn.com/2005/WORLD/meast/10/12/syria.minister/index.html; BBC News, "Syrian minister 'commits suicide'", online at: news.bbc.co.uk/2/hi/middle_east/4334442.stm. See also Goldsmith, "Syria's Alawites", 47.
62 Goldsmith, "Syria's Alawites", 44.
63 Goldsmith, "Syria's Alawites", 44.
64 Goldsmith, "Syria's Alawites", 45.
65 Shadid, "Death of a Syrian Minister", cited in Goldsmith, "Syria's Alawites", 47.
66 Goldsmith, "Syria's Alawites", 48.

67 Goldsmith, "Syria's Alawites", 48–9.
68 Goldsmith, "Syria's Alawites", 42. See also Ilsley, "Syria: Hama Massacre", cited in Goldsmith, "Syria's Alawites", 42.
69 Hussein, "Five Possible Scenarios for Syria".
70 Ibn Khaldūn, *Al-Muqaddimah*, I, 207 [I, 264].
71 See: www.ft.com/cms/s/0/e29a73f8-6b78-11e0-a53e-00144feab49a.html#axzz27XqI4hAA. I would like to thank Linda Matar for referring me to this article.
72 See *Al-Akhbar English* at: http://english.al-akhbar.com/node/9621.

9 Towards a Khaldūnian sociology of the state

1 MacIver, *The Modern State*; Nettl, "The State as a Conceptual Variable"; Sorokin, *Society, Culture, and Personality*, 203–11.
2 Sabine, *A History of Political Theory*, 351.
3 Ibn Khaldūn, *Al-Muqaddimah*, I, 328 [I, 387–8].
4 Rabīʿ, *The Political Theory of Ibn Khaldūn*, 141.
5 Ibn Khaldūn, *Al-Muqaddimah*, I, 327–8 [I, 387].
6 Ben Salem, "La notion de pouvoir", 309.
7 Ibn Khaldūn, *Al-Muqaddimah*, I, 327 [I, 387].
8 Ibn Khaldūn, *Al-Muqaddimah*, II, 221 [II, 285].
9 Ibn Khaldūn, *Al-Muqaddimah*, II, 82 [II, 106–7].
10 Ortega, *The Revolt of the Masses*, 120.
11 Ortega, *The Revolt of the Masses*, 117–21.
12 Ortega, *The Revolt of the Masses*, 123.
13 Ali ibn Abu Talib, *Nahjul Balagha*, 500.
14 Black, "Classical Islam and Medieval Europe", 95.
15 Gellner, "Cohesion and Identity", 207.
16 von Kremer, "Ibn Chaldun und seine Kulturgeschichte der Islamischen Reiche"; Flint, *History of the Philosophy of History*, 158ff.; Gumplowicz, *Soziologische Essays*, 90–114; Maunier, "Les idées économiques d'un philosophe arabe"; Oppenheimer, *System der Soziologie*, Vol. II, 173ff., Vol. IV, 251ff.; Ortega, "Abenjaldún nos revela el secreto".
17 Becker and Barnes, *Social Thought from Lore to Science*, Vol. I, 266–79.
18 For a discussion on the relevant concepts see Chase-Dunn and Hall, "Conceptualizing Core/Periphery Hierarchies".
19 Turchin, *Complex Population Dynamics*; Turchin and Hall, "Spatial Synchrony Among and within World-Systems".
20 Turchin and Hall, "Spatial Synchrony Among and within World-Systems", 53.
21 For studies on the role of nomads in the historical evolution of core/periphery hierarchies see Hall, "Civilizational Change"; and Chase-Dunn and Hall, *Core/Periphery Relations*.
22 Khatibi, "Hierarchies Pre-Coloniales", 120–1.
23 Romein, "Theoretical History", 54.
24 Romein, "Theoretical History", 58.
25 Talbi, "Ibn Khaldun", 829.
26 Ibn Khaldūn, *Al-Muqaddimah*, I, 9–10 [I, 11].
27 Ibn Khaldūn, *Al-Muqaddimah*, I, 5–6 [I, 6].
28 Ibn Khaldūn, *Al-Muqaddimah*, I, 6 [I, 6].
29 Ibn Khaldūn, *Al-Muqaddimah*, I, 6 [I, 6].
30 Ibn Khaldūn, *Al-Muqaddimah*, I, 5–6 [I, 6].
31 Ibn Khaldūn, *Tārīkh*, Vol. 6, 225–9 [Vol. 2, 161–73]. Page numbers in brackets refer to the French translation of the *Kitāb al-ʿIbar* by de Slane.
32 See Ibn Khaldūn, *Tārīkh*, Vol. 6 [Vol. 2].

33 Ben Salem, “Esquisse d’une théorie khaldunienne de l’Etat maghrébine”, 3.

34 Since the late 1990s, more works that can be considered as non-Eurocentric readings of Ibn Khaldūn have appeared. See, for example, Tehranian, “Pancapitalism and Migration”; Ruthven “The Eleventh of September and the Sudanese Mahdiya in the Context of Ibn Khaldun’s Theory of Islamic History”. See also various issues of the *Journal of North African Studies*, including the special issue on Ibn Khaldūn entitled “The Worlds of Ibn Khaldūn”, Vol. 13(3), 2008.

35 Djeghloul, “Ibn Khaldoun: Mode d’emploi les problèmes d’un heritage”, 42–3.

36 See Raḥīmlū, “Ibn Khaldūn”; Shaykh, *Dar Muṭāla‘āt Taṭbīqī dar Falsafah-i Islāmī*; Ṭabāṭabā‘ī, *Ibn Khaldūn va ‘Ulūm-i Ijtimā‘ī.*

37 Connell, *Southern Theory*, 22–4.

38 Connell, *Southern Theory*, 24.

39 Alatas and Sinha, “Teaching Classical Sociological Theory”.

40 Scott, *Sociological Theory*, 1.

41 Talbi, “Ibn Khaldun”, 829; Lawrence, “Introduction: Ibn Khaldun and Islamic Ideology”, 156–7.

42 Lawrence, “Introduction: Ibn Khaldun and Islamic Ideology”, 157.

10 Bibliographic remarks and further reading

1 Those who wish to gain a more extensive introduction to Ibn Khaldūn may consult the following bibliographies: Al-Azmeh, “Bibliography”; ‘Biblioghrāfiyyah ‘Abd al-Raḥmān b. Khaldūn”; Fischel, “Ibn Khaldūniana”; Pérès, “Essai de Bibliographie”; and Tixier-Wieczorkiewicz, *L’œuvre d’Ibn Khaldun dans la recherché contemporaine depuis 1965.*

2 Ibn Khaldûn, *Peuples et nations du monde, la conception de l’histoire les Arabes du Machrek et leurs contemporains les Arabes du Maghrib et les Berbères extraits des ‘Ibar’traduit de l’arabe et presents par Abdesselam Cheddadi.*

3 Rosenthal, “Ibn Khaldun in his Time”, 167.

4 Roussillon, “La représentation de l’identité”, 56, n.48.

5 Roussillon, “Durkheimisme et réformisme”, 5; Abaza, *Debates on Islam and Knowledge*, 146.

6 Zāyid, “Saba‘ūn ‘Āmā”, 14.

7 ‘Izzat, *Etude comparée d’Ibn Khaldun et Durkheim*; Gellner, “Cohesion and Identity”; Khayrī, “Tā’sīs ‘Ilm al-Ijtimā‘”; Stowasser, *Religion and Political Development*; Al-‘Arawī, “Ibn Khaldūn wa Mākyāfīlī”; Laroui, “Ibn Khaldun et Machiaval”; Wāfī, *Al-falsafah al-Ijtimā‘iyyah li Ibn Khaldūn wa Aujust Kumt*; Baali, *Ilm al-Umran and Sociology*; Baali and Price, “Ibn Khaldun and Karl Marx”; Bousquet, “Marx et Engels se sont-ils intéressés aux questions Islamiques?”; Hopkins, “Engels and Ibn Khaldun”; Goodman, “Ibn Khaldūn and Thucydides”.

8 This was translated into English by Bukhsh in 1927 as “Ibn Khaldûn and his History of Islamic Civilization”.

9 Rosenthal, “Ibn Khaldūn”.

10 Hassan, “Sociology of Islam”.

11 Ghazoul, “The Metaphors of Historiography”.

12 Al-Wardī, *Manṭiq Ibn Khaldūn.*

13 Rabī‘, *The Political Theory of Ibn Khaldūn.*

14 Al-Jābirī, *Arab-Islamic Philosophy*; “Ibistīmūlūjiyā al-Ma‘qūl”.

15 ‘Afīfī, “Mawqif Ibn Khaldūn min al-Falsafah wa-l-Taṣawwuf”; Badawī, “Ibn Khaldūn wa Arastū”; Al-Marzūqī, “Minhajiyyah Ibn Khaldūn wa Ijtimā‘ahu al-Naẓarī”; Al-Sā‘ātī’, “Al-Minhaj al-‘Ilmī fī Muqaddimah Ibn Khaldūn”; Ṭāhā, “An al-Istidlāl fī al-Naṣṣ al-Khaldūnī”; Al-Ṭālbī, “Minhajiyyah Ibn Khaldūn al-Tārīkhiyyah wa Atharuhā fī Diwān <<Al-‘Ibar>>”.

16 Brett, "The Way of the Nomad", 252ff.
17 Gibb, "The Islamic Background".
18 Mahdī, *Ibn Khaldûn's Philosophy of History.*
19 Al-Azmeh, *Ibn Khaldun.*
20 Cheddadi, "Ibn Khaldūn: anthropologue ou historien?"
21 Gellner, *Muslim Society*, Ch. 1.
22 Messier, "Re-thinking the Almoravids, Re-thinking Ibn Khaldun".
23 Alatas, "Ibn Khaldun and the Ottoman Modes of Production"; "A Khaldunian Perspective on the Dynamics of Asiatic Societies".
24 Turchin, *Complex Population Dynamics*, Chapter 7; Turchin and Hall, "Spatial Synchrony", 53.
25 Turchin and Hall, "Spatial Synchrony", 53.
26 Abdesselem, *Ibn Khaldun et ses lecteurs*.

Bibliography

Works of Ibn Khaldūn

In Arabic

Ibn Khaldūn (2005) *Al-Muqaddimah*, 5 vols, 'Abd al-Salām al-Shaddādī (Abdesselam Cheddadi), Casablanca: Bayt al-Funūn wa al-'Ulūm wa-l-Ādāb.

Ibn Khaldūn (1850 AD) *Kitāb al-'Ibar wa-al-Dīwān al-Mubtadā' wa-al-Khabar fī Ayyām al-'Arab wa-al-'Ajam wa-al-Barbar* (Book of Examples and the Collection of Origins of the History of the Arabs and Berbers), ed. Shaykh Nasr al-Hūrūnī, Cairo: Bulaq.

Ibn Khaldūn (1391 AH/1971 AD) *Tārīkh Ibn Khaldūn*, 7 vols, Beirut: Muassasat al-A'lami li-l-Maṭbū'āt.

Ibn Khaldoun (2006) *Autobiographie: Al-Sīrat Al-Dhātiyyah aw Ibn Khaldūn wa Riḥlatuhu Gharban wa Sharqan*, ouvrage présenté, traduit et annoté par Abdesselam Cheddadi, Témara: Maison des Arts, des Sciences et des Lettres.

Ibn Khaldūn (1958) *Shifā' al-Sā'il fī Tahdhīb al-Masā'il*, ed. M. al-Tanjī, Istanbul: n.p.

In translation

Issawi, Charles (1950) *An Arab Philosophy of History: Selections from the Prolegomena of Ibn Khaldun of Tunis (1332-1406)*, translated and arranged by Charles Issawi, London: John Murray.

Kay, Henry Cassels (1892) *Yaman, its early medieval history by Najm ad-Din Omarah Al-Hakami. Also the abridged history of its dynasties by Ibn Khaldun. And an account of the Karmathians of Yaman by Abu Abd Allah Baha ad-Din Al-Janadi*, London: Edward Arnold.

Ibn Khaldoun (1968–69) *Histoire des Berbères et des dynasties musulmanes de l'Afrique septentrionale*, new edn, tr. Le Baron de Slane, Paris: P. Geuthner.

Ibn Khaldûn (1997) *Discours sur l'histoire universelle: Al-Muqaddima*, traduit de l'arabe, présenté et annoté par Vincent Monteil, 3rd edn, Paris: Sindbad.

Ibn Khaldûn (1967) *The Muqaddimah: An Introduction to History*, 3 vols, translated from the Arabic by Franz Rosenthal, London and Henley: Routledge and Kegan Paul.

Ibn Khaldûn (1967) *The Muqaddimah: An Introduction to History* (abridged edition), translated and introduced by Franz Rosenthal, abridged and edited by N. J. Dawood, London: Routledge and Kegan Paul.

Ibn Khaldûn (1986) *Peuples et nations du monde, la conception de l'histoire des Arabes du Machrek et leurs contemporains les Arabes du Maghrib et les Berbères extraits des 'Ibar' traduit de l'arabe et presentés par 'Abdesselam Cheddadi*, 2 vols, Paris: Sindbad.

de Sacy, Antoine Isaac Silvestre, Baron, ed. and tr. (1810) "Extraits de Prolégomènes d'Ebn Khaldoun", in de Sacy, *Relation de l'Egypt, par Abd-Allatif, médecin arabe de Bagdad*, Paris, pp. 509–24 (translation) and 558–64 (Arabic text).

de Slane, William MacGuckin (1862–68) *Prolégomènes historiques d'Ibn Khaldoun, traduit en Français et commentés. Notice et extraits des manuscripts de la Bibliothèque Impériale, Académie des Inscriptions et Belles-Lettres, vol. xix–xxi*, Paris.

Cited works

Abaza, Mona (2002) *Debates on Islam and Knowledge in Malaysia and Egypt: Shifting Worlds*, London: Routledge Curzon.

Abaza, Mona and Stauth, Georg (1990) "Occidental Reason, Orientalism, Islamic Fundamentalism: A Critique", in Martin Albrow and Elizabeth King, eds, *Globalization, Knowledge and Society: Readings from International Sociology*, London: Sage Publications.

Abdel-Malek, A. (1963) "Orientalism in Crisis", *Diogenes* 11(44): 103–40.

Abdesselem, Ahmed (1983) *Ibn Khaldun et ses Lecteurs*, Paris: Presses Universitaires de France.

Abir, Mordechai (1987) "The Consolidation of the Ruling Class and the New Elites in Saudi Arabia", *Middle Eastern Studies* 23(2): 150–71.

Abrahamian, E. (1974) "Oriental Despotism: The Case of Qajar, Iran", *International Journal of Middle East Studies* 5(3–31), 6.

Abrahamian, E. (1975) "European Feudalism and Middle Eastern Despotisms", *Science and Society* 39(2): 129–56.

Abun-Nasr, Jamil N. (1971) *A History of the Maghrib*, 2nd edn, Cambridge: Cambridge University Press.

'Afīfī, Abī al-'Alā (1962) "Mawqif Ibn Khaldūn min al-Falsafah wa-l-Taṣawwuf", in A'māl Mahrajān Ibn Khaldūn (Proceedings of the Ibn Khaldun Symposium), Cairo: National Centre for Social and Criminological Research, pp. 135–43.

Afshari, Mohammad Reza (1983) "The Pīshivarān Merchants in Precapitalist Iranian Society: An Essay on the Background and Causes of the Constitutional Revolution", *International Journal of Middle East Studies* 15(2): 133–55.

Akat, Asaf Savas (1981) "Proposal for a Radical Reinterpretation of the Asiatic Versus the European Social Formation", in Anouar Abdel Malek, ed., *The Civilizational Project: The Visions of the Orient*, Mexico City: El Colegio de Mexico, pp. 69–79.

Akhavi, Shahrough (1986) "State Formation and Consolidation in Twentieth Century Iran: The Reza Shah Period and the Islamic Republic", in Ali Banuazizi and Myron Weiner, eds, *The State, Religion, and Ethnic Politics: Afghanistan, Iran and Pakistan*, Syracuse: Syracuse University Press.

Alatas, Syed Farid (1990) "Ibn Khaldun and the Ottoman Modes of Production", *Arab Historical Review for Ottoman Studies* No. 1–2: 45–63.

Alatas, Syed Farid (1993) "A Khaldunian Perspective on the Dynamics of Asiatic Societies", *Comparative Civilizations Review* 29: 29–51.

Alatas, Syed Farid (2006) *Alternative Discourses in Asian Social Science: Responses to Eurocentrism*, New Delhi: Sage.

Alatas, Syed Farid (2007) "The Historical Sociology of Muslim Societies: Khaldūnian Applications", *International Sociology* 22(3).

Alatas, Syed Farid (2013) *Ibn Khaldun*, New Delhi: Oxford University Press.

Alatas, Syed Farid and Vineeta Sinha (2001) "Teaching Classical Sociological Theory in Singapore: The Context of Eurocentricism", *Teaching Sociology* 29(3): 316–31.

Alatas, Hussein (Syed Hussein Alatas) (1954) "Objectivity and the Writing of History", *Progressive Islam* 1(2): 2–4.

Aldila Isahak (2006) "The Influence of Ibn Khaldūn's Political Thought on Ibn al-Azraq: A Comparative Exposition of the *Muqaddimah* and *Badā'i' al-Silk fī Ṭabā'i' al-Mulk*", International Conference: Ibn Khaldun's Legacy and its Contemporary Significance, International Institute of Islamic Thought and Civilization (ISTAC), Kuala Lumpur, 20–22 November.

Aldila Isahak (2010) *Ibn al-Azraq's Political Thought: A Study of Bad'i' al-Silk fi Taba'i' al-Mulk*, Saarbrücken: VDM Verlag Dr Müller.

Ali ibn Abu Talib (1967) *Nahjul Balagha*, Poona: Nahjul Balagha Publications Committee.

Amanat, Abbas (2001) "The Kayanid Crown and Qajar Reclaiming of Royal Authority", *Iranian Studies* 34(1–4): 17–30.

Amin, Samir (1975) *Unequal Development*, New York: Monthly Review Press.

Amin, Samir (1989) *Eurocentrism*. London: Zed.

Andreski, S. (1969) *The Uses of Comparative Sociology*. Berkeley and Los Angeles: University of California Press.

Ansari, Hamied N. (2009) "Civilization and its Enemy", in Osman Bakar and Baharuddin Aḥmad, eds, *Ibn Khaldūn's Legacy and Its Significance*, Kuala Lumpur: International Institute of Islamic Thought and Civilization (ISTAC), International Islamic University Malaysia (IIUM), pp. 79–86.

Al-'Arawī, 'Abdallāh (Laroui, Abdallah) (1979) "Ibn Khaldūn wa Mākyāfīlī", in *A'māl Nadwah Ibn Khaldūn*, Rabat: Faculty of Letters and Human Sciences, pp. 183–204.

Ardıç, Nurullah (2008) "Beyond 'Science as a Vocation': Civilisational Epistemology in Weber and Ibn Khaldun", *Asian Journal of Social Science* 36: 434–64.

Arjomand, Said Amir (1984) *The Shadow of God and the Hidden Imām: Religion, Political Order, and Societal Change in Shi'ite Iran from the Beginning to 1890*, Chicago: Chicago University Press.

Arjomand, Said Amir (1985) "The Clerical Estate and the Emergence of a Shi'ite Hierocracy in Safavid Iran", *Journal of the Economic and Social History of the Orient*, 28: 169–219.

Asad, T. and Wolpe, H. (1976) "Concepts of Modes of Production", *Economy and Society* 5(4): 470–506.

Ashraf, Ahmad (1970) "Historical Obstacles to the Development of a Bourgeoisie in Iran", *Iranian Studies* 2(2/3): 54–79.

Astre, Georges-Albert (1947) "Un précurseur de la sociologie au XIVe siècle: Ibn Khaldoun", in *L'Islam et L'occident*, Paris: Cahiers du Sud, pp. 131–50.

Al-Attas, Syed Muhammad al-Naquib (1977) "Preliminary Thoughts on the Nature of Knowledge and the Definition and Aims of Education", paper presented at the First World Conference on Muslim Education, Makkah al-Mukarramah, 1397/1977, organized by King Abdul Aziz University.

Al-Attas, Syed Muhammad al-Naquib (1978) *Islam and Secularism*, Kuala Lumpur: ABIM.

Al-Attas, Syed Muhammad al-Naquib (1979) *Aims and Objectives of Islamic Education*, London: Hodder and Stoughton.

Al-Attas, Syed Muhammad Al-Naquib (1980) *The Concept of Education in Islam: A Framework for an Islamic Philosophy of Education*, Kuala Lumpur: ABIM.

Al-Attas, Syed Muhammad Naquib (1989) *Islam and the Philosophy of Science*, Kuala Lumpur: International Institute of Islamic Thought and Civilization.

Ayad, Kamil (1930) *Die Geschichts- und Gesellschaftslehre Ibn Haldūns*, Stuttgart & Berlin: Colta.

Ayubi, Nazih (1995) *Over-Stating the Arab State: Politics and Society in the Middle East*, London: I.B. Tauris.

El-Azmeh, Aziz (1979) "The *Muqaddima* and *Kitab Al'Ibar*: Perspectives from a Common Formula", *The Maghreb Review* 4(1): 17–20.

Al-Azmeh, Aziz (1981) *Ibn Khaldun in Modern Scholarship: A Study in Orientalism*, London: Third World Centre.

Al-Azmeh, Aziz (1981) "Bibliography", in Aziz Al-Azmeh, *Ibn Khaldun in Modern Scholarship: A Study in Orientalism*, London: Third World Centre, pp. 229–318.

Al-Azmeh, Aziz (1982) *Ibn Khaldūn: An Essay in Reinterpretation*, London: Frank Cass.

Al-Azmeh, Aziz (1993) *Ibn Khaldun*, Cairo: American University in Cairo Press.

Al-Azmeh, Aziz (1997) *Muslim Kingship: Power and the Sacred in Muslim, Christian, and Pagan Polities*, London and New York: I.B.Tauris.

Al-Azraq, Abū 'Abdallāh Muḥammad bin al-Azraq al-Andalusī (1977), *Badā'i' al-Silk fī Ṭabā'i' al-Mulk (The Wonders of State Conduct and the Nature of Kingship)*, ed. Muḥammad bin 'Abd al-Karīm, Tunis: Al-Dār al-'Arabiyyah li-l-Kitāb.

Baali, F. (1986) *Ilm al-Umran and Sociology: A Comparative Study*, Annals of the Faculty of Arts, Kuwait University, 36th Monograph, Vol. 7.

Baali, F. (1988) *Society, State, and Urbanism: Ibn Khaldūn's Sociological Thought*, Albany: State University of New York Press.

Baali, F. (1992) *Social Institutions: Ibn Khaldūn's Social Thought*, Lanham: University Press of America.

Baali, F. and Price, B. (1982) "Ibn Khaldun and Karl Marx: On Socio-Historic Change", *Iqbal Review* 23(1): 17–36.

Baali, F. and Wardi, A. (1981) *Ibn Khaldun and Islamic Thought-Styles*, Boston: G. K. Hall.

Babayan, Kathryn (2002) *Mystics, Monarchs and Messiahs: Cultural Landscapes of Early Modern Iran*, Cambridge: Harvard Center for Middle Eastern Studies.

Bacon, E. E. (1954) "Types of Pastoral Nomadism in Central and Southwest Asia", *Southwestern Journal of Anthropology* 10(1): 44–68.

Badawī, 'Abd al-Raḥman (1962) "Ibn Khaldūn wa Arastū", in *A'māl Mahrajān Ibn Khaldūn* (Proceedings of the Ibn Khaldūn Symposium), Cairo: National Centre for Social and Criminological Research, pp. 152–62.

Badawī, Al-Sayyid Muḥammad (1979) "Al-Mūrfūlūjiyā al-Ijtimā'iyyah wa Asasuhā al-Minhajiyyah 'inda Ibn Khaldūn", in *A'māl Nadwah Ibn Khaldūn*, Rabat: Faculty of Letters and Human Sciences, pp. 173–82.

Baer, G. (1970) "The Administrative, Economic and Social Functions of Turkish Guilds", *International Journal of Middle East Studies*, 1(1): 28–50.

Banani, Amin (1978) "Reflections on the Social and Economic Structure of Safavid Persia at its Zenith", *Iranian Studies* 11: 83–116.

Bandar bin Sultan, *al-Watan*, 1 June 2004, tr. MEMRI, online at: www.memri.org/bin/articles.cgi?Page=countries&Area=saudiarabia&ID=SP72504 (accessed 19 March 2013).

Barkan, O. L. (1956) "Turkiye' de Sarvaj var mi idi?" ("Was there serfdom in Turkey?"), *Turk Tarih Kurumu Belletin* 20(1–3): 237–46.

Barnes, H. E. (1917) "Sociology before Comte: A Summary of Doctrines and an Introduction to the Literature", *American Journal of Sociology* 23(2): 174–247.

Barnes, H. E. (1948) "Ancient and Medieval Social Philosophy", in *An Introduction to the History of Social Philosophy*, ed. H. E. Barnes, Chicago and London: University of Chicago Press.

Barthold, V. (1968) *Turkestan down to the Mongol Invasion*, London: Luzac.

Bashir, Shahzad (2006) "Shah Isma'il and the Qizilbash: Cannibalism in the Religious History of Early Safavid Iran", *History of Religions* 45(3): 234–56.

Batatu, Hanna (1981) "Some Observations on the Social Roots of Syria's Ruling, Military Group and the Causes for its Dominance", *Middle East Journal* 35(3): 331–44.

Batatu, Hanna (1999) *Syria's Peasantry, the Descendants of its Lesser Rural Notables and their Politics*, Princeton: Princeton University Press.

Becker, Howard and Barnes, Harry Elmer (1961) *Social Thought from Lore to Science*, 3 vols, New York: Dover Publications.

Bedford, Ian (1987) "Parasitism and Equality: Some Reflections on Pastoral Nomadism and Long-Distance Trade", *Mankind* 17(2): 140–52.

Bel, A. (1913) "Almohades", *The Encyclopaedia of Islam: A Dictionary of the Geography, Ethnography and Biography of the Muhammadan Peoples*, eds, M. Th. Houtsma, T. W. Arnold, R. Basset and R. Hartmann, Vol. 1, Leyden: Brill and London: Luzac.

Ben Salem, Lilia (1973) "La notion de pouvoir dans l'oeuvre d'Ibn Khaldūn", *Studia Islamica*, 293–314.

Ben Salem, Lilia (1982) "Esquisse d'une théorie Khaldunienne de l'état Maghrébine", in *Actes du Colloque International sur Ibn Khaldūn*, Centre National des Etudes Historiques, Algiers, Majallat al-Tārīkh, SNED, pp. 255–62.

Ben Salem, Lilia (1983) "Interet des analyses d'Ibn Khaldoun pour l'étude des hierarchies sociales des sociétiés du Maghreb", in *Actes du Premier Colloque International sur Ibn-Khaldoun*, Frenda, 1–4 September. El-Annaser, Kouba: Centre National d'Etudes Historiques, pp. 5–16.

Ben Salem, Lilia (1996) 'Ibn Khaldoun, père de la sociologie?', in *Les Savoirs en Tunisie*, Tunis: Editions Alif.

"Biblioghrāfiyyah 'Abd al-Raḥmān b. Khaldūn (1960–1980)", *al-Hayāt al-Thaqāfiyyah*, 9 (1980): 247–72.

Black, A. (1993) "Classical Islam and Medieval Europe", *Political Studies* 41(1): 58–69.

Blackstone, P. W. and Hoselitz, B. F., eds (1952) *The Russian Menace to Europe*, Glencoe, IL: Free Press.

Bombaci, Alessio (1946) "La Dottrina Storiografica di Ibn Haldūn", *Annali della Scuola Normale Superiore di Pisa* 15(3–4): 159–85.

Bottomore, T. (1983) *A Dictionary of Marxist Thought*, Cambridge, MA: Harvard University Press.

Boulakia, Jean David C. (1971) 'Ibn Khaldûn: A Fourteenth Century Economist', *Journal of Political Economy* 79(5): 1105–18.

Bousquet, G.-H. (1979) "Marx et Engels se sont-ils intéressés aux questions Islamiques?", *Studia Islamica* 30: 119–30.

Brett, M. (1972) "Ibn Khaldūn and the Dynastic Approach to Local History: The Case of Biskra", *Al-Qantara* 12: 157–80.

Brett, M. (1999) "The Way of the Nomad", in M. Brett, *Ibn Khaldūn and the Medieval Maghrib*, Aldershot: Ashgate, pp. 251–69.

Al-Bukhārī (1979) *Ṣaḥīḥ al-Bukhārī: Arabic-English*, 9 vols, ed. Muhammad Muhsin Khan, Lahore: Kazi Publications.

Burke III, Edmund (1972) "The Image of the Moroccan State in French Ethnological Literature: A New Look at the Origin of Lyautey's Berber Policy", in Ernest Gellner and C. Micaud, eds, *Arabs and Berbers: From Tribe to Nation in North Africa*, London: Duckworth.

Buzpınar, Ş. Tufan (1996) "Opposition to the Ottoman Caliphate in the Early Years of Abdülhamid II: 1877–1882", *Die Welt des Islam* 36(1): 59–89.

Buzpınar, Ş. Tufan (2004) "Osmanlı Hilâfet, Hakkında Bazı Yeni Tespitler ve Mülahazalar (1725–1909)", *Türk Kültürli İncelemeleri Dergisi* 10: 1–38.

Buzpınar, Ş. Tufan (2005) "The Question of Caliphate under the last Ottoman Sultan", in Itzchak Weismann and Fruma Zacks, eds, *Ottoman Reform and Muslim Regeneration*, London: I.B.Tauris, pp. 1–18.

Cafadar, Cemal (1995) *Between Two Worlds: The Construction of the Ottoman State*, Berkeley: University of California Press.

Cahen, C. (1971). "Ikta'", in B. Lewis, V.I. Menage, C. Pellat, J. Schacht, eds, *Encyclopedia of Islam*, Vol. 3. Leiden: Brill and London: Luzac.

Carré, Olivier (1979–80) "Ethique et politique chez Ibn Khaldûn, juriste Musulman: actualité de sa typologie des systèmes politique'", *L'Annee sociologique* 30: 109–27.

Carré, Olivier (1988) "A propos de vues néo-Khalduniennes sur quelques systèmes politiques Arabes actuels", *Arabica* 35(3): 368–87.

Centre National d'études Historiques (1978) *Actes du Colloque Internationale sur Ibn Khaldoun*, 21–26 June, Algier: Centre National d'études Historiques.

Chase-Dunn, Christopher and Hall, Thomas D., eds (1991) *Core/Periphery Relations in Precapitalist Worlds*, Boulder, CO: Westview.

Chase-Dunn, Christopher and Hall, Thomas D. (1991) "Conceptualizing Core/Periphery Hierarchies for Comparative Study", in Chase-Dunn and Hall, eds, *Core/Periphery Relations in Precapitalist Worlds*, Boulder, CO: Westview, pp. 5–44.

Cheddadi, Abdesselam (1980) "Le Système du Pouvoir en Islam d`après Ibn Khaldun", *Annales, Eco. So. Civ.* 3–4: 534–50.

Cheddadi, Abdesselam (1986) "Ibn Khaldūn: Anthropologue ou Historien?", in Ibn Khaldūn, *Peuples et Nations du Monde*, Vol. 1, Paris: Sindbad, pp. 13–56.

Cheddadi, Abdesselam (2006) *Actualité d'Ibn Khaldûn: Conférences et entretiens*, Témara: Maison des Arts, des Sciences et des Letteres.

Cheddadi, Abdesselam (2006) *Ibn Khaldûn: L'Homme et le Theoretician de la Civilization*, Paris: Gallimard.

Cook, Weston Franklin (1990) *The Hundred Years War for Morocco, 1465–1580: Warfare and State Building in the Early Modern Maghrib*, Vols I and II, PhD Dissertation, Georgetown University, UMI.

Coon, C. S. (1960) "Badw", in H. A. R. Gibb, J. H. Kramers, E. Levi-Provencal, J. Schachts, eds, *Encyclopedia of Islam*, new edn, Vol. 1, Leiden: Brill and London: Luzac.

Connell, Raewyn (2007) *Southern Theory: The Global Dynamics of Knowledge in Social Science*, Sydney: Allen and Unwin.

Conyers, James E. (1972) "Ibn Khaldun: The Father of Sociology?", *International Journal of Contemporary Sociology* 9(4): 173–81.

Cory, Stephen (2008) "Breaking the Khaldunian Cycle? The Rise of Sharifianism as the Basis for Political Legitimacy in Early Modern Morocco", *Journal of North African Studies* 13(3): 377–94.

Cuisenier, Jean (1976) "Kinship and Social Organization in the Turko-Mongolian Cultural Area", in Elborg Foster and Orest Ranum, eds, Elborg Foster and Patricia Ranum, trs,

Family and Society: Selections from the Annales Economies, Sociétés, Civilisations. Baltimore: Johns Hopkins University Press, pp. 204–36.

Dale, Stephen Frederic (2006) "Ibn Khaldun: The Last Greek and the First Annaliste Historian", *International Journal of Middle East Studies* 38: 431–51.

Dhaouadi, Mahmoud (1990) "Ibn Khaldun: The Founding Father of Eastern Sociology", *International Sociology* 5(3): 319–35.

Dickson, Martin B. (1962) "The Fall of the Ṣafavi Dynasty", *Journal of the American Oriental Society* 82(4): 503–17.

van Ditsmarsch, Hans P. (2008) "Logical Fragments in Ibn Khaldūn's *Muqaddimah*", in S. Rahman, Tony Street and Hassan Tahiri, eds, *The Unity of Science in Arabic Tradition*, Dordrecht: Springer Science and Business Media B.V., pp. 281–94.

Divitçioğlu, S. (1967) *Asya Üretim Tarzı ve Osmanlı Toplumu* (*Ottoman Society and the Asiatic Mode of Production*), Istanbul: Istanbul Universitesi Yayinlarindan.

Djeghloul, Abdelkader (1983) "Ibn Khaldoun: Mode d'Emploi. Les Problèmes d'un Heritage", in *Actes du Premier Colloque International sur Ibn-Khaldoun*, Frenda, 1–4 September. El-Annaser, Kouba: Centre National d'Etudes Historiques, pp. 35–43.

Durkheim, E. (1933) *The Division of Labour in Society.*, New York: Free Press.

Enan, Muhammad Abdullah ('Inān, Muḥammad 'Abdallāh) (1941) *Ibn Khaldun: His Life and Work*, Lahore: Muhammad Ashraf.

Engels, Frederick (1975) "On the History of Early Christianity", in Karl Marx and Frederick Engels, *On Religion*, Moscow: Progress Publishers, pp. 275–300. First published in *Die Neue Zeit*, Vol. 1, 1894–95, pp. 4–13, 36–43.

Ersanlı, Buşra (2002) "The Empire in the Historiography of the Kemalist Era", in Fikret Adanır and Suraiya Faroqhi, eds, *The Ottomans and the Balkans: A Discussion of Historiography*, Leiden: Brill, pp. 115–54.

Faculty of Letters and Human Sciences (1979) *A'māl Nadwah Ibn Khaldūn* (*Proceedings of the Ibn Khaldūn Seminar*), 14–17 February, Rabat: Faculty of Letters and Human Sciences.

Faghirzadeh, Saleh (1982) *Sociology of Sociology: In Search of Ibn Khaldun's Sociology Then and Now*, Tehran: Soroush Press.

Falsafi, N. (1953) *Zindigānī-yi Shāh 'Abbās Avval* (*The Life of Shah Abbas I*), Vol. 1, Tehran: Tehran University.

Farmayan, Hafez F. (1969) *The Beginning of Modernization in Iran: The Policies and Reform of Shah Abbas I (1587–1629)*, Salt Lake City: Middle East Center, University of Utah.

Al-Faruqi, Ismail R. (1981) "Islamizing the Social Sciences", in Ismail R. Al-Faruqi, ed., *Social and Natural Sciences: The Islamic Perspective*, Jeddah: Hodder and Stoughton and King Abdulaziz University.

Al-Faruqi, Ismail R. (1982) *Islamization of Knowledge: General Principles and Work Plan*, Herndon, Virginia: International Institute of Islamic Thought.

Al-Faruqi, Ismail R. (1988) "Islamization of Knowledge: Problems, Principles and Prospective", in *Islam: Source and Purpose of Knowledge*, Herndon, Virginia: International Institute of Islamic Thought.

Fischel, Walter J. (1952) *Ibn Khaldūn and Tamerlane*, Berkeley and Los Angeles: University of California Press.

Fischel, Walter J. (1954) "Ibn Khaldun's Use of Jewish and Christian Sources", in *Proceedings of the 23rd International Congress of Orientalists*, Cambridge: Royal Asiatic Society, pp. 332–3.

Fischel, Walter J. (1961) "Ibn Khaldūn's Use of Historical Sources", *Studia Islamica* 14: 109–19.

Fischel, Walter J. (1967) *Ibn Khaldūn in Egypt – His Public Functions and His Historical Research (1382–1406): A Study in Islamic Historiography*, Berkeley and Los Angeles: University of California Press.

Fischel, Walter J. (1967) "Ibn Khaldūniana: A Bibliography of Writings on and Pertaining to Ibn Khaldūn", in Walter J. Fischel, *Ibn Khaldūn in Egypt – His Public Functions and His Historical Research (1382–1406): A Study in Islamic Historiography*, Berkeley and Los Angeles: University of California Press, pp. 171–212.

Fleischer, Cornell (1983) "Royal Authority, Dynastic Cyclism, and 'Ibn Khaldunism' in Sixteenth-Century Ottoman Letters", *Journal of Asian and African Studies* 18(3–4): 198–220.

Fletcher, Ronald (1971) *The Making of Sociology: A Study of Sociological Theory, Vol. 1: Beginnings and Foundations*, London: Michael Joseph.

Flint, Robert (1893) *History of the Philosophy of History in France, Belgium, and Switzerland*, Edinburgh.

Floor, Willem (1999) *The Persian Textile Industry in Historical Perspective*, Paris: Harmattan.

Floor, Willem (2000) *The Economy of Safavid Persia*, Wiesbaden: Reichert Verlag.

Foran, John (1988) "The Modes of Production Approach to Seventeenth Century Iran", *International Journal of Middle East Studies* 20(3): 345–63.

Foran, John (1992) "The Long Fall of the Safavid Dynasty: Moving beyond the Standard Views", *International Journal of Middle East Studies* 24(2): 281–304.

Forster-Carter, A. (1978) "The Modes of Production Controversy", *New Left Review*, 107: 47–77.

Fragner, Bert (1986) "Social and Internal Economic Affairs", in Peter Jackson and Laurence Lockhart, eds, *The Cambridge History of Iran, Vol. VI: The Timurid and Safavid Periods*, Cambridge: Cambridge University Press, pp. 491–567.

Frank, A. G. (1967) *Capitalism and Underdevelopment in Latin America*, New York: Monthly Review Press.

Fusfeld, Warren (1983) "Naqshabandi Sufism and Reformist Islam", *Journal of Asian and African Studies* 18(3–4): 241–62.

Gautier, E. F. (1937) *Le Passé de l'Afrique du Nord*, Paris: Payot.

Gellner, Ernest (1969) *Saints of the Atlas*, London: Weidenfeld and Nicolson.

Gellner, Ernest (1975) "Cohesion and Identity: The Maghreb from Ibn Khaldun to Emile Durkheim", *Government and Opposition* 10(2): 203–18.

Gellner, Ernest (1981) *Muslim Society*, Cambridge: Cambridge University Press.

Ghazoul, Ferial (1986) "The Metaphors of Historiography: A Study of Ibn Khaldūn's Historical Imagination", in A. H. Green, ed., *In Quest of an Islamic Humanism: Arabic and Islamic Studies in memory of Mohamed al-Nowaihi*, Cairo: American University in Cairo Press, pp. 48–61.

Gibb, H. A. R. (1933) "The Islamic Background of Ibn Khaldūn's Political Theory", *Bulletin of the School of Oriental and African Studies* 7: 23–31.

Gibbons, Herbert Adams (1916) *The Foundation of the Ottoman Empire: A History of the Osmanlis up to the Death of Bayezid I (1300–1403)*, Oxford: Clarendon Press.

Giese, Friedrich (1924) "Das Problem der Enstehung des osmanischen Reiches", *Zeitschrift für Semitistik und verwandte Gebiete* 2: 246–71.

Gökyay, Orhan Şail (2002) "Kâtib Celebi", *Islâm Ansiklopedisi*, vol. 25, Ankara: Türkiye Diyanet Vakfı, pp. 36–40.

Goldsmith, Leon (2011) "Syria's Alawites and the Politics of Sectarian Insecurity: A Khaldunian Perspective", *Ortadoğu Etütleri* 3(1): 33–60.

Goldstone, Jack A. (1991) *Revolution and Rebellion in the Early Modern World*, Berkeley and Los Angeles: University of California Press.

Goodman, Lenn Evan (1972) "Ibn Khaldūn and Thucydides", *Journal of the American Oriental Society* 92(2): 250–70.

Griffiths, Liz (2004) "Farming to Halves: A New Perspective on an Absurd and Miserable System", *Rural History Today* 6: 5.

Gumplowicz, Ludwig (1899/1928) *Soziologische Essays: Soziologie und Politik*, Innsbruck: Universitats-Verlag Wagner.

Habib, John (1978) *Ibn Sa'ud's Warriors of Islam: The Ikhwan of Najd and Their Role in the Creation of the Sa'udi Kingdom, 1910–1930*, Leiden: Brill.

Hall, Thomas D. (1991) "Civilizational Change: The Role of Nomads", *Comparative Civilizations Review* 24: 34–57.

Hamès, Constant (1987) "La filiation généalogique (*nasab*) dans la société d'Ibn Khaldūn", *L'Homme* 27(2): 99–118.

Hannoum, Abdelmajid (2003) "Translation and the Colonial Imaginary: Ibn Khaldūn Orientalist", *History and Theory* 42: 61–81.

Hashmi, Al-Hajj Dr Yusuf Abbas (1984) *Kitābu'r-Rasūl – The Constitutional Dictation of Muhammad*, Karachi: University of Karachi.

Hassan, Riaz (2000) "Sociology of Islam", *Encyclopaedia of Sociology*, New York: Macmillan, pp. 2937–53.

Al-Hayāt al-Thaqāfiyyah (1980) No. 9: 241–75.

Helfgott, Leonard M. (1977) "Tribalism as a Socioeconomic Formation in Iranian History", *Iranian Studies* 10(1–2): 36–61.

D'Herbelot de Molainville, Barthélemy (1697) "Khaledoun", in *Bibliotheque Orientale*, Paris.

Himmich, Bensalem (2004) *The Polymath*, Roger Allen, trans., Cairo: The American University in Cairo Press. First appeared in 2001 in Arabic as *Al-'Allama*.

Hindess, B. and Hirst, P. (1975) *Pre-Capitalist Modes of Production*, London: Routledge and Kegan Paul.

Hinz, Walther (1936) *Tashkīl-i Daulat-i Mellī dar Irān: Hukūmat-i Āqa Quyūnlū va Ẓuhūr-i-Daulat-i Ṣafavī* (*The Formation of the National State in Iran: The Āqa Quyūnlū and the Emergence of the Safavid State*), Tehran: Khvārazmī.

Hodgson, Marshall G. S. (1974) *The Venture of Islam: Conscience of History in a World Civilization*, Chicago: University of Chicago Press.

Hopkins, Nicholas S. (1990) "Engels and Ibn Khaldun", *Alif* (Cairo) 10: 9–18.

Horrut, Claude (2006) *Ibn Khaldûn, un Islam des <<Lumières>>*, Paris: Editions Complexe.

Hourani, George F. (1982) "Ibn Khaldūn's Historical Methodology", *The Maghreb Review* 7(5–6): 99–102.

Hume, David (1976) *The Natural History of Religion*, Oxford.

Hurewitz, J. C. (1968) "Military Politics in the Muslim Dynastic States, 1400–1750", *Journal of the American Oriental Society* 88(1): 96–101.

Hussein, Safa A. (2012) "Five Possible Scenarios for Syria, and their Impact on Iraq", Daily Star (Lebanon), 6 April. Online at: www.dailystar.com.lb/Opinion/Commentary/2012/Apr-06/169390-five-possible-scenarios-for-syria-and-their-impact-on-iraq.ashx#ixzz1tj0ktLvB (accessed 2 May 2012).

Hussein, Taha (1918) *La Philosophie Sociale d'Ibn-Khaldoun: Étude Analytique et Critique*, Paris.

Ilsley, Omar (2011) "Syria: Hama Massacre", in Herbert Adam, ed., *Hushed Voices, Unacknowledged Atrocities of the 20th Century*, Berkshire: Berkshire Academic Press, pp. 125–37.

İnalcık, H. (1969) "Capital Formation in the Ottoman Empire", *Journal of Economic History*, 29: 97–140.

İnalcık, H. (1979–80) "The Khan and the Tribal Aristocracy", *Harvard Ukranian Studies* 34: 447–58.

İnalcık, H. (1981–82) "The Question of the Emergence of the Ottoman State", *International Journal of Turkish Studies* 2(2): 71–9.

İnalcık, H. (1994) *The Ottoman Empire: The Classical Age 1300–1600*, London: Phoenix.

İnalcık, H. (1999) "The Problem of the Foundation of the Ottoman State" (in Turkish), *Doğu Bati* 7.

İnalcık, Şevkiya (1948) "Ibn Hacer'de Osmanlılara Dair Haberler", *Ankara Üniversitesi Dil Tarih Coğrafya Fakültesi Dergisi* 6.

'Inān, Muḥammad 'Abdallāh (Enan, Muhammad Abdullah) (1953) *Ibn Khaldūn: Hayātuhu wa turāthuhu al-fikrī*, Cairo: Al-Maktabat al-Tijāriyat al-Kubrā.

Irons, W. (1972) "Variation in Economic Organisation: A Comparison of the Pastoral Yomut and the Basseri", in W. Irons and N. Dyson-Hudson, eds, *Perspectives on Nomadism*. Leiden: Brill.

Islamoğlu, H. and Keyder, C. (1977) "Agenda for Ottoman History", *Review* 1(1): 21–55, 37–44.

Issawi, Charles (1950) "Introduction", in Issawi, *An Arab Philosophy of History: Selections from the Prolegomena of Ibn Khaldun of Tunis (1332–1406)*, tr. and arr. by Charles Issawi, London: John Murray.

Issawi, Charles, ed. (1971) *The Economic History of Iran 1800–1914*, Chicago: University of Chicago Press.

Ivanov, M. S. (1356 AH/1977 AD) *Tārīkh-i Nuvīn-i Irān* (*Modern History of Iran*), Stockholm: Tudeh Publishing Center.

'Izzat, 'Abd al-'Azīz (1947) *Ibn-Khaldoun et sa science sociale*, Cairo.

'Izzat, 'Abd al-'Azīz (1952) *Etude Comparée d'Ibn Khaldun et Durkheim*, Cairo: Al-Maktabat Al-Anglo Al-Misriyyah.

Ja'fariyān, Rasūl (1370 AH) *Dīn va Siyāsat dar Dawrah-i Ṣafavī*, Qom: Anṣāriyān.

Al-Jābirī, Muḥammad 'Ābid (1971) *Al-'Aṣabiyyah wa al-Dawlah* (*Group Feeling and the State*), Beirut: Dār al-Ṭalī'ah li al-Ṭabā'ah wa al-Nashr.

Al-Jābirī, Muḥammad 'Ābid (1979) "Ibistīmūlūjiyā al-Maqūl wa al-Lāmaqūl fī Muqaddimah Ibn Khaldūn", in *A'māl Nadwah Ibn Khaldūn*, Rabat: Faculty of Letters and Human Sciences, pp. 73–132.

Al-Jabri, Mohammed 'Abed (Al-Jābirī, Muḥammad 'Ābid) (1999) *Arab-Islamic Philosophy: A Contemporary Critique*, Austin: Center for Middle Eastern Studies, University of Texas.

Jennings, R. C. (1986) "Some Thoughts on the Gazi-Thesis", *Wiener Zeitschrift für die Kunde des Morgenlandes* 76: 151–61.

Kasravi, Aḥmad (1305–6 AH/1926 AD) "Najhād va Tabār-i Ṣafaviyyah", *Āyandah* 2(5): 357–65.

Kâtib Çelebi (Kātib Çelebī) (1982) *Düstūrü'l-amel li-ıslāhı'l-halel* (*The Mode of Procedure for Rectifying the Damage*), Ankara: Kültür ve Turizm Bakanlığı Yayınları.

Keddie, Nikki R. (1978) "Class Struggle and Political Power in Iran since 1796", *Iranian Studies*, 11: 305–30.

Keyder, C. (1976) "The Dissolution of the Asiatic Mode of Production", *Economy and Society* 5(2): 178–96.

Khadduri (1984) *The Islamic Conception of Justice*, Baltimore: Johns Hopkins University Press.

Ibn al-Khaṭīb, Lisān al-Dīn (1973–74) *Al-Iḥāṭah fī Akhbār Gharnāṭah* (*A Comprehensive History of Granada*), Cairo: Mu'assasāt al-Khanjī.

Khatibi, Abdelkebir (1971) "Hierarchies pre-coloniales: les théories", *Bulletin Economique et Sociale du Maroc* 33(120–1): 27–61.

Khayrī, Majīd al-Dīn 'Umar (1991) "Tā'sīs 'Ilm al-Ijtimā': Ishkāliyyat al-Mawḍū' wa al-Minhaj 'inda Ibn Khaldūn wa Aujust Kumt wa Imīl Durkāym", *Dirāsāt* (Amman) 28(4): 185.

Khazanov, A. M. (1984) *Nomads and the Outside World*, Cambridge: Cambridge University Press.

Khvāndamīr, Amīr Maḥmūd (1991) *Tārīkh-i Shāh Ismā'īl va Shah Ṭahmāsb-i Ṣafavī*, Tehran: Gostardeh.

Ḳınalızade 'Alī Çelebi (1248 AH/1833 AD) *Ahlāḳ-i 'Alā'ī*, Bulaq.

Köprülü, M. Fuat (1992) *The Origins of the Ottoman Empire*, ed. and tr. G. Leiser, Albany: State University of New York Press.

Köprülü, M. Fuat. (1992) "Anadolu'da Islamiyet: Türk Istailasından Sonra Anadolu Tarih-i Dinisine Bir Nazar ve Bu Tarihin Menba'ları", *Darüfünun Edebiyat Fakültesi Mecmuası* 2: 281–311, 385–420, 457–486.

Köprülü, M. Fuat (1993) *Islam in Anatolia after the Turkish Invasion*, ed. and tr. G. Leiser, Salt Lake City: University of Utah Press.

Kostiner, James (1985) "On Instruments and their Designers: The Ikhwān of Najd and the Emergence of the Saudi State", *Middle Eastern Studies* 21(3): 298–323.

Krader, L. (1963) *Social Organisation in Mongol-Turkic Pastoral Nomads*, The Hague: Mouton.

von Kremer, Alfred (1879) "Ibn Chaldun und seine Kulturgeschichte der Islamischen Reiche", *Sitzunsberichte der Kaiserlichen Akademie der Wissenschaften* (Philosoph.-histor. Klasse) (Vienna): 93.

von Kremer, Alfred (1927) "Ibn Khaldûn and his History of Islamic Civilization", *Islamic Culture* (Hyderabad) 1: 567–607. English translation of von Kremer's "Ibn Chaldun und seine Kulturgeschichte der Islamischen Reiche" by S. Khuda Bukhsh.

Laclau, E. (1971) "Feudalism and Capitalism in Latin America", *New Left Review* 67:19–38.

Lacoste, Yves (1984) *Ibn Khaldun: The Birth of History and the Past of the Third World*, London: Verso.

Lambton, A. K. S. (1953) *Landlord and Peasant in Persia*, London: Oxford University Press.

Lambton, A. K. S. (1965) "Reflections on the Iqta'", in G. Makdisi, ed., *Arab Studies in Honor of Hamilton A. R. Gibb*, Leiden: Brill.

Lambton, A. K. S. (1967) "The Evolution of the Iqta' in Medieval Iran", *Iran (Journal of the British Institute of Persian Studies)* 5: 41–50.

Lambton, A. K. S. (1987) *Qajar Persia*, London: I.B. Taurus.

Landau, R. (1958) *Islam and the Arabs*, London: George Allen and Unwin.

Laroui, Abdallah (1977) *The History of the Maghrib: An Interpretive Essay*, Princeton: Princeton University Press.

Laroui, Abdallah (1980) *L'etat dans le Monde Arabe Contemporain*, Louvain: Université Catholique.

Laroui, Abdallah (1987) *Islam et Modernité*, Paris: Editions la Découverte.

Laroui, Abdallah (1987) "Ibn Khaldun et Machiaval", *Islam et Modernité*, Paris: Editions la Découverte, pp. 97–125.

Lawrence, Bruce (1983) "Introduction: Ibn Khaldun and Islamic Ideology", *Journal of Asian and African Studies* 18(3–4): 154–65.

Lawrence, Bruce (1983) "Ibn Khaldun and Islamic Reform", *Journal of Asian and African Studies* 18(3–4): 221–39.

Lewis, B. (1968) *The Emergence of Modern Turkey*, London: Oxford University Press.

Lewis, B. (1993) *Islam in History: Ideas, People, and Events in the Middle East*, Chicago: Open Court.

Lockhart, Laurence (1958) *The Fall of the Safavī Dynasty and the Afghan Occupation of Persia*, Cambridge: Cambridge University Press.

Lowry, Heath W. (2003) *The Nature of the Early Ottoman State*, Albany: State University of New York Press.

MacIver, R. M. (1964) *The Modern State*, London: Oxford University Press.

Mahdi, Muhsin (1957) *Ibn Khaldūn's Philosophy of History*, London: George Allen and Unwin.

Mandel, E. (1968) *Marxist Economic Theory*, tr. B. Pearce, London: Merlin Press.

Marçais, George (1946) *La Berbérie Musulmane et L'Orient au Moyen Age*, Paris: Aubier.

Marcinkowski, Muhammad Ismail (2002) *Mīrzā Rafī'ā's Dastūr al-Mulūk: A Manual of Later Safavid Administration*, Kuala Lumpur: International Institute of Islamic Thought and Civilization.

Martinez-Gros, Gabriel (2006) *Ibn Khaldûn et les sept vies de l'Islam*, Paris: Sindbad.

Marx, Karl (1964) *Pre-Capitalist Economic Formations*, tr. E. Hobsbawm, London: Lawrence and Wishart.

Marx, K. (1967) *Capital: A Critique of Political Economy, Vol. 1: The Process of Capitalist Production*, New York: International Publishers.

Marx, K. (1970) *Capital, Vol. 3*. London: Lawrence and Wishart.

Marx, K. (1970) *A Contribution to the Critique of Political Economy*, Moscow: Progress Publishers.

Marx, K. and Engels, F. (n.d.) *Selected Correspondence*. Moscow: Foreign Languages Publishing House.

Marx, K. and Engels, F. (1952) *The Russian Menace to Europe*, ed. P. W. Blackstone and B. F. Hoselitz, Glencoe, IL: Free Press.

Marx, K. and Engels, F. (1974) *On Colonialism*, Moscow: Progress Publishers.

Al-Marzouki Abu Yaareb (Al-Marzūqī, Abū Ya'rub) (2003) "Ibn Khaldun's Epistemological and Axiological Paradoxes", in Ahmed Ibrahim Abushouk, ed., *Ibn Khaldun and Muslim Historiography* (Kuala Lumpur: Research Centre, International Islamic University Malaysia, 2003), pp. 47–82.

Al-Marzūqī, Abū Ya'rub (1982) "Minhajiyyah Ibn Khaldūn wa Ijtimā'ahu al-Naẓarī", *Al-Majallat al-Tārīkhiyyah al-Maghribiyyah* 27–28: 247–76.

Matthee, Rudi (2012) *Persia in Crisis: Safavid Decline and the Fall of Isfahan*, London: I.B. Tauris.

Matthes, Joachim (2000) "Religion in the Social Sciences: A Socio-Epistemological Critique", *Akademika* 56: 85–105.

Matuz, J. (1982) "The Nature and Stages of Ottoman Feudalism", *Asian and African Studies* 16: 281–92.

Maunier, René (1913) "Les Idées Économiques d'un Philosophe Arabe au XIVe siècle", *Revue d'Histoire Économique et Sociale* 6.

Maus, Heinz (1962) *A Short History of Sociology*, New York: Philosophical Library. First published in German in Ziegenfuss' Handbuch der Soziologie, Stuttgart: Enke Verlag, 1956.

Mazzaoui, Michael M. (1972) *The Origins of the Ṣafawids: Šī'ism, Ṣūfism and the Ġulāt*, Wiesbaden: Franz Steiner Verlag.

Merad, Ali (1956) "L'Autobiographie d'Ibn Khaldûn", *IBLA* (Tunis) 19(1): 53–64.

Meredith, Colin (1971) "Early Qajar Administration: An Analysis of its Development and Functions", *Iranian Studies* 4(2/3): 59–84.

Messier, Ronald A. (2001) "Re-thinking the Almoravids, Re-thinking Ibn Khaldun", in Julia Clancy Smith, ed., *North Africa, Islam and the Mediterranean World: From the Almoravids to the Algerian War*, London: Routledge, pp. 59–80.

Meuleman, Johan H. (1991) "La causalité dans la *Muqaddimah* d'Ibn Khaldun", *Studia Islamica* 74: 105–42.

Michaud, Gerard (1981) "Caste, confession et société en Syrie: Ibn Khaldoun au chevet du 'Progessisme Arabe", *Peuples Méditerranéens* 16: 119–30.

Minorsky, V. (1942) "The Poetry of Shāh Ismail I", *Bulletin of the School of Oriental and African Studies* 10(4): 1006a–53a.

Minorsky, V. (1943) *Tadhkirat al-Muluk: A Manual of Safavid Administration (circa 1137/1725)*, London: E. J. W. Gibb Memorial.

Mīrahmadī, Maryam (1990) *Dīn va Daulat dar 'Asr-i Ṣafavī* (*Religion and State in the Safavi Period*), Tehran: Amir Kabir.

Montagne, Robert (1931) *The Berbers: Their Social and Political Organisation*, London: Frank Cass.

Monteil, Vincent (1978) "Introduction à la sociologie religieuse d'Ibn Khaldûn (1332–1406)", *Social Compass* 25(3–4): 343–58.

Moodey, Richard W., ed. (1989) *Resource Book for Teaching Sociological Theory*, 2nd edn, Washington, DC: American Sociological Association.

Moore Jr, Barrington (1966) *Social Origins of Dictatorship and Democracy: Lord and Peasant in the Making of the Modern World*, Boston: Beacon.

Morris, James Winston (2009) "An Arab Machiavelli? Rhetoric, Philosophy and Politics in Ibn Khaldun's Critique of Sufism", *Harvard Middle Eastern and Islamic Review* 8: 242–91.

Mourad, Kamal-Eddine (1972) *Le Maroc à la Recherche d'une Revolution*, Paris: Sindbad.

Moussalli, Ahmed (2009) *Wahhabism, Salafism and Islamism: Who is the Enemy?* Beirut, London and Washington: Conflicts Forum. Online at: http://conflictsforum.org/briefings/Wahhabism-Salafism-and-Islamism.pdf (accessed 28 March 2012).

Nasr, Seyyed Hossein (1968) *Science and Civilization in Islam*, Cambridge, MA: Harvard University Press.

Nasr, Seyyed Hossein (1976) *Islamic Science: An Illustrated Study*, London: World of Islam Festival Trust.

Nasr, Seyyed Hossein (1980) "Reflections on Methodology in the Islamic Sciences", *Hamdard Islamicus* 3(3): 3–13.

Nasr, Seyyed Hossein (1981) *Knowledge and the Sacred: The Gifford Lectures, 1981*, Edinburgh: Edinburgh University Press.

Nasr, Seyyed Hossein (1993) *The Need for a Sacred Science*, Surrey: Curzon Press.

Needham, Joseph (1969) "The Dialogue of East and West", in Joseph Needham, *Within the Four Seas: The Dialogue of East and West*, London: George Allen and Unwin. Adapted from the Presidential Address to the Britain–China Friendship Association, 1955.

Nettl, J. P. (1968) "The State as a Conceptual Variable", *World Politics* 20(4): 559–92.

Newby, Gordon D. (1983) "Ibn Khaldun and Frederick Jackson Turner: Islam and the Frontier Experience", *Journal of Asian and African Studies* 18(3–4): 274–85.

Newman, Andrew J. (1993) "The Myth of the Clerical Migration to Safawid Iran: Arab Shiite Opposition to 'Ali al-Karaki and Safawid Shiism", *Die Welt des Islams* 33(1): 66–112.

Nomani, Farhad (1976) "Notes on the Origins and Development of Extra-Economic Obligations of Peasants in Iran, 300–1600 AD", *Iranian Studies* 9(2/3): 121–41.

Nomani, Farhad (1977) "Notes on the Economic Obligations of Peasants in Iran, 300–1600 AD", *Iranian Studies*, 10(1–2): 62–83.

Oppenheimer, Franz (1922–35) *System der Soziologie*, Jena.

Ortega y Gasset, José (1932) *The Revolt of the Masses*, New York: Norton.

Ortega y Gasset, José (1976–78) "Abenjaldún nos revela el secreto", *Revista del Instituto Egicio de Estudios Islámicos en Madrid* 19: 95–114. First published in 1934 in El Espectador 7: 9–53.

Ortega y Gasset, José (2000) "Ibn Khaldūn Reveals His Secrets to Us", translated from the Spanish by Saida del Moral Llobat, unpublished manuscript, International Institute of Islamic Thought and Civilization (ISTAC), Kuala Lumpur.

Osman Bakar (1984) "The Question of Methodology in Islamic Science", in Rais Ahmad and S. Naseem Ahmad, eds, *Quest for New Science*, Aligarh: Centre for Studies on Science.

Owen, Roger (1981) *The Middle East in the World Economy, 1800–1914*, London and New York: Methuen.

Oumlil, Ali (1979) *L'Histoire et son Discours: Essai sur la Méthodologie d'Ibn Khaldoun*, Rabat: Ed. Techniques Nord-Africaines.

Oweiss, Ibrahim M. (n.d.) "Ibn Khaldun, the Father of Economics". Online at: www9.georgetown.edu/faculty/imo3/ibn.htm (accessed 20 March 2013).

Pérès, Henri (1956) "Essai de Bibliographie sur la Vie et l'Oeuvre d'Ibn Khaldūn", in *Studi Orientalistici in Onore di Giorgio Levi della Vida*, Rome: Istituto per l'Oriente, pp. 304–29.

Petruchevsky, I. P. (1968) "The Socio-Economic Condition of Iran Under the Il-Khans", in J. A. Boyle, ed., *The Cambridge History of Iran, Vol. 5: The Saljuq and Mongol Periods*, Cambridge: Cambridge University Press, pp. 483–537.

Pigulevskaya, N. V., Yakubsky, A. Y., Petruchevsky, I. P. and Striyeva, L. V. (1354 AH/1975 AD) *Tārīkh-i Irān az Dawrah-i Bāstān tā Pāyān-i Sadi-ye Hijdahumin-i Mīlādī (History of Iran From Ancient Times Till the End of the Eighteenth Century)*, Tehran: Payam Press.

Poggi, G. (1978) *The Development of the Modern State: A Sociological Introduction*, Stanford, CA: Stanford University Press.

Poliak, A. N. (1936) "La féodalité Islamique", *Revue de Etudes Islamique*, Cahier 3, 251–3.

Qadir, M. Abdul (1941) "The Social and Political Ideas of Ibn Khaldūn", *Indian Journal of Political Science* 3: 117–26.

Quinn, Sholeh A. (1996) "The Dreams of Shaykh Ṣafī al-Dīn and Safavid Historical Writing", *Iranian Studies* 29(1–2): 127–47.

Rabī', Muhammad Mahmoud (1967) *The Political Theory of Ibn Khaldūn*, Leiden: Brill.

Radloff, V. V. (1883) *Ethnographische Ubersicht der Turkenstamme Sibiriens und der Mongolei. Besonder Abdruck aus der vergleichenden Grammatik der Nordlichen Turkensprachen von Wilhelm Radloff*, Leipzig: T. O. Weigel. Cited in J. Cuisenier, (1976) "Kinship and Social Organization in the Turko-Mongolian Cultural Area", in E. Forster and O. Ranum, eds, *Family and Society: Selections from the Annales Economies, Societies, Civilisations*, Baltimore and London: Johns Hopkins University Press.

Rahīmlū, Yūsif (1990) "Ibn Khaldūn", in Kāẓim Mūsavī Bujnūrdī, ed., *Dā'irat al-Ma'ārif-i Buzurg-i Islāmī*, Vol. III, Tehran: Markaz-i Dā'irat al-Ma'ārif-i Buzurg-i Islāmī.

Al-Rasheed, Madawi (2002) *A History of Saudi Arabia*, Cambridge: Cambridge University Press.

Al-Rayḥānī, Amīn (1964) *Najd wa-l-Mulḥaqātihā* (*Najd and its Dependencies*), Beirut: Dar al-Rayḥānī Publishing.

Reid, James J. (1978) "The Qajar Uymaq in the Safavid Period, 1500–1722", *Iranian Studies* 11: 117–43.

Reid, James J. (1978) *Tribalism and Society in Islamic Iran, 1500–1629*, Los Angeles: University of California Press.

Reid, James J. (1979) "Comments on 'Tribalism as a Socioeconomic Formation'", *Iranian Studies* 12(3–4): 275–81.

Ritter, Hellmut (1948) "Irrational Solidarity Groups: A Socio-Psychological Study in Connection with Ibn Khaldûn", *Oriens* 1: 1–44.

Ritzer, George (2000) *Classical Sociological Theory*, 3rd edn, Boston: McGraw-Hill.

Romein, Jan (1948) "Theoretical History", *Journal of the History of Ideas* 9(1): 53–4.

Rosenthal, Erwin I.J. (1932) *Ibn Khalduns Gedanken über den Staat; ein Beitrag zur Geschichte der mittelalterlichen Staatslehre*, Munich: R. Oldenbourg.

Rosenthal, Erwin I.J. (1979) "Ibn Khaldūn as a Political Thinker", *Maghreb Review* 4(1): 1–5.

Rosenthal, Franz (1967) "Translator's Introduction", in *Ibn Khaldun: The Muqadimmah – An Introduction to History*, 3 vols, translated from the Arabic by Franz Rosenthal, London: Routledge and Kegan Paul, pp. xxvii–cxv.

Rosenthal, Franz (1967) "Ibn Khaldūn's Life", in *Ibn Khaldun: The Muqadimmah – An Introduction to History*, 3 vols, translated from the Arabic by Franz Rosenthal, London: Routledge and Kegan Paul, pp. xxvii–lxvii.

Rosenthal, Franz (1983) "Ibn Khaldun in his Time (May 27, 1332–March 17, 1406)", *Journal of Asian and African Studies* 18: 166–78.

Rosenthal, Franz (1997) "Ebn K̲aldūn, Abū Zayd 'Abd-Al-Raḥmān", *Encyclopaedia Iranica*, ed. Ehsan Yarshater, New York: Encyclopaedia Iranica Foundation, Vol VIII, pp. 32–5.

Roussillon, Alain (1992) "La Représentation de l'Identité par les Discours Fondateurs de la Sociologie Turque et Egyptienne: Ziya Gökalp et 'Ali Abd Al-Wahid Wafi'", in *Modernisation et Mobilisation Sociale II*, Egypte-Turquie, Cairo: Dossier du CEDEJ, pp. 31–65.

Roussillon, Alain (n.d.) "Durkheimisme et Réformisme: Fondation Identitaire de la Sociologie en ūgypte", unpublished manuscript, Cairo: CEDEJ.

Ruthven, Malise (2002) "The Eleventh of September and the Sudanese Mahdiya in the Context of Ibn Khaldun's Theory of Islamic History", *International Affairs* 78(2): 339–51.

Al-Sā'ātī, Ḥasan (1962) "Al-Minhaj al-'Ilmī fī Muqaddimah Ibn Khaldūn", in *A'māl Mahrajān Ibn Khaldūn* (Proceedings of the Ibn Khaldun Symposium), Cairo: National Centre for Social and Criminological Research, pp. 203–27.

Sabine, G. H. (1937) *A History of Political Theory*, New York: Holt, Rinehart and Winston.

Said, Edward (1979) *Orientalism*, New York: Vintage Books.

Salame, Ghassan (1990) "'Strong' and 'Weak' States: A Qualified Return to the *Muqaddimah*", in Giacomo Luciani, ed., *The Arab State*, London: Routledge, pp. 29–64.

Sarī' al-Qalam, Maḥmūd (1389 AH) *Farhang-i Siyāsī-yi*. Tehran: Farzān.

Sarkar, Benoy Kumar (1985) *The Positive Background of Hindu Sociology*, Delhi: Motilal Banarsidass. First published in 1914 in Allahabad.

Āl Sa'ūd, Fayṣal ibn Mash'al ibn Sa'ūd ibn 'Abd al-'Azīz, *Rasā'il A'immah Da'wah al-Tawḥīd,* 79. Online at: http://isbn2book.com/9960-39-511-1/rasa%C2%AEil_a%C2%AEimmat_da%C2%B0wat_al-tawhid/ (accessed 20 March 2013).

Savory, Roger (1968) "Notes on the Safavid State", *Iranian Studies* 1(3): 96–103.

Savory, Roger (1974) "The Safavid State and Polity", *Iranian Studies* 7(1–2): 179–212.

Savory, Roger (1980) *Iran Under the Safavids*, Cambridge: Cambridge University Press.

Schmidt, N. (1926) "The Manuscripts of Ibn Khaldun", *Journal of the American Oriental Society* 46: 171–6.

Schmidt, N. (1930) *Ibn Khaldūn: Historian, Sociologist and Philosopher*, New York.

Scott, John (1995) *Sociological Theory: Contemporary Debates*, Aldershot: Edward Elgar.

Seddon, David (1977) "Tribe and State: Approaches to Maghreb History", *Maghreb Review* 2(2): 23–40.

Serjeant, R. B. (1964) "The 'Constitution of Medina'", *Islamic Quarterly* 8(1–2): 3–16.

Sha'bānī, Riḍa (1369 AH) *Mabāni-yi Tārīkh-i Ijtimā'ī-yi Irān*, Tehran: Qūmis.

Shadid, Anthony (2005) "Death of a Syrian Minister Leaves Sect Adrift in a Time of Strife", *Washington Post*, 31 October.

Shatzmiller, Maya (1984) "Unity and Variety of Land Tenure and Cultivation Patterns in the Medieval Maghreb", *Maghreb Review* 8: 24–8.

Shatzmiller, Maya (1992) "Al-Muwaḥḥidūn", *The Encyclopaedia of Islam*, new edn, eds, G. E.Bosworth, E. van Donzel, W. P.Heinrichs and Ch. Pellat, Vol. VII. Leiden: Brill.

Shatzmiller, Maya (1997) "Women and Wage Labour in the Medieval Islamic West: Legal Issues in an Economic Context", *Journal of the Economic and Social History of the Orient* 40(2): 174–206.

Shatzmiller, Maya (2000) *The Berbers and the Islamic State: The Marēnid Experience in Pre-Protectorate Morocco*, Princeton: Markus Wiener.

Shaugannik, Hassan (1985) "Mode of Production in Medieval Iran", *Iranian Studies* 18(1): 75–94.

Shaw, S. J. (1976) *History of the Ottoman Empire and Modern Turkey, Vol. 1: Empire of the Gazis: The Rise and Decline of the Ottoman Empire, 1280–1808*, Cambridge: Cambridge University Press.

Shaykh, Sa'īd (1930) *Dar Muṭāla'āt Taṭbīqī dar Falsafah-i Islāmī*, Tehran: Intishārāt-i Khārazmī.

Shukrī, Yad Allāh (1943) *'Ālam Ārā-yi Ṣafavī*, Tehran: Ittilā'āt.

Siddiqui, Kalim (1976) *The Islamic Movement: A Systems Approach*, Slough: The Muslim Institute.

Silverfarb, Daniel (1982) "Great Britain, Iraq, and Saudi Arabia: The Revolt of the Ikhwan, 1927–1930", *International History Review* 4(2): 222–48.

Simon, Heinrich (1978) *Ibn Khaldun's Science of Human Culture*, Lahore: Sh. Muhammad Ashraf.

Von Sivers, Peter (1980) "Back to Nature: The Agrarian Foundations of Society According to Ibn Khaldūn", *Arabica* 27(1): 68–91.

Soofi, Abdol (1995) "Economics of Ibn Khaldun Revisited", *History of Political Economy* 27(2): 387–404.

Sorokin, Pitirim A. (1962) *Society, Culture, and Personality: Their Structure and Dynamics*, New York: Cooper Square Publishers.

Spengler, Joseph J. (1963–64) "Economic Thought of Islam: Ibn Khaldun", *Comparative Studies in Society and History* 6(3): 268–306.

Spickard, J. V. (2001) "Tribes and Cities: Towards and Islamic Sociology of Religion", *Social Compass* 48(1): 103–16.

Spooner, B. (1971) "Towards a Generative Model of Nomadism", *Anthropological Quarterly* 44(3): 198–210.

Stowasser, Barbara (1983) *Religion and Political Development*, Washington, DC: Center for Contemporary Arab Studies, Georgetown University, 1983.

Ṭabāṭabā'ī, Javād (1995) *Ibn Khaldūn va 'Ulūm-i Ijtimā'ī*, Tehran: Tarḥ-i Naw.

Ṭāhā, 'Abd al-Raḥmān (1979) "An al-Istidlāl fī al-Naṣṣ al-Khaldūnī", *A'māl Nadwah Ibn Khaldūn*, Rabat: Faculty of Letters and Human Sciences, pp. 57–72.

Talbi, M. (1967) "Ibn Kaldun et le sens de l'histoire", *Studia Islamica* 26: 73–148.

Talbi, M. (1971) "Ibn Khaldun", *The Encyclopaedia of Islam*, new edn, eds B. Lewis, V. L. Ménage, C. Pellat and J. Schach, Vol. III, Leiden: Brill and London: Luzac, pp. 825–31.

Talbi, M. (1973) *Ibn Khaldūn et l'histoire*, Tunis: MTD.

Al-Ṭālbī, Muḥammad (1980) "Minhajiyyah Ibn Khaldūn al-Tārīkhiyyah wa Atharuhā fī Diwān <<Al-'Ibar>>", *Al-Hayāt al-Thaqāfiyyah* 9: 6–26.

Tapper, R. (2011) "Confederations, Tribal", *Encyclopaedia Iranica*. Online at: www.iranicaonline.org/articles/confederations-tribal (accessed 20 March 2013).

Tehranian, Majid (1998) "Pancapitalism and Migration in Historical Perspective", *International Political Science Review* 19(3): 289–303.

Teitelbaum, Joshua (2005) "Terrorist Challenges to Saudi Arabian Internal Security", Middle East Review of International Affairs (MERIA) Journal 9(3): 1–11. Online at: http://meria.idc.ac.il/journal/2005/issue3/jv9no3a1.html (accessed 2 May 2012).

Thomas, Lewis V. (1972) *A Study of Naima*, ed. Norman Itzkowitz, New York: New York University Press.

Tibawi, A. L. (1963) "English Speaking Orientalists", *Muslim World* 53: 185–204, 298–313.

Tibawi, A. L. (1979) "Second Critique of English-Speaking Orientalists and Their Approach to Islam and the Arabs", *Islamic Quarterly* 23(1): 3–54.

Togan, Zeki Veli (1957) "Sur l'Origine des Safavides", in *Mélanges Louis Massignon*, Vol. III, Damascus: Institut Française de Damas.

Tokei, F. (1964) "Le Mode de Production Asiatique dans l'Oeuvre de K. Marx et F. Engels", *La Pensee*, 114: 7–32.

Tomar, Cengiz (2008) "Between Myth and Reality: Approaches to Ibn Khaldun in the Arab World", *Asian Journal of Social Science* 36(3–4): 590–611.

Torr, D., ed. (1942) *The Correspondence of Marx and Engels*, New York: International Publishers.

Toynbee, Arnold J. (1935) *A Study of History*, vol. 3. London: Oxford University Press.

Turchin, Peter (2003) "Scientific Prediction in Historical Sociology: Ibn Khaldun Meets Al Sa'ūd". Online at: http://cliodynamics.info/PDF/Khaldun- Saud.pdf (accessed 14 February 2012).

Turchin, Peter (2003) *Complex Population Dynamics: A Theoretical/Empirical Synthesis*, Princeton: Princeton University Press.

Turchin, Peter (2003) *Historical Dynamics: Why States Rise and Fall*, Princeton: Princeton University Press.

Turchin, Peter and Hall, Thomas D. (2003) "Spatial Synchrony Among and within World-Systems: Insights from Theoretical Ecology", *Journal of World-Systems Research* 9(1): 37–64. Online at: http://jwsr.ucr.edu/archive/ (accessed 20 March 2013).

Turner, B. S. (1971) "Sociological Founders and Precursors: The Theories of Religion of Emile Durkheim, Fustel de Coulanges and Ibn Khaldun", *Religion* 1: 32–48.

Turner, B. S. (1978) *Marx and the End of Orientalism*, London: George Allen and Unwin.

Turner, B. S. (1989) "From Orientalism to Global Sociology", *Sociology* 23(4): 629–38.

Turner, B. S. (1984) *Capitalism and Class in the Middle East: Theories of Social Change and Economic Development*, London: Heinemann Educational.

Urvoy, Dominique (1974) "La pensée d'Ibn Tūmart", *Bulletin d'Etudes Orientales* 28: 19–44.

Vassiliev, Alexei (1998) *The History of Saudi Arabia*, London: Saqi Books.

Wāfī, 'Alī 'Abd al-Wāḥid (1951) *Al-Falsafah al-Ijtimā'iyyah li Ibn Khaldūn wa Aujust Kumt*, Cairo.

Wāfī, 'Alī 'Abd al-Wāḥid (1962) "Ibn Khaldūn, Awwal Mu'assis li 'Ilm al-Ijtimā'", in *A'māl Mahrajān Ibn Khaldūn (Proceedings of the Ibn Khaldūn Symposium)*, Cairo: National Centre for Social and Criminological Research, pp. 63–78.

Wallerstein, Immanuel (1996) "Eurocentrism and its Avatars: The Dilemmas of Social Science", paper given at the KSA-ISA Joint East Asian Regional Colloquium, *The Future of Sociology in East Asia*. Korea Sociological Association, 22–23 November.

Walzer, Richard (1963) "Aspects of Islamic Political Thought: Al-Fārābī and Ibn Khaldūn", *Oriens* 16: 40–60.

Wansborough, John (1968) "The Decolonization of North African History", *Journal of African History* 9(4): 643–50.

Al-Wardī, 'Alī (1962) *Manṭiq Ibn Khaldūn*, Cairo: Institute of Arabic Studies.

Waterbury, John (1970) *Commander of the Faithful*, London: Weidenfeld and Nicolson.

Weber, Alfred (1925) *History of Philosophy*, tr. Frank Thilly, New York: Charles Scribner's Sons.

Weber, M. (1978) *Economy and Society: An Outline of Interpretive Sociology*, 2 vols, eds G. Roth and C. Wittich, Berkeley, Los Angeles and London: University of California Press.

Wittek, P. (1925) "Der Stammbaum der Osmanen", *Der Islam* 14: 94–100.

Wittek, P. (1938) *The Rise of the Ottoman Empire*, London: Royal Asiatic Society.

Wittek, P. (1938) "De la Défaite d'Ankara a la Prise de Constantinople (Un Demi-siècle d'Histoire Ottomane)", *Revue des Études Islamiques* 12: 1–34.

Wittek, P. (1982) "Le Role de Tribus Turques dans l'Empire Ottoman", in *La Formation de l'Empire Ottoman*. London: Variorum Reprints.

Wolf, Eric (1982) *Europe and the People Without History*, Berkeley: University of California Press.

Wylie, Diana (2008) "Decadence? The Khaldunian Cycle in Algeria and South Africa", *Journal of North African Studies* 13(3): 395–408.

Zaid Aḥmad (2003) *The Epistemology of Ibn Khaldūn*, London: Routledge Curzon.

Zāyid, Aḥmad (1996) "Saba'ūn 'Āmā li-l-'Ilm al-Ijtimā' fī Misr" ("Seventy Years of Sociology in Egypt"), *Majallat Kulliyat al-Ādāb* (Cairo University) 56(4): 1–38.

Index